After the Enlightenment

After the Enlightenment is the first attempt at understanding modern political realism as a historical phenomenon. Realism is not an eternal wisdom inherited from Thucydides, Machiavelli, or Hobbes, but a twentieth-century phenomenon rooted in the interwar years, the collapse of the Weimar republic, and the transfer of ideas between continental Europe and the United States. This book provides the first intellectual history of the rise of realism in America, as it informed policy and academic circles after 1945. It breaks through the narrow confines of the discipline of International Relations and resituates realism within the crisis of American liberalism. Realism provided a new framework for foreign policy thinking and transformed the nature of American democracy. This book sheds light on the emergence of "rational choice" as a new paradigm for political decision-making and speaks to the current revival in realism in international affairs.

Nicolas Guilhot is research professor at the CNRS (Centre National de la Recherche Scientifique) and visiting scholar at NYU. His work sits at the intersection of political theory, the history of political thought, and international relations. His publications include *The Democracy Makers: Human Rights and the Politics of Global Order* (2005) and *The Invention of International Relations Theory: Realism, the Rockefeller Foundation, and the 1954 Conference on Theory* (2011).

After the Enlightenment

*Political Realism and International Relations
in the Mid-Twentieth Century*

NICOLAS GUILHOT

CAMBRIDGE
UNIVERSITY PRESS

University Printing House, Cambridge CB2 8BS, United Kingdom

One Liberty Plaza, 20th Floor, New York, NY 10006, USA

477 Williamstown Road, Port Melbourne, VIC 3207, Australia

4843/24, 2nd Floor, Ansari Road, Daryaganj, Delhi – 110002, India

79 Anson Road, #06-04/06, Singapore 079906

Cambridge University Press is part of the University of Cambridge.

It furthers the University's mission by disseminating knowledge in the pursuit of education, learning, and research at the highest international levels of excellence.

www.cambridge.org
Information on this title: www.cambridge.org/9781107169739
DOI: 10.1017/9781316755181

© Nicolas Guilhot 2017

This publication is in copyright. Subject to statutory exception and to the provisions of relevant collective licensing agreements, no reproduction of any part may take place without the written permission of Cambridge University Press.

First published 2017

Printed in the United States of America by Sheridan Books, Inc.

A catalogue record for this publication is available from the British Library.

ISBN 978-1-107-16973-9 Hardback
ISBN 978-1-316-62111-0 Paperback

Cambridge University Press has no responsibility for the persistence or accuracy of URLs for external or third-party Internet Web sites referred to in this publication and does not guarantee that any content on such Web sites is, or will remain, accurate or appropriate.

Contents

Acknowledgments		*page* vi
	Introduction	1
1	The Realist Gambit – or the End of Political Science	28
2	American *Katechon*: Christian Realism and the Theological Foundations of International Relations Theory	69
3	The Making of the Realist Tradition: Felix Gilbert and the Reclaiming of Machiavelli	115
4	The Kuhning of Reason: Political Realism and Decision-Making after Thomas Kuhn	152
5	Cyborg Pantocrator: At the Origins of Neorealism	184
6	The Americanization of Realism: Kenneth Waltz, the Security Dilemma, and the Problem of Decision-Making	220
Index		249

Acknowledgments

I have benefited over the years from discussions with many colleagues. The list is long and I am sure I have forgotten a few – I hope they can pardon me: Sonja Amadae, Jenny Andersson, Andrew Arato, Lucian Ashworth, Volker Berghahn, Didier Bigo, Nehal Bhuta, Craig Calhoun, Carlo Invernizzi Accetti, Nomi Claire Lazar, Philippe Fontaine, Stefanos Geroulanos, Hunter Heyck, Daniel Steinmetz Jenkins, Patrick Thaddeus Jackson, Robert Jervis, Tjorborn Knutsen, David Long, Mark Mazower, Alison McQueen, Thomas Meaney, Philip Mirowski, Anthony Molho, Samuel Moyn, Nate Mull, Olivier Nay, Inderjeet Parmar, Benoît Pelopidas, Jacques Revel, Or Rosenboim, Daniel Sabbagh, William Scheuerman, Brian Schmidt, Jack Snyder, Mark Solovey, Anders Stephanson, Yanis Varoufakis, Srdjan Vucetic, Patrick Weil, Stephen Wertheim, Colin Wight, Michael Williams, Olivier Zajec, and Michael Zank.

Robert Jervis and Ronald Rogowski kindly accepted my request to discuss their use of Kuhn when I was working on Chapter 4. The late Kenneth Waltz generously reminisced about the 1956–57 seminar on theory at Columbia. Daniel Bessner has been an invaluable accomplice in thinking through the emergence of neorealism described in Chapter 6. I am very much indebted to him for allowing me to reproduce a large chunk of the essay we originally wrote together, and the ideas expressed in it owe very much to him. I cannot express enough my gratitude to John Mearsheimer, who has commented on many of the original papers, and whose intellectual generosity and conversation have influenced my thinking in more ways than I can acknowledge here. He single-handedly makes realism respectable. I have a special debt toward Robert Vitalis, whose superb work on IR theory has set a benchmark that I cannot emulate and who has on many occasions offered his brilliant wit and criticism.

At the Rockefeller Archive Center, James Allen Smith and his outstanding team of archivists have demonstrated an uncanny capacity for blurring the distinction between work and leisure. I owe special thanks to Tom Rosenbaum and Erwin Levold. At the archives of Harvard University, Timothy Driscoll was instrumental in securing my access to the papers of the Bureaucratic Politics Group. I also want to thank the archivists of the Mudd Manuscript Library Princeton and Jodi Boyle at the M.E. Grenander Department of Special Collections & Archives at SUNY Albany for their invaluable help.

At Cambridge University Press, my editor Robert Dreesen and his assistants made the publication of this book a most pleasant process. I am also indebted to Peter Dimock, my first editor, who has helped me many times find my voice, even when I could no longer stand the sound of it.

A Rockefeller Archive Center Grant-In-Aid made it possible for me to get a first glimpse of the actual history of postwar realism back in 2005.

The research leading to these results has received funding from the European Research Council under the European Community's Seventh Framework Programme (FP7/2007–2013) Grant Agreement no. [284231].

Introduction

This book brings together in a revised, augmented, and updated form six essays about political realism written in the course of the past ten years or so. Although they have been written as discrete pieces, it became clear over time that they told episodes of a single story. Their publication as a single volume gives me the opportunity to spell out the larger argument that runs through them, and to state why I believe that argument continues to matter. The reason why the history of political realism is relevant to us today becomes obvious when one reads what self-declared realists were saying about their own predicament. Here is one of them:

> We are still ... capable of great uprisings *against* a recognized threat or danger. But we are so confused in our thoughts as to which *positive* goals should guide our action that a general fear of what will happen after the merely *negative* task of defense against danger has been performed paralyzes our planning and thinking in terms of political ideas and ideals.

These words could have been written today, and yet they were written in 1951 by John Herz, a refugee scholar from Germany, in the introduction to his book *Political Realism and Political Idealism*. More than sixty years separate us from these remarks, which nonetheless resonate uncannily with our present situation. Today, we too have become engulfed by our own concern with security and confused about the more general meaning and purpose of politics. Since 9/11, security has become the universal framework of political thinking and the primary deliverable of any policy, foreign or domestic, often overriding well-established constitutional rights and provisions. It often seems to foreclose all alternative values whose breadth, reach, and controversial implications once were central to political life. Facing and confronting "a recognized threat or danger" has become the essence of government as well as a new source of legitimacy. References to a permanent state of exception now sound like academic platitudes glossing over the obvious.

The ideals that once seemed capable of mobilizing political energies behind transformative projects seem now thoroughly discredited, or watered down beyond recognition. Instead, security itself has become an ideal – maybe the only ideal left. Increasingly, former "positive goals" have been engulfed by the "negative tasks," giving an appealing shine to the latter, as the notion of security has expanded to become the all-encompassing horizon of human experience. Even the spread of democracy, humanitarian assistance, and human rights are now seen as the functional components of a global security mix rather than ends valuable in themselves. Human development, long discredited by the neoliberal policies of the "Washington consensus" of the 1990s, has come back as a fundamental security measure in the many counterinsurgencies in which the West is currently engaged. And if there is anything new in contemporary humanitarianism, it is indeed its discovery of political realism.[1]

It is not a coincidence that political realism and indeed Herz himself are coming back into fashion.[2] Herz thought that the search for security was

---

[1] See for instance Ruti G. Teitel, *Humanity's Law* (Oxford: Oxford University Press, 2011); David W Kennedy, *The Dark Side of Virtue: Reassessing International Humanitarianism* (Princeton: Princeton University Press, 2004); Peter Redfield and Erica Bornstein, eds., *Forces of Compassion: Humanitarianism between Ethics and Politics* (Santa Fe: SAR Press, 2011).

[2] On Herz, see Casper Sylvest, "John H. Herz and the Resurrection of Classical Realism," *International Relations* 22, no. 4 (2008): 441–55; Peter M. R. Stirk, "John H. Herz and the International Law of the Third Reich," *International Relations* 22, no. 4 (2008): 427–40. The literature on political realism is ballooning, but for a few examples, see Robert M. A. Crawford, *Idealism and Realism in International Relations: Beyond the Discipline* (London: Routledge, 2000); Jack Donnelly, *Realism and International Relations* (Cambridge: Cambridge University Press, 2000); Stefano Guzzini, "The Enduring Dilemmas of Realism in International Relations," *European Journal of International Relations* 10, no. 4 (2004): 533–68; Stefano Guzzini, *Power, Realism and Constructivism* (Oxon: Routledge, 2013); Oliver Jütersonke, *Morgenthau, Law and Realism* (Cambridge: Cambridge University Press, 2010); Alison McQueen, *Political Realism in Apocalyptic Times* (New York: Cambridge University Press, forthcoming); Philip Mirowski, "Realism and Neoliberalism: From Reactionary Modernism to Postwar Conservatism," in *The Invention of International Relations Theory: The Rockefeller Foundation, Realism, and the 1954 Conference on Theory*, ed. Nicolas Guilhot (New York: Columbia University Press, 2011); Seán Molloy, *The Hidden History of Realism: A Genealogy of Power Politics* (New York: Palgrave Macmillan, 2006); William Scheuerman, *Hans Morgenthau: Realism and Beyond* (Cambridge: Polity, 2009); Brian C. Schmidt, "Realism as Tragedy," *Review of International Studies* 30, no. 3 (2004); Michael C. Williams, ed. *Realism Reconsidered:*

a basic fact of human life. He also suggested that it was the reason why conflicts and wars would remain an ever-present possibility, notwithstanding the intentions of the parties to such conflicts: What defines security for some may be perceived as a threat by others, and thus can trigger an escalation that spirals into open conflict. He called this basic condition of human life the "security dilemma" and thought it was intractable. He named the fundamental type of political thinking that took the security dilemma as its foundational premise "political realism." Today, this is still the intellectual foundation of the discipline that teaches cohorts of students to think about international affairs.

Herz thought that taking these "'gladiatorial' facts" into account was the *sine qua non* for the pursuit of any ideal or value. He wanted to put realism at the service of moral and political progress, to strike a balance between the grim necessities of power and the striving for ideals, and to reconcile security with the realization of collective values. Far from endorsing a pessimistic and limiting vision of human possibilities, often tied to conservative or reactionary ideologies, Herz wanted to formulate what he called interchangeably a "liberal realism" or "realist liberalism."[3] And yet, Herz's attempt at reconciling realism with a progressive sense of history and politics failed. Like many other realists, he ended up developing the same critique of liberalism, socialism, or internationalism.

Although he had been a student of Hans Kelsen, the great Viennese representative of legal positivism, Herz had gradually drifted toward the intellectual positions of Kelsen's nemesis in Weimar, the archconservative jurist Carl Schmitt. By the end of his life, Herz had become a willing participant in the Schmitt-revival launched by the journal *Telos*. He conceded that his "realist liberalism" was nothing more than an attempt at preserving some of Schmitt's fundamental insights.[4] Herz

---

The Legacy of Hans J. Morgenthau in International Relations (Oxford: Oxford University Press, 2007); Duncan Bell, "Introduction: Under an Empty Sky – Realism and Political Theory," in *Political Thought and International Relations: Variations on a Realist Theme*, ed. Duncan Bell (Oxford: Oxford University Press, 2008).

[3] See for instance John Herz, "Political Ideas and Political Reality," *The Western Political Quarterly* 3, no. 2 (1950): 161–78; John Herz, "Idealist Internationalism and the Security Dilemma," *World Politics* 2, no. 2 (1950): 157–80; John Herz, *Political Realism and Political Idealism: A Study in Theories and Realities* (Chicago: University of Chicago Press, 1951).

[4] He recounts the episode in his memoirs: John Herz, *Vom Überleben. Wie ein Weltbild entstand Autobiographie* (Düsseldorf: Droste Verlag, 1984). On how Schmitt influenced his conception of realism, see John Herz, "Looking at Carl Schmitt from the Vantage Point of the 1990s," *Interpretation* 19, no. 3 (1992): 307–14. Herz's correspondence with *Telos* editors can be found in his papers, at the M.E. Grenander Department of Special Collections & Archives at SUNY.

found his own progressive hopes for his liberal realism blocked in the political dead-end he had so clearly identified.

Herz's example tells us something important about the nature of modern realism as a political ideology. It suggests that realism places limits upon the kind of political goals that one can pursue and indeed makes it difficult if not impossible to pursue positive or transformative goals. It informs a certain kind of political outlook, at the cost of excluding others. It also suggests that when we talk about realism, we are really talking about two different things that the rise of political realism in the mid-twentieth century has sought to conflate in the process of establishing its historical legitimacy.

The first is realism as an ethical attitude, a reflexive relationship to one's actions that relies on prudential conduct in the pursuit of whatever ends one has chosen. It is normatively neutral and does not preclude any political or moral end. It is the realism of Machiavelli, for instance, a realism that can perfectly accommodate a search for glory that any contemporary realist would consider folly. It is a realism that does not imply a pessimistic anthropology or a regressive social ontology. It is naturalistic, pragmatic, and concrete.

The second is "realism" in the modern sense that is more familiar to us. It goes beyond the practical wisdom known to philosophers as *phronesis*. Above all, it is an "-ism," an ideology. It involves a specific conception of human nature and of historical time. It places limits upon what one can hope to achieve. These limits are not dictated by a concrete situation; they are metaphysical limits, constitutive of human nature and built into a historical process that, in the last instance, is considered to be in the hands of God – or at least not in those of men. This realism stifles the capacity to elaborate any political project beyond the maintenance of order – it is, by definition, a conservative realism. It developed essentially as a reaction to conceptions of science, history, and politics that emerged in the late eighteenth century and informed the great movements of democratization of the nineteenth century. It developed against these specific foes and could not have existed before the advent of modernity. It is this realism with which we now must come to terms.

Today, realism seems to offer something that looks to many like the promise of better politics. A mixture of idealistic vision and realistic execution has always characterized if not the truth of American foreign policy, at least of the narcissistic self-image of the American foreign policy establishment.[5] But

---

[5] The point is perfectly captured in Perry Anderson, *American Foreign Policy and Its Thinkers* (London and New York: Verso, 2015).

the current intellectual revival of realism cuts deeper and points at an exhaustion of alternatives. International relations theorists and intellectual historians are going back to classical postwar realism and exhuming an intellectual tradition that according to them has not lost any of its relevance but remains a perennial source of wisdom for navigating the politics of our times. This is not just a reaction against the impoverishment of a discipline that since the 1960s has gradually severed its ties to history and political theory as it became increasingly caught up with purely formal methodologies.[6] In recovering the complexity and richness of mid-century realist thought, historians and political theorists have contributed to its contemporary resurgence and, more or less wittingly, to its re-enchantment. Once considered a quietist ideology, skeptical if not critical about the very possibility of reforming international politics, realism is today being reclaimed as a potentially progressive intellectual project.[7] It seems to many to be the only grand narrative we have left with which to make sense of international politics. Interventions gone awry in the Middle East and a dangerous stand-off with Russia are today not condemned on the basis of anti-imperialist arguments or because they constitute breaches of international law. They are criticized because they ignore the basic precepts and wisdom of political realism. The degeneration of the soft-power policies of "democracy promotion" of the 1980s into the militarized democracy promotion of the G. W. Bush administration have made global transformative agendas an easy target of realist critique. Increasingly, realism seems to be the only language left if one is to impugn imperial adventurism and its moral contradictions while being taken seriously within policy-making and opinion circles. Very tellingly, realism seems to have captured the imagination of some on the Left, for whom it

---

[6] The literature is growing at a fast pace. See for instance Michael C. Williams, *The Realist Tradition and the Limits of International Relations* (Cambridge: Cambridge University Press, 2005); Williams, *Realism Reconsidered*; Duncan Bell, ed. *Political Thought and International Relations: Variations on a Realist Theme* (Oxford: Oxford University Press, 2008); Michael Cox, "Hans J. Morgenthau, Realism, and the Rise and Fall of the Cold War," in *Realism Reconsidered*, ed. Michael C. Williams (Oxford: Oxford University Press, 2007); Donnelly, *Realism and International Relations*; Stefano Guzzini, *Realism in International Relations and International Political Economy* (London: Routledge, 1998); Guzzini, "The Enduring Dilemmas of Realism in International Relations"; Molloy, *The Hidden History of Realism: A Genealogy of Power Politics*; Scheuerman, *Hans Morgenthau*.

[7] See William Scheuerman, *The Realist Case for Global Reform* (Cambridge: Polity Press, 2011); Vibeke Schou Tjalve, *Realist Strategies of Republican Peace: Niebuhr, Morgenthau, and the Politics of Patriotic Dissent* (New York: Palgrave Macmillan, 2008).

represents the only possible counterpoint to depoliticized visions of a neoliberal world order.[8]

The contemporary attraction to realism as perhaps the last genuinely "political" form of thinking with which to oppose neoliberal depoliticization fundamentally misunderstands realism and ignores how much it has in common with neoliberalism. There is no doubt that postwar realism was a reaction against the economic understanding of history inherited from nineteenth-century liberalism and its utopian pretense to eventually displace politics.[9] But this opposition between realism and economics remains superficial and obscures a deeper convergence, for neoliberalism too was a reaction against its nineteenth-century predecessor ideology. In *After Utopia*, her brilliant and still unsurpassed description of the liberal-conservative postwar moment, Judith Shklar touches upon this convergence. She bundles together economists such as Wilhelm Röpke, political theorists such as Bertrand de Jouvenel, and historians such as Jacob Talmon as exponents of a backlash against a form of liberalism that traced its roots to the Enlightenment. She may as well have added international relations intellectuals such as Hans Morgenthau, John Herz, Kenneth Thompson, George Kennan, and Reinhold Niebuhr. A few years earlier, in one of the first articles ever published on neoliberalism, her mentor Carl Friedrich had characterized this intellectual movement as a form of political realism: The distinction, for him, was almost non-existent.[10] Neoliberalism too was a defensive movement. Like many realists, neoliberals thought that "European society has been deteriorating steadily since the French Revolution," resulting in twentieth-century totalitarianism.[11] The movement emerged as a reaction against administered rationality, planning, and its alleged authoritarianism. The neoliberals also embraced a neo-Burkean vision of social development that was pitted against any form of Enlightenment rationalism. For them, "'human nature' or the interdependence of human factors provide[d] insuperable barriers to the best intentioned reforms."[12] These were exactly the views of political realists. In individualized exchanges in the market as in

---

[8] Scheuerman, *The Realist Case for Global Reform*; Danilo Zolo, *Cosmopolis: Prospects for World Government* (Cambridge, MA: Polity Press, 1997).
[9] Judith N. Shklar, *Legalism: Law, Morals, and Political Trials* (Cambridge, MA: Harvard University Press, 1964), 123.
[10] Carl J. Friedrich, "The Political Thought of Neo-Liberalism," *The American Political Science Review* 49, no. 2 (1955): 509–25.
[11] Judith N. Shklar, *After Utopia: The Decline of Political Faith* (Princeton: Princeton University Press, 1957), 36.
[12] Shklar, *After Utopia*, 237–38.

international relations, an infinity of interactions that took place in a space deprived of central authority and which could not be entirely comprehended by a single mind constantly generated new patterns of order. Yet, for order to emerge, these interactions could not be simply left to spontaneity. A carefully crafted framework had to be maintained through political means – whether a framework of full economic competition, or an artfully maintained balance of power.[13] Realism and neoliberalism were twin ideological movements born in the crisis of the 1930s that reacted to the crisis of liberalism and to the rise of totalitarianism. Both were attempts at saving liberalism from its own deficiencies and from its enemies. Both recognized the primacy of politics and of political power but also their potential for unleashing universal human catastrophe. Both assumed that the fundamental liberal provisions that organized social life in the West could survive only if they were supplemented by forms of politics that were not liberal. Both thought of politics and economics in terms of concretely managed order. Both shared intellectual references, from Walter Lippmann's essays to some strands of Catholic thought. Both sought to insulate from democracy core domains of decision-making, including foreign and economic policy, and to entrust them to a select elite of expert decision-makers. Both assumed that public opinion was essentially irrational – whether it was manipulated by intellectuals or incapable of grasping the issues of high politics. Both were moved by a deep distrust of "scientific man," whom they considered a dictator in the making. Both redefined what "rationality" meant and eventually came to rely on some version of "rational choice" to legitimize economic and political decisions. The current return to realism as an antidote to neoliberal depoliticization is bound to fail because it refuses to recognize the shared ideological framework of decision-making upon which this attempted recovery of politics rests.

REALISM'S TAKEOFF

In the early afternoon of May 7, 1954, a military jet taxied to the end of the runway at Maxwell Field, Alabama, home of the Air War College.

---

[13] The intellectual history of neoliberalism has hardly been written yet. But for a few serious attempts, see for instance Philip Mirowski and Dieter Plehwe, *The Road from Mont Pèlerin: The Making of the Neoliberal Thought Collective* (Cambridge: Harvard University Press, 2009); François Denord, *Néo-libéralisme version française. Histoire d'une idéologie politique* (Paris: Demopolis, 2007); Pierre Dardot and Christian Laval, *The New Way of the World: On Neoliberal Society* (London: Verso, 2013); Serge Audier, *Néo-libéralisme(s). Une archéologie intellectuelle* (Paris: Grasset, 2012).

After a few minutes, the aircraft, a decommissioned Lockheed F94 Starfire, reached the entrance of the runway and slowly pivoted until its nose pointed in the direction of the long asphalted strip. Once in position, the pilot brought the jet to a standstill, engaged the brakes, and pushed the throttle until the central turbofan geared up to its maximum thrust, compressing air into the engine, where the jetfuel sprayed in the combustion chamber was ignited. Spitting a hissing stream of burning gases, the plane dashed along the runway. After a short run, it lifted its twelve thousand pounds into the air with a deafening roar, retracted its landing gear, and started climbing steeply toward its cruising altitude until it became a mere dot in the distance. Soon, it was engulfed by the morning mist, leaving behind a faint trail of exhaust fumes as it headed toward Washington, DC.

Besides the pilot, the two-seat interceptor aircraft had a most unusual passenger: a professor of political science at the University of Chicago, Hans J. Morgenthau, who had started his US academic career in 1936 after escaping from Nazi Germany and is today considered the founding father of the academic discipline known as international relations theory. Morgenthau had just given an address on the "Problems of Integrating the Factors of National Strategy" to the military brass gathered at Maxwell's Air War College for the 1954 National Security Forum. Leaving on a military jet was not a common practice for guest speakers and the Air Force did not have the habit of offering such complimentary perks to its visitors. This was indeed an exceptional circumstance. The flight had been arranged by Dean Rusk, who had recently left Acheson's State Department to become president of the Rockefeller Foundation. Morgenthau's presence was urgently required in Washington, where he was to join a small gathering of academics, policymakers, and journalists invited by the Foundation to discuss over two days the need for building a "theory" of international politics that could be taught across the campuses of the country.[14] The meeting had already started on the morning of May 7, and few believed that any such theory could see the light of day without the Chicago professor, widely regarded as a wise man when it came to understanding what politics is all about. Although the pilot may have been unaware of it, the flight was also a combat mission: By transporting Morgenthau to Washington, he was actually delivering

---

[14] On the particulars of this meeting, see the contributions in Nicolas Guilhot, ed. *The Invention of International Relations: The Rockefeller Foundation, Realism, and the Making of IR Theory* (New York: Columbia University Press, 2011).

a weapon on a specific target. The target, in this case, was the cultural currency of science, the cult of technology, and the resulting erosion of politics.

The 1950s were the age of science: To be taken seriously, any intellectual enterprise had to be scientific, and to be legitimate, any political decision had to be based on scientific evidence. The times were forward-looking, confident in the power of science and technology to solve social, economic, and political issues at home and abroad. World War II had ended with the defeat of the forces of irrationality and political romanticism, reason had reclaimed its rights over human affairs, and progress had resumed its course unimpaired. The interwar zeal for social engineering and scientific management was boosted by the civilian conversion of wartime Research & Development capacities. Even the political conflicts of these new times were of a different nature: The Cold War enemy was rational and therefore tractable. The Soviets too had adopted Science as their politics and did politics in the name of their science.

Science had come out of World War II fortified and tightly enmeshed with the governance of industrial societies. Governmental bureaus, universities, and philanthropic bureaucracies were replete with economists, statisticians, sociologists, psychologists, physicists, mathematicians, and engineers. Philanthropic foundations, like the Rockefeller and the Ford foundations, invested their munificent resources in an effort to establish the social sciences on par with the natural sciences. The social sciences thought of themselves as "social physics" and approached society as a second Nature, yet to be charted by explorers of the modern times, its vast resources lying untapped under the familiar landscape of everyday life. Scientists made visible its deepest recesses and summoned into being new entities such as unemployment, voting behavior, consumption patterns, social stratification, and public opinion. Knowledge of their interrelationship gave the key to their manipulation, and their manipulation would improve society. Statistical sampling and polling techniques developed since the 1930s inaugurated new ways to aggregate individual situations into unified representations of the nation. As it churned out increasing amounts of social data that not only represented the country but fostered "social integration," science was now woven into the very fabric of American society.[15]

---

[15] Emmanuel Didier, *En quoi consiste l'Amérique? Les statistiques, le New Deal et la démocratie* (Paris: La Découverte, 2009); see also David Paul Haney,

The age of science, as if by design, also seemed to usher in the twilight of politics. Postwar science constituted itself partly by professing detachment from, and indifference to, social values – that is, by understanding itself as being the opposite of politics.[16] The international crisis of the 1930s and the ensuing world conflagration had shown the devastating effects and the irrationality of power politics. Political decisions were messy, irrational, and arbitrary: scientific calculations were precise, rational, and incontrovertible. A cool-headed rationality was to replace the disorderly passions of politics, enlightened technical experts would formulate better judgments than volatile and emotional publics, scientific precision would substitute give-and-take arrangements, and technological solutions would overcome social and political conflicts.

The most enthusiastic scientific modernists of all, the sociologists celebrated the dawn of a post-political age. By the mid-1950s, many announced with confidence the "end of ideology" in Western industrial nations, as rationally administered welfare states were fulfilling basic social needs while at the same time spreading the values of efficiency and rationality associated with the age of science. The scientific management of production and income distribution had confined the politics of class struggle to the dustbin of history. Fundamental issues were considered settled, and all that was left to be done was for social engineers to improve existing social processes and institutions. Politics, it seems, was no longer an existential affair. At least not for science, which, as sociologist Paul Lazarsfeld once noted, did not distinguish between the socialist vote and the choice of a particular brand of soap.[17]

The Americanization of Social Science: Intellectuals and Public Responsibility in the Postwar United States (Philadelphia: Temple University Press, 2008).

[16] Andrew Jewett, *Science, Democracy, and the American University: From the Civil War to the Cold War* (New York: Cambridge University Press, 2012), 272.

[17] Daniel Bell, *The End of Ideology. On the Exhaustion of Political Ideas in the Fifties* (Cambridge, MA: Harvard University Press, 2000); Seymour Martin Lipset, *Political Man: The Social Bases of Politics* (London: Heinemann, 1960). See also Chaim I. Waxman, ed. *The End of Ideology Debate* (New York: Funk & Wagnalls, 1968). At about the same time, politics also disappeared from US history, as historians observed the existence of a deep-seated liberal consensus constitutive of the nation. For classical statements, see Louis Hartz, *The Liberal Tradition in America: An Interpretation of American Political Thought since the Revolution* (New York: Harcourt, Brace and Company, 1955); Richard Hofstadter, *The American Political Tradition and the Men Who Made It*, 1st edn. (New York: Alfred A. Knopf, 1948). Socialism too was a scientific way to overcome politics – a point emphasized by authors as diverse as Aron and Foucault. For the former, socialism had no political theory, while for the latter it had no concept of government. Raymond Aron, "Science et théorie de la politique," *Revue Française de*

For all these reasons, the age of science viewed mass politics with suspicion. Since the first half of the century, the social sciences considered that politics "had become outdated, falling prey to the mass appeals and backroom deals frequently thought to characterize it."[18] Deliberative visions of democracy tended to wane and the sphere of public intersubjectivity was increasingly seen as a potential threat to individual freedom. The behavioral social science movement was premised on "doubts about the average citizen's capacity to take an active political role."[19]

While sociologists mulled over the social pathologies of mass society, economists elevated the inability of its members to make collectively rational decisions to the status of Nobel Prize-worthy insight. The "voice of the people" was better left in the hands of a professional caste of haruspices inspecting the innards of society with scientific tools and second-guessing the direction of its future development. No longer expressed exclusively by parliamentary technologies, it was increasingly captured by sampling techniques that developed alongside, but also challenged, traditional political representation.

These scientific devices summoned new entities such as "public opinion" and the "common man," passive proxies for a public that could not actively engage with the complexities of the age of science, and that Walter Lippmann had relegated to the rank of a passive ectoplasm in *The Phantom Public*. Science, by representing the body politic and exercising government in its name, suddenly displaced centuries of political theory: *vox scientiae, vox populi*. The denizens of the age of science did not have to be actively engaged, since most of their lives were optimally allocated by rational social planning. When they were not presented with readymade choices between politicians or bars of soap, their free will turned out to be a real burden. After having dropped off the bureaucratic grid when administrative bottlenecks delayed his drafting by the military for a year, Saul Bellow's *Dangling Man* is "unwilling to admit that [he] do[es] not know how to use [his] freedom."[20]

Science Politique 11, no. 2 (1961): 265–66; Michel Foucault, *Naissance de la biopolitique. Cours au Collège de France 1978–1979* (Paris: Gallimard-Seuil, 2004).

[18] John M. Jordan, *Machine-Age Ideology: Social Engineering and American Liberalism, 1911–1939* (Chapel Hill: University of North Carolina Press, 1994), 7.

[19] Jewett, *Science, Democracy, and the American University*, 358.

[20] Paul F. Lazarsfeld, "An Episode in the History of Social Research: A Memoir," in *The Intellectual Migration: Europe and America, 1930–1960*, eds., Donald Fleming

THE REALIST COUNTER-ENLIGHTENMENT

But could science really replace politics altogether? Could politics be made entirely rational? Could science substitute for moral choice and political decision? What some contemporary modernizers saw at the time as the rationalization of political life appeared to Morgenthau and other intellectual critics a dangerous exercise in self-delusion. These critics thought they were witnessing the dangerously naïve American dream of the liberal mind lulled by the technological utopias of modernity. Although the crisis of the 1930s and the war had shaken the moral foundations of liberalism and made more pressing the need to rebuild a vision of history and politics that no longer relied on the certainties of the past, a number of prominent political thinkers refused to abandon the hopes associated with the Enlightenment project. From Hannah Arendt to Harold Lasswell and David Easton, a number of political theorists and political scientists sought to rebuild a more sober and less utopian version of the Enlightenment tradition. They were determined to pursue the informed search for a positive, empirical social scientific knowledge that would strengthen and protect liberal democracy against its enemies and its ills while acknowledging its imperfections. Beyond the individual differences, this movement represented what Ira Katznelson has aptly called a "political studies Enlightenment."[21]

The essays collected here seek to understand the significance for the present of another group of influential thinkers who, in sharp contrast, took advantage of this historical juncture to launch an attack on the Enlightenment and on its resurrection as a program of scientific governance in modern societies. Because of their anti-utopian positions, these thinkers came to be seen and eventually to describe themselves as political "realists." Unable to countermand the powerful trends that were redefining what it meant to do political and social science in their time, they nevertheless successfully established their sway over the nascent intellectual enclave known as international relations theory. In private discussions and in their published writings, thinkers such as Hans Morgenthau, John Herz, George Kennan, Herbert Butterfield, Reinhold Niebuhr, and others explicitly put the blame on the Enlightenment for the

---

and Bernard Bailyn (Cambridge: Belknap Press of Harvard University Press, 1969); Walter Lippmann, *The Phantom Public* (New Brunswick: Transaction Books, 1993); Saul Bellow, *Dangling Man* (London: Penguin, 2006), 3.

[21] Ira Katznelson, *Desolation and Enlightenment: Political Knowledge after Total War, Totalitarianism, and the Holocaust* (New York: Columbia University Press, 2003), 2.

ills and tragedies of the twentieth century. Far from representing the negation of human reason, fascist or communist totalitarianism was the ultimate outcome of a secular culture that had displaced traditional authorities in favor of an infatuated belief in the omnipotence of rationality. Despite representing a very diverse group, these political theorists, historians, diplomats, and theologians shared a critical diagnosis of modernity, and in particular a deep suspicion of the postwar scientific ethos that sustained an updated vision of liberal governance in America. For them, the value-neutrality that defined science after 1945 was correlated to a moral relativism that had proven to be the Achilles' heel of liberal regimes.

Among this group, German and central European Jewish émigrés were particularly vociferous, as they had witnessed firsthand the collapse of a regime that had proved unable to extricate itself in time from the paralyzing strictures of legal positivism and its neutral approach to constitutionalism.[22] But their Protestant colleagues, who were often associated with the neo-orthodox movement, were no less unwavering in their attack on the social sciences, in which they saw a utopian and hubristic project to organize and govern societies on the basis of scientific rationalism. They saw this attempt as a symptom of the spiritual crisis of secular modernity and a misguided and potentially authoritarian bid to artificially instantiate progress, in blind defiance of the natural limitations of human nature. Whether it set government on the totalitarian course of administered rationality, or whether it corroded the moral and normative resources necessary for political decision-making adequate to the totalitarian threat, the scientific approach to politics paved the way for totalitarian outcomes.

But there was much more going on beneath the rhetorical surface of this opposition to totalitarianism. What makes it sometimes difficult to understand the nature of realism is that disciplinary historians have often

---

[22] For an overview, see Bernhard Schlink and Arthur J. Jacobson, eds., *Weimar: A Jurisprudence of Crisis* (Berkeley and Los Angeles: University of California Press, 2000); John P. McCormick, "Legal Theory and the Weimar Crisis of Law and Social Change," in *Weimar Thought: A Contested Legacy*, eds., Peter E. Gordon and John P. McCormick (Princeton: Princeton University Press, 2013); Augustin Simard, *La loi désarmée. Carl Schmitt et la controverse légalité/légitimité sous Weimar* (Québec: Presses de l'Université de Laval, 2009); Ellen Kennedy, *Constitutional Failure: Carl Schmitt in Weimar* (Durham: Duke University Press, 2004); Olivier Beaud, *Les derniers jours de Weimar. Carl Schmitt face à l'avènement du nazisme* (Paris: Descartes & Cie, 1997); David Dyzenhaus, *Legality and Legitimacy: Carl Schmitt, Hans Kelsen and Hermann Heller in Weimar* (Oxford: Oxford University Press, 1997).

considered the criticisms that the realists have addressed to the social sciences exclusively as methodological quarrels, overlooking their ideological implications. In part, this is the result of a limitation intrinsic to disciplinary history as practiced by international relations scholars.[23] But it may also be because these discussions took place at a time when the place of science in American society was being transformed and its connection to the liberal project was becoming less visible.

During the 1920s, prevailing views of science were tethered to a normative concern with democracy and its publics. Exemplified by the works of John Dewey, this concern inspired those who Andrew Jewett has recently called "scientific democrats." Scientific democrats believed that "science could dramatically improve democratic practice not only by fostering technological growth, improving administrative techniques ... and giving the citizens the technical information needed to participate constructively in policy debates, but also ... by shaping their moral character."[24]

By the 1950s, however, this explicit alliance between science and democracy had morphed into a more complicated picture, in which a socially secluded scientific culture could profess its value neutrality to the extent that it operated in the wider context of an underlying normative consensus around liberal values.[25] Nominally value-free technocratic expertise could thus coexist with an implicit commitment to liberal politics. The behavioral social sciences captured this new articulation between

---

[23] There has been a wonderfully rich historiography of IR in the past fifteen years. However, to the extent that it is almost exclusively practiced by international relations scholars rather than intellectual historians (with a few exceptions), it has tended to remain trapped in the accepted cannon of the discipline, even when it was revisiting it. As a result, it has usually ignored the writings of the historians, theologians, and public intellectuals who are not considered to belong to the past of the discipline, even though they contributed – sometimes more powerfully than political theorists – to the emergence of a realist vision in American politics. For a recent exception to this tendency that considerably reframes the history of the discipline by taking into account the place of race in it, see Robert Vitalis, *White World Order, Black Power Politics: The Birth of American International Relations* (Ithaca: Cornell University Press, 2015).

[24] Jewett, *Science, Democracy, and the American University*, 10.

[25] As Jewett shows, the consensus historians solved a number of epistemological and cultural problems for the scientific communities to the extent that by positing a generally shared liberal consensus at the basis of the American polity, they allowed natural and social scientists to operate without having to worry about their normative commitments, since "value-neutralists viewed themselves as spokespersons for a normative consensus." He suggests that the consensus historians retrospectively sought to reintegrate the New Deal with its administered economy and technocratic government within a liberal tradition. Jewett, *Science, Democracy, and the American University*, 55.

science and its wider cultural context and presented themselves as the latest effort to modernize the Enlightenment tradition, sometimes explicitly so. Behavioral social scientists represented the latest instantiation of "scientific democrats," albeit with an elitist technocratic ethos and a more sober attitude toward the mobilization of the public.

The realists' attack on science was thus, *de facto*, an attack on modern mass democracy. It was a more or less deliberate attempt at limiting mass democracy's political reach and divesting it from some forms of authority. It is no coincidence that realists allied themselves with such erstwhile critics of the "scientific democrats" as Walter Lippmann. Even their analysis of totalitarianism was premised upon a critique of its democratic origins. "Fascism," Morgenthau wrote, "can be considered the consummation of the equalitarian and fraternal tenets of 1789."[26] British historian Herbert Butterfield, who headed the British Committee on International Relations, subscribed to the same view. The realists' critique of democratization and of its dangerous consequences, their aristocratic nostalgia for eighteenth-century style diplomacy and more generally for unaccountable forms of decision-making, their positive attitudes toward traditional, and in particular religious, authorities all point at a well-known ideological repertoire that mobilized the traditional themes of the counter-Enlightenment. The realists saw their own rise in academic and policy circles as an opportunity to settle the score with the Enlightenment and to close a historical parenthesis that had started with the French revolution and had led directly to twentieth-century totalitarianism. Rapidly establishing a foothold in the fledgling discipline of International Relations but receiving reinforcements from historians and theologians and pronouncing upon all things political, they articulated a powerful intellectual program that blended anti-liberal and Christian conservative elements with a rhetoric of the defense of liberalism. They saw American political culture as essentially deficient and bereft of the moral and political resources necessary to confront the totalitarian threat. The notions that law and democracy were the foundations of government appeared to them extremely dangerous in dangerous times.

These men considered that liberalism, if left to its own devices, was incapable of ensuring its own survival. Whenever the survival or the security of the regime was at stake, what was needed, they thought, was

---

[26] Hans J. Morgenthau, *Truth and Power: Essays of a Decade, 1960–70* (New York: Praeger, 1970), 376. The excerpt is from a review of Ernst Nolte's *Three Faces of Fascism: Action Française, Italian Fascism, National Socialism*, published in 1966.

a capacity to exercise power unconstrained by law, individual morality, or democratic procedures. This necessitated nothing short of an intellectual revolution, and the rehabilitation of some pre-liberal if not anti-liberal forms of political authority capable of making timely decisions in critical situations. As Judith Shklar observed at the time, the result was a conservative or defensive liberalism that had "joined the ancient enemies of the Enlightenment."[27]

This book tells the story of the realist counter-Enlightenment and of its intellectual and political success in Cold War America. Ironically, the notion of "counter-Enlightenment" was coined by one of the staunchest fellow travelers of this movement, someone who was indeed very close to the realists, the British philosopher Isaiah Berlin. A declared enemy of rationalistic visions of history and politics who shared with the realists a diagnosis of totalitarianism as the ultimate outcome of Enlightenment rationalism, Berlin dedicated a famous essay to the ideas that had shaped the reaction to the French Enlightenment.[28] Wary of finding himself on the wrong side of history, however, he had cautiously expanded the counter-Enlightenment in order to include in it not just Catholic reactionaries, but a much longer skeptical tradition spanning centuries and including more palatable thinkers, such as Vico, Montesquieu, and Montaigne. Berlin's essay was a clear indictment of the false hope that the scientific method could be applied to politics and ethics, and more generally a warning against faith in any form of administered rationality. Earlier, Berlin had similarly written about political realism with the very same intentions.[29] He was a representative of the Cold War counter-Enlightenment along with other philosophers, such as Michael Oakeshott. Their outlook was shared by a number of political thinkers involved in the development of international relations theory.

Existing studies of the postwar counter-Enlightenment usually focus on the same figures: Berlin, most often, and occasionally Jacob Talmon. These studies have all but neglected the political realists.[30] This may be the result of a retrospective disciplinary bias, but if so it is certainly

---

[27] Shklar, *After Utopia*, 255–56.
[28] See "The Counter-Enlightenment," in Isaiah Berlin, *Against the Current* (Princeton: Princeton University Press, 2013), 1–32.
[29] See "Realism in politics" in Isaiah Berlin, *The Power of Ideas* (Princeton: Princeton University Press, 2000), 163–72.
[30] See Zeev Sternhell, *The Anti-Enlightenment Tradition* (New Haven: Yale University Press, 2009), 372–421; Graeme Garrard, *Counter-Enlightenments from the Eighteenth Century to the Present* (London: Routledge, 2006).

unwarranted, since at the time the theory of international politics was not clearly differentiated yet from political theory or, indeed, from history. In fact, the realists considered Berlin an intellectual ally, to the point of inviting him to the conference to which Morgenthau was being flown. Not only were they as emphatic as Berlin or Talmon in their critique of the Enlightenment, but in the 1950s they succeeded in establishing new academic fields on counter-Enlightenment ideological foundations. A reinterpretation of modern political realism and international relations theory as branches of this tradition is overdue. In providing this genealogy of realism, however, my goal is not to reduce realism to a strand of an immutable intellectual tradition.[31] It is to understand realism as an active ideological force that has creatively reinterpreted the counter-Enlightenment tradition and successfully adapted it to the modern world, and in particular to the liberal and scientific culture of Cold War America.

What is so fascinating about the postwar realist movement is that, unlike Isaiah Berlin's or Zeev Sternhell's static counter-Enlightenments, it did not stand solely in tension with Western rationalism and Enlightenment values. Its lasting intellectual success, its capacity to shape an entire academic discipline and to penetrate the security establishment of Cold War America to become its intellectual and moral compass was due in no small measure to the compromises it made with scientific culture and with political liberalism. The realist counter-Enlightenment, in other words, was also the tail end of this reactionary tradition and its irreversible transformation into a component of liberal modernity.

American realism signaled a deep transformation of a set of European ideas about authority and tradition, which, when transplanted on American soil, powerfully modified dominant notions of liberal governance. It gave these ideas a conservative inflection but also transformed them in the process. The result was the emergence of an unprecedented ideological hybrid for which we still lack a descriptive term, although some have been proposed occasionally, from Judith Shklar's "conservative liberalism" to "authoritarian liberalism" or even "neoliberalism."

---

[31] Sternhell – like Berlin – tends to remain locked into a frontal opposition between two ever-resurgent worldviews, a sort of unending eighteenth century in which the intellectual clash between Kant and Herder never ceases to be replayed through proxies, to the point of becoming a transcendental structure of modern history. For a more historical account of the counter-Enlightenment, see Darrin M. McMahon, *Enemies of the Enlightenment: The French Counter-Enlightenment and the Making of Modernity* (New York: Oxford University Press, 2001).

REALISM, DECISION-MAKING AND THE RISE OF RATIONAL CHOICE

What made the main characters of this book "realists" was a general wariness about any claims of being able to replace politics with rationalistic or scientific schemes. For them, power and conflict were intrinsic to the human condition, and as such an absolute horizon beyond which it was impossible to pass. Politics was ultimately the sphere of fundamental decisions over human affairs, one in which rationalism had little purchase beyond self-preservation. Political decisions were rooted in a universal struggle for power, which Morgenthau considered an anthropological fact and the signature of man's destitute condition. Political decisions were decisions over war and peace; decisions that discriminated between friends and foes and thus preceded and defined social order itself; decisions that were not bound by preexisting rules, but, on the contrary, specified the rules of political existence in the first place.

This was a pre-rational, existential dimension of the human condition that could not be entirely understood through scientific categories or transcended with social technologies. Politics would never go away, and fantasies of replacing it with technical fixes jeopardized the capacity to deal politically with any given situation. For many realists, the 1930s had tragically demonstrated the impotence of rationalist approaches to politics. A science of politics was ultimately a delusional project, since the political condition had no "outside" from which politics could be apprehended scientifically. As a result, the value-neutrality that defined science could never obtain in politics. "A science of politics," Morgenthau wrote disparagingly, "deals with a subject that is existentially alien to it."[32]

The realists viewed politics as an existential engagement in a *concrete* situation that could not be captured through rationalist abstractions. This was true of the way they conceived the study of politics as well, in the sense that it could not abstract from what Morgenthau called the *Standort*, the perspective of the actor engaged in the situation. For them, politics always took place within a determined space, within a singular configuration of forces and a historically unique distribution of things, entitlements, claims, and power.

The world of politics was not the *tabula rasa* of rationalist templates that could be manipulated at will as long as it remained a projection of the

---

[32] Hans J. Morgenthau, *Science: Servant or Master?* (New York: New American Library, 1972), 34.

mind. It was not the flat and transparent world preexisting the philosophical Big Bang of the social contract. It was a grainy, textured world of embodied and tangible powers, crisscrossed by different intensities and forces. It was a world that was always already politicized, a world that was inhabited by powers whose authority was not grounded in reason but in the existence of power itself and in the fact it had survived historical vicissitudes. In other words, it was an *old* world.

Just as the space of politics was not the Euclidean space of science but a concrete territory, the time of politics was not some Cartesian abstraction. While science looked for laws and regularities, political time was elastic and incommensurable with itself. The art of politics was essentially a matter of timeliness, a sensitivity to what Machiavelli called *la qualità dei tempi*. Political time too was something concrete, qualified by unfolding events that gave it its rhythm, its pace, and that had the ability to compress or dilate it, to accelerate it or bring it to a standstill.[33] What was political about a situation was thus entirely contained in its unique character, in what early realists called its "historical individuality," which was precisely what science could never capture since science was comprised of abstractions and lawful generalities. The scientific approach to politics was bound to fail because in the real world of politics, all things were not commensurable and would never be made equal.

It is not that rationalism or science cannot be applied to political processes: much of what is called "politics" is nothing else than the routine application of established rules to current affairs or the scientific management of resources. Yet, as Mannheim (whom many among the realists had read closely) had argued, this was a mistaken use of the word: The "routine affairs of the state" conducted "in accordance with existing rules" in a "rationalized sphere consisting of settled and routinized procedures" were not politics but, more strictly, administration.[34] Politics proper designated a domain of social life where such routine was not possible: "dominance in national and international life is achieved through struggle, in itself irrational, in which chance plays an important part. These irrational forces in society form that sphere of social life which

---

[33] Niccolò Machiavelli, *Il Principe*, in *Opere I*, ed. Corrado Vivanti (Torino/Paris: Einaudi-Gallimard, 1997). See in particular ch. 25, "Quantum Fortuna in rebus humanis possit et quomodo illis sit occurrendum."
[34] Karl Mannheim, *Ideology and Utopia: An Introduction to the Sociology of Knowledge* (London: Routledge and Kegan Paul, 1936), 100–01.

is unorganized and unrationalized, and in which conduct and politics become necessary."[35]

Politics and prudence were *de rigueur* when social life was neither organized, not rationalized. Politics took place when established rules and templates no longer provided a reliable guide for action and even hampered it. It was no coincidence, then, that in the postwar years the discipline of international relations became the fulcrum of political realism. It designated a domain where rules were few and unreliable, uncertainty high, organization almost absent, and the possibility of lethal conflict ever present. In this sphere of emergencies, existential threats, and constant possibility of war, realism found its most powerful intellectual foundation.

From a realist perspective, politics took essentially the form of authoritative decisions. Thinking of politics as decision means accepting the disjunction between politics and rationality. The need for a political decision arises in critical times when established rules and rational frameworks no longer provide a guide for action. Etymology connects the word "crisis" to the Greek verb *krinein*, which means "to decide," "to discriminate," "to arbitrate." Crises call for decisions because established routines are no longer effective or because outcomes are claimed by competing sets of rules. Emergencies also call for decisions to be taken without the leisure of considering all their logical consequences. Political decisions are thus fundamentally different from the application of a preexisting rule or a calculation.

A true decision, Jacques Derrida once suggested, bears upon what is not entirely subject to rational determination: "a decision that would not experience the undecidable would not be a free decision, it would be only the programmable application or the continuous unfolding of a calculable process."[36] This experience of the undecidable occupies a place of choice in Western political lore and is never very far from any hagiography of leadership. It is precisely the capacity to cut through the thick tangle of rational determinations and to overcome the narrow limits set by established rules that our political culture sees as the distinctive mark of the great decision-maker. "Turn him to any cause of policy, / The Gordian knot of it he will unloose / Familiar as his garter..." says the Bishop of Canterbury about the political virtuoso Henry the

---

[35] Mannheim, *Ideology and Utopia*, 103. These considerations are located in the first section of Chapter 2: "Why is there no science of politics?"

[36] Jacques Derrida, *Force de loi* (Paris: Galilée, 1994), 53.

Fifth.[37] And just as Alexander's feat ushered in a new historical era through a forceful decision unconstrained by the science of knots, a true political decision moves beyond the narrow limits of rationality and uses power to create a new reality and a new beginning.

Nowhere was this awareness of the disconnect between politics and rationality more present that in the newborn discipline of international relations, which, as an influential report put it at the time, was premised on the possibility that "force and not social science will be employed to solve disputes," not unlike the way the Macedonian king had dealt with the Gordian knot.[38] And no one was more prominent in this field than Hans Morgenthau, who had published *Politics among Nations* in 1948 and who was widely regarded as the founding father of this new academic enterprise. But how could this truth be told? How could this vision of politics as decision be defended in the age of science? And who wanted to hear that Politics had little to do with Reason after the disturbing episode of World War II? Extolling political will over rational constraints was better left to Leni Rieffenstahl's propaganda movies and to Carl Schmitt. His name is associated with the doctrine known as "decisionism," and he was once one of Morgenthau's major intellectual references. He had become a fervent Nazi supporter in 1933, while a few years later, Morgenthau had been forced to escape to Switzerland and the United States.

As he jetted through the American skies on the morning of May 7, 1954, Morgenthau had cause for worry. An old European wisdom about statecraft was entering its crepuscule as science purported to replace politics with "systems," "cybernetic steering," "strategic interactions" captured by "game theory," and other inventions that substituted sovereign decisions with machine codes. The very aircraft on which he was being transported was a technological artifact around which much research had been done to transform human decisions into a servo-mechanical ersatz operating through feedback loops and other mathematized control mechanisms.

What Morgenthau could not foresee, however, was that within a matter of years, political realism would gradually morph into

---

[37] William Shakespeare, "Henry V," in *The Complete Works* (Oxford: Oxford University Press, 2005), 597, 1.1.48–50.
[38] Bryce Wood, "The Program of the Division of the Social Sciences in the Field of International Relations," Folder 67, Box 8, Series 910, Research Group (RG) 3, Rockefeller Foundation Archives (RF), Rockefeller Archive Center, Tarrytown, NY (hereafter RAC), 1947, p. 24.

a pseudo-science. The realist message, like Morgenthau himself, would soon be delivered through high-tech means; the drive for power inherent to a flawed human nature would become a structural "security dilemma" amenable to systemic representations and cybernetic schematics deprived of agency; concrete political decisions taken in the fog of war or the emergency of the moment would be recast as instances of "rational choice" entirely deprived of moral dilemmas. Primordial political authority – the kind of Schmittian decision that could grasp the *kairos* of the moment and cut through the paralyzing loops of rational elaboration – would soon be recast as the ultimate instance of rationality.

Authority, Carl Friedrich wrote, was rational precisely because it bridged rationality and action across the contingency of circumstances. This kind of authority was, according to him, "potential rationality ... in a condensed form."[39] The sovereign *fiat* taken under the pressure of circumstances, in the darkest and most secluded corridors of power, was on its way to become "rational choice" in a dramatic transformation of the language of political theory that is still with us today. Political realism in America followed a trajectory very similar to that of Morgenthau in his jet plane: An old doctrine of prudence, a conservative theory of sovereignty and authority, was soon encased in a high-tech exoskeleton and resold as a product of modernity.

THE SCIENCE OF RATIONAL DECISION-MAKING AND ITS HISTORY

How did political realism leave behind its contempt for science and rationalism? How did it take the form of a political "science"? What are the implications of this transformation? Certainly, the increasing entanglement of science and politics that characterized the Cold War science regime contributed to blur the distinction between "truth" and "power." In 1946, Morgenthau had launched a vitriolic attack on the politically debilitating effects of scientific rationalism in *Scientific Man vs. Power Politics*. By the 1950s, his scientific man had moved very much to the center of power politics and was probably dependent on Air Force funding

---

[39] The only way to escape the undecidability of the rational decision, Friedrich goes on, is to reintroduce authority: Carl J. Friedrich, "On Rereading Machiavelli and Althusius: Reason, Rationality, and Religion," in *Rational Decision*, ed. Carl J. Friedrich, Nomos (New York: Prentice-Hall, 1964), 180.

for his research.⁴⁰ He was also working on problems that gave a new meaning to what being "rational" meant. Even though it seemed to refer to a universal and atemporal attribute, the idea of "rationality" that emerged after 1945 had not existed before. As Thomas Schelling later put it, "defining 'rational' ... is itself part of the business of game theory."⁴¹ Rationality now developed operational meanings closely connected to concrete strategic problems. It was much less constraining than prior references to the all-powerful "Reason" of the philosophical tradition and it proved to be much more accommodating of the designs of the powers that be when it was not directly subservient to them. Rationality cast doubt over the capacity of democratic publics to attain a rationality that seemed to be confined to the rarefied atmosphere of high office.⁴²

The postwar years also witnessed a backlash against scientific positivism across the disciplines. This backlash did not only take the form of a return to theological or metaphysical thinking about politics, although the realist movement indulged in both. It also translated into new sociological accounts of science – notably Thomas Kuhn's – the suggestion that scientific authority was really not that different from other forms of social authority. Scientific programs no longer were synonymous with mobilizing a constraining, positive notion of reality. On the contrary, science now dwelt on artificiality and simulation: Game theory, cybernetics, and general systems theory penetrated a number of disciplines. They profoundly transformed the analysis of strategic and security problems. These programs in turn had a profound influence on political theory and

---

⁴⁰ On the relationships between scientific research and military R&D, see Mark Solovey, *Shaky Foundations: The Politics-Patronage-Social Science Nexus in Cold War America* (New Brunswick: Rutgers University Press, 2013).
⁴¹ Thomas C. Schelling, *Choice and Consequence: Perspectives of an Economist* (Cambridge, MA: Harvard University Press, 1984), 215.
⁴² Histories of "rationality" are very recent. See in particular Paul Erickson et al., *How Reason Almost Lost Its Mind: The Strange Career of Cold War Rationality* (Chicago: The University of Chicago Press, 2013); Philip Mirowski, *Machine Dreams: Economics Becomes a Cyborg Science* (Cambridge: Cambridge University Press, 2002); Sonja M. Amadae, *Rationalizing Capitalist Democracy: The Cold War Origins of Rational Choice Liberalism* (Chicago: University of Chicago Press, 2003); S. Belletto, "The Game Theory Narrative and the Myth of the National Security State," *American Quarterly* 61, no. 2 (2009): 333–57; Hunter Heyck, "Producing Reason," in *Cold War Social Science: Knowledge Production, Liberal Democracy, and Human Nature*, eds. Mark Solovey and Hamilton Cravens (New York: Palgrave, 2012); Robert Leonard, *Von Neumann, Morgenstern, and the Creation of Game Theory: From Chess to Social Science, 1900–1960* (Cambridge: Cambridge University Press, 2012).

political science, which has not been fully gauged yet. They entirely transformed the way theorists thought about decision-making.⁴³ They provided a new language for thinking about authority and justifying political decisions.

According to this new protocol of legitimation, "rationality" compensated for an absent public. It posited that by virtue of being rational, decisions could potentially receive unanimous consent. Beyond its diverse methodological forms, rational choice provided the new basis on which political decisions could be taken without democratic mandate. Though it was implicitly the exclusive attribute of far-sighted statesmen and defense intellectuals, rationality provided an adequate substitute for an absent public.

These changing conceptions of science eventually contributed to making it less antithetic to traditional conceptions of political authority. Over time, the realists were able to abandon their opposition to science and political rationalism. The result was an updated and modernized form of political realism, known as "neorealism," which did not shun the language of science and rationality but, on the contrary, mobilized it successfully to safeguard a traditional vision of politics and authority in the age of high modernism.

The publication of Kenneth Waltz's *Theory of International Politics* in 1979 signaled the successful completion of this disciplinary intellectual conversion. In the field of political theory, neorealism was indeed a conservative revolution – one that perfectly illustrated the motto of the young Tancredi, eager to maintain the privileges of his family by joining the revolutionary forces in di Lampedusa's novel *Il gattopardo*: "If we want things to stay the same, everything will have to change."

As political realists sought to become more modern by embracing science, they also scrambled to appear legitimate by inventing a more glorious lineage than the one running through the counter-Enlightenment and culminating in the anti-liberal and theological reaction of the 1930s. In their effort to establish the validity of limitations on liberal constitutionalism and to rehabilitate dictatorial decision-making in times of crisis, they turned to classical authors rather than Carl Schmitt, despite their intellectual indebtedness to him. They did not seek to enroll counter-revolutionary thinkers either, even though in private some of

---

⁴³ For the case of economics, see Mirowski, *Machine Dreams*. For security studies and nuclear deterrence, see Sonja M. Amadae, *Prisoners of Reason: Game Theory and Neoliberal Political Economy* (Cambridge: Cambridge University Press, 2016).

them did not hide their admiration for Burke. Instead, they conscripted Thucydides, Machiavelli, and Hobbes into the role of precursors or pioneers of a "realist tradition" that soon became central to the disciplinary lore – even though some of these authors had never been considered "realists" until then. The case of Machiavelli, in particular, exhibited a spectacular reversal. A thinker whom twentieth-century realists without exception had condemned until the mid-1950s became the first exemplar of modern political realism.

Such developments were paralleled by excavations into the American past by historians and political theorists eager to exhume the remnants of an indigenous realism going back to the founding of the republic, and allegedly recovered by successive layers of isolationist ideology or messianic idealism.[44] These intellectual archaeologies were the work of émigré scholars – including Felix Gilbert and Hans Morgenthau – who brought to the United States ideas that they thought were sorely lacking in their adoptive country. *Historia magistra vitae*: Reading these ideas into the American past made perfect sense if one wanted to establish their cultural currency. These historiographical maneuvers of the 1950s had a deep impact on perceptions of American foreign policy. Realist ideas authorized new ways of thinking about politics. Taken together, they outlined a continuous tradition running from the tumultuous politics of sixteenth-century Italian city-states to the troubled birth of the American republic. Realists uncovered a "republican" tradition that made exceptions to morality or democratic custom not only permissible but necessary when the preservation of freedom was at stake.

These historiographical operations took place in the context of a broader conversation about the vexed relationship between security and liberal constitutionalism, and in particular of efforts to rehabilitate dictatorship as a form of governance that could be occasionally warranted under the specific circumstances of the Cold War.[45] The emergence of

---

[44] See for instance Felix Gilbert, *To the Farewell Address: Ideas of Early American Foreign Policy* (Princeton: Princeton University Press, 1961); Hans J. Morgenthau, "The Mainsprings of American Foreign Policy: The National Interest vs. Moral Abstractions," *The American Political Science Review* 44, no. 4 (1950): 833–54. See also Norman Jacobson, "Political Realism and the Age of Reason: The Anti-Rationalist Heritage in America," *The Review of Politics* 15, no. 4 (1953): 446–69.

[45] The main arguments of this discussion can be found in Clinton Rossiter, *Constitutional Dictatorship: Crisis Government in the Modern Democracies* (Princeton: Princeton University Press, 1948); Carl J. Friedrich, *Constitutional Reason of State: The Survival of the Constitutional Order* (Providence, RI: Brown University Press, 1957). For an earlier analysis of dictatorial powers, see Frederick Watkins, *The Failure of*

a "republican" paradigm in political thought also functioned as an argument in favor of the possibility of articulating in non-contradictory ways dictatorial measures in the defense of freedom. This new political history suggested that such a possibility was not only defensible in terms of constitutional doctrine, but that it had a long history and latency in American political culture. The nascent historiography of republicanism was very much an intellectual development associated with the Cold War and the rise of political realism as the dominant foreign policy ideology.[46]

What makes political realism such an elusive ideology is that the price it had to pay to become influential in America consisted in making compromises not only with liberalism but also with the scientific culture of the Cold War university. Starting in the late 1950s, it successfully established itself as an academic discipline by adopting the trappings of rationalistic social science, with rational choice, systems theory, and cybernetics serving as new legitimation protocols for political decision-making. This transformation of realism was the condition of its success. But this also made it difficult to decipher realism's ideological underpinnings. By the late 1970s, realism seemed to be hardly more than a set of assumptions and a formal method for the analysis of international politics that did not imply any specific normative preferences. And yet, as this book suggests, in its scientific, modernized form, realism carries along with it very specific visions of history, politics, and human nature tied to the counter-Enlightenment tradition. Such visions may have become almost unrecognizable in their current technocratic forms, but they are nonetheless fundamental components of our political imagination.

ABOUT THIS BOOK

Chapter 1 is an updated and augmented version of "The Realist Gambit: Postwar American Political Science and the Birth of IR Theory," initially published in *International Political Sociology* 2(4), 2008, pp. 281–304. Chapter 2 was published as "American Katechon: International Relations

---

Constitutional Emergency Powers under the German Republic (Cambridge, MA: Harvard University Press, 1939). See the discussion in Chapter 6.

[46] Renzo Pecchioli, *Dal "mito" di Venezia all' "ideologia americana". Itinerari e modelli della storiografia sul repubblicanesimo dell'età moderna* (Venezia: Marsilio, 1983). This has been usually overlooked by disciplinary historians, who have tended to take at face value the "republican" aspects of realism, while they were in fact a by-product of this historiographical operation. See for instance Tjalve, *Realist Strategies of Republican Peace*.

Theory as Secularized Political Theology," in *Constellations: An International Journal of Critical and Democratic Theory*, 17(2), 2010, pp. 224–53. Chapter 3 appears in a slightly modified form as "The 'First Modern Realist': Felix Gilbert's Machiavelli and the Making of the Realist Tradition in International Relations," in *Modern Intellectual History*, 2015, DOI: 10.1017/S1479244314000870. Chapter 4 was published as "The Kuhning of Reason: Realism, Rationalism, and Political Decision in IR Theory after Thomas Kuhn," in the *Review of International Studies*, 42(1), 2016, pp. 3–24. Chapter 5 is a modified version of "Cyborg Pantocrator: Or how IR Theory turned Decisionism into Rational Choice," which was published in *The Journal of the History of the Behavioral Sciences*, 47(3), 2011, pp. 1–23. Chapter 6 is a substantially rewritten and augmented version of an article co-written with Daniel Bessner and published as "How Realism Waltzed Off: Liberalism and Decision-Making in Kenneth Waltz's *Theory of International Politics*," in *International Security*, 40(2), 2015, pp. 87–118.

I

The Realist Gambit – or the End of Political Science

POLITICAL SCIENCE AND INTERNATIONAL RELATIONS AFTER 1945

The lack of differentiation between political science and international relations theory is one of the striking aspects of postwar disciplinary debates. Whether they studied domestic or international politics, scholars at the time belonged to a hardly differentiated disciplinary field. Indeed, the study of international politics was identified as one of the thriving areas of political science after 1945. The collaboration between political scientists and government agencies during the war had widened the interest of the profession in all things international. Dramatic international developments and soaring enrolment numbers following the demobilization of the armed forces contributed to creating a strong demand for courses in international relations. Summing up wartime developments in the discipline, Harvard political scientist Carl Friedrich observed that "among the more specialized organizations, those in the international field are most numerous, and indeed are highly significant for the progress of political science in the United States."[1] For sure, the thriving field of International Relations (IR) may have seemed ill-defined compared with an established discipline that had its own association since 1903, a dedicated journal, and academic departments in prestigious universities. A lot of ink was spent trying to delineate the contours of the expanding field of IR by defining its core contents as well as its research methods, and

---

[1] Carl J. Friedrich, "Instruction and Research: Political Science in the United States in Wartime," *The American Political Science Review* 41, no. 5 (1947): 985.

the immediate postwar years were a period of sustained reflection about the organization of international knowledge.² In most accounts, practitioners and observers alike concurred that it had strong affinities with political science, but that it also needed to mobilize other branches of the social sciences, such as geography, economics, international law, diplomatic history, social psychology, and anthropology. "The IR specialist," according to Klaus Knorr, "is a specialist in one of the basic fields, ordinarily political science, who is compelled to draw upon the relevant research work of specialists in other subsidiary fields."³ The specificity of IR resided not in a method, but rather in the particular assemblage of materials and techniques it represented, in the "patterns of equipment" it brought to bear upon the study of power.⁴

These perplexities were not confined to a neatly delineated field of IR. The discussions about its nature only reflected locally a status anxiety that was felt throughout the discipline of political science. In the late 1940s, IR appeared to "command ... no methodology of its own," but neither did political science.⁵ Writing the same year as Knorr, Friedrich pointed out that "the development of a central core of sound theory is perhaps the greatest need of American political science today. Its most obvious weakness in comparison with economics is the lack of interest of political scientists in the development of such an agreed foundation in theory."⁶ A 1948 report by the research committee of the American Political Science Association tried to cast the situation in a more optimistic light and considered that "there is no longer any single technique methods and designs must be blended and kept in elastic touch and mutual penetration."⁷ The situation does not seem to have substantially improved in the early 1950s when Harold Lasswell pointed out "the existence among academicians of conflicting conceptions of the scope

---

² This concerned not only IR theory, but also area studies. See Hans J. Morgenthau, "Area Studies and the Study of International Relations," *International Social Science Bulletin* 4, no. 4 (1952): 647–55. For an overview, see David L. Szanton, *The Politics of Knowledge: Area Studies and the Disciplines* (Berkeley: University of California Press, 2004).
³ Klaus Knorr, "Economics and International Relations: A Problem in Teaching," *Political Science Quarterly* 62, no. 4 (1947): 552.
⁴ Frederick S. Dunn, "The Present Course of International Relations Research," *World Politics* 2, no. 1 (1949): 85.
⁵ Knorr, "Economics and International Relations," 552.
⁶ Friedrich, "Instruction and Research," 980.
⁷ Ernest S. Griffith, ed. *Research in Political Science; the World of the Panels of the Research Committee, American Political Science Association* (Chapel Hill: University of North Carolina Press, 1948).

and method of political science." Because the discipline was defined by its "subject-matter" rather than by an agreed method, "most valuable work has been done by other than academically trained political scientists."[8] The same criticism was addressed to IR, to the extent that the field was also defined by "the nature of the questions" it dealt with rather than a consensual methodology, which resulted in much relevant work being done within neighboring disciplines.[9] In 1955, Morgenthau seems to have formulated a common complaint when he lamented the "inorganic growth and haphazard character of political science," a discipline that had developed "not by virtue of an intellectual principle germane to the field, but in response to pressures from the outside."[10] His criticism of the state of IR, however, was couched in the very same terms, because he saw no difference between the two fields: for him, they ought to be part of a general theory of politics. A few years later, Stanley Hoffmann deplored that "without theory, we will have to take whatever other disciplines w[ill] see fit to dump onto our plate, and we will have indigestion from smörgåsbord."[11] In other words, the lack of a theoretical core was a generic problem of political science that, by extension, also marred IR but was not specific to it. This has important implications for the argument followed here, for it means that the protracted search for a theory was not so much about clarifying the professional identity of IR as it was part of a discipline-wide conversation involving all the branches of political science. Postwar statements about IR theory must be understood primarily as contributions to a wider contest over the nature and the method of political science itself.

What was really at stake in these debates was the legitimacy of political science as a scientific project. That this project was in crisis was something that many contemporaries acknowledged and tried to address. Pondering what the discipline had to offer in the current world situation, Quincy Wright started by pointing out "the insistence by many that a science of politics is impossible," an objection that he then proceeded to counter.[12]

---

[8] Harold D. Lasswell, "The Immediate Future of Research Policy and Method in Political Science," *The American Political Science Review* 45, no. 1 (1951): 133.
[9] Frederick S. Dunn, "The Scope of International Relations," *World Politics* 1, no. 1 (1948): 144.
[10] Hans J. Morgenthau, "Reflections on the State of Political Science," *Review of Politics* 17, no. 4 (1955): 437.
[11] Stanley Hoffmann, "International Relations: The Long Road to Theory," *World Politics* 11, no. 3 (1959): 348.
[12] Quincy Wright, "Political Science and World Stabilization," *The American Political Science Review* 44, no. 1 (1950): 2.

Writing a few years later, Fred Kort, a political scientist at the University of Connecticut, stressed "the contested status of the science of politics" and the fact that those who wanted to turn the study of politics into a science remained "on the defensive" as they grappled with the twin problems of the unpredictability of human behavior and the difficulty of ascertaining what would be the criteria of a science of politics.[13] Morgenthau himself was explicit about the fact that the struggle to define international relations theory was actually a struggle to define political science *in toto*: "the controversy about the nature and the proper place of international relations and area studies as academic disciplines is a manifestation of that division of opinion concerning the fundamental problem of understanding politics."[14] His ambivalence about the desirability of establishing IR theory as a separate field only reflected his conviction that political science as a whole needed to be organized around the concept of power, not just the study of international affairs. The existence of a separate field of IR only provided a modicum of solace once it became clear that political science would move in the opposite direction.

As Morgenthau's diagnosis suggested, most of the discussions about the nature and identity of the discipline revolved around two contested issues: the role of values, and the problem of the rationality of politics, which revolved around the concept of "power." The possibility of a science of politics was indexed on the prevailing conception of science at the time, and this conception was premised on value relativism. A true science did not pronounce on ultimate ends, only on the causal sequences allowing for their realization. As long as science was considered to be part of a modernizing historical process that could also be described in terms of moral and political progress, value-relativism was not an issue. There was also a strong association in interwar American culture between science and democracy.[15] Yet, after World War II had witnessed the power of science and technology unleashed at the service of the darkest purposes, narratives of historical progress could no longer be taken for granted. An increasingly vocal critique of value-relativism and scientific positivism, articulated in particular by émigré scholars, set the stage for the postwar

---

[13] Fred Kort, "The Issue of a Science of Politics in Utilitarian Thought," *The American Political Science Review* 46, no. 4 (1952): 1140.
[14] Hans J. Morgenthau, "Prospect for a New Foreign Policy," in *Politics in the 20th Century* (Chicago: The University of Chicago Press, 1958), 88.
[15] Jewett, *Science, Democracy, and the American University*.

debate on political science. For these critics, the moral blindness of scientific positivism had prevented scientists from discriminating between democracy and totalitarianism.[16] Unable to resist their harnessing to the most sinister political projects, the social sciences had been in no position to contribute in any meaningful way to the fight against fascism, when they did not serve it. Arnold Brecht, a legal scholar who had found refuge at the New School in 1933, reported on a 1946 roundtable on relativism in political theory starting with a dramatic personal note:

> modern science and modern scientific methods ... have led to an ethical vacuum, a religious vacuum, and a philosophical vacuum.... For they have offered little or nothing to distinguish between good and evil, right and wrong, justice and injustice. All social sciences are involved in this calamity, but none has been so deeply affected as political science, which had to face the new creeds of Communism, Fascism, and Nazism as political phenomena of tremendous power. They settled down in the area abandoned by science, taking full advantage of the fact that, scientifically speaking, there was a vacuum.[17]

Whether they deplored the demise of the social sciences, like Brecht, or suggested that there was a dialectic connivance between scientific positivism and totalitarianism, like members of the Frankfurt School, émigré scholars leveled a charge that forced political scientists defending the traditional image of the discipline to make explicit a number of methodological assumptions previously taken for granted.[18] The charge against value-relativism was indeed at odds with the basic image of science in the United States: true science stemmed from a commitment to empiricism and rational inference, and to an objectivism untainted by the assumption of normative preferences. Value-relativism, in fact, was the very criterion of science. Faced with the rejection of value-relativism, many political scientists struggled to maintain the image of a value-free social science in a context where normative orientations could no longer be ignored, solicited as they were by the ideological tensions of the Cold War.

---

[16] A good example is the attack by Voegelin and the reply by Kelsen: Eric Voegelin, *The New Science of Politics* (Chicago: The University of Chicago Press, 1952); Hans Kelsen, Eric Voegelin, and Eckhart Arnold, *A New Science of Politics: Hans Kelsen's Reply to Eric Voegelin's "New Science of Politics": A Contribution to the Critique of Ideology* (Piscataway, NJ: Transaction Books, 2004).

[17] Arnold Brecht, "Political Theory: Beyond Relativism in Political Theory," *The American Political Science Review* 41, no. 3 (1947): 470.

[18] On this issue, see John G. Gunnell, "American Political Science, Liberalism, and the Invention of Political Theory," *The American Political Science Review* 82, no. 1 (1988): 71–87; as well as John G. Gunnell, "Relativism: The Return of the Repressed," *Political Theory* 21, no. 4 (1993): 563–64.

Steeped in the early twentieth-century Deweyan tradition of "scientific democracy," Harold Lasswell, for instance, considered that the preference for democratic values was "obvious" and that it did not need, therefore, to "interfere with objectivity" in scientific activity.[19] Taking a rather exceptional position among émigré scholars, Hans Kelsen defended in no uncertain terms the principle of value-free political science: the scientist "must not presuppose any value" and this "principle of objectivity applies to social science as well as to natural science, and in particular to so-called political science." If scientific statements had involved the endorsement of values, they would become "political ideology" and "there w[ould] never be a real political science."[20] In the interwar years, as Morgenthau later reminisced, "the epic struggle between Kelsen ... and his politically oriented enemies [had] provided the great issues in political science."[21] Eager to prevent any encroachment of politics on the territory of law and to establish the scientific basis of legal theory, he had developed the most rigorous form of positivism. But the intellectual fortunes of this program waned after 1945, and Kelsen found himself on the losing side of the postwar debate about international politics. His brand of legal positivism – which, by entirely dissociating law from justice, recognized the legal nature of the National Socialist state – was violently criticized.[22] His enemies scored a paradoxical intellectual victory precisely when they had been defeated politically. Adding insult to injury, Kelsen saw some of his own disciples – like his former student John Herz – gradually drift toward the legal realism of his intellectual nemesis Carl Schmitt.[23] Even Morgenthau, who had frequented Kelsen in Geneva, had written his *Habilitationsschrift* as an attempt to overcome what he saw as the deficiencies of Kelsen's normativism, before moving much further away

---

[19] Harold D. Lasswell and Daniel Lerner, *The Policy Sciences: Recent Developments in Scope and Method* (Stanford: Stanford University Press, 1951), 135.
[20] Hans Kelsen, *General Theory of Law and State* (New York: Russell & Russell, 1961), 641, 46–47.
[21] Hans J. Morgenthau, *Dilemmas of Politics* (Chicago: The University of Chicago Press, 1958), 21.
[22] See Kelsen's observations about Bolshevism, Fascism, and National Socialism as legal orders in Hans Kelsen, *General Theory of Law and State* (New Brunswick: Transaction, 2006), 5.
[23] On Kelsen's waning influence after 1945, see William E. Scheuerman, "Professor Kelsen's Amazing Disappearing Act," in *Émigré Scholars and the Genesis of International Relations*, ed. Felix Rösch (Basingstoke: Palgrave Macmillan, 2014). John Herz tells of his gradual disillusion with Kelsenian legal theory in his memoir: Herz, *Vom Überleben*, 94–103. For Herz's relation to Schmitt, see Herz, "Looking at Carl Schmitt."

from legal formalism.[24] Despite his important role in the legal architecture of the United Nations, Kelsen rapidly became an isolated voice in post-1945 debates, preaching in the desert and often used as a foil and proxy for an American scientific culture to which he was alien.

Trying to obviate the problem, Wright distinguished between the value-relativism of "pure science," and "applied science" that could "assume the values of a particular group and seek formulae useful in achieving these values."[25] These latter values could be of the most general kind (such as human welfare) and political science could move freely between its status as a pure science and its practical applications. In his article on the possibility of a scientific study of politics, Kort suggested that both natural and social phenomena were subject to the same scientific method of inquiry. The difference was in the "lower degree of probability" that hypotheses could achieve in political science, because of the number of uncontrolled variables intervening.[26] To a large extent, behavioralism would be the explicit formulation and defense of a number of assumptions that were implicit in traditional American social science but became increasingly contested in the postwar years.[27]

The second issue that the proponents of a science of politics had to deal with was the rationality of their subject matter and, more broadly, the relation between reason and power. Here again, the discussion must be resituated against the backdrop of the war and the unprecedented combination of bureaucratic rationality and calls to irrational impulses that distinguished the exercise of power in Fascist and Nazi regimes. As the rational nature of politics could no longer be taken for granted, and as the state could no longer be considered as the embodiment of a rational good, the problem was to determine whether politics could be entirely characterized and accounted for through rational categories. This whole discussion crystallized around the notion of "power." Power, of course, was not a new subject in the discipline, but it fulfilled specific functions within the

---

[24] For a discussion of Morgenthau's debt to Kelsen, see Jütersonke, *Morgenthau, Law and Realism*, in particular chapter 3.
[25] Wright, "Political Science and World Stabilization," 3–4.
[26] Kort, "The Issue of a Science of Politics in Utilitarian Thought," 1151.
[27] John G. Gunnell, *The Descent of Political Theory: The Genealogy of an American Vocation* (Chicago: The University of Chicago Press, 1993); Robert Adcock, "Interpreting Behavioralism," in *Modern Political Science: Anglo-American Exchanges since 1880*, eds., Robert Adcock, Mark Bevir, and Shannon C. Stimson (Princeton: Princeton University Press, 2007); Robert Adcock, "The Historiography of a Centenarian Field: Contexts and the History of Political Science," paper given at the Annual Meeting of the American Political Science Association, New Orleans, 2012.

postwar disciplinary debates. First, power was meant to *separate* political science from other disciplines, not *integrate* them. In the minds of those who thought in terms of "power politics," power provided an organizing focus that would set a theory of politics apart from other disciplines. But power was not just any concept: It was also meant to protect political theory from being taken over by quantitative methods. These methods, Morgenthau suggested, were inadequate when it came to understanding "phenomena which are determined by historic individuality, rational or moral choice."[28] Power was precisely such a phenomenon, which could not be satisfactorily analyzed in formal conceptual terms: It was "a quality of interpersonal relations that can be experienced, evaluated, guessed at, but that is not susceptible to quantification."[29] In order to be understood, it had to be resituated within a concrete situation. Unless, as Judith Shklar correctly saw, one would adopt a radical view of power as something always indexed to an existential peril: "The only occasion in which it can be said to appear in 'pure' form, unconditioned by a host of circumstances, is in active combat. Here power means destroying an enemy physically or subordinating him to one's will by the threat of destruction. That is why the only perfectly clear definition of politics-as-power is that of Carl Schmitt."[30] Some cognoscenti, such as Arnold Wolfers, quickly realized that the dramatization of power politics and its associated vision of inimical interstate relations was essentially as a "German view" that could be traced back to Schmitt or Ratzenhofer and was a bit problematic (not least because of Wolfer's own past, as we shall see).[31] Yet, American realists, Shklar noted, were "anything but fascists" and even though they longed for a central concept of politics, they did not want to pay "the full price" for it.[32] Rather than exposing their debt to Schmitt, they turned to more acceptable concepts, some borrowed from Christian thought, which was going through a powerful revival in the 1940s and 1950s, and in particular notions of a fallen human nature, marred by a sinful *animus dominandi* of Augustinian descent. At this rate, power could be virtually anything and it was certainly restive to any attempt at formal quantification or model-building.

The notion of power was thus increasingly used to stress the incapacity of scientific rationalism to comprehend politics. It gave strong leverage to

---

[28] Morgenthau, *Dilemmas of Politics*, 18.   [29] Morgenthau, *Truth and Power*, 245.
[30] Shklar, *Legalism*, 125.
[31] Arnold Wolfers, "Statesmanship and Moral Choice," *World Politics* 1, no. 2 (1949): 181.
[32] Shklar, *Legalism*, 125.

those who wanted to detach political science from the naturalistic model of scientific analysis and keep the analysis of politics within the ambit of the historical disciplines. Analyzing politics or the state "in terms of power" meant introducing irrational elements such as psychological drives, charisma, or a deep-seated *libido dominandi*. In a programmatic article on the study of power in which he discussed recent trends in American political science, Franz Neumann made the case that power was an "elusive concept." Because it was not merely physical coercion but also an appeal to rational and emotional faculties, its "two-sided character ... already marks political science off from natural sciences. It makes it impossible (even if it were desirable) to measure power relationships as one measures the behavior of external nature."[33] The concept of power was not digestible by theorists of a more systemic slant who wanted to study complex interactions, systemic feedbacks, but could not come to terms with a transitive and linear notion that presupposed some mysterious source and smacked of metaphysics or theology.[34]

The new focus on power, in other words, was very much the symptom of the crisis of confidence of scientific rationalism. In September 1951, *The American Political Science Review* dedicated a special section to the issue of "Political Science and Political Power" in which the issues at stake in the vogue of power politics, both for political science at large and IR, became visible. Writing about "the present-day tendency to think and to speak of the state almost exclusively in terms of power," Walter Sandelius accepted the view that the reality of power was more than just physical coercion: "the power of propaganda, of prestige, and the like are variously documented and analyzed in the search for political realities."[35] Citing Morgenthau's view of power as "the evil lust for domination over men," he proceeded to mount a defense of scientific rationalism by refuting the idea that what was historical or psychological was not rational. Ultimately, the analysis of power could still be conducted within the framework of scientific rationalism. At the other end of the spectrum, Thomas Vernor Smith expounded a social-Darwinistic, ontological view of power as ubiquitous and running through nature and society alike, but

---

[33] Franz L. Neumann, "Approaches to the Study of Power," *Political Science Quarterly* 65, no. 2 (1950): 162.

[34] For an example of such qualms about "power," see Herbert A. Simon, "Notes on the Observation and Measurement of Political Power," *The Journal of Politics* 15, no. 4 (1953).

[35] Walter E. Sandelius, "Reason and Political Power," *The American Political Science Review* 45, no. 3 (1951): 704.

finding in nationalism and the national interest its highest moral expression.[36] This anti-rationalist manifesto written by a philosopher embodied a lot of what was wrong with the metaphysical view of power. For most in the political science profession, the focus on power politics entailed the risk of moving away from the standards of naturalistic science and regressing to speculative and ideational constructions or, worse, to some kind of *Lebensphilosophie* associated with reactionary German romanticism.

International relations scholars obviously took part in these debates, but they did not speak with one voice. Divergences of opinion as to the direction in which the field should develop were underscored by a growing uncertainty about its identity. As the demand for IR courses grew, many political scientists were "not at all certain about what material to cover or what approach to use."[37] This context triggered a protracted discussion about the study of IR, and the late 1940s saw a proto-disciplinary conversation take shape in journal articles, conferences, and reports of various kinds.[38] The twin issues of relativism and rationalism thus resonated within an ongoing reflection about the nature of international politics. The framework of this discussion was a relative consensus about the fact that IR was primarily defined by its topic and not by its method. It was "applied science" (Wolfers); "an unsystematic putting-together and presentation of material" from other fields, a "hodgepodge" (Gurian); it commanded "no methodology of its own" (Knorr); maybe it was only "the non-domestic side of the traditional disciplines" (Dunn). A few years later, Quincy Wright still claimed that IR was based on "at least eight disciplines," and Stanley Hoffmann that it was a "flea market."[39] As I pointed out earlier, such perplexities were not confined to IR, as similar doubts assailed other regions of political science, if not the whole discipline. But by making IR an applied field where analytical tools were imported from the social sciences, interdisciplinarity tended to impose the dominant criteria of scientific rationalism prevailing in other disciplines.

---

[36] T. V. Smith, "Power: Its Ubiquity and Legitimacy," *The American Political Science Review* 45, no. 3 (1951): 699.

[37] Russell H. Fifield, "The Introductory Course in International Relations," *The American Political Science Review* 42, no. 6 (1948): 1189.

[38] Brian C. Schmidt, "The Rockefeller Foundation Conference and the Long Road to a Theory of International Politics," in *The Invention of International Relations Theory: Realism, the Rockefeller Foundation, and the 1954 Conference on Theory*, ed. Nicolas Guilhot (New York: Columbia University Press, 2011).

[39] Quincy Wright, *The Study of International Relations* (New York: Appleton-Century-Crofts, 1955), 33; Hoffmann, "International Relations," 348.

Most scholars seeking to strengthen IR by promoting the application of social science research techniques to the study of international politics therefore subscribed to value-relativism as a principle of scientific work. They also tended not to advocate disciplinary autonomy, in the name of the same ideal of scientific unity. Arnold Wolfers, for instance, considered that "discussing whether IR constitutes a separate discipline" was a moot point, since "the problem is how to apply the resources of the social sciences most effectively to matters concerning international affairs." And "as a social scientist," the student of IR had "no special competence to judge the moral merits of ends or means," and was therefore committed to the ideal of value-free social science.[40] Similar views, mitigated by a commitment to social reform characteristic of the "policy science" approach, ran through much of Frederick Dunn's writing during the same years, and in particular the idea that IR should be subjected to the same criteria of validity as any other science, meaning logical induction and subsequent testing of hypotheses through empirical research.[41]

In this context, the push for a distinct "theory" of international relations overlapped with the pursuit of a specific agenda, focused on securing a place for power politics in postwar academe. If many students of international affairs saw the future of the field within the orbit of a scientific method cutting across traditional disciplines, the realists who subscribed to power politics were obviously dismayed by such prospects. Early proponents of a theory of IR were not parsimonious of critical pronouncements upon political science, and were aware that the institutional location of IR within political science departments was a thorny issue. The "advisability of this solution," Morgenthau sternly wrote, depended upon "whether a department of political science actually puts the study of politics in the centre of its endeavors or whether as most of them do it merely offers a disparate collection of courses whose common denominator is a vague and general relation to the activities of the state."[42] The emphasis on power politics required an altogether different approach, remote from the functional analysis defended, for instance, by Lasswell. Scholars opposed to value relativism and to the rationalist view of power sought to move the field away from its interdisciplinary

---

[40] Arnold Wolfers, "International Relations as a Field of Study," *Columbia Journal of International Affairs* 1, no. 1 (1947): 24–26.
[41] Dunn, "The Scope of International Relations"; Dunn, "The Present Course of International Relations Research."
[42] Morgenthau, "Area Studies and the Study of International Relations," 655.

stage, which subjected it to the dominant trends in political science. It gradually became clear that the only way to achieve this was to pursue disciplinary autonomy. The rejection of relativism and rationalism thus provided the common denominator for the forces that converged into the project of building a theory of international relations.

One of the earliest objections against considering IR as a mere subfield of other social sciences was formulated by Waldemar Gurian. A long-neglected and recently rediscovered figure in the development of postwar political science, Gurian was an important player in the rise of political realism in the United States.[43] A Russian Jewish emigrant to Germany, where he converted to Catholicism at a young age, he was among the early German disciples of the neo-Catholic French intellectual Jacques Maritain. A gifted Catholic publicist, he was also, in the words of Hannah Arendt, "a pupil of Max Scheler, the philosopher and of Carl Schmitt, the famous professor of constitutional and international law who later became a Nazi."[44] Initially an ardent critic of democracy and liberalism, Gurian eventually distanced himself from his erstwhile mentor Schmitt and in the 1930s became, if not a *Vernunftrepublikaner*, at least an advocate of a tactical alliance with democrats against the civilizational threat represented by Communism. He auspicated the emergence of an "authoritarian democracy" reinvigorated by traditional Christian values.[45] After the war, Gurian's neo-traditionalism converged with the intellectual agenda of those who opposed value-relativism in politics and in the study of politics. His critique of modernity, now reshuffled as a critique of totalitarianism – a leitmotiv extremely common among realists, found for instance in the works of Herbert Butterfield in England or in those of Morgenthau in the United States – fueled the

---

[43] Contemporary appraisals of Gurian, usually written by people close to him, include Hannah Arendt, "The Personality of Waldemar Gurian," *The Review of Politics* 17, no. 1 (1955): 33–42; and John U. Nef, "The Significance of the Review of Politics," *The Review of Politics* 17, no. 1 (1955): 24–32. For recent and more nuanced intellectual portraits of Gurian, see Heinz Hürten, "Modernitätskritik und Totalitarismustheorie im Frühwerk Waldemar Gurians," in *Totalitarismus. Eine Ideengeschichte des 20. Jahrhunderts*, eds., Alfons Söllner, Ralf Walkenhaus, and Karin Wieland (Berlin: Akademie Verlag, 1997); Ellen Thümmler, "Totalitarian Ideology and Power Conflicts – Waldemar Gurian as International Relations Analyst after the Second World War," in *Émigré Scholars and the Genesis of International Relations: A European Discipline in America?*, ed. Felix Rösch (Basingstoke: Palgrave Macmillan, 2014); and especially Udi Greenberg, *The Weimar Century: German Émigrés and the Ideological Foundations of the Cold War* (Princeton: Princeton University Press, 2014).
[44] Arendt, "The Personality of Waldemar Gurian," 34.
[45] Greenberg, *The Weimar Century*, 133.

anti-liberal *revanchisme* of the postwar years, and found an influential vehicle in *The Review of Politics*, which Gurian had established in 1939. Writing in 1946 about the study of international relations, he cautioned that the objections against considering IR a separate branch of knowledge should not be accepted. IR may have no method of its own, Gurian conceded, but it was nonetheless defined by "a special point of view" focusing on the relations between separate political units. These units did not have to be states: They were first and foremost communities of purpose, and thus could be supranational organizations like the Catholic Church or the labor movement. In this watered-down rendition of an existential concept of the "political" as the primary focus of IR, Gurian could not fail to attack the dominant conceptions of science preventing IR from developing in the way he adumbrated: the instruction of IR should be "free of a spirit of relativistic nihilism" and acknowledge that "views on the nature of men become decisive."[46] The same year, Morgenthau's *Scientific Man vs. Power Politics* made a much more adamant case for the specificity of international politics and the inadequacy of the scientific method. Later, he would explicitly connect the project of a theory with the rejection of value relativism: the "denial of the existence and intelligibility of a truth about matters political that exists regardless of time and place implies a denial of the possibility of political theory."[47]

SPONSORING THE COUNTER-ENLIGHTENMENT: THE ROCKEFELLER FOUNDATION AND THE DEVELOPMENT OF INTERNATIONAL RELATIONS THEORY

An important milestone in this conversation was a series of regional conferences organized by the Council on Foreign Relations in April and May 1946, whose conclusions were summarized in a volume later published by Grayson Kirk, a professor of government at Columbia University.[48] Compared with interwar surveys, the Kirk report was characterized by its criticism of the infatuation of academics with Wilsonianism: a "disproportionate amount of time and energy was given to discussing 'international cooperation,' while the analyses of the

---

[46] Waldemar Gurian, "On the Study of International Relations," *The Review of Politics* 8, no. 3 (1946): 280.
[47] Morgenthau, "Reflections on the State of Political Science," 452.
[48] Grayson Kirk, *The Study of International Relations in American Colleges and Universities* (New York: Council on Foreign Relations, 1947).

forces of conflict in society, and of the institution of war, were subordinated and tainted with the stigma of moral reproach." Much of interwar scholarship thus amounted to "propaganda," however well meaning.[49] The report also expressed dissatisfaction with the division of the field between international law, international organization, and international politics: To the extent that law and international forums could become politicized at any time, international politics was really "the nucleus" of the field. While leaving open the question of the disciplinary status of IR, Kirk also advocated "a special method and approach" and suggested that its real focus should be power politics.[50] If the Kirk report provided "a kind of consensual springboard into the second postwar era," it was in part because it was ambiguous and could be construed in different ways.[51] On the one hand it still subscribed to the view of IR as an interdisciplinary enterprise, whose subject matter was "drawn from a variety of specialized fields."[52] Yet, it criticized the reformist inclinations of IR and made clear that the field revolved around the political, understood as a phenomenon that could displace the orders of morality and law. Although the Kirk report sanctioned the dominance of the realist mood, it did not do much to arbitrage between its internal divisions. This was probably unavoidable, due to its nature as a synthesis document reflecting the views of the profession. But it certainly emboldened the active minority that opposed the widespread acceptance of value-relativism and rationalism in the study of politics that resulted from the methodological subordination of IR to other disciplines. Although the scholars of that persuasion fought an uphill battle against the opinion prevailing in such prestigious centers as Yale's Institute of International Studies or Princeton's Woodrow Wilson School of Public and International Affairs, and against the general direction in which political science was developing, their inferiority was compensated by the support they received from the Rockefeller Foundation. By assembling a network of scholars who shared similar views but belonged to different institutional or disciplinary areas, the Foundation contributed to the emergence of an intellectual counterforce to what was perceived as the liberal bias of the social science movement, in

---

[49] Kirk, *The Study of International Relations*, 4. For an example of an interwar survey of the field, see Edith E. Ware, *The Study of International Relations in the United States* (New York: Columbia University Press, 1938).
[50] Kirk, *The Study of International Relations*, 10–12.
[51] William C. Olson and A. J. R. Groom, *International Relations Then and Now: Origins and Trends in Interpretation* (London: HarperCollins, 1991), 108.
[52] Kirk, *The Study of International Relations*, 15.

particular when it came to the study of international politics. As the hub of this network, the Division for the Social Sciences of the Rockefeller Foundation acted as the midwife of IR theory.

In retrospect, the support granted by the Rockefeller Foundation to realist scholars may seem puzzling. Why indeed would a foundation support the intellectual current that called into question the key premises of most of its past and present activities? The idea of scientific reform based on the use of rational knowledge to solve social conflicts was anathema to critics of scientific rationalism such as Morgenthau. It embodied all the illusions of the liberal pretense to master the historical process through technical means. Moreover, postwar realism primarily defined itself against the legalist approach to IR that was the stock-in-trade of philanthropic foundations. In the wake of the nineteenth-century peace movement, foundations had played an important role in articulating the key instances of the legalist vision of international affairs, and in particular international arbitration, customary law, disarmament, and peace conferences.[53] If these efforts were retrospectively ridiculed by the postwar advocates of power politics, they reflected less a naive pacifism than a complex and pragmatic institutional project. Imbued with Wilsonian internationalism, and inspired by Victorian-era liberalism and a belief in the political benefits of free trade, this project saw the development of economic forces as one of the pillars of a peaceful and rational international order.[54] In the United States, its advocates were the new industrial elites and their legal advisors. It consisted essentially in applying to international conflicts the methods that they had successfully applied to industrial conflicts. For the officers of the philanthropic foundations, and in particular of the Carnegie Endowment for International Peace and the Rockefeller Foundation, the methods allowing for the rational management of large organizations (corporations, army, etc.), so successfully implemented during World War I and in the management of industrial conglomerates, could be applied to a wider range of social institutions (universities, cities, research institutions, economic planning, etc.) The "social science" that the foundations sought to promote was essentially understood as a reform technology, devised by experts and capable of providing technical solutions (usually industrial or

---

[53] Francis A. Boyle, *Foundations of World Order: The Legalist Approach to International Relations, 1898–1922* (Durham, NC: Duke University Press, 1999).

[54] See Lucian Ashworth, *Creating International Studies: Angell, Mitrany and the Liberal Tradition* (Aldershot: Ashgate, 1999).

organizational, rather than political) to the conflicts that travailed industrial societies. Just like social conflicts, international conflicts were considered as the outcome of a lack of rational organization. They could be avoided or solved through a rationalization of political behavior and a more efficient social organization. This internationalist and reformist vision found a powerful echo among foundations, governments, and international-minded experts in the wake of the Versailles conference and its architecture of collective security. It was based on the idea that war has its roots in misunderstandings between nations, and that the rational, cool-headed, and collective analysis of international issues made it possible to defuse tensions. By developing better knowledge of economics needs, raw material resources, demographics, populations, and external trade, and by developing this knowledge collectively, in internationalized settings, the study of international relations was thus supposed to foster a "scientific" arbitrage of international questions by limiting the role of politics. Scientific internationalism was de facto conflated with the study of international relations.

This intellectual project had both a pedagogical and a scientific dimension. By educating the public opinions of democratic countries and by encouraging the rational and dispassionate analysis of current international affairs, it was meant to create the conditions for peace. Essentially, the post-1919 approach to international relations was self-consciously opposed to the secretive practices of traditional diplomacy and to the intrigues of the chancelleries. The discussion of international issues had to be moved to public spaces where it could be rationalized. These public spaces may have been the purview of a restricted elite, made up of experts, authorized representatives of the public, civil servants, etc. but it was nonetheless a relatively open space of discussion, more inclusive and strongly internationalized. The study of international relations and the management of international affairs were thus understood as a question of social and international organization. The collective study of current international affairs was supposed to become itself a channel for the coordination of foreign policies, in particular through international congresses and conferences. The birth of international relations as a field of study indeed reflected the effervescence of cooperation initiatives spawned by the League of Nations. If there was any methodology to the study of IR at the time, it was to the extent that it followed an institutional method: The study of international relations was nothing else than another possible domain of international cooperation and thus another subject waiting to be standardized, just like the study of rabies, research against syphilis, passports, maritime commercial tonnage, polling techniques, the fight against the opium trade, the nomenclature of vitamins, or sanitary regulations – to name many of the issues that provided the subject of international conferences during the period. Like these issues, international politics had to be brought within international standards and legal norms.

Starting in the 1920s, the Rockefeller Foundation thus pursued the objective of "facilitat[ing] the amicable adjustment of differences between nations" and promoting the "permanent conference" between them, which was the symbol of the regime of publicity and rationality under which international affairs were supposed to be discussed.[55] It sponsored a network of groups and institutions, in the United States and in Europe, affiliated with or close to the League of Nations' International Institute for Intellectual Cooperation. Scientific internationalism was directly an instrument of pacification of interstate relations. As French sociologist Célestin Bouglé, whose Center for Sociology received support from the Rockefeller Foundation, put it, international scientific cooperation consisted in "placing the social sciences at the service of peace" and in "bringing the minds of men closer together above national borders."[56] The legacy of this approach was still felt after World War II. In 1945, for instance, the Division of Social Sciences of the Rockefeller Foundation still considered that raising education about IR contributed to peace by avoiding misconceptions, and in 1946 its most important financial appropriation still went to the League of Nations, then poised to become the United Nations, making its support to realist critics of international reform all the more paradoxical.

Two major factors explain the support granted by the Rockefeller Foundation to the realist vision of international affairs. The first is the revision that took place within its Division for Social Sciences after 1945. The invigorated critique of the policy science model that implicitly defined much of American social science was heard at the Foundation, which had longstanding ties with the émigré scholars who usually formulated it. The crisis of scientific rationalism placed at the service of social reform was very much the crisis of the philanthropic model, and this crisis led to

---

[55] Rockefeller Foundation, *Annual Report* (New York: Rockefeller Foundation, 1930), 227; Rockefeller Foundation, *Annual Report* (New York: Rockefeller Foundation, 1932), 278.
[56] Raymond Aron et al., eds., *Les sciences sociales en France: Enseignement et recherche* (Paris: Paul Hartmann, 1937), 6–7.

a reappraisal of previous programs by the Division for Social Sciences. The second factor was the intellectual orientation of the Program on International Relations that was established in 1953–1954: The Program was based on a de facto alliance with Hans Morgenthau, whose views of the field of IR and of the need for a theory it entirely endorsed. The Rockefeller Foundation thus became not only the architect of a new academic field, but also a player occupying a very specific position within this field.

In promoting the efforts of a group of political realists to define the academic discipline around their own vision of politics, however, the Foundation was not reneging on its earlier commitment to international law, and its support for realists could plausibly be seen in the continuity of its previous policies. Realism was indeed building critically upon legalistic approaches to international affairs. This perception rested partly on a professional continuity: Most of the German émigrés who reinvented themselves as scholars of international relations in American political science departments were usually trained as jurists in Germany, if not recognized lawyers.[57] They gave realism the credentials it needed for appearing as superior to, and improving on, the legalist vision of international affairs. They also found a receptive context among those in the United States who pushed for a less idealistic stance in foreign policy matters and could finally take advantage of the fact that, as Kenneth Thompson noted, international law had "stumbled down from [its] high estate" after 1945. Realism thus developed also as a promising revision of the dominant intellectual approach in the area of international law, and it was characterized by a "vigorous sociological approach" that insisted that "the legal rule be seen in relationship to a given social reality."[58] That international law was now considered "sociologically" meant that the Foundation had decided that legal positivism was no longer an approach worthy of its support. This was an important development in legal thinking that not only contributed to defining IR theory but would also reshape the field of legal studies in the United States, since the same logic would eventually culminate in the creation of the Law and Society Association in 1964, supported by the Rockefeller Foundation as a direct offshoot of the

---

[57] Alfons Söllner, "Vom Völkerrecht zur Science of International Relations. Vier typische Vertreter der politikwissenschaftlichen Emigration," in *Exil, Wissenschaft, Identität: Die Emigration deutscher Sozialwissenschaftler 1933–1945*, ed. Ilja Srubar (Frankfurt am Main: Suhrkamp, 1988), 164–65.

[58] Kenneth W. Thompson, "International Law as a Target Area in RFs International Relations Program," January 17, 1955, Folder 67, Box 8, Series 910, RG 3.1, RF, RAC.

legal realism of the 1950s and under the same program of Legal and Political Philosophy, headed by Kenneth Thompson.[59] This program acted as "a counterweight to the growing power of social science in the study of politics," and its decisive role in the emergence of both IR theory and legal realism suggests a very deliberate anti-positivistic orientation and the endorsement of the most radical anti-formalistic trends in the study of law.[60] Legal positivism defined itself as the exclusion of any non-legal factor from the analysis of law, starting indeed with moral, social, and political factors. While the signature emphasis on "power" characteristic of realism may indeed have been vague, it is certainly true, as Judith Shklar later noted, that its primary appeal rested in its nature as a reaction against the application of legal positivism to the field of international law. Shklar, whose seemingly dispassionate analysis of realism blended into a hardly concealed affinity if not an explicit sympathy, expressed a realist viewpoint when she later wrote that by bracketing out social values, legalism functioned essentially as "a substitute for foreign policy, for taking a stand on issues, for thinking about international relations."[61] This was exactly the position articulated by Morgenthau, Herz, Schwarzenberger, and others after 1945.

The reappraisal of IR programs started early on. In his 1945 memorandum on the foundation's policy in the field of IR, Joseph Willits, the director of the Division for Social Sciences, expressed mixed feelings about past achievements. The massive investments made in developing international studies (almost ten million dollars from 1926 to 1945) appeared in retrospect as "an infinity of small dabs at many things."[62] More significantly, the traditional emphasis on the education of public opinion was

---

[59] Bryant G. Garth, "James Willard Hurst as Entrepreneur for the Field of Law and Social Science," *Law and History Review* 18, no. 1 (2000): 37–58.

[60] Emily Hauptmann, "From Opposition to Accommodation: How Rockefeller Foundation Grants Redefined Relations between Political Theory and Social Science in the 1950s," *The American Political Science Review* 100, no. 4 (2006): 648. On IR theory as a force of deformalization, see Martti Koskenniemi, *The Gentle Civilizer of Nations: The Rise and Fall of International Law, 1870–1960* (Cambridge: Cambridge University Press, 2002), 459 ff.

[61] Shklar, *Legalism*, 135. Her critique of Kelsen is extremely significant and indicates her own normative orientation. Shklar's position was essentially that of the "defensive" liberals she described in her earlier work, *After Utopia*. Her motivation was a desire to save liberalism from legalism by reintroducing in liberalism a capacity for thinking politically: "as part of the liberal ethos legalism has only proved itself a liability, preventing liberalism from facing up to the realities of contemporary politics." (Ibid., p. 142.)

[62] Joseph H. Willits, Memorandum on Postwar Policy in the Support of International Relations, May 14, 1945, Folder 67, Box 8, Series 910, RG 3, RF, RAC, p. 2.

now questioned: With the rise of mass media and their increased coverage of world affairs the programs of "adult education" were no longer an area where the Foundation could make a difference. Instead, it should identify the "points of strategic importance" for IR in the new postwar context. Along with other institutions, such as the Social Science Research Council (SSRC), which established a Committee on International Relations Research in 1948, the Rockefeller Foundation became part of the disciplinary conversation of the 1940s as it sought to generate reliable surveys of current work and foster the development of the field. In this context, it financed the 1946 cycle of regional conferences organized by the Council on Foreign Relations and subsequently took its cues from the Kirk report.

The translation of the Kirk report into operational guidelines was the work of Bryce Wood.[63] Wood was asked to write an internal report for the Foundation outlining possible courses of action. The Foundation, he wrote, had to decide whether it wanted to continue support for expertise in international law and research on international organization, which he defined as "strictly non-political international activities," or whether instead it would seek to strengthen the capacities of US foreign policy-making. The question raised was really about the possibility, as the international situation was becoming increasingly polarized, to maintain the prewar internationalist perspective and to stay outside of politics. He suggested that, while peace efforts remained worth supporting, the reorientation of Rockefeller programs away from internationalism and toward a better capacity to define the national interest was not only desirable, but, in fact, already underway. This process had already begun in 1935, Wood argued, when the foundation had made a grant to the Yale Institute of International Studies, which was one of the early receptacles of realism in the United States.[64] This decision was part of a wider trend, which consisted of "the strengthening of anti-totalitarian foreign policies" next to the traditional interest in international peace.[65] In the postwar context, this policy should be continued and expanded,

---

[63] Bryce Wood, "The Program of the Division of the Social Sciences in the Field of International Relations," August 1947, Folder 67, Box 8, Series 910, RG 3, RF, RAC.

[64] On the Yale institution, see Inderjeet Parmar, "'To Relate Knowledge and Action ... ': The Rockefeller Foundation's Impact on Foreign Policy Thinking during America's Rise to Globalism, 1939–45," *Minerva* 40, no. 3 (2002): 235–63; Inderjeet Parmar, *Foundations of the American Century: The Ford, Carnegie, and Foundations in the Rise of American Power* (New York: Columbia University Press, 2012).

[65] Wood, "The Program," 28.

Wood suggested. Beyond the circumstantial argument that the Cold War forced politicization and that the experience of the Rockefeller Foundation with international law would not prevent it from being drawn into politics, the Wood report actually reiterated an idea that had been developed by the most ferocious critics of legalism: Law was not a bulwark against politics, because it could become politicized at any moment. It also made two further claims that strengthened the case for conceiving of IR theory as an alternative to social science. First, as a branch of knowledge, IR was concerned with the "possibility that force and not social science will be employed to solve disputes," that is, it took for granted the limits of scientific rationalism.[66] Second, Wood argued that the "anti-statistical nature of diplomacy" called for different methods: the secrecy of diplomatic transactions – a recurrent theme in realist thought – the small number of statesmen and other factors made international politics unfit for the kind of quantitative analysis that was gaining ground in other social sciences.[67] The Wood report was an important policy document that paved the ground for the alliance between realists and the Rockefeller Foundation. It explains why support for the interdisciplinary option and for the scientific rationalism that came attached to it seems to have declined considerably by the early 1950s.[68]

Paving the way toward an autonomous discipline, the decision to strengthen a "theory of international politics" was taken in 1953 and officialized in the President's report to the trustees. The "Program for International Studies" drafted by Kenneth W. Thompson for the Division for Social Science was entirely pitted against the "aimless humanitarianism" of interwar scholarship, which it contrasted with the objective study of power politics. Only by shedding its past ways could the study of international politics reach the status of a scientific field of study. While acknowledging that "no serious student would presume to claim the study of IR had arrived at the stage of an independent academic discipline," the Program, however, suggested that all the requirements were met: the field had a core focus (the state and power politics); efforts were made toward developing an appropriate methodology; and "inventories have been drawn up by individual scholars, universities and institutes, of topics

---

[66] Wood, "The Program," 24.   [67] Wood, "The Program," 44.
[68] Joseph H. Willits to Dean Rusk, "Some point for intensive exploration," December 28, 1953, Folder 61, Box 7, Series 910, RG 3, RF, RAC.

and concrete projects which would best serve the development of general principles in the field and their validation through systematic inquiry."[69] Obviously, interdisciplinarity – what Thompson called "blending fragments of knowledge and isolated techniques from the humanities and the natural sciences" – was not the way forward.

MAPPING OUT THE FIELD: THE CHICAGO VIEW

If conversations within the Rockefeller Foundation pointed at the need to establish disciplinary autonomy, they did not specify in detail the lines along which the emerging discipline should develop. Yet, curiously, the views of IR theory promoted by the Rockefeller Foundation in the mid-1950s consistently echoed those of Hans J. Morgenthau. This is all the more surprising since earlier contacts between Morgenthau and the officers of the Rockefeller Foundation had not been good. In 1950, Morgenthau had approached the Foundation with a proposal requesting support for his newly established Center for the Study of American Foreign Policy at the University of Chicago.[70] Following consultations with Pendleton Herring, the president of the SSRC, who thought Morgenthau's work was "highly personal and dogmatic," and with Philip Mosely, who did not show more enthusiasm, the proposal was turned down. Morgenthau's strong views, which he expressed during a meeting with Willits, certainly accounted for this lack of understanding: He had criticized the "pragmatic and anti-philosophical" American tradition for the poverty of political philosophy in the country, and attributed the crisis of the tradition of political thought to the "scientific spirit." "The Foundation," he suggested, "could make a great contribution, if it set up an institute of political philosophy, and break up the stranglehold which public administration has on political science and philosophy."[71] This early attempt at countering the social sciences, however, did not succeed.

The situation changed dramatically three years later, when Kenneth W. Thompson, a young political scientist at Northwestern, was hired as

---

[69] Thompson, "A Program for International Studies."
[70] Hans J. Morgenthau, "Application to the Rockefeller Foundation for aid in establishing a Center for the Study of American Foreign Policy under the direction of Hans J. Morgenthau Professor of Political Science at the University of Chicago 1950," Folder 4874, Box 411, Series 200S, RG 1.1, RF, RAC.
[71] Joseph H. Willits, Interview notes from a meeting with Hans J. Morgenthau, August 16, 1950, Folder 4874, Box 411, Series 200S, RG 1, RF, RAC.

a consultant in charge of the IR program of the Rockefeller Foundation. The appointment of the man Morgenthau considered "the best student he ever had," and who reciprocated his admiration, brought Morgenthau back into the good graces of the Foundation, albeit indirectly, and gave him considerable intellectual influence over the formulation of the IR program.[72] After joining the Division for Social Science as a consultant in 1953, Thompson subsequently became Assistant Director (1955–1957), Associate Director (1957–1960), Director for Social Sciences (1960–1961), and Vice-President for International Programs (1961–1974). Born in 1921, Thompson had studied history before joining the army as an infantry and counterintelligence officer. He later enrolled at the University of Chicago, where he took a Ph.D. in political science in 1950, with a dissertation on the political philosophy of Toynbee. More importantly, he was a disciple and close colleague of Morgenthau, with whom he had published the reader *Principles and Problems of International Politics*.[73] It is hard to overstate the role played by Thompson in aligning the IR program with the views elaborated in Chicago against the legalistic teaching of Quincy Wright. If Morgenthau was the thinker, Thompson was the academic entrepreneur and philanthropic manager who decisively contributed to establishing the discipline on a theoretical agenda inspired by Morgenthau.[74]

The picture of the field that emerges from Thompson's papers bears witness to the strong anti-behaviorist bias that oriented the RF Program for International Studies. His analysis of the academic landscape was crucial for determining the institutional loci and the research efforts on which the Program would concentrate its resources. Writing at the end of 1953, Thompson observed that one of the obstacles to the development of a theory of IR was the absence of appropriate outlets. *World Politics*, which had been founded in 1949 at Yale and whose editor was William T. R. Fox, had been "taken over by the behavioral scientists," the *American Political Science Review* had obligations to "five or six fields," and *International Organization* was essentially about "the factual

---

[72] Joseph H. Willits, Interview notes from a meeting with Hans J. Morgenthau, September 14, 1953, Microfilm, Reel 1, RG 12.1–12.2, RF, RAC.
[73] Kenneth W. Thompson and Hans J. Morgenthau, eds., *Principles and Problems of International Politics: Selected Readings* (New York: Alfred A. Knopf, 1950).
[74] On Thompson, see Farhan Rajae's useful if largely hagiographic biography: Farhang Rajae, *Kenneth W. Thompson, the Prophet of Norms* (New York: Palgrave Macmillan, 2013).

description of United Nations' affairs."[75] A month later, reporting to Dean Rusk on the Foundation's Program in International Studies, Thompson delineated what he saw as the strategic alternative for the Foundation. The old Yale group, which the RF had supported since 1935, had migrated en masse to Princeton's Center of International Studies in 1951. But since 1943, these scholars had developed an interest in a practical approach to foreign policy decisions. Decision-making, however, was the kind of issue that lent itself most to the development of quantitative research tools and rational-choice methodologies after the war. The "Princeton school," Thompson wrote, had thus developed "behavioral constructs," which, he added somewhat scornfully, had aroused little interest.[76] Next to the behavioral approach to international politics, however, there was another school of thought that emphasized the national interest as the interpretive standard of rational political action. "If Princeton is the capitol [sic] city of behaviorism," Thompson went on, "Chicago and Columbia are the centers of this second approach at the present time."[77] "Is it of interest to the foundations and to scholarly progress in general that the growth of a 'party-line' at major institutions has been a dominant characteristic of the field? Or is this, to the contrary, a force contributing to progress through intense specialization? Can we steer a middle course between extremes?"[78] The question was purely rhetorical and the conclusion was foregone: "If what is sought is diversity in approach then perhaps Columbia or Chicago or Stanford–Berkeley has much to offer."[79] Yet, the middle course envisaged by Thompson proved rather partisan in then end.

A list of centers and scholars doing research in IR drafted in February 1954 sheds some light on what Thompson himself meant by "Chicago" and "Columbia."[80] At Chicago, the Program considered exclusively the Center for the Study of American Foreign Policy. The department of political science, with its strong empirical tradition going back to Charles Merriam and its contribution to behavioralism, was simply excluded from the list, and virtually no mention was made of the

---

[75] Thompson to Willits, "Theory of International Politics," December 28, 1953, Folder 61, Box 7, Series 910, RG 3, RF, RAC.
[76] Kenneth W. Thompson, Report to Dean Rusk on the RFs Program in International Studies, January 12, 1954, Folder 61, Box 7, Series 910, RG 3, RF, RAC, p. 8.
[77] Ibid., p. 10.   [78] Ibid., p. 9.   [79] Ibid., p. 8.
[80] Thompson to Rusk, "Academic Competence in International Relations," February 17, 1954, Folder 61, Box 7, Series 910, RG 3, RF, RAC.

work of Quincy Wright, who represented the main alternative to Morgenthau. This is all the more significant, since the department had provided cohorts of IR scholars to Yale's Institute of International Studies, and, through the Institute, to Princeton, Columbia, the MIT, and the Rand corporation.[81] Chicago, in other words, meant essentially Morgenthau's kind of classical realism. As for Columbia, what Thompson had in mind was primarily the Institute of War and Peace Studies. Opened in 1952 under the direction of William T. R. Fox and established within the School of International Affairs, the Institute's mandate was to deal with "basic research" on issues of national security rather than with policy-making.[82] The other major figure at Columbia was Reinhold Niebuhr, at the Union Theological Seminary, another critic of liberalism and scientific rationalism. The same list of institutions and individuals reveals a bleak view of the work done at Princeton's Center for International Studies. The same bias drove the process of shortlisting potential participants in the conversation that Thompson was staging on the "theory" of IR. Names were initially circulated during informal discussions between Thompson, Wolfers, and Fox. None of the Princeton scholars suggested by Fox (Harold Sprout, Klaus Knorr, and Frederick Dunn) were included in the shortlist, while some of Wolfers' suggestions (John Herz) were also discarded.[83] The invitations extended to foreign policy practitioners obeyed the same logic: the exhaustive Rockefeller listing of "Academic competence in international relations" included a number of nonacademic institutions with an interest in foreign policy, such as the Council on Foreign Relations, the Brookings Institution, the Carnegie Endowment for International Peace, and the Rand Corporation. Among those, only the Foreign Service Educational Foundation was retained as a valid provider of participants. Often nicknamed the "Policy Planning Staff in Exile," the Foreign Service Education Foundation of 1954 was the fiefdom of Paul Nitze, and also included George Kennan.

---

[81] Gabriel A. Almond, "Who Lost the Chicago School of Political Science?" *Perspectives on Politics* 2, no. 01 (2004): 91–93.

[82] L. Gray Cowan, *A History of the School of International Affairs and Associated Area Institutes Columbia University* (New York: Columbia University Press, 1954), 90–92.

[83] It is difficult to guess why Herz was not invited. It may have to do with the fact that his book *Political Realism and Political Idealism*, published in 1951, was viewed by most of his colleagues as a half failure.

THE REALIST METHODENSTREIT: THE 1954 CONFERENCE ON THEORY

The strategy pursued by the foundation officers was not limited to an "exploratory search" identifying scholars and research in the field. It entailed an exercise in social engineering that consisted of getting together like-minded theorists to discuss the content of the theory and its institutional dimension. A major step in that direction was taken in May 1954, with the organization of a "conference on international politics" convened to discuss the possibility and the nature of a theory of international politics, its relevance to foreign policy-making, and the institutional resources available: Ph.D. opportunities, publication outlets, regular seminars, departmental bases, relations with statesmen and policy-makers, etc. The 1954 conference is unique in that it gathered the luminaries of international politics to have them discuss the nature, the boundaries, and the future of their field. The participants included Hans Morgenthau, Reinhold Niebuhr, William T. R. Fox, Arnold Wolfers, Dean Rusk, Paul Nitze, Kenneth W. Thompson, and Dorothy Fosdick, along with influential commentators of international affairs such as Walter Lippmann or the journalist John Reston. Some were indeed seasoned diplomats, such as Rusk, Nitze, Kennan, or Fosdick, who also came from the Policy Planning Staff (she would become foreign policy adviser to Henry "Scoop" Jackson the following year). Compared with the conferences of the late 1940s, the 1954 seminar was highly selective in terms of thematic and professional range: It excluded scholars associated with the study of international law and organizations; more importantly, it firmly located the interest in theory within a network of scholars and practitioners committed to the study of power politics. It also gave pride of place to believers in the political virtues of traditional diplomacy, opposed to any notion of public scrutiny or democratic control over foreign policy decisions, and to the idea that diplomacy could be somehow overcome in favor of more rational, less interest-driven approaches to international politics. In fact, a number of participants had a very dim view of democracy itself, starting with Kennan who did not hide his distaste for it and thought that some form of "benevolent despotism had greater possibilities for the good."[84] Morgenthau, of course, had already articulated the most powerful critique of the weaknesses of a foreign policy crafted under democratic and deliberative conditions: "if one wanted to overstate the

---

[84] Quoted in Anderson, *American Foreign Policy and Its Thinkers*, 39.

case, one might say that a democratically conducted foreign policy is of necessity bad foreign policy."[85] As he attended the meeting, Walter Lippmann was probably mulling about the deficiencies of democratic publics, which he would expose at length in his *Essays in the Public Philosophy*, published the year after. Mostly concerned with examples drawn from international politics, the book inveighed against the corrosion of executive authority by democracy. "The people of democracies ... have made it increasingly difficult for their governments to prepare for war." "Strategic and diplomatic decisions," Lippmann suggested, "call for a kind of knowledge – not to speak of an experience and a seasoned judgment – which cannot be had by glancing at newspapers, listening to snatches of radio comment, watching politicians perform on television, hearing occasional lectures, and reading a few books."[86] Recycling the major themes of interwar antiparliamentarianism, and in particular the critique of parties and pluralism, Lippmann acted as an important wingman of postwar realists. Although not an international relations theorist proper, he wrote prolifically about international matters and, like William T. R. Fox who also attended the meeting, had gone through a realist epiphany in the 1940s that led him to endorse interventionist positions and shed any idealistic leftovers in favor of power politics.[87] The composition of the group ensured that the nascent "theory" of international relations was joined at the hip with an attempt to limit the reach of democracy and exempt foreign policy decisions from public accountability, in the name of state authority.

The gathering was thus designed as a counterpoint to the reformist conferences of experts in international law and organizations that had punctuated the interwar years.[88] A common theme running through the different contributions was the inadequacy of previous approaches to international politics and the need to strengthen the "theory" of international relations. Morgenthau, for instance, claimed that none of the hitherto prevailing modes of dealing with the subject, "history, reform, or pragmatic manipulation," could claim scientific status, as they were not

---

[85] Morgenthau, *Dilemmas of Politics*, 326.
[86] Walter Lippmann, *Essays in the Public Philosophy* (Boston: Little, Brown and co., 1955), 25.
[87] For Lippmann's conversion to interventionism and an assertive foreign policy, see the narrative of his conversion in the introduction to Walter Lippmann, *U.S. Foreign Policy: Shield of the Republic* (Boston: Little, Brown and Co., 1943).
[88] Kenneth W. Thompson, "Conference on Theory of International Politics," May 7, 1954, Folder 69, Box 8, Series 910, RG 3, RF, RAC.

dealing with "general laws."[89] Arnold Wolfers pointed at political science and the social sciences in general as the relevant pool of tools for analyzing international affairs. William Fox and Kenneth Thompson made similar claims. On the face of it, these debates seemed to suggest that, in contrast to the amateurish reformism of the past, the development of an academic interest in a theory of international politics was a bid for scientific supremacy.

The opposition between the rational and scientific status of postwar IR theory and interwar "idealist" internationalism is well known and belongs to the official lore of the discipline. Like any foundational legend, however, it builds upon carefully selected historical facts but conceals others. A wholly different image takes shape when we understand the genesis of the discipline in its own terms, and the transcript of the 1954 conference provides a solid ground to assess these terms.[90] Behind the consensual and largely rhetorical claims to "science" that supported the attack against the legal-historical approach to international relations lay divisions within realism that, over time, would only increase, to the point of entirely reshaping the disciplinary landscape over the next five decades.

But a closer look at the May 1954 conference suggests that, as an intellectual project, the "theory" of international relations was essentially conceived as a device meant to insulate the field from the surrounding behavioral sciences. It was not meant to make it more scientific, but, quite the contrary, immune to science. Claims to scientific status in the analysis of international politics were made by two competing projects: classical realism and behavioralism. Morgenthau may indeed have heralded a "science" of international politics in some of his publications and indeed in the second edition of *Politics among Nations* published the same year, in 1954, but this must be understood against the backdrop of the excoriating attack delivered against the social sciences in *Scientific Man vs. Power Politics*, where the belief in "the power of science to solve all problems" was portrayed as the cause of the "decay" of the Western world.[91] By modeling themselves on the natural sciences, the social sciences had produced the illusion of a mastery over social progress and

---

[89] Hans J. Morgenthau, "The Theoretical and Practical Importance of a Theory of International Relations," May 7, 1954, Folder 69, Box 8, Series 910, RG 3, RF, RAC, p. 1.
[90] For a more detailed analysis of this conference, see the contributions collected in Guilhot, *The Invention of International Relations*.
[91] Hans J. Morgenthau, *Scientific Man vs. Power Politics* (Chicago: The University of Chicago Press, 1946), vi.

of "scientific solutions" to the moral dilemmas of politics when, in fact, the kind of certainty they could produce was limited and irrelevant to such dilemmas. Far from subsiding, this polemic against the social sciences emerged as a rather consensual leitmotiv of the 1954 meeting. Morgenthau, of course, could be expected to warn against the "social science tendency," which he regarded as "the greatest present pitfall" to theory-building.[92] But he was joined by the other participants in his critique of behavioralism. Kenneth Thompson identified objective, empirical, data-gathering social science as the main obstacle to the development of a proper theory of international politics.[93] In his position paper on the topic, Paul Nitze expressed "little patience with those behaviorist theories which maintain that there is no such thing as a better or worse decision in foreign affairs."[94] Because the social sciences claimed to be value-free, they could not address the issue of moral judgment that constituted the essence of politics, nor could they understand the nature of decisions that did not solve such dilemmas but simply put an end to them through robust action. They assumed, as Niebuhr vehemently argued, "that the proper 'scientific technics' can assure men mastery over their historical fate," when both the course and the meaning of history were not opened to human scrutiny.[95] Not all was to be discarded in the social sciences, however: Morgenthau envisioned their role as a subordinate one, limited to mining data for the theorist. The social scientific approach, he concluded, "must be contained within very narrow limits."[96] The final report, written by Kenneth Thompson, finessed what may have been slightly more open views of the social sciences and devoted a whole section to the criticism of "presuppositionless social science."[97]

The rhetoric of "general laws" of international politics and "rationality" in the conduct of international affairs was obviously associated with a continuing critique of history and legal scholarship. Against the latter, it was meant to suggest that the introduction of the political in the analysis of international law was not the irruption of irrational factors. On the contrary, the declared intention to spell out "laws" or "principles" of

---

[92] "Conference on International Relations," p. 36.   [93] Ibid., p. 39.
[94] Paul Nitze, "The Implication of Theory for Practice in the Conduct of Foreign Affairs," May 7, 1954, Folder 69, Box 8, Series 910, RG 3, RF, RAC, p. 5.
[95] Reinhold Niebuhr, "The Moral Issue in International Relations," May 1954, Folder 69, Box 8, Series 910, RG 3, RF, RAC, p. 7.
[96] "Conference," p. 36.
[97] Kenneth W. Thompson, "Toward a Theory of International Politics," Folder 69, Box 8, Series 910, RG 3, RF, RAC.

what defined international politics had to be justified in terms very close to those that in the nineteenth century supported the development of legal science.⁹⁸ But by the time the Rockefeller group convened in Washington to discuss theory, the dissociation of IR from international law was already foregone: In the mid-1950s, the real fight was internal to political science departments, and it was a fight against the behavioral social science movement. The two aspects were not unrelated: American social science had developed out of the social reform movement of the turn of the century, and produced the belief in the capacity of science and rational planning to achieve economic progress and overcome conflict.⁹⁹ Wilsonianism and the international law movement extended this belief to the international sphere. The same rational methods used to harmonize domestic interests would solve the problems of international politics, and IR would become a province of the social sciences. But this was precisely the liberal fallacy denounced by Morgenthau, which assumed that "the social structures of international and domestic society are essentially identical" and that the former was also amenable to peaceful social engineering.¹⁰⁰ The critique of interwar liberal internationalism, in the eyes of many realists, could not be complete without a simultaneous critique of the behavioral sciences, which were considered to be a force of depoliticization that prevented American liberalism from absorbing the lessons taught by the Weimar experience.¹⁰¹ The academic context was thus quite hostile to the realist enterprise. Behavioralism promoted a unified conception of the social sciences under the experimental method, and promised unlimited scientific progress, usually leading its advocates to make grand programmatic statements.¹⁰² Such claims also involved a bid to institutional supremacy. In the run-up to the creation of the National Science Foundation in 1950, the sociologist Talcott Parsons had tried to have the new public agency endorse behavioral standards

---

⁹⁸ Judith Shklar thus noted that realism attempted to separate politics from legality in the same way that legalism had tried to separate law from morality. Shklar, *Legalism*, 126.
⁹⁹ Dorothy Ross, *The Origins of American Social Science* (Cambridge: Cambridge University Press, 1991).
¹⁰⁰ Morgenthau, *Scientific Man vs. Power Politics*, 108–09.
¹⁰¹ Alfons Söllner, "German Conservatism in America: Morgenthau's Political Realism," *Telos* 72 (1987): 161–72.
¹⁰² See for instance Robert A. Dahl, "The Behavioral Approach in Political Science: Epitaph for a Monument to a Successful Protest," *The American Political Science Review* 55, no. 4 (1961): 763–72; and Gabriel A. Almond, "Introduction: A Functional Approach to Comparative Politics," in *The Politics of the Developing Areas*, eds., Gabriel A. Almond and James S. Coleman (Princeton: Princeton University Press, 1960).

for social science research.¹⁰³ In a similar fashion, Daniel Lerner and Harold Lasswell had stressed the methodological unity of the sciences of which IR was part.¹⁰⁴ As if this was not threatening enough, the new paradigm also benefited from the support of the Ford Foundation, which set up a Behavioral Sciences Program in 1952 and invested its massive resources in the institutionalization of the social sciences at home and abroad.¹⁰⁵

In this context, the purpose of the 1954 conference was essentially defensive. Reporting on the debates, Kenneth Thompson wrote that "theory in the study of international politics may deserve a special priority because of the stringency of the debate generated in part by the imperialism of competing approaches each claiming to have pre-empted the field."¹⁰⁶ The point of discussing "theory" was to establish a demarcation line vis-à-vis the behavioral sciences and to build into such theory the antibodies that would prevent the capture of IR by the behavioral social science movement and the loss of its political dimension, painstakingly established against and wrested from legalism. The items on the agenda included a discussion not only of the "nature" of theory but also, more significantly perhaps, of its "limits": a clear reminder, against the cognitive pretensions of the social sciences, that power politics was restive to complete rationalization.¹⁰⁷ In fact, IR theory not only had limits: It was essentially defined by these limits. Niebuhr insisted on the necessity for theory to be open to the contingent. A "prudent self-interest" was the highest attainable degree of rationality and morality.¹⁰⁸ Morgenthau emphasized the incommensurability between theoretical statements and political practice. Politics was always about concrete decisions engaging with a world of unpredictable contingencies: "A theory of international relations," Morgenthau wrote, "must, then,

---

¹⁰³ Samuel Z. Klausner and Victor M. Lidz, eds., *The Nationalization of the Social Sciences* (Philadelphia: University of Pennsylvania Press, 1986).

¹⁰⁴ Daniel Lerner and Harold D. Lasswell, *The Policy Sciences: Recent Developments in Scope and Method* (Stanford: Stanford University Press, 1951).

¹⁰⁵ Peter J. Seybold, "The Ford Foundation and the Triumph of Behavioralism in American Political Science," in *Philanthropy and Cultural Imperialism: The Foundations at Home and Abroad*, ed. Robert F. Arnove (Boston: G.K. Hall, 1980).

¹⁰⁶ Kenneth W. Thompson, "Toward a Theory of International Politics," 1954, Folder 69, Box 8, Series 910, RG 3, RF, RAC.

¹⁰⁷ "Agenda II: Outline for Structuring the Discussion," Folder 69, Box 8, Series 910, RG 3, RF, RAC.

¹⁰⁸ Reinhold Niebuhr, "The Moral Issue in International Relations," Folder 69, Box 8, Series 910, RG 3, RF, RAC, p. 3.

guard against the temptation to take itself too seriously and to neglect the ambiguities which call it into question at every turn. A theory of IR which yielded to that temptation would become a metaphysic, superimposing a logically coherent intellectual scheme upon a reality which falls far short of such coherence. *A theory of international relations, to be theoretically valid, must build into its theoretical structure, as it were, those very qualifications which limit its theoretical validity and practical usefulness.*[109] "Prudence" was the best one could hope for. As Morgenthau put it in the course of the debates, "in reality you can only rely on a series of informed hunches."[110] The theory may provide a rational representation of a given situation, but it remained stylized and, indeed, an abstraction. The actual engagement with the concrete political situation was a matter of Machiavellian *virtù*. It called for a decision that cut across conflicting judgments: a Gordian decision that cut across an infinite tangle of factors and blazed a trail in the darkness of the historical future. The social scientific approach to politics and the very idea that a political "science" was possible were delusional because they ignored entirely this concrete moment and pretended to replace it with scientific technologies assuming the transparency of the historical situation. Politics entailed an existential dimension restive to its reduction to a set of computable variables. It was a constitutive dimension of the human condition that could not be suppressed by social engineering, and that was always in excess of any rational categorization. Truly political decisions could not be subsumed under preexisting rules, precisely because they lay out the rules of political existence in the first place. And they did so from a concrete position, not from a normative standpoint. Only by taking this specific location into account was it possible to discuss politics rationally. Drawing on a German tradition that distinguished strongly between the sciences of nature and the sciences of the spirit, Morgenthau understood "science" in a way fundamentally different from, and actually opposed to, what his American colleagues had in mind, and he was perfectly aware of this difference: For him, a "social" science was such precisely because it reflected "both the social *Standort* and the particular intellectual interest of the observer."[111] But the behavioral social sciences movement was the exact opposite and dreamt of

---

[109] Hans J. Morgenthau, "The Theoretical and Practical Importance of a Theory of International Relations," Folder 69, Box 8, Series 910, RG 3, RF, RAC, p. 4. Emphasis mine.
[110] "Conference," p. 31.   [111] Morgenthau, *Dilemmas of Politics*, 93.

a unified scientific method independent from both its subject and its practitioner. As a result, as Morgenthau later put it, "a science of politics thus deals with a subject that is existentially alien to it."[112]

The only exception to the anti-behaviorist consensus was Arnold Wolfers, whose case deserves a brief mention. His views were somewhat at odds with the rest of the group, and the debates that ensued help illuminate the real stakes of a distinct IR theory. A Swiss, Wolfers (1892–1968) was trained as a legal scholar, like many of his fellow émigrés. He took his diploma in Zurich and practiced law before pursuing his doctorate in Giessen. Following a lecturing tour in the United States, he came to Germany in 1925 as a *Privatdozent* at the University of Berlin, before joining the Rockefeller-funded *Deutsche Hochschule für Politik* in Berlin and becoming, successively, its studies supervisor and its director (1930–1933). The school represented a "modern" political science against traditional German historical-legal scholarship, and although it was nominally free from partisan influence, its president, Ernst Jaeckh, promoted very conservative politics and a de facto alliance with the nationalists in a frontal opposition to Weimar and Versailles.[113] Wolfers was already an old Rockefeller hand when he joined the faculty at Yale in 1933. Yet, by the 1950s, the Yale group, and Wolfers himself, had developed an interest in behavioral methods. From the perspective of the behavioral sciences, the question of "theory" was indeed solved in advance: No domain of human action could indeed claim exemption from a universally applicable scientific method. Realists attracted by behavioral methodologies and by political "science" had no particular incentive to develop IR as a distinctive discipline. This explains why IR theory did not crystallize around Yale and Princeton, in spite of the important work done in these institutions. The views Wolfers expressed in 1954 were essentially those he held already in the late 1940s, when he had called for the implementation of social science techniques in the study of international politics, and they attracted much criticism: In the pre-circulated paper, he suggested that "the main job of the theorist qua theorist is ... the creative elaboration of fruitful hypotheses which bear on the relationship between

---

[112] Morgenthau, *Science: Servant or Master?*, 34.
[113] On Wolfers, see Hannah Caplan and Melinda Rosenblatt, eds., *International Biographical Dictionary of Central European Émigrés 1933–1945*, vol. II: The Arts, Sciences, and Literature (Munich: K.G. Saur, 1983); see also Rainer Eisfeld, "From the Berlin Political Studies Institute to Columbia and Yale: Ernst Jaeckh and Arnold Wolfers," in *Émigré Scholars and the Genesis of International Relations*, ed. Felix Rösch (Basingstoke: Palgrave Macmillan, 2014).

specified variables."[114] He reiterated this pro-behavioral position during the discussions, adding that the concept of political "behavior" allowed for a greater degree of certainty: "as soon as you begin to talk about behavior, however, you are pretty safe," he said, to which Morgenthau immediately quipped that such an analysis then became "meaningless."[115]

But the "hunches" Morgenthau had in mind when discussing the "theory" of international relations were much more than educated guesses of a prudential type. They harked back to nothing short of a mystique of sovereignty that carried into postwar realism a good deal of Weimar-style decisionism, a vision of politics that privileged authority over democracy and the public use of reason, and gave pride of place to the concrete and unconditioned decision over the predictability and calculability of institutional routines and codified arrangements. It is because the political decision was always in excess of any previously stipulated norm or principle, and constrained by circumstances that no prior knowledge could encompass, that a social scientific approach to politics was simply irrelevant and emptied politics of its true substance. Morgenthau's occasional descriptions of the statesman placed at the center of politics not a technology of power, nor a set of abstract rules or laws of politics, but the unconditioned decision, shrouded in the *arcana imperii* and irreducible to computable risk calculations: The political decision was "a decision taken in the face of the unknown and the unknowable ... The statesman ... must be capable of staking the fate of the nation upon a hunch. He must face the impenetrable darkness of the future and still not flinch from walking into it, drawing the nation behind him ... "[116] Paradoxically, the "theory" of international relations that participants of the 1954 Rockefeller conference were calling for was a theory of what could not be much theorized about. Its main purpose was to preserve, by giving it an acceptable academic form, the legacy of a conservative and anti-democratic vision of politics. Thinking of politics as decision was

---

[114] Arnold Wolfers, "Theory of International Politics: Its Merits and Advancement," Folder 69, Box 8, Series 910, RG 3, RF, RAC, p. 5.
[115] "Conference," p. 33.
[116] Hans J. Morgenthau, *The Restoration of American Politics*, vol. 3 of *Politics in the 20th Century* (Chicago: The University of Chicago Press, 1958), 102–3. Compare with Derrida: "Even if time and prudence, the patience of knowledge, and the mastery of external conditions were by hypothesis without limits, the decision would be structurally finite, however late it is taken – a decision of urgency and precipitation, acting in the night of non-knowledge and non-rule." Derrida, *Force De Loi*, 58.

indeed the best bulwark against any temptation to treat politics as an object of social-scientific enquiry. This, as we shall see, would be an enduring problem for the project of preserving the realist message in a cultural context entirely won over to the lures of science and technology.

THE POLITICS OF THEORY

Underwritten by the Rockefeller Foundation, the realist "theory" of international relations emerged in the mid-1950s as a symptomatic reaction to the evolution of American political science. This reactive aspect runs through the minutes of the 1954 meeting, which saw the emergence of what was an essentially negative consensus. What this "theory" exactly meant may not have been very clear to the participants in the May 1954 conference – in his subsequent report, Kenneth Thompson wrote euphemistically that the state of theory was compounded by "vigorous debate" and "little unanimity on points of detail"[117] – but the necessity of having a theory was unanimously recognized, as it provided a rallying cry for the opponents of behavioralism, and more generally for the opposition to scientific rationalism as an instrument of liberal governance. In spite of the inconclusive nature of the debates, therefore, the 1954 workshop was considered a very stimulating event that ought to be followed up by others. Following the circulation of Thompson's report, William Fox wrote to say that Morgenthau, Niebuhr, Nitze, Wolfers, and himself were willing to engage in "more formal discussions," which would hopefully involve English scholars such as Martin Wight or Herbert Butterfield, and asked for the support of the Rockefeller Foundation.[118] In order to secure the regular participation of Niebuhr, who was regarded as a major source of intellectual inspiration, it was decided that these regular discussions would take place at Columbia's Institute of War and Peace Studies (since Niebuhr was at the Union Theological Seminary). Starting in 1957, Columbia's inter-university seminar gave a stable form to the network that coalesced during the 1954 workshop and established the legitimacy of international relations theory as an intellectual project.[119]

---

[117] Kenneth W. Thompson, "Toward a Theory of International Politics," *The American Political Science Review* 49, no. 3 (1955): 746.

[118] Fox to Thompson, January 21, 1955, Folder 4,128, Box 493, Series 200S, RG 1.2, RF, RAC, p. 1.

[119] Some of the seminar papers were later published by William T. R. Fox. The importance of this seminar for the subsequent development of the discipline is further underscored

Yet, while it did not really advance research methods or theory-building, the 1954 workshop brought into the open a lot of "unresolved problems."[120] Its real significance may have been more ideological than scientific. It fostered the emergence of a group that, in spite of its diversity, was bound by a common understanding of politics and left a deep imprint on the discipline. The postwar realists were united by their negative view of the social sciences: They saw in scientific rationalism the same utopian drive that characterized the legalist vision of international affairs in the interwar years. Their opposition to behavioralism entailed much more than a battle over the future direction of political science. It pointed at a shared understanding of history and politics.

When Niebuhr inveighed against the social sciences and their pretense to deliver compelling judgments and conclusions, he was in fact attacking the idea of a "historical science" that assumed the presence of "normative structures in history analogous to the norms of nature."[121] Once carried into politics, the scientific method blended with ideology and supported liberal governance that purported to replace all politics with rational norms and deliberation or, worse, a form of government that pretended to fulfill the *telos* of history because it had discovered its "laws" and availed itself of a universal and messianic significance.[122]

As they sought to identify the cause of the crisis that had engulfed the world – and for the émigré scholars, very much their own world – since the 1930s, their diagnosis became overtly political. During the run-up to the May conference, Thompson had mentioned as a possible participant Isaiah Berlin, who may have been in the United States at the time of the meeting. This was a timely choice: Berlin too was mulling over political realism in 1954 and developing ideas remarkably similar to those voiced in the Rockefeller conclave, which he would publish in the December issue of the *Spectator*. His view of realism was indeed a plea in favor of a political attitude that did not believe that "the lives of men, as every object of nature, conformed to certain regularities of behavior which could be codified in

---

by the presence among this early group of intellectual entrepreneurs of a young Kenneth Waltz, serving as the rapporteur of the group. See Chapter 6.

[120] William T. R. Fox, ed. *Theoretical Aspects of International Relations* (Notre Dame: University of Notre Dame Press, 1959), xi.

[121] Reinhold Niebuhr, "Ideology and the Scientific Method," in *The Essential Reinhold Niebuhr*, ed. Robert McAfee Brown (New Haven: Yale University Press, 1986), 212.

[122] To quote Morgenthau: "The distinction between ideology and morality becomes blurred as does the distinction between ideology and theory. The advocate of the national crusade appears not only to promote universal moral values but also to have discovered theoretical truth." Morgenthau, *Dilemmas of Politics*, 52.

laws" and that "statecraft was a science like engineering or agriculture." This optimistic attitude was discredited, Berlin went on, "by the failure of the French Revolution, which somewhat undermined the prestige of the philosophy of the Enlightenment." "Nevertheless," he went on, "the conviction that history does obey laws, that the acts of human beings are calculable, that it is possible to develop a natural science of human behaviour, is a perennial human obsession." The piece was called "Realism in politics."[123]

For the participants of the 1954 conference, the rationalist project that sought to rebuild liberal governance on the basis of the social sciences was clearly identified as an Enlightenment leftover that would not disappear unless its root cause was thoroughly defeated. Much more than an academic critique of scientific rationalism and liberalism, the nascent theory of international relations carved out an academic and intellectual enclave for a distinct political mood that explicitly considered itself as a form of counter-Enlightenment. Berlin may have been right that the idealism of the eighteenth century was discredited "less by the arguments of its opponents – theologians, political reactionaries, anti-rationalist Romantics – than by the failure of the French Revolution."[124] But the postwar attack on the Enlightenment was a strange conjuncture, which blurred many ideological frontlines and generated unexpected alliances.[125] Born in the 1950s, international relations theory was no longer feeding on the errors of the French Revolution nor even from the failure of the Bolshevik one: It was, *pace* Berlin, a project informed also by theologians, reactionaries, and political romantics.

While some participants of the 1954 conference can be described as "conservative" or "defensive" liberals, others could hardly be placed in this category. Wolfers, who had supported the authoritarian policies of Hitler's immediate predecessors, had a benevolent relationship – indeed, for an émigré, an enthusiastic one – to the Nazi regime, which he thought was only a robust form of national community-building. Even after emigrating to the United States, it seems that any reservations about Hitler Wolfers may have had were tempered if not trumped by a sympathy for the *Führer*'s anti-Communism and a lasting admiration for the social and national significance of the Nazi movement.[126] Wolfers

---

[123] Berlin, *The Power of Ideas*, 164–65.   [124] Ibid.
[125] Seán Molloy speaks of the "contramodern attitude of the Realist tradition." Molloy, *The Hidden History of Realism*, 35–36. See also Shklar, *After Utopia*.
[126] Eisfeld, "From the Berlin Political Studies Institute to Columbia and Yale," 114. Wolfers, who knew the United States well, saw the rising national socialist movement as a mass movement that would give Germany the stability that the middle-classes gave

had been instrumental in giving an academic foothold at the *Hochschule* to the revolutionary-conservative intellectual project and in turning the school into a place of intellectual opposition to Weimar and Versailles (Carl Schmitt, for instance, regularly taught there). As late as 1932, while defending Hindenburg's and von Papen's policies like his boss Ernst Jaeckh, Wolfers saw the Nazi party as a "force making for democracy."[127] And once his status as a *Mischling* forced him into emigration, he still assured his American audiences that Hitler was a valuable bulwark against "Asiatic bolshevism." As late as 1934, in a cable to Berlin, the German embassy in Washington described Wolfers as a reliable spokesperson for the "New Germany."[128] His good disposition vis-à-vis Germany would continue into World War II.[129]

Although he did not attend the meeting, Herbert Butterfield's influence also loomed large over the discussions that surrounded the 1954 conference. The British historian would shortly afterward become the contact person of the Rockefeller network in the United Kingdom, and Thompson would convince him to chair the Rockefeller-sponsored British Committee on International Relations in 1959.[130] A conservative Methodist, Butterfield had developed a vision of historiography deeply shaped by Christian realism. His providentialist understanding of history made him deeply critical of liberal optimism and, indeed, of any kind of "whig" history.[131] His cultural pessimism led him to deplore the

---

to America. On the parallels between the New Deal and European fascism, see Wolfgang Schivelbusch, *Three New Deals: Reflections on Roosevelt's America, Mussolini's Italy, and Hitler's Germany, 1933–1939* (New York: Picador, 2006). See also the discussion in Ira Katznelson, *Fear Itself: The New Deal and the Origins of Our Time* (New York: Liveright, 2013).

[127] Quoted in Eisfeld, "From the Berlin Political Studies Institute to Columbia and Yale," 119.
[128] Ibid., pp. 120, 123.
[129] Wolfers eventually pursued a successful academic career but he was also very well connected to the policy planning and intelligence communities.
[130] On the "English School," see in particular Tim Dunne, *Inventing International Society: A History of the English School* (London: MacMillan, 1998).
[131] Butterfield has gone down in the history of science as the historian who coined the expression "whig history." On Butterfield, see in particular Michael Bentley, *The Life and Thought of Herbert Butterfield: History, Science, and God* (Cambridge; New York: Cambridge University Press, 2011); Robert J. Delahunty, "Herbert Butterfield, Christianity, and International Law," *University of Detroit Mercy Law Review* 86 (2009): 615–58; Ian Hall, "History, Christianity and Diplomacy: Sir Herbert Butterfield and International Relations," *Review of International Studies* 28, no. 4 (2002): 719–36; Kenneth B. McIntyre, *Herbert Butterfield: History, Providence, and Skeptical Politics* (Wilmington: ISI Books, 2011); Karl W. Schweizer and Paul Sharp,

materialism and spiritual vacuity of modern society. While he never explicitly stated his political views, in the 1930s Butterfield was drawn into the orbit of the neo-traditionalist and often pro-fascist circles of Corpus Christi College. He never quite expressed support for the Nazi regime, but he maintained a very cozy relationship with its academic and cultural dignitaries until 1938. His political quietism led him to adopt repeatedly conciliatory positions, and after the war, apologetic ones vis-à-vis Nazi Germany. Making an argument that would be picked up much later by the conservative historian Ernst Nolte, Butterfield claimed that Nazism was a defensive reaction against the Communist threat coming from the East. Bolshevik utopianism was the real evil, and Germany was a bulwark of European civilization against the most fanatical and extreme expression of a secularized modernity.[132]

Certainly, these views were not shared by all postwar realists. But they were perfectly acceptable to them, because they were motivated by a common condemnation of the Enlightenment, and of its twins, liberalism and Marxism. The realists understood the international situation through the prism of the critical diagnosis of modernity typical of all counter-Enlightenment doctrines, and they all shared the belief that "European society has been deteriorating steadily since the French Revolution."[133] The international crisis, as Thompson reported from the debates, resulted from an "unfounded optimism," which "derived, undoubtedly, from the philosophy of the enlightenment and from its step-child, the peace-movement of the nineteenth century ..."[134] The time had come to reassert the legitimacy of self-interest, to shed the "cult of internationalism" and to accept that politics was essentially power politics, the expression of a flawed human nature that no degree of social engineering could ever redeem. Even when the realists condemned totalitarianism, they were condemning what they saw as the consummate manifestation of the Enlightenment project: For them,

---

eds., *The International Thought of Herbert Butterfield, Studies in Diplomacy and International Relations* (Basingstoke: Palgrave Macmillan, 2007). For a superb dissection of Butterfield's relationship to German conservatism, see Martina Steber, "Herbert Butterfield, der Nationalsozialismus und die deutsche Geschichtswissenschaft," *Vierteljahrshefte für Zeitgeschichte* 55, no. 2 (2007): 269–307. On the connections between IR and history, I refer the reader to Nicolas Guilhot, "Portrait of the Realist as a Historian: On Anti-Whiggism in the History of International Relations," *European Journal of International Relations* 21, no. 1 (2015): 3–26.

[132] In 1953, Butterfield wrote to his colleague Adam Watson that "communism incorporates the anti-Christ of our time, and I also think that communism is the prior evil that provoked Nazism and Fascism." Quoted in Steber, "Herbert Butterfield," 282, 97.

[133] Shklar, *After Utopia*, 236.   [134] Thompson, "A Program for International Studies."

"rationalism sooner or later must and did lead to totalitarianism."[135] The product of democratization and of a vacuous scientific culture, totalitarianism was nothing else than "the facile heresy of the self-educated in a scientific age."[136]

Postwar realism subscribed to a specific understanding of Western history that located the ultimate cause of the decline of the West in the French Revolution and its intellectual legacy. It provided one of the political arms – at least where international affairs were concerned – of a historiographical movement that asserted itself in the postwar years and subjected the Enlightenment to an unsparing critique. Political realism was part of this ideological restoration, and it drew for international politics the lessons of this movement. "The paramount problem for contemporary study of international relations," Niebuhr suggested to the other conference participants, "is to supplant the illusions which we have inherited from the French enlightenment ... with the wisdom of Edmund Burke."[137] The same neo-traditionalism surfaced in the writings of Morgenthau, and could be found in the pronouncements of virtually all the participants in the 1954 conference. Morgenthau, for instance, adopted the classical counter-revolutionary view of the Enlightenment as a de-civilizing attack on the throne and the altar that undermined the Christian foundations of the *ancient régime* and was thus directly responsible for the "decline of the cosmopolitan aristocratic society and of the restraining influence of its morality over international politics" and for the diffusion of secular nationalism.[138] The realists' vision of the previous two centuries of European history were part of a wider denunciation of utopian thought that historians such as Jacob Talmon or Reinhart Koselleck were developing at the same time, and often in conversation with political and international relations theorists.[139] In fact, conservative, and often Christian,

---

[135] Shklar, *After Utopia*, 239.
[136] Herbert Butterfield, *Christianity and History* (London: G. Bell and Sons, 1949), 6. Through the concept of totalitarianism, a long tradition of counter-Enlightenment thought was carried over into Cold War anticommunism, but also into a conservative refoundation of liberalism at home. Alfons Söllner, Ralf Walkenhaus, and Karin Wieland, eds., *Totalitarismus. Eine Ideengeschichte des 20. Jahrhunderts* (Berlin: Akademie Verlag, 1997); Abbott Gleason, *Totalitarianism: The Inner History of the Cold War* (New York: Oxford University Press, 1995).
[137] Reinhold Niebuhr, "The Moral Issue in International Relations," Folder 69, Box 8, Series 910, RG 3, RF, RAC, p. 8.
[138] Hans J. Morgenthau, *Politics among Nations: The Struggle for Power and Peace* (New York: Alfred A. Knopf, 1948), 189, 310.
[139] See in particular Jacob L. Talmon, *The Origins of Totalitarian Democracy* (London: Secker & Warburg, 1952) and Reinhart Koselleck, *Critique and Crisis: Enlightenment*

historians played a decisive role in the early development of international relations theory: Herbert Butterfield in England or Jean-Baptiste Duroselle in France were instrumental in securing the first institutional bases of academic realism in their respective countries, the former with the British Committee on International Relations, the latter with the Centre d'Etudes et de Recherches Internationales (CERI) at the Institut d'Etudes Politiques in Paris.[140] Others, such as Felix Gilbert, whom we will meet in Chapter 4, played an important role in developing – indeed, inventing – a realist "tradition" that would provide realism with the historical pedigree it lacked. All entertained a bleak and wary view of modernity.

And yet, what makes it difficult to pronounce upon the ideological orientation of postwar realism is that its critique of the Enlightenment was couched in the language of the defense of liberalism. Postwar realists, whether they dealt with international affairs or domestic matters, were convinced that liberalism, if left to its own devices, was unable to secure its own survival. Achieving security, however, could not be done through liberal means. The defense of a free, liberal order implied the carving out of spaces for political decisions that were not constrained by democratic procedures. It meant restoring a capacity to decide at critical moments, unencumbered by the strictures of liberal constitutionalism, parliamentarianism, and deliberative, democratic politics, and without the dangerous illusions that a "science" of government and politics could provide any guidance. Politics was an art, performed not by technical specialists, but by a few men of good judgment, an elite seasoned in the arcane wisdom of statecraft. This vision not only inspired the small group of founding fathers brought together by the Rockefeller Foundation: It was embodied by it. With their successful bid to establish the autonomy of international relations theory on the basis of its realism, a specific kind of anti-liberal *revanchisme* lodged itself at the heart of the postwar policy planning establishment.

---

and the Pathogenesis of Modern Society (Cambridge, MA: MIT Press, 2000). Koselleck had expressed his admiration for Butterfield's political Christology: Reinhart Koselleck, "Rezension Zur Herbert Butterfield," *Archiv für Rechts- und Sozialphilosophie* 41 (1955): 591–99.

[140] On Duroselle, see Nicolas Guilhot, "The French Connection: Jean-Baptiste Duroselle, Raymond Aron et l'essor des relations internationales en France," *Revue Française de Science Politique* 67, no. 1, in press 2017.

2

American *Katechon*: Christian Realism and the Theological Foundations of International Relations Theory

"One word alone comes to us clearly, so far, out of the darkness ahead, as a prophecy of the age to come; but in this word, as it seems to me, we have a reliable clue to the whole spirit and temper of the new age. This word is *realism*."
  Walter Marshall Horton, *Realistic Theology* (New York: Harper, 1934), 10.

"It is a defect of many modern text books on international relations that they underestimate the profound influence of religious forces and ideas (sometimes hidden in anti-religious guise or masked in a purely secular indifferentism) on international relations, and on the concepts of the future society and its order."
  Waldemar Gurian, "On the Study of International Relations," *The Review of Politics* 8, no. 3 (1946): 280.

One of the defining features of the Enlightenment was its pretense to have freed politics from the yoke of traditional authorities and, in particular, ecclesial and religious authorities. Its politics would be grounded in Reason, not Revelation. "It is an undeniable fact that the extraordinary progress science has achieved in modern times is, in the first place, the result of its emancipation from the bonds in which theology had held it during the Middle Ages": thus wrote Kelsen, one of the greatest and last defenders of scientific positivism, in his systematic rebuttal of Eric Voegelin's *New Science of Politics*.[1] If political realism was central to the postwar counter-Enlightenment, it is because it represented a

---

[1] Kelsen, Voegelin, and Arnold, *A New Science of Politics*, 11.

re-theologization of political thought that rejected this pretense. Grieving over the postwar pushback against positivism, Kelsen clearly saw its retrenchment as a pendulum movement swinging back to theology: "When the foundations of the established social order are shaken by wars and revolutionary movements and the need for an absolute, not merely relative, justification of that order becomes urgent, religion, and with religion theology and other metaphysical speculations are brought to the front of intellectual life and become ideological instruments of politics."[2] Shaped by two decades of political and intellectual crisis, postwar realism was precisely one of these ideological instruments that brought back theology to the frontlines of intellectual life and structured visions of world order: after two centuries of unfounded optimism and rationalistic *hubris*, it called for political atonement and intellectual contrition.

As they sought to ground their vision of international politics outside the Enlightenment tradition, the postwar realists did not turn exclusively to counter-revolutionary thinkers like Burke. Another intellectual icon of the movement was Augustine, who often surfaced in the writings of Reinhold Niebuhr, Hans Morgenthau, or members of the English school of international relations such as Herbert Butterfield or Martin Wight: With its pessimistic anthropology, its denial of mundane progress, and the absolute separation it established between the universal values of the City of God and the relative claims of earthly kingdoms, Augustinism provided an important political language for Anglo-American protestant circles thinking about international politics in the wake of World War II.[3] Augustine was not, however, the only theological marker of political realism. Even the movement's rejection of the social sciences had a specific theological background. In the United States, the reformist impulse behind the development of the social sciences in the 1920s and 1930s was rooted in the progressive theology of the social gospel, which assumed that social injustices associated with industrial

---

[2] Ibid.
[3] On political Augustinism, see in particular Roger Epp, "The 'Augustinian Moment' in International Politics: Niebuhr, Butterfield, Wight and the Reclaiming of a Tradition," in *International Politics Research Papers* (Aberystwyth: Department of International Politics, University College of Wales, 1991); Roger Epp, "The Ironies of Christian Realism: The End of an Augustinian Tradition in International Politics," in *The Christian Realists: Reassessing the Contributions of Niebuhr and His Contemporaries*, ed. Eric Patterson (Lanham: University Press of America, 2003); Charles A. Jones, "Christian Realism and the Foundations of the English School," *International Relations* 17, no. 3 (2003): 371–87.

capitalism could be redeemed through benevolent and rational interventions.[4] It ignored the doctrine of the original sin and assumed God's immanence in all progress. The arguments against empirical social science that we encountered in the last chapter were a direct attack on the liberal theology of the 1920s, which took for granted God's self-revelation in history and looked confidently at the future. Political realism, in other words, must be resituated against the background of what Maurice Cowling has called "the anti-liberal theological movement of the twenties."[5]

In the immediate postwar years, this theological substratum was still an explicit background for the discussion of international politics on realist terms. This discussion involved not only political theorists but also public intellectuals, diplomats, historians, and, last but not least, theologians, many of whom were indeed "Christian realists." Obviously, the figure of Reinhold Niebuhr loomed large over these discussions. One of the most influential commentators of international events of the 1940s and 1950s and, in the words of Kennan expressing the feeling of many other realists, "the father of us all," Niebuhr certainly represented a realistic approach to international affairs informed by theological considerations. But such considerations pervaded the entire effort to secure an academic recognition for the theory of international relations and were common to those who actively discussed the shape of the future discipline. In this respect, the Rockefeller gathering was indeed a cenacle of Christian realists. Niebuhr is an obvious case in point, but a number of other participants had very similar views: Kenneth Thompson (who would later publish *Christian Ethics and the Dilemmas of Foreign Policy*), Dorothy Fosdick (who, in full-fledged intellectual rebellion against her father, the liberal pastor Harry Emerson Fosdick, and fresh from a stint at the Policy Planning Staff, would take her theological cues from Niebuhr in her *Common Sense and World Affairs*, published in 1955), or indeed George Kennan, who did not shy away from the occasional foray into theological matters. On the other side of the Atlantic, Herbert Butterfield was probably the most outspoken advocate of a Christian realist approach to politics, which he had recently defended in *Christianity and History* (1949).

---

[4] Ross, *The Origins of American Social Science*; Guy Alchon, *The Invisible Hand of Planning: Capitalism, Social Science, and the State in the 1920s* (Princeton, NJ: Princeton University Press, 1985).
[5] Maurice Cowling, *Religion and Public Doctrine in Modern England*, 3 vols., vol. 1 (Cambridge: Cambridge University Press, 1980), 199.

Yet, as the discussion of international politics became an academic specialty enclosed in political science departments, this background was progressively bracketed out. The publication of Kenneth Waltz's *Man, the State, and War* in 1959 signaled the end of the theological moment. The link between political order, the destiny of man and God's self-revelation in history was severed, and the theological underpinnings of IR theory were safely excised from the nascent "science" of international relations. By decoupling the question of war from the metaphysical question of evil and human nature, Waltz was removing the need for an explicit theodicy that was still a central preoccupation for Morgenthau or Niebuhr and sustained their concept of politics and statecraft. Like the early modern jurists, the academic IR theorists secured the recognition of their expertise only by restating the *silete theologi in munere alieno*.

The silence of the theologians, however, did not mean that religious schemes ceased to operate within the nascent discipline. Secularization is never a process of absolute separation between the religious and the profane, but rather a complex, non-linear mechanism of transfer, translation, and anamorphosis of religious patterns.[6] After 1945, an unpalatable theology of sovereign power was transposed into the technical and disciplinary language of the theory of international relations. It is probably a testimony to the success of this transposition that the theological premises of many IR concepts have been lost and only survive as a source of metaphors in a few current titles.[7] Despite a recent surge of interest in classical realism, recent scholarship has been surprisingly blind to the theological dimension of IR theory, with few notable exceptions.[8]

---

[6] On secularization, see Jean-Claude Monod, *La querelle de la sécularisation de Hegel à Blumenberg* (Paris: Vrin, 2002).

[7] Fred M. Kaplan, *The Wizards of Armageddon* (New York: Simon and Schuster, 1983); Richard K. Betts, "Should Strategic Studies Survive?" *World Politics* 50, no. 1 (1997): 7–33; Campbell Craig, *Glimmer of a New Leviathan: Total War in the Realism of Niebuhr, Morgenthau, and Waltz* (New York: Columbia University Press, 2003); Nicholas Rengger, "Realism, Tragedy, and the Anti-Pelagian Imagination in International Political Thought," in *Realism Reconsidered: The Legacy of Hans J. Morgenthau in International Relations*, ed. Michael C. Williams (Oxford: Oxford University Press, 2007).

[8] See in particular Epp, "The 'Augustinian Moment' in International Politics"; Epp, "The Ironies of Christian Realism"; Michael Loriaux, "The Realist and Saint Augustine: Skepticism, Psychology, and Moral Action in International Relations Thought," *International Studies Quarterly* 36, no. 4 (1992): 401–20; Rengger, "Realism, Tragedy, and the Anti-Pelagian Imagination"; Nicholas Rengger, "On Theology and International Relations: World Politics Beyond the Empty Sky," *International Relations* 27, no. 2 (2013): 141–57.

And yet, to the extent that modern international law took shape in reaction to the scholasticism of the theologians, it should not come as a surprise that the theory of international relations, which emerged essentially as a critique of international law, displayed strong theological accents.[9]

A first line of argument developed here is that until the late 1950s the search for a theory of international relations was suffused with theological themes. One reason for this was, of course, the absence of well-defined disciplinary boundaries, as a result of which the discussion of international politics was not yet monopolized by political theorists. But another was the fact that by the mid-1930s political realism had already come to define the neo-orthodox reaction against liberal Protestantism in the United States. As a result, the search for a theory of international relations was largely influenced by Christian realism. By weaving a number of religious themes in the project of articulating an academic or "scientific" theory of international relations, the realists articulated what was essentially a "theology of international engagement."[10] To the extent that it primarily sought to insulate the study of power from the rationalist idea of a *science* of politics, early IR was often swayed toward positions where rationalism was countered by an emphasis on the non-transparency of the historical process and the irrationality of the human drives that made politics necessary. From the outset, many realist scholars saw the "elemental, undisguised, and all-pervading" struggle for power lurking "under the surface of legal and institutional arrangements" as exceeding any possibility of containing politics within the limits of reason.[11] There was a strong theological element in this vision of politics and history. First, it rehabilitated the doctrine of the original sin, which was a signature of the neo-orthodox movement, along with "the transcendence of God" and "the essential difference between God's Word and any human expression or institution."[12] Second, political theology can be broadly defined as a challenge, on the basis of the idea of revelation, to rationalist pretenses to the self-justification, self-foundation, and teleological meaning of the

---

[9] On international law and scholasticism, see Richard Tuck, *The Rights of War and Peace: Political Thought and the International Order from Grotius to Kant* (Oxford: Oxford University Press, 1999). On the relationship between law and IR, see the excellent analysis by Koskenniemi, *The Gentle Civilizer*, ch. 4.
[10] Heather A. Warren, *Theologians of a New World Order: Reinhold Niebuhr and the Christian Realists, 1920–1948* (New York: Oxford University Press, 1997), 3.
[11] Morgenthau, "Reflections on the State of Political Science," 454.
[12] Warren, *Theologians of a New World Order*, 50.

political.[13] In a warm review of the German translation (1953) of Butterfield's *Christianity, Diplomacy and War*, the historian Reinhart Koselleck, who recognized in the work of his British colleague a critique of the Enlightenment congenial to his own, captured the nexus between theology and politics that was the signature of Christian realism. What Butterfield added to the critique of utopian ideologies was a distinctive "Christological historical ontology" that blocked any attempt at articulating politics with moral righteousness. Far from being a realm of emancipation and autonomy, politics could only operate within the limits set by theology. The Enlightenment had set modern politics on a catastrophic course precisely because it had severed this connection: "theological errors," Koselleck wrote, "reveal themselves as political mistakes."[14] From a theologico-political point of view, revelation alone, not reason, provides the legitimacy of the political order. Rationalist conceptions of politics failed to understand that the ultimate meaning of history was beyond their reach, and that any attempt at fulfilling some historical teleology under the political guidance of reason was bound to fail. This failure had already engulfed liberalism and its belief in the possibility of reforming domestic and international society. No longer the instrument of progress, politics was thus confined to the maintenance of a modicum of order and stripped of any eschatological significance. Somebody like Kennan thus spoke as a political theologian when he asserted that the Kingdom would not be realized "in the workings of the state, with its imperfect justice, its pretense to moral infallibility, its purely external enemies, and its absurd claim to be a law and a purpose unto itself."[15]

But the theological roots of realism in Protestant neo-orthodoxy and the mid-century Augustinian vogue among realists in the English-speaking world may well be the tree that hides the Teutonic forest. Focusing on "political theology" proper introduces a second line of argument, which summons the sulfurous figure of Carl Schmitt, one of the most important German jurists of the twentieth century – and a Catholic – who rallied the Nazi regime in 1933. Published in 1922, Schmitt's *Political Theology* is a concise treatise that offers both a theory of sovereignty and an

---

[13] Heinrich Meier, "Was Ist Politische Theologie?" in *Politische Theologie zwischen Ägypten und Israel*, ed. Jan Assman (Munich: Carl Friedrich von Siemens Stiftung, 1991).
[14] Koselleck, "Rezension Zur Herbert Butterfield," 592.
[15] George Kennan, "Foreign Policy and Christian Conscience," *The Atlantic Monthly*, May 1959, 44–49.

interpretation of political concepts that emphasizes the theological nature of *all* politics. "All significant concepts of the modern theory of the state," Schmitt proclaimed, "are secularized theological concepts not only because of their historical development (...) but also because of their systematic structure."[16] In exposing the isomorphism between the theological and the political-legal orders, political theology represents a fundamental challenge to the Enlightenment's pretense of having freed politics from religion, and thus to the very core of liberal modernity. Schmitt's political theology represented a strand of Catholic conservatism that resonated with the ideological program of Protestant neo-orthodoxy.

During the 1930s and the 1940s, an entire conception of power and politics developed in a more or less critical dialogue with Schmitt reached the United States with the cohorts of legal scholars who had left Germany or Austria, some of whom became key figures in the emergence of IR theory. Although Schmitt dropped out of the intellectual limelight after 1945, his influence certainly did not wane, but followed indirect and subterranean pathways.[17] "Schmittian perspectives," Martti Koskenniemi has argued, became "absolutely central for international relations 'realism.'"[18] Among these perspectives, the theological one was certainly central to this influence, and extended beyond a few individual cases to a wider intellectual milieu, where it became the default mode of theorizing about international politics in the early years of the discipline.

---

[16] Carl Schmitt, *Political Theology: Four Chapters on the Concept of Sovereignty* (Chicago: Chicago University Press, 2005), 36.

[17] Jan-Werner Müller, *A Dangerous Mind: Carl Schmitt in Post-War European Thought* (New Haven: Yale University Press, 2003).

[18] Koskenniemi, *The Gentle Civilizer*, 494. The conceptual lineage linking Schmitt, through Morgenthau, to the rise of IR theory has been recently exposed by various commentators besides Koskenniemi. See in particular William Scheuerman, "Carl Schmitt and Hans Morgenthau: Realism and Beyond," in *Realism Reconsidered: The Legacy of Hans J. Morgenthau in International Relations*, ed. Michael C. Williams (Oxford: Oxford University Press, 2007); H. K. Pichler, "The Godfathers of 'Truth': Max Weber and Carl Schmitt in Morgenthau's Theory of Power Politics," *Review of International Studies* 24, no. 2 (1998): 185–200; Chris Brown, "'The Twilight of International Morality'? Hans J. Morgenthau and Carl Schmitt on the End of the Jus Publicum Europaeum," in *Realism Reconsidered: The Legacy of Hans J. Morgenthau in International Relations*, ed. Michael C. Williams (Oxford: Oxford University Press, 2007); Daniel Steinmetz Jenkins, "Why Did Raymon Aron Write That Carl Schmitt Was Not a Nazi? An Alternative Genealogy of French Liberalism," *Modern Intellectual History* 11, no. 3 (2014): 549–74; Jodok Troy, "Freund oder Feind? Die Aktualität des Politischen nach Carl Schmitt in der internationalen Politik," in *Der Feind – Darstellung und Transformation eines Kulturbegriffs*, eds., Paul Ertl and Jodok Troy (Vienna: Schriftenreihe der Landesverteidigungsakademie, 2008).

Christian realism offered a very fertile soil for the acclimation of Schmitt's political theology, which could be translated into the readily available and legitimate language of neo-orthodoxy and political Augustinism. Another series of tropes, in particular Schmitt's ambivalent critique of secularization, were morphed after 1945 into a more fashionable critique of nationalism by Morgenthau, but without any substantial change. As a result, political theology was deployed unfettered because it no longer had to reveal its problematic origins – with the paradoxical effect that its influence increased precisely as Schmitt ceased to be an acceptable interlocutor. Among the émigré scholars and the Americans familiar with Schmitt's work, however, few were fooled by this exercise in translation. The nascent discipline of international relations thus encapsulated an imported doctrine of sovereignty, a theologically grounded decisionism that exempted sovereignty from the rule of law. This anti-legalistic discourse was obviously central to the development of the discipline. But it was also functional to the exercise of global hegemony by the United States after 1945: it provided a rationale for coming to terms with power in ways that were not bound by an excessive attachment to international law or, in other words, with sovereignty as a fact rather than a construct, without, however, having to openly endorse the embarrassing author of this doctrine. Celebrated under the aegis of the Rockefeller Foundation's committee on theory, which included exponents of both traditions, realist Christian political theology set the discipline on a very specific course.

AUGUSTINE AND BEYOND: POLITICAL THEOLOGY IN THE POSTWAR YEARS

In his study of the "Augustinian moment" that shaped international thought in the mid-twentieth century, Roger Epp identifies a coherent ideological constellation centered mainly on Anglo-American circles critical of liberalism, whose principal figures were the theologian Reinhold Niebuhr in the United States, and, on the British side, historian Herbert Butterfield and the scholar of international politics Martin Wight. This transatlantic reclamation of Augustine took place in the context of "a revival of intellectual interest in and commitment to Christianity dating back to the 1930s" that gained momentum as the dominant ideologies of progress entered a protracted crisis.[19] The combined effects of the economic recession and of the deterioration of the international situation,

---

[19] Epp, "The 'Augustinian Moment' in International Politics."

along with the rise of Nazism in Germany and the entrenchment of Stalinism in the Soviet Union, undermined the hopes placed in the creation of a rational international order and the very idea that mankind was on a path to material and moral progress. The postwar years saw this skeptical mood gather momentum and become explicitly articulated as a credible ideological and intellectual alternative to the liberal mainstream. Liberal Protestantism, which had held sway in the 1920s, was increasingly coming under criticism.

Involved in Wilsonian internationalism and pacifism, distrusting of "power politics," wedded at times to isolationism, liberal Protestantism was characterized by an optimistic outlook that saw human values realized through social progress. It infused a variety of activist movements and systematic efforts at improving social conditions, in an era of rapid industrialization that threatened to disrupt both the social fabric and the national imaginary rooted in American exceptionalism. It informed philanthropic efforts to develop a more scientific kind of humanitarianism through managerial institutions and expert knowledge that resulted in the development of the modern social sciences. By the same token, however, liberal Protestantism also became a secular religion, heavily invested in, and therefore dependent upon, the material fortunes of American society. As long as it found a plausible validation in its development, this elite vision remained dominant and pervasive. But the economic upheavals of the 1930s undermined its foundations, and the deterioration of the international situation leading up to the war further contributed to its crisis. The most visible reaction to this liberal mystique was the rise of a neo-orthodoxy inspired in particular by European theologians such as Paul Tillich or Karl Barth, and associated with Reinhold Niebuhr, Walter Horton, Francis Miller, Henry Van Dusen, or John Bennett in the United States. Neo-orthodoxy was essentially a reaction against the secular entrapment of liberal Protestantism.[20] It sought to "disentangle Christian thought from its alliance with nineteenth-century secular civilization," out of the conviction that the vicissitudes of the epoch yielded neither the ultimate meaning of history nor the promise of salvation.[21]

---

[20] Donald B. Meyer, *The Protestant Search for Political Realism, 1919–1941*, 2nd edn. Wesleyan 1988 edn. (Berkeley: University of California Press, 1960).

[21] Walter Marshall Horton, *Realistic Theology* (New York and London: Harper & Brothers Publishers, 1934).

Much of the neo-orthodox critique was thus directed against the moral bankruptcy of a scientific culture and an industrial civilization that had substituted eschatology with material progress and given rise to "political religions" that pretended to fulfill history. Liberalism and Communism were such political religions, although the differences were acknowledged. The very idea of the perfectibility of man was anathema to the neo-orthodox mindset, which systematically opposed the ideas of original sin and providence to the notion of progress, and emphasized the transcendence of God against any optimism placed in social and political institutions. Meyer is indeed right to point out that neo-orthodoxy was essentially a *negative* movement that did not give positive political content to the Gospel, but instead deprived politics of theological significance. These two elements – the critique of scientific culture and the critique of progressive politics – converged after 1945 in denouncing the conflation of politics and technology that came to define postwar liberalism and would find in the tremendous development of the social sciences a new lease of life. For realist neo-orthodoxy, there was no such things as "mandarins of the future," to borrow Nils Gilman's apt title of his study of modernization theory, but only hubristic and flawed pretenses at social engineering.[22] As Niebuhr later warned, such theories

> fail to observe the creaturely limitations of the elite who are assigned to the role of masters of history (...) Unfortunately, the clear refutation of the policies, which rest upon the presupposition that human history can and must be mastered, had not deterred bold scientists in the liberal world from projecting various scientific programs for manipulating historical events as if they were in the dimension of nature.[23]

A recurrent theme of Niebuhr's cultural criticism was the misleading idea that the human sciences should be modeled after some kind of physics of society, in which he saw a direct manifestation of the naïve and utopian drive of much American social science.

This return to the values and meanings of Christianity could not fail to influence academic debates, as they provided a common ground for those who shared Niebuhr's dissatisfaction with the social sciences. For some, like the political scientist John Hallowell, the turn toward Christianity was an attempt at reconstituting liberalism on a religious basis by

---

[22] Nils Gilman, *Mandarins of the Future: Modernization Theory in Cold War America* (Baltimore: The Johns Hopkins University Press, 2003).
[23] Reinhold Niebuhr, *Christian Realism and Political Problems* (New York: Charles Scribner's Sons, 1953).

reconnecting it to its cultural roots.[24] For others, like the Catholic historian Carlton Hayes, it served the purpose of attacking liberalism as a force that had corroded the communal bonds of Western civilization.[25] In all cases, however, the Christian revival was to be reckoned with as a counterpoint to the search for a positive, empirical and exact science of social processes that would culminate in the behavioral paradigm of the 1950s. In political theory but also, as we shall see, in international relations theory, theological motives gained traction in the context of a more general reaction against a liberal, pragmatic and positivist mainstream.[26]

Political realism must be resituated against the background of this intellectual and religious ferment. The call for a "realist" approach to contemporary issues first resonated in theological circles of the 1930s, long before it became a stable category in the discussion of political theory. A stream of publications contributed to carving out an ideological space both counteracting the secularization of Protestant liberalism and bringing international issues under a theological lens. These included, among others, Douglas Macintosh's edited volume *Religious Realism* (1931), Reinhold Niebuhr's *Moral Man and Immoral Society* (1932), Walter M. Horton's *Realistic Theology* (1934), and John C. Bennett's *Christian Realism* (1941). In most of these writings, realism was not so much a well-articulated doctrine as a general *Zeitgeist* understood to transform simultaneously politics, literature, science, and philosophy. Realism, Horton wrote, was primarily "a certain temper of mind which craves objectivity and fears subjectivism; which prefers objective realities, however disagreeable, to subjective fancies, however glorious"[27] – words that would later find an echo in Carr's definition of realism as a mindset able "to distinguish the analysis of what is from the aspiration about what should be."[28] Realist theology was fundamentally rooted in the contemporary historical situation: realism made sense as a situated response to the crisis of liberalism, not as a long-established tradition. The first chapter of Bennett's *Christian Realism* was entitled "Our New Situation" and was, in his own words, "most influenced by events since

---

[24] Gunnell, *The Descent of Political Theory*, 213.
[25] Peter Novick, *That Noble Dream: The "Objectivity Question" and the American Historical Profession* (Cambridge: Cambridge University Press, 1998), 243–44.
[26] On IR and political theory, see in particular Bell, *Political Thought and International Relations*.
[27] Horton, *Realistic Theology*.
[28] Edward Hallett Carr, *The Twenty Years' Crisis, 1919–1939* (London: Macmillan, 1939), 13.

the invasion of the Low Countries."²⁹ Horton's *Realistic Theology* was clearly grounded in the "disintegration" of liberalism in World War I and in the insufficiencies of the "Jazz Age."³⁰ Later, Niebuhr's *Christian Realism and Political Problems* (1953), which comprises essays written between 1948 and 1953, was still informed by the discussion of current events and the crisis of the 1930s.

In this context, a number of theologians and political thinkers turned to Augustine for inspiration in their attempt at rethinking the relationship between religious orientations and worldly affairs. But this reclaiming did not take place within a pre-established tradition inherited from the past: rather, it was the product of a historical analogy. The writings of the bishop of Hippo were congenial to the ideological program of neo-orthodoxy, in particular to the attempt at delinking religion from existing political projects. Niebuhr, Horton, Bennett, and others found echoes of their own concerns in Augustine's monumental attempt at salvaging Christianity from its investment in the worldly fortunes of the Roman Empire. "There is much in the present plight of Western civilization to remind us of the days of St. Augustine," Horton wrote. Twenty years after Western civilization had "reached the peak of its glory, [it] threatened to succumb to external and internal forces which have loosened its whole fabric, and put many of our most cherished values into jeopardy."³¹

Mid-century Augustinism was arguably a crucial element in the development of "realism." It offered an alternative to the teleological and progressive vision of politics associated with liberalism. By disconnecting the realization of eschatological designs and ideals of justice from the fortunes of mundane politics, it also provided an intellectual compass for navigating the uncertainties of the postwar order. Progress no longer found a legible translation in history. What mid-century thinkers retained from Augustine was the fact that he "broke with classical rationalism," as well as a conception of politics as an essentially conflictual arena that could, at best, ensure a fragile modicum of peace allowing the denizens of the *civitas terrena* to peregrinate toward the *civitas dei*.³² The relation to transcendental values was thus shifted from the imperfect realm of politics, where they remained unattainable, to the conscience of the believer. This irresolvable tension between the imperfect necessities of politics and individual ethics was indeed at the center of many early

---

[29] John C. Bennett, *Christian Realism* (New York: Charles Scribner's Sons, 1941), x.
[30] Horton, *Realistic Theology*, 6.   [31] Horton, *Realistic Theology*, 160.
[32] Niebuhr, *Christian Realism and Political Problems*, 121.

discussions of statecraft among realist scholars.³³ In reclaiming Augustine as "the first great 'realist' in western history," Niebuhr was in fact engaged, along with others, in the *invention* of a realist tradition that was first and foremost a product of its time, rather than a legacy of the past.³⁴

By focusing on Augustinism as a rhetorical tradition, in the manner of Pocock, however, one runs the risk of turning Augustinism into a preexisting, self-evident paradigm with a force of its own, and of giving precedence to the paradigm itself over its strategic uses. By taking this "tradition" as a starting point, commentators have also tended to be biased in their selection of the authors supposed to exemplify the theological dimension of international relations: The result has been an excessive focus on "Protestant theologians and Protestant-dominated ecumenical forums" and on Anglo-American thinkers.³⁵ The problem with this approach is that it leaves out the contribution of German émigrés, even though some of them brought into the nascent theory of international relations powerful strains of continental political theology and engaged in sustained theological dialogue with Niebuhr. It seems more fruitful, then, to consider Augustinism as a loose political language that lent itself to a variety of different purposes. According to who did the talking – a British dissenting Methodist like Butterfield who "moved easily in the thought-world of Catholicism" or a German Jewish émigré like Morgenthau – it could be spoken with very different inflexions.³⁶

What then becomes clear is that the Augustinian language characteristic of Protestant neo-orthodoxy also functioned as a proxy for another tradition, another opposition to liberal Protestantism, but one that came from largely Jewish and Catholic quarters. More specifically, it was Jewish in its sociological composition, but largely Catholic in its theological equipment. For sure, political theology in Weimar was also rooted in a rich tradition of Jewish philosophy, which transpires in the works of

---

³³ Hans J. Morgenthau, "The Evil of Politics and the Ethics of Evil," *Ethics* 56, no. 1 (1945): 1–18; Wolfers, "Statesmanship and Moral Choice."
³⁴ Niebuhr, *Christian Realism and Political Problems*, 120–21. That there was no such preexisting tradition in which Augustine was read as a "realist" is striking when one considers that, a few decades earlier, Meinecke was reading Augustine as the author delivering "a final crushing judgement" against the ancient tradition of reason of state and of power politics, not as an exponent of this tradition: Friedrich Meinecke, *Machiavellism: The Doctrine of Raison d'Etat and its Place in Modern History* (New Brunswick: Transaction Books, 1998), 27.
³⁵ Epp, "The Ironies of Christian Realism," 200.
³⁶ Jones, "Christian Realism," 376.

Sholem, Benjamin, Rosenzweig, or Strauss, to name but a few.[37] But this is not the tradition with which the émigrés who contributed to the birth of international relations theory were associated. Before retooling themselves as IR scholars in US political science departments, most of them were jurists, and as such much more familiar with the works of Schmitt than with this philosophical tradition.[38] Through a process of reception that was more or less critical, their theological equipment was chiefly inherited from Carl Schmitt's influential formulation of the theologico-political problem. Morgenthau, for instance, was well acquainted with the theology of crisis, and in particular the works of Martin Buber and Paul Tillich, but he had also developed early on a sustained intellectual engagement with Schmitt's work.[39] Waldemar Gurian, whom we encountered in the previous chapter and who turned the *Review of Politics* into a platform for the critique of scientism and the development of political realism, was a protégé of Schmitt. He was the advocate of an "uncompromising realism," in which Arendt saw "the natural result of Christian teachings and Catholic training."[40] Arnold Wolfers was well acquainted with the work of Schmitt, who had taught at the Hochschule für Politik. John Herz, late in his life, revealed the extent of Schmitt's relevance for postwar realists, and once done with the *de rigueur* criticisms acknowledged his intellectual debt.[41] This receptive environment for Schmitt's ideas has long remained absent from the standard genealogies of international relations theory and political realism. Some of the key figures in this environment occupied important strategic positions: Gurian's *Review of Politics*, for instance, was closely aligned with the Committee on Social Thought at the University of Chicago.[42]

---

[37] On this tradition, see Eric Jacobson, *Metaphysics of the Profane: The Political Theology of Walter Benjamin and Gershom Sholem* (New York: Columbia University Press, 2003); Benjamin Lazier, "On the Origins of 'Political Theology': Judaism and Heresy between the World Wars," *New German Critique* 35, no. 3 (2008): 143–64.

[38] For an empirical appraisal of the shift from law to political science among German Jewish émigrés to the United States, see the analysis by Söllner, "Vom Völkerrecht zur Science of International Relations," 165.

[39] Roger L. Shinn, "The Continuing Conversation between Hans Morgenthau and Reinhold Niebuhr," in *One Hundred Year Commemoration of the Life of Hans Morgenthau*, ed. G. O. Mazur (New York: Semenenko Foundation, 2004), 84.

[40] Arendt, "The Personality of Waldemar Gurian," 42. Arendt's very positive opinion of Gurian may have had something to do with her own silent dialogue with Schmitt over political theology and secularism Samuel Moyn, "Hannah Arendt on the Secular," *New German Critique* 35, no. 3 (2008): 71–96.

[41] Herz, "Looking at Carl Schmitt."

[42] Nef, "The Significance of the Review of Politics."

Augustine and beyond: Political Theology in the Postwar Years

It was also instrumental in giving exposure to Morgenthau's version of realism. The University of Chicago was the fulcrum of this opposition to mainstream liberalism, in both its secular and Protestant instantiations. While Chicago had been the cradle of the empirical social science movement under such figures as Charles Merriam or Robert Park, the nomination of the neo-Thomist Robert Maynard Hutchins as chancellor in 1929 opened a deep ideological rift within the institution and gave political theology a new impetus. Highly skeptical of the value of social sciences modeled after physics, Hutchins opened the university to the staunchest critics of liberal modernity, such as Leo Strauss or Hans Morgenthau (whose recruitment in 1943 took place in opposition to the liberal internationalist Quincy Wright). Shortly after the beginning of Hutchins's term, "word spread around the country that the University of Chicago was a former Baptist school where Jewish professors were now teaching Catholic theology to atheists."[43]

Yet, if Schmittian ideas could remain influential, it is also because they found in the United States a cultural receptacle in the neo-orthodoxy represented by Niebuhr and the Christian realists. Once translated in the indigenous language of conservative Christian realism, this import became undetectable. By bringing together some of these émigrés with Niebuhr, Kennan, Butterfield, or Thompson – all Christian realists – for the purpose of discussing and defining the "theory" of international relations in the early 1950s, the Rockefeller Foundation played a crucial role in producing this ideological blend fit for home consumption and yet explicitly conceived in opposition to the Enlightenment tradition. For the Christian realists, "the entire Enlightenment project, from the 18th century onwards – the French as much as the Russian revolution – had been fundamentally misguided in its worship of reason and humanity and the expense of faith and God."[44] As the project of a new, international political theory congealed, the production of a realist "tradition" reaching back to Augustine, and eventually enriched by the addition of Machiavelli, Hobbes, or Thucydides, further contributed to masking the immediate roots of IR theory in the reactionary canon of the interwar years.

---

[43] Martin Gardner, *The Night Is Large: Collected Essays, 1938–1995* (New York: St. Martin's Griffin, 1996), 511.

[44] Jones, "Christian Realism and the Foundations of the English School," 375.

CARL SCHMITT'S POLITICAL THEOLOGY

The strong contingent of German legal scholars among the first international relations theorists in the United States ensured that Schmitt was an interlocutor in the postwar debate, albeit a silent one, since the disrepute into which he fell after 1945 confined him to the backstage of the intellectual scene.[45] Yet, in the fields of politics and law, but also in geography and history, there is evidence that he was not totally ignored and that he, in turn, followed closely some US debates over international law after World War II.[46] In international relations theory, his influence chiefly took the form of a not so "hidden dialogue" between Schmitt and Morgenthau. As William Scheuerman has aptly observed, the commentary of Morgenthau's precise relation to the intellectual heritage of Carl Schmitt has become in recent years a "small cottage industry."[47] This abundant commentary certainly sheds new light on the antecedents of IR theory and leaves no doubt as to the importance of Morgenthau's "Schmittian intellectual baggage," although this baggage is obviously not the only one he carried along.[48] Recently, various commentators have explored the meanders and the full reach of this influence on Morgenthau's thought.[49] If most of them have insisted on the conception of the political, the critique of liberalism and international law, or the contempt for rationalism and the technological or scientific mindset that are common to both authors – not to mention the more trivial dispositions

---

[45] Müller, *A Dangerous Mind*.

[46] Mira Siegelberg, "Between Regionalism and Universalism: Carl Schmitt in Postwar America" (unpublished paper, Harvard University, 2008).

[47] Scheuerman, "Carl Schmitt and Hans Morgenthau," 87 fn. 2.

[48] Scheuerman, "Carl Schmitt and Hans Morgenthau," 86. The political orientations of Morgenthau during his Weimar years and the extent of his intellectual affinities with Schmitt are – and will certainly remain – a subject of debate. See Michael C. Williams, "Why Ideas Matter in International Relations: Hans Morgenthau, Classical Realism, and the Moral Construction of Power Politics," *International Organization* 58, no. 4 (2004): 633–65. William Scheuerman, who was among the first to emphasize the role of Schmitt in the development of Morgenthau's thought, has recently produced a much more nuanced account that significantly downplays Schmitt's influence in favor of social-democratic ideas to which Morgenthau was exposed when he worked in a labor law practice; Scheuerman, *Hans Morgenthau*. No matter what the final word may be on these matters, Scheuerman was certainly right to claim that Morgenthau's relation to Schmitt entailed an element of "bad conscience."

[49] Christoph Frei, *Hans J. Morgenthau: An Intellectual Biography* (Baton Rouge: Louisiana State University Press, 2001); Koskenniemi, *The Gentle Civilizer*; Pichler, "The Godfathers of 'Truth'"; Williams, "Why Ideas Matter in International Relations"; Michael C. Williams, "Foreword," in *The Concept of the Political*, ed. Hans J. Morgenthau (Basingstoke: Palgrave Macmillan, 2012); Jütersonke, *Morgenthau, Law and Realism*.

of elitist conservatives, such as a distaste for abstract art and a contempt for middle class culture[50] – no one has yet traced the modulation of the politico-theological tradition as it reached the southern shores of Lake Michigan.[51] But more importantly, as I have suggested, the real issue is to understand the extent to which Schmitt's political theology has been influential beyond the single case of Morgenthau, by permeating a milieu that had been exposed to his most influential writings of the interwar years and percolating into IR theory. First, however, a brief reconstruction of this aspect of his thought is in order.

Carl Schmitt's style has been alternatively praised or condemned for being, at times, deliberately esoteric and suggestive, preferring incisive statements and fulgurating metaphors to analytical developments. No matter the respective merits and defects of his manner, it certainly makes full use of the evocative power of language to qualify the most abstract concepts. An attentive reader cannot fail to notice that Schmitt's discussion of political concepts is peppered with a vocabulary of sharpness and clarity of vision: the political quality of such concepts lies in their capacity to establish "distinctions," "categorizations" that are "intense"; they operate as a "criterion" in what is essentially a discriminating activity; the political implies a capacity for "clearly evaluating" situations. But "clarity" for Schmitt is not so much an abstract or notional attribute as it is a sensorial, almost existential quality: Political concepts are concepts that allow for a clear perception of who is a friend and who is an enemy. As a result, such clarity of perception can only obtain in concrete situations: "only the actual participants can correctly recognize, understand, and judge the concrete situation and settle the extreme case of conflict."[52] It is when the threat materializes into an actual possibility of lethal conflict that political distinctions are made. Political concepts are, by definition, concepts that *deal* practically with such situations. Because they are indexed to a friend–enemy situation, political concepts cannot be neutral. Instead, they must introduce distinctions and discriminate. "[A]ll

---

[50] These aspects of "reactionary modernism" are very salient in Schmitt's *Nordlicht* (1916). Yet, they also surface in some of Morgenthau's writings: attack on middle class culture in *Scientific Man vs. Power Politics*, and explicit contempt for modern art in Morgenthau, "Reflections on the State of Political Science," 443. On Morgenthau as an exemplar of "reactionary modernism," see Mirowski, "Realism and Neoliberalism."

[51] For an exception that, however, focuses on Strauss see Heinrich Meier, *Leo Strauss and the Theological-Political Problem* (Cambridge; New York: Cambridge University Press, 2006).

[52] Carl Schmitt, *The Concept of the Political* (Chicago: Chicago University Press, 2007), 27.

political concepts, images, and terms have a polemical meaning."[53] A concept that does not find its place within a system of oppositions, a concept for which there is no counter-concept, is not a political concept.[54] Such is, for instance, the case with the notion of "humanity," which is not taken within a concrete antagonism and does not, therefore, designate a political entity: It can be political only when it is used for "cheating." If Schmitt's concepts have been described as "sharp," it is because they are essentially weapons.

To the extent that the capacity for discrimination is always situated, it cannot be contained either within *a priori* rationalizations. No abstract rationality can generate the clarity of perception that Schmitt has in mind when he defines the political. Taking sides in the friend–enemy situation cannot be dictated by law, whose dynamics is precisely to abstract from the concrete, to disconnect concepts and situated meanings: It is an existential decision that requires no further or external justification and is the basis of all subsequent justifications. Schmitt sees sovereign political communities essentially as "decisive human grouping[s]" that give a legal and institutional form to their political life on the basis of a preexisting decision.[55] This existential decision precedes and exceeds the legal order: There is no superior norm in the eyes of which it could be "wrong," while the decision is the source of all norms. Political realism, in its true sense, is based on an original nondistinction between what is and what ought to be. For a true realist, political existence is authoritative *per se*: The political entity "exists or does not exist. If it exists, it is the supreme, that is, in the decisive case, the authoritative entity."[56] The very existence of the legal order is thus premised on the sovereign decision: Not only does the sovereign decide upon what constitutes an exceptional case that warrants suspending the normal operation of law, but, by extension, the situation is normal as long as it is judged to be so: "the legal order rests on a decision and not on a norm."[57] The decision is the true foundation of the political order. As long as this form of sovereign judgment can be exercised, the political capacity for distinctions is safeguarded.

---

[53] Schmitt, *The Concept of the Political*, 30.
[54] This intuition was successfully developed by Reinhardt Koselleck in his program for *Begriffsgeschichte*. See Melvin Richter, *The History of Political and Social Concepts: A Critical Introduction* (New York: Oxford University Press, 1995).
[55] Schmitt, *The Concept of the Political*, 38.
[56] Schmitt, *The Concept of the Political*, 44.
[57] Schmitt, *Political Theology*, 10. See also Roberto Esposito, *Due. La Macchina Della Teologia Politica E Il Posto Del Pensiero*, Piccola Biblioteca Einaudi (Torino: Einaudi, 2013), 42–48.

Schmitt's study of the concept of sovereignty is where his critique of liberalism most clearly evolves out of a politico-theological predicament.[58] His *Political Theology* (1922) is indeed drafted as the Weimar Republic's liberal constitutionalism appears increasingly ill-adapted and paralyzing in a situation that would require strong political decisions – a topic that is central to Schmitt's vast production as a publicist during the interwar years.[59] Schmitt's main concern is the incapacity of liberal constitutional orders to make political distinctions and to discriminate between friend and foe, an incapacity that is, according to him, the main pathology of the "neutral state" of the nineteenth century. With its guaranteed individual freedoms and institutionalized *laissez-faire*, the liberal state is in fact defined by its indifference vis-à-vis social and economic interests. Schmitt identifies legal positivism as the juristic ideology of this indifference, since it envisions law by explicitly insulating it from sociology and from any concrete situation. Kelsen's "pure" theory of law, where this insulation is articulated, is here Schmitt's direct target. Identified with its own constitution, the liberal state becomes contained within the rule of law and unable to rise above it when the exception arises. It is neutral because its concepts no longer relate to a concrete situation, since the concrete situation has been carefully bracketed out of its juristic representation. By the same token, it ceases to be a genuine state: "the state simply transforms itself into an association which competes with other associations." Unable to discriminate between friend and foe on the basis of its own interests, the liberal state is in a state of irredeemable decay: "the incapacity or the unwillingness to make this distinction is a symptom of the political end."[60]

THE ARCH-REALIST: SCHMITT'S KATECHON

Why is the liberal state unable to instantiate sovereignty? Although Schmitt does not provide a succinct, univocal answer, but rather distillates it throughout his works, it is possible to encapsulate his diagnosis into one word: secularization. Schmitt himself suggests this explanation when he borrows the expression *stato neutrale ed agnostico* to scold liberal

---

[58] Steven Ostovich, "Carl Schmitt, Political Theology, and Eschatology," *KronoScope* 7 (2007): 49–66.
[59] See Carl Schmitt, *Positionen und Begriffe: Im Kampf mit Weimar-Genf-Versailles, 1923–1939* (Berlin: Duncker & Humblot, 1988).
[60] Schmitt, *The Concept of the Political*, 44, 68.

constitutionalism, which faced with the imperative of the decision remains as hesitant as Buridan's ass.[61] His characterization of the neutral state as "agnostic" points at a systematic understanding of the morphological development of the European state in relation to theology, first exposed in the third chapter of *Political Theology* (1922) and later briefly developed in *Ex Captivitate Salus* (1945) and *The Nomos of the Earth* (1950). The statement that "all significant concepts of the modern theory of the state are secularized theological concepts" is indeed followed by an analysis of modern constitutionalism as the juristic equivalent of deism, replacing deity within the immanent order of nature. The neutral state of modern liberalism is unable to understand and effectuate sovereignty because sovereignty is essentially defined by its transcendent relationship to law. A state that is entirely contained within the rule of law is indeed a fully secularized state, held in the illusion of self-grounding and operating on the basis of concepts whose theological roots are concealed by a positivistic legal ideology. The liberal state, in other words, no longer operates in the framework of political theology.

Schmitt's critique of liberalism suggests that "political theology" not only designates a method for the sociology of legal concepts of the state, but also involves a specific view of the historical process of secularization. Notwithstanding later claims to the contrary, during the interwar period Schmitt viewed "political theology" as something more than a metaphor or a methodological principle based upon the structural analogies between political and theological concepts: "this relationship [between, e.g. monarchy and monotheism, constitutionalism and deism] can be explained neither materialistically as mere 'ideological superstructure,' reflex, or 'reflection,' nor, on the other hand, idealistically or spiritually as 'material substructure.'"[62] A metaphorical or heuristic use of the notion of "political theology" would indeed imply a clear distinction and a separation between the two dimensions. Yet, such a separation is precisely what is negated with the concept of political theology, which seeks to contain secularization. As Heinrich Meier has noted, "political theology" is also a political concept, and as such it has indeed a "polemical meaning": it is the counter-concept of secularization. Political theology is

---

[61] Carl Schmitt, "The Age of Neutralizations and Depoliticizations (1929)," in *The Concept of the Political* (Chicago: Chicago University Press, 2007), 88.
[62] Carl Schmitt, "State Ethics and the Pluralist State," in *Weimar: A Jurisprudence of Crisis*, eds., Arthur J. Jacobson and Bernhard Schlink (Berkeley: University of California Press, 2000), 302.

secularization seen from the other side. While secularization is premised on the separation of the religious and the political, political theology refutes this possibility because any absolute separation would mean the end of the political itself. And this is precisely the diagnosis of the neutral state of modern liberalism: a secular state that is utterly "depoliticized" and unable to make political "decisions" because it can no longer understand sovereignty. What secularization sees as the possibility of rational self-grounding, political theology sees as a drift away from the only real foundation, and hence as a deficit of legitimacy. Jacob Taubes, arguably one of the most insightful readers of Schmitt's political theology, has perfectly expressed the meaning of secularization for the Catholic jurist: "it's an illegitimate category. That something is secularized implies that it has been transferred from a legitimate place to an illegitimate one."[63] Ultimately, legitimacy is to be found in revelation, not reason – and the sovereign decision is its equivalent in the domain of politics. It is the theological background of Western Christendom against which the state has developed as a principle of concrete territorial ordering that can provide legitimacy. Absolute secularization can only lead to the collapse of this principle. Trapped in its self-referentiality, the state of the rule-of-law cannot revert to the legitimating decision that stands behind its legality. It is unable to decide upon the exception, and thus doomed to be undone by the forces of chaos.

What the Schmittian "political theology" makes clear is that the battle against secularization is a battle for the state. It is important to emphasize that Schmitt does not advocate a re-theologization of politics: rather, he defends the autonomy of the political, but also warns that this autonomy is premised on the historical constitution of a territorial order distinct from, *but coexisting with*, the moral order embodied by the ecclesial institutions of Christianity. Should secularization proceed to the extent that the state no longer understands itself in relation (and in tension) with this background and conflate its own interests with morality itself – as in the case of liberalism – then it would assume again religious attributes and give rise to dangerous political religions.[64] By the same token, it would cease to act politically. The end product of secular modernity, in fact, is

---

[63] Jacob Taubes, *The Political Theology of Paul* (Stanford: Stanford University Press, 2004), 69.

[64] Heinrich Meier, *The Lesson of Carl Schmitt: Four Chapters on the Distinction between Political Theology and Political Philosophy* (Chicago: The University of Chicago Press, 1998), 122–27; William Rasch, "Messias oder Katechon? Carl Schmitts Stellung zur Politischen Theologie," in *Politische Theologie: Formen und Funktionen im 20.*

a state that is unable to prevent its own collapse. For what lies at the center of Schmitt's paradox of the sovereign is that any legal *order*, in order to maintain itself, presupposes an element that exempts itself from it and stands in relation to it as God in relation to his creature. This is what nineteenth-century legal positivism has forgotten because it is "un-Christian and atheistic."[65] The survival of the state as a historical counterforce to chaos is what is really at stake in the historical unfolding of secularization. This battle, however, is not a final, eschatological battle resulting in perpetual peace and the unification of humanity – Schmitt's critique of humanity as a non-political concept that is, at best, a self-delusion, at worst a "cheat," a false universalism allowing for more wars and predation, does not need to be repeated here. The battle against chaos knows only limited victories; it is circumscribed and always started all over again in the realm of human finitude. Separation and difference – or, in other words, enmity – cannot be canceled in a mundane world bound to remain a "pluriverse."[66]

Schmitt encapsulates this pessimistic vision of statecraft in the perplexing figure of the *katechon*, variously translated as "restrainer," "delayer," or "withholder." Mentioned in the second epistle to the Thessalonians, in which Paul seeks to curb the eschatological enthusiasm of the local Christians that threatens to disrupt public order, the *katechon* is the mundane force that delays the arrival of the Antichrist (the "lawless one"), which precedes the return of Christ and the *parousia* (2 Thessalonians 2:1–12). The existence of the *katechon* explains why the time of the Kingdom of God is not imminent and why historical time is possible: It holds back the reign of lawlessness that precedes and announces the end of times. One can easily figure why Schmitt saw in the *katechon* a metaphorical vehicle for his own vision of sovereignty and statecraft: It operates in the downtrodden realm of imperfection; it does not prepare or gradually establish the kingdom of God in a progressive or teleological sense: It merely delays it by fighting chaos and maintaining order until the Day comes, thus opening the possibility of history.

Although the precise significance of the *katechon* for Schmitt's representation of history has generated a lot of commentary, this Biblical

Jahrhundert, eds., Jürgen Brokoff and Jürgen Fohrmann (Paderborn: Ferdinand Schöningh, 2003).
[65] Carl Schmitt, *The Nomos of the Earth in the International Law of the Jus Publicum Europaeum* (New York: Telos, 2006), 76.
[66] It is worthwhile observing that Schmitt's critique of the "Babylonian unity" of mankind anticipated the post-1945 realist critique of world government and the UN.

metaphor seems to fulfill two functions within the general economy of his *oeuvre*.⁶⁷ First, the *katechon* makes a de-theologized form of politics possible. By holding back, postponing, or delaying the end of times, it embodies a form of politics that does not accomplish eschatological goals, but is detached from them. It represents, as it were, a sort of middle-range theory of politics. It protects the community from the illusions of both absolute perfection and absolute evil, and squarely locates politics on a *realistic* ground that is immune to utopian cues. As William Rasch points out, "to accept the political can only be nihilistic if one hopes to replace here and now the City of Men by the City of God, and if one cannot conceive of a third position between absolute good and absolute evil."⁶⁸ Such a "third position," it should be noted, is also at the center of the realist argument about the discrepancy between politics and morality.⁶⁹ The *katechon*, in that sense, is indeed a proto-realist. A second concern expressed in this iconic figure seems to be a concern with history as a succession of specific political orders.⁷⁰ For each historical epoch, Schmitt posited the existence of a *katechon*, of an ordering force that gave the age its concrete structure and its relative stability. It is not a coincidence that Schmitt introduces this allegory in 1942 and that the *katechon* kept surfacing in his works thereafter, precisely when the shape of the world order to come was anything but clear. By choosing a Biblical allegory, Schmitt was both indicating the historical necessity of a "restrainer" and confessing that its current identity remained concealed. In many ways, the *katechon* gave a theological coating to the question of the balance of power after 1945.

PROVIDENTIALISM AND THE BALANCE OF POWER

In 1950, the *katechon* resurfaced in *The Nomos of the Earth*, Schmitt's major postwar work, in which he proceeded to reconstruct the emergence of a European legal order based on an international society of monarchs, and its subsequent decline as the legally sanctioned notions of legitimate adversary and limited warfare that characterized it gave way to the "total wars" of the twentieth century, waged in the name of universal causes

---

[67] See Günter Meuter, *Der Katechon: Zu Carl Schmitts fundamentalistischer Kritik der Zeit* (Berlin: Duncker & Humblot, 1994); Felix Grossheutschi, *Carl Schmitt und die Lehre vom Katechon* (Berlin: Duncker & Humblot, 1996); Esposito, *Due*, 83–89.
[68] Rasch, "Messias oder Katechon? Carl Schmitts Stellung zur politischen Theologie," 53.
[69] Morgenthau, "The Evil of Politics and the Ethics of Evil."
[70] Meier, *The Lesson of Carl Schmitt*, 160–73.

rather than limited interests. Schmitt described the *jus publicum Europaeum* as a concrete order, based on the twin foundations of a concrete land-space and a universal morality embodied by the ecclesiastical authorities, and considered it the highest achievement of European civilization. While the rationalization of this spatial order took the form of states ensuring the "detheologization of public life" and thus limiting violence to codified interstate encounters, these states still remained part of "the same European family" and their international law derived its strength from its being rooted in a common Christian background.[71] As long as this order persisted, it channeled disputes into limited military confrontations based on divergences between identifiable and concrete interests, and kept these confrontations strictly exempt from any moral content. This Eurocentric order was also confined to a space delimited by "global lines" beyond which conquest was a legitimate activity, not bound by the niceties of European international law.[72]

Woven into this stylized historical tapestry was a polemical argument contrasting this supposed golden age of European politics with the rise of liberalism in the nineteenth century, the colonization of the state by social interests, and the replacement of the concrete legal order of the *jus publicum Europaeum* with moral abstractions and the legal utopia of a world community, the enemies of which had then to be annihilated in unlimited wars waged with unlimited means. No matter the degree of historical stylization involved in its narrative as well as its serious limitations, *Nomos* offered a compelling analysis of the world-historical situation of the mid-twentieth-century.[73] But it was also a forward-looking work oriented by the question of the *nomos* that would succeed the old Eurocentric order destroyed by liberalism. "Where do we stand today?" Schmitt asked in a subsequent rejoinder, refusing to see in the Cold War a concrete political order and considering it as a transitional phase.[74] Schmitt envisaged three possible scenarios: the unlikely and worrying triumph of one of the Cold War contenders; the rise of America as a balancer inheriting the role previously performed by Britain; or the constitution of autonomous world regions, or *Grossraüme*, which he favored.

---

[71] Schmitt, *Nomos*, 140. [72] Schmitt, *Nomos*, 86–100.

[73] For a discussion of these approximations, see Martti Koskenniemi, "International Law as Political Theology: How to Read Nomos Der Erde?" *Constellations* 11, no. 4 (2004): 492–511.

[74] Schmitt, *Nomos*, 354.

It is, of course, tempting to discount Schmitt's vision as the idiosyncratic rambling of a bitter and defeated reactionary. But Schmitt was not alone in raising the pressing question of who would be the new *katechon*, the restraining force that would contain disorder and generate a new balance of power. The question of the balance was on many minds on both sides of the Atlantic, and the fact that *The Nomos of the Earth* was actually engaging a number of themes at the center of American discourse about international law and organization has gone largely unnoticed. Yet, a number of American authors whom Schmitt read carefully "shared many of Schmitt's assumptions about the impossibility of a universal international law" and about the need for a concrete spatial order.[75] The entire project of developing a theory and a discipline of international relations, in particular, was supposed to reintroduce the question of the balance of power – rather than an abstract international legalism – into the doctrine and practice of statecraft. But although this question resonated throughout the early postwar development of IR theory, it remained unanswered and revealed a deep-seated anxiety: could it be that the postwar order was deprived of a balance? Could it be that there was no *katechon* giving the epoch its order and its historical form? Did the crisis of the 1930s and World War II signal the end of an era and the descent into political anomie?

As Schmitt was deploring the disappearance of the old European *nomos* and scrutined in vain the political horizon for a possible balancer, other voices were formulating similar concerns. Morgenthau regretted that the balance of power had lost "the vital energy which transformed it from a metaphor into a living principle of international politics." The reduction of the number of really independent states and the emergence of two superpowers had deprived the balance of its flexibility. Alliances no longer made any difference in the distribution of power between the two main contenders. As a result, Morgenthau suggested with a real anxiety, it may be the case that "the place itself [of the "holder" of the balance] no longer exists."[76] In a letter to Joseph Willits urging the Rockefeller Foundation to prepare Americans for their new international responsibilities, Arnold Toynbee warned that the two World Wars had precipitated the "transfer of power" between Britain and America: but America was unprepared to assume its new hegemonic responsibilities, and if this unpreparedness was combined with "the obvious inability of

---

[75] Siegelberg, "Between Regionalism and Universalism," 2.
[76] Morgenthau, *Politics among Nations*, 270, 274.

Great Britain, Belgium and the Netherlands to continue to carry the whole of their previous responsibilities," this may lead to a "political vacuum," a dangerous "interregnum."[77] This image of the empty space, of the unoccupied position, of the absent *katechon*, surfaced in a number of conversations about the balance of power. Paradoxically, the nascent theory of international relations enshrined the concept of balance precisely when (and, arguably, because) its historical existence became uncertain. By pointing out the absence of an element or a subject that endowed historical situations with meaning and orientation, early realists were in fact articulating locally a concern that dominated postwar intellectual debates. The disappearance of the balance of power was not only jeopardizing the capacity to make sense of the current historical situation: it was also undermining the capacity to make sense of history itself. As Schmitt's *katechon* suggested, the succession of political orders, each generated by a balancer, made sense within a wider eschatological scheme characterized by a form of Providentialism. The angst-ridden discussion of the balance of power after 1945 must be understood as the local manifestation of a generalized crisis of political eschatology, powerfully captured at the time by Karl Lowith or Jacob Taubes.[78]

In order to recover this specific meaning of the balance of power, one has to peel away layers of abstraction that the concept has subsequently developed. Only once its core is laid bare do its theological foundations become visible. The balance of power has provided the model for the kind of formal modeling of political rationality that developed as IR gradually evolved into a social science in the course of the 1960s.[79] Overtime, it has become a systemic, structural concept that could function as a model for deterrence or strategic equilibriums in the nuclear age.[80] Yet, the balance was initially understood as a specific historical formation, not as an abstract configuration of forces. Early realists considered the balance of power as the main achievement of the European order of the eighteenth century, and offered it as a model of political organization capable of

---

[77] Arnold Toynbee to Joseph H. Willits, May 16, 1947, Folder 61, Box 7, Series 910, RG 3, RF, RAC.

[78] Karl Löwith, *Meaning in History: The Theological Implications of the Philosophy of History* (Chicago: University of Chicago Press, 1949); Jacob Taubes, *Abendländische Eschatologie* (München: Matthes & Seitz, 1991).

[79] For a survey of the concept, see Richard Little, *The Balance of Power in International Relations: Metaphors, Myths and Models* (Cambridge: Cambridge University Press, 2007). See also the classical study by Alfred Vagts, "The Balance of Power: Growth of an Idea," *World Politics* 1, no. 1 (1948): 82–101.

[80] Craig, *Glimmer of a New Leviathan*.

generating a modicum of order and peace. For both Schmitt and Morgenthau, the balance was the only thing left of the idea of politics as a concrete spatial ordering, as opposed to the abstractions of international law. A change in the balance, Schmitt wrote in a language pitting against each other the repertoires of legality and factuality, does not only affect "the contractual parties (...) but all participants." Its character as a leftover of the *jus publicum Europaeum* appears in the fact that the balance of power contains the idea of a spatial order: it "expresses spatial viewpoints (...) and illuminates the idea of a comprehensive spatial order inherent in this balance. Therein (...) lies the great practical superiority of the concept of balance, because therein lies its capacity to achieve a bracketing of war."[81] In that sense, the balance of power was indeed a realist concept, indexed to the concrete situation of a Eurocentric and Christian order.

Morgenthau offered a very similar understanding when he suggested that the balance was the mere "instrumentality" of an "intellectual and moral tradition of the Western world." It was made possible not only by a "moral climate," but also by the capacity of European powers to expand their power by grabbing land on "the wide expanses of three continents [that] offered that opportunity: Africa, the Americas, and the part of Asia bordering on the Eastern oceans"[82] – a reminder that racialized and imperial land-partitions were the implicit background of many IR concepts, and indeed fundamental to the development of the entire discipline of international relations.[83] With the passing of this tradition, the collapse of the liberal order that had succeeded it, and the impending end of colonial empires, the existence and the shape of the balance of power were called into question. Despite the fact that the antagonism between the United States and the Soviet Union would later be viewed as a balancing system of mutual deterrence by a discipline of international relations won over by formalistic modeling techniques, the postwar realists certainly did not consider the Cold War as a form of balance of power that could prevent the occurrence of another devastating conflict. For them, the concept of balance could not be applied to just any situation

---

[81] Schmitt, *The Nomos of the Earth*, 188–89.
[82] Morgenthau, *Politics among Nations*, 267, 278.
[83] Vitalis, *White World Order, Black Power Politics*; David Long and Brian C. Schmidt, eds., *Imperialism and Internationalism in the Discipline of International Relations* (Albany: State University of New York Press, 2005); Nicolas Guilhot, "Imperial Realism: Postwar IR Theory and Decolonization," *International History Review* 36, no. 4 (2014): 698–720.

involving a plurality of potentially divergent interests, for it referred to a very specific, and maybe historically unique, European land ordering.

This Eurocentric understanding of the balance of power was also tethered to a providential view of history that sanctioned European supremacy. In an address at Chatham House in 1951, Butterfield had suggested that the European balance of the eighteenth century represented "a special civilized area and a *providential* order."[84] A providential order, for Butterfield, meant that the balance of power was not the result of some human design, for men are not "sovereign makers of history" and cannot contemplate the large-scale consequences of their actions, but of a Providence that "moves over history with the function of creating good out of evil," i.e. out of the self-interest of states and rulers. It was not political virtue, but providential dispensation that endowed the Christian nations of Europe with an orderly balance of power. Butterfield distinguished between "the Providence which lies in the very constitution of things" and imposes its constraints upon any action, and a form of Providence that allows for the uncoordinated actions of multitudes of men to result in what retrospectively appears as an order – an "ordaining and reconciling" Providence. The very possibility of order in history was the signature of Providence, the sign that "in the workings of history there must be felt the movement of a living God." In the realm of politics, the balance of power was the providential order *par excellence*. Even the materialistic eighteenth century and its science of diplomacy "kept that conception of a providential order which it was thought necessary in general to maintain – a conception which like a number of other things seemed to survive as a kind of shell after the religion, which had given it some reality, had evaporated out of it."[85] Along with Niebuhr's, Butterfield's was probably the most developed articulation of what was still a very common interpretation of the concept of balance among the postwar theorists of international relations.

The transatlantic discussion of the balance of power in the 1940s was thus steeped in what Giorgio Agamben has called the "theological paradigm" of providential government.[86] As Butterfield's treatment suggestively illustrates, the question of the balance was informed by

---

[84] Herbert Butterfield, "The Scientific versus the Moralistic Approach in International Affairs," *International Affairs* 27, no. 4 (1951): 418.
[85] Butterfield, *Christianity and History*, 98, 111, 01–02.
[86] Giorgio Agamben, *Il Regno e la Gloria: Per una Genealogia Teologica dell'Economia e del Governo* (Torino: Bollati Boringhieri, 2009).

a theological tradition in which the presence of God in history took the form not of an external, transcendent, and sovereign intervention, but of an immanent order, of a design that takes shape through the seemingly unconstrained movement of things and men when they are permitted to follow their own nature and inclinations. This tradition sought to reconcile the idea of the undivided sovereignty of a transcendent being with its actual effectiveness, and therefore with its mundane operation and its distributed agency through a multiplicity of beings. It produced the notion of Providence, which came to designate the generous divine dispensation that ensured that the nature of the creation contained the intrinsic possibility of a harmonious order. An immanent *order* thus became the manifestation of a transcendent principle of *coordination* – or rather, order was thinkable only to the extent that it was premised on a transcendent authority. The legacy of this theological tradition has been the providential postulate implicit in any concept of spontaneous order, whether conceived of as "equilibrium" or as "balance."

Interestingly, Agamben suggests that this set of questions defined the domain of "economics," understood as the government of things and men: the Fathers of the Church referred to it as the divine *oikonomia*,[87] a term that survived until the Middle Ages, and starting in the eighteenth century, modern economics inherited the question of the natural order of things – or, to use a more contemporary language, of how equilibrium is achieved without a principle of central allocation. The influence of providentialism on classical economics is well known, and finds its most suggestive expression in the idea that the optimal distribution of wealth is equivalent to allocation by an "invisible hand."[88] Yet, Agamben's brief foray into modern economics can be extended to political science, for the notions of "equilibrium" and of "balance" refer to the same class of problems. The problem of reaching equilibrium in the absence of a central principle of allocation is strictly equivalent to the problem of achieving balance of power in the absence of a central principle of authority or, to

---

[87] According to Agamben, the tradition of the theological *oikonomia* was derived from the doctrine of the Trinity: it was motivated by a concern "to avoid a split within monotheism, which would have reintroduced a plurality of divine figures and, as a result, polytheism." God was thus said to be one ontologically, but plural from the point of view of his economy, or praxis. Agamben, *Il Regno e la Gloria*, 69.

[88] Lisa Hill, "The Hidden Theology of Adam Smith," *The European Journal of the History of Economic Thought* 8, no. 1 (2001): 1–29; Jacob Viner, *The Role of Providence in the Social Order* (Philadelphia: American Philosophical Society, 1972). I am grateful to Yanis Varoufakis for pointing out these similarities to me.

put it differently, in a situation of anarchy: "stability and restraint arise through the process of conflict in a way similar to the operation of Adam Smith's invisible hand."[89] Just as the immanent order reflects a transcendent principle, the "balance" of power is the placeholder for an absent central authority. Ultimately, the question upon which the entire discipline of international relations was founded in the postwar era – what Brian Schmidt calls "the enigma of politics in the absence of central authority"[90] – is essentially a theological question.[91]

But while economics made the hand invisible and eventually turned Providence into efficiency theorems and equilibrium equations, the early language of IR theory assumed the existence of a mundane – and sometimes, heavy – providential hand: At different times, the Roman or Germanic Empire, England, or another power secured the possibility of the balance and was the force that created order and defined a *nomos*. A closer reading of Morgenthau's writings suggests that for each historical epoch the balance was, literally, "held" by a particular political subject or power. This allegorical representation appears clearly in *Politics among Nations* when Morgenthau systematically posits the existence of a "holder" of the balance, a "balancer." This personalization of the balance is a crucial feature of the concept, for it suggests that the balance of power was initially a concept of *providential agency*, not an exclusively spatial concept (and even less so the systemic and purely formal concept it would become in the 1960s).

The balance implies a balancing subject, a historical agent that "holds" the balance and thus prevents anomy. It is hard not to read into Morgenthau's rendition of the balance of power echoes of Schmitt's *katechon* (not least because Schmitt himself occasionally intertwined the two notions). While the *katechon* is the "restrainer," the one who "withholds" historical time and thus acts as a bulwark against chaos and disorder, Morgenthau writes of the "restraining task of the 'holder' of the

---

[89] Robert Jervis, "A Political Science Perspective on the Balance of Power and the Concert," *The American Historical Review* 97, no. 3 (1992): 716–24.

[90] Brian C. Schmidt, *The Political Discourse of Anarchy: A Disciplinary History of International Relations* (Albany: State University of New York Press, 1998), 41.

[91] It is not fortuitous, therefore, that old economic doctrines of government premised on Providentialism – and in particular the eighteenth-century *économie politique*, for which the best government is the one that assists the natural order produced by the eternal laws that Providence has placed into things – find echoes in the realist vision of statecraft, and in particular in Morgenthau's claim that the good statesman is the one who adjusts his actions to the reality of power seeking (as opposed to moral abstractions).

balance."⁹² These "handling" metaphors are the clearest indication that the postwar discussion of the balance of power was not yet detached from theology. They belong to a well-established eschatological repertoire that associated divine government with the imagery of a *manus gubernatoris*, which ran through the writings of Schmitt, Morgenthau, Butterfield, Niebuhr, Thompson, Toynbee, and other major contributors to the emergence of a realist discipline of international relations. Such metaphors were much more than luxuriant rhetoric, and their theological meaning was immediately intelligible at the time. Writing in *Social Research* in 1955, the Biblical scholar Jacob Taubes (who was then spending two years at the New School on a Rockefeller fellowship) perfectly articulated this dimension of the balance in modern political science: "The idea of balance of power had a transcendent, a transmundane point of reference, which in deistic theology is interpreted as a function of divine providence. In the deistic vocabulary, there is still a 'hand' that 'holds' the balance."⁹³ Taubes's reference to the Paulinian *qui tenet* was not fortuitous and suggested that the eschatological significance of the balance of power was not lost to the participants in this conversation.⁹⁴ Set against this background, the anxiety of many postwar theorists of international relations about the possible end of the traditional system of the balance of power acquires another, deeper dimension: the end of the balance may have been, ultimately, the surest sign of the triumph of secularism. In a hostile intellectual context won over to secularism, depoliticization, and technology, international relations theory stood as the last stronghold of political theology .

"LIBERALISM'S EMPTY SKIES": MORGENTHAU'S CRITIQUE OF SECULARISM

That Morgenthau shared some of Schmitt's fears should come as no surprise, for his analysis of the situation was strikingly similar. As Schmitt was about to publish his *Nomos*, Morgenthau was busy peddling the same notion of "the political," appropriately repackaged as "power politics"

---

[92] Morgenthau, *Politics among Nations*, 274.
[93] Jacob Taubes, "Theology and Political Theory," *Social Research* 22, no. 1 (1955): 64.
[94] Schmitt writes "The decisive historical concept of this continuity [between medieval law and the Roman Empire] was that of the restrainer: *katechon*. 'Empire' in this sense meant the historical power to *restrain* the appearance of the Antichrist and the end of the present eon; it was a power that withholds (*qui tenet*) as the Apostle Paul said in his Second Letter to the Thessalonians." Schmitt, *Nomos*, 59–60.

for American audiences.⁹⁵ Morgenthau's ambivalent intellectual relation to Carl Schmitt is well known and goes back to Morgenthau's doctoral dissertation, which discussed and refined Schmitt's concept of the political. Morgenthau had sent his work to the senior jurist, and received a complimentary reply and an invitation – although no acknowledgment followed when Schmitt borrowed his definition of the political as an "intensity" of feeling rather than a separate sphere in the third (1932) edition of his book.⁹⁶ Despite an unpleasant meeting, this perplexing dialogue continued as Morgenthau published *La notion du "politique" et la théorie des différends internationaux* in 1933, a further reflection on the indeterminacy of international law and a critique of its depoliticizing tendencies.⁹⁷ Completed in 1940, *Scientific Man and Power Politics* is a long diatribe against modernity that can largely be read, as Scheuerman aptly put it, as a "popularized version of Schmitt."⁹⁸ Beyond the anti-modern ranting, it also adopted a Schmittian concept of the political as essentially indexed to a concrete situation. For Morgenthau as much as for Schmitt, genuine political concepts always refer to a concrete situation, a further proof of the depoliticized nature of liberalism: "while nonliberal political concepts, such as 'Roman Empire,' 'new order,' 'living space,' 'encirclement,' 'national security,' 'haves vs. have-nots,' and the like, show an immediately recognizable relationship to concrete political aims; liberal concepts, such as 'collective security,' 'democracy,' 'national self-determination,' 'justice,' 'peace,' are abstract generalities which may be applied to any political situation but which are not peculiar to any particular one."⁹⁹ And in spite of Morgenthau's nonchalance with sources, there is evidence that he kept abreast of Schmitt's intellectual production well after 1945.¹⁰⁰ Set against this backdrop, attempts at turning Morgenthau into a consistent critique of Schmitt remain unconvincing, as they tend to bypass much of his prolific production of the

---

⁹⁵ Söllner, "German Conservatism in America."
⁹⁶ The episode would be revealed by Morgenthau himself in a 1977 autobiographical sketch. Hans J. Morgenthau, "Fragment of an Intellectual Autobiography: 1904–1932," in *A Tribute to Hans Morgenthau*, ed. Kenneth Thompson and Robert J Myers (Washington, DC: The New Republic Book Company, 1977).
⁹⁷ On which see Williams, "Foreword."
⁹⁸ William Scheuerman, *Carl Schmitt: The End of Law* (Lanham, MD: Rowman & Littlefield, 1999), 244.
⁹⁹ Morgenthau, *Scientific Man vs. Power Politics*, 72.
¹⁰⁰ William Scheuerman, "Was Morgenthau a Realist? Revisiting Scientific Man Vs. Power Politics," *Constellations* 14, no. 4 (2007): 65, fn. 11.

1940s and 1950s and overlook the fact that his understanding of sovereignty and of the relation of sovereignty to law was still entirely modeled after Schmitt's.[101]

Morgenthau's reconstruction of the European balance of power and its decline shares many traits with Schmitt's own rendition, and both thinkers look back wistfully at the glorious and orderly tableau of the classical age. The development of the modern territorial state in Europe had allowed for the emergence of a notion of sovereignty in which the sovereign was "the sole source of man-made law" but "not himself subject to it," Morgenthau wrote in 1948, in his own rendering of the capacity to decide upon the exception.[102] Sovereignty, indeed, was a political fact before being a doctrine that liberalism sought to encase into abstract norms. Bounded spatially, this absolute power derived its legitimacy from its embeddedness within an "international society" formed by a web of legal and moral relations with similar states.[103] The existence of this supranational aristocratic society was the concrete foundation upon which an effective legal

---

[101] The most consistent attempt at recasting Morgenthau as a democrat and as an intellectual opponent of Schmitt has been made by Michael Williams. For sure, in *La notion du "politique" et la théorie des différends internationaux* (1933), Morgenthau dedicates fifteen pages to the distinction between his concept of the political and Schmitt's. Yet, Morgenthau's critical excursus may be understood primarily as a personal reaction after Schmitt's unfair behavior and their disappointing encounter. Rather than a matter of substantial difference, it is indeed a striking example of what Freud called the "narcissism of small differences": for Morgenthau, cultivating his own distinctiveness was all the more necessary since his position was largely identical with Schmitt's. In the deteriorating climate of the 1930s, as Schmitt was on his way to becoming the *Kronjurist* of the Reich, minor conceptual differences acquired huge symbolic significance. But even there, Morgenthau still defined the political as a notion that has "no fixed content," a quality that may affect "any given object" Hans J. Morgenthau, *La notion du "politique" et la théorie des différends internationaux* (Paris: Sirey, 1933), 32. It is hard to concur with Williams when he attributes to Morgenthau a "clear delineation [of politics] from other spheres," Williams, "Why Ideas Matter in International Relations: Hans Morgenthau, Classical Realism, and the Moral Construction of Power Politics," 649, while Morgenthau, in the section dedicated to Schmitt, explicitly states that the political is not a sphere but a particular intensity of feeling that can arise in any given social sphere: Morgenthau, *La notion du "politique"*, 44. On both counts, Morgenthau and Schmitt develop essentially an identical understanding of the political. It is also hard to see Morgenthau as a democrat when he had very few positive things to say about democracy in the 1940s and 1950s, apart from one article, in which, however, he cynically considered democracy as a political ideology, i.e. as an instrument in the wider struggle for power between states Hans J. Morgenthau, "A Positive Approach to a Democratic Ideology," *Proceedings of the Academy of Political Science* 24, no. 2 (1951): 79–91. Williams is right, however, to the extent that Morgenthau will gradually develop a more positive view of American democracy.

[102] Morgenthau, *Politics among Nations*, 244.

[103] Morgenthau, *Politics among Nations*, 184 ff.

order restraining the amplitude of political conflicts was premised. Its cultural and moral cohesion provided the required degree of concrete social "homogeneity" that made its international jurisprudence both determinate and valid – an ambiguous argument when one considers that Schmitt had previously suggested that the effectiveness and determinacy of legal norms required a homogeneous political community, a point he later used to support the Nazi policies of aryanization of the legal professions.[104] As this European order started dissolving after 1848, it was replaced by the Nation-State as the ultimate container of moral allegiances, and the aristocratic control over foreign policy was often replaced by democratic government – which saw power politics and war as the residual corollaries of a conservative form of elite rule, and hence proceeded to criminalize them: The nation thus became "the starting-point of a universal mission whose ultimate goals reaches to the confine of a political world."[105] In a world no longer bound by supranational standards of morality, international legality could only become the instrument of – rather than the impediment to – unlimited conflicts between political entities no longer conceiving of their actions as related to finite interests, but as means toward universal ends. The alliance of democracy and universalism, for Morgenthau, was the primary cause for the collapse of the old European order and for the destructive and morally corrupt nature of modernity.[106]

Morgenthau's diagnosis of this collapse overlapped with Schmitt's on a number of critical counts: first, echoing Schmitt's analysis of the role of "amity lines," he also attributed the erosion of the *jus publicum Europaeum* to the exhaustion of the "wide expanses of three continents" that offered European powers the opportunity for aggrandizement without risking a general conflagration on their continent.[107] Second, Morgenthau pointed unambiguously at the rise of liberalism and at political developments "in the English-speaking world" that "disavow[ed] the political fact of sovereignty" by equating it with the rule of law and dissolving it in the corrosive bath of legal self-referentiality.[108] This was

---

[104] Morgenthau, *Politics among Nations*, 190; Scheuerman, *Carl Schmitt*, 126–27.
[105] Hans J. Morgenthau, "World Politics in the Mid-Twentieth Century," *The Review of Politics* 10, no. 2 (1948): 269.
[106] Morgenthau, *Politics among Nations*, 190–91.
[107] Morgenthau, *Politics among Nations*, 278.
[108] Hans J. Morgenthau, "The Problem of Sovereignty Reconsidered," *Columbia Law Review* 48, no. 3 (1948): 341–42. The article is an earlier version of Chapter XVII in Politics among Nations.

exactly the analysis of liberal depoliticization and neutralization that Schmitt had distillated throughout the interwar period. Finally, Morgenthau denounced the democratic rise of the middle classes to government and its corollary: the substitution of politics with legal relations modeled after contractual arrangements between private interests and, ultimately, the erosion of state authority as the state became an association among others. Pluralism was an enemy he had in common with Schmitt.

The parallel reconstruction of the Eurocentric legal order that runs through Schmitt's *Nomos* and Morgenthau's postwar writings has been stressed by several commentators. However, the theological element of Morgenthau's arguments has largely gone unnoticed.[109] A closer reading reveals a complex, yet consistent, line of argument that is developed in the shadow of Schmitt's political theology, as Morgenthau proceeds to a critique of nationalism that ultimately reveals itself to be a critique of secularism.

Some key sections of *Politics among Nations* bear witness to the importance that the theme of nationalism had acquired for Morgenthau during the 1940s. Morgenthau understood the stability of the European system of sovereign territorial states as premised on the existence of a supranational society united by common "moral standards of conduct" and "shared beliefs and common values" that placed limitations on warfare and disconnected state interests from morality.[110] This ethical universe started dissolving when "the one international society of the seventeenth and eighteenth centuries has been replaced by a number of national societies which provide for their members the highest principle of social integration." By making the nation the ultimate container of moral allegiances, nationalism had dealt "the final, fatal blow" to the restraints on the destructive power of politics. As national allegiances prevailed over supranational ones, nationalism aggregated all loyalties and no longer knew of any superior moral authority. "For the nationalistic universalism of the mid-twentieth century the nation is but the starting-point of a universal mission whose ultimate goal reaches to the confines of the political world."[111] The ultimate repository of

---

[109] Chris Brown, for instance, claims that the "theological dimension" of Schmitt's analysis "mean[t] nothing to Morgenthau, who resisted the notion of giving a theological twist to his work." Brown, "the Twilight of International Morality," 50.
[110] Morgenthau, *Politics among Nations*, 186, 193.
[111] Morgenthau, *Politics among Nations*, 269.

morality, the modern nation-state is justified in all its external actions, and its wars become total wars of annihilation that can be waged in the name of humanity.

Morgenthau's earlier critique of the liberal international order was thus targeting only a symptom of "the great positive force which shapes the political face of our age: nationalism."[112] Morgenthau's critique of nationalism as a phenomenon that totalizes the different dimensions of belonging and allegiance can be juxtaposed to Schmitt's analysis of the rise of the "total state," just as his warnings against the tendency of modern wars to become unrestrained, total wars waged in the name of nationalistic universalism echo Schmitt's. But it is also clear that "the supra-national forces ... which bind individual together across national boundaries" that Morgenthau refers to are of a religious kind.[113] The "one universal moral code" to which European societies gave "unquestioning allegiance" is that of Christianity, and the international society of the seventeenth and eighteenth centuries was "one" because it "had united the monarchs and the nobility of Christendom." With nationalism, however, this real, concrete universalism grounded in religion and mediated by ecclesial institutions was replaced by "a multiplicity of morally self-sufficient national communities" that represented as many brands of false, unauthentic universalism.[114]

What is the process whereby the nation-state becomes the sole container of morality, and the *pro patria mori* the ultimate moral virtue? Morgenthau's analysis of nationalism, in fact, morphs into a critique of secularization. Nationalism destroys the remnants of the European *respublica Christiana* when the national state usurps the place traditionally occupied by religion – and this can happen only in a secular age: "for an age that believes no longer in an immortal God, the state becomes the only God there is."[115] That Morgenthau's real and intended target is not nationalism *per se* but rather the secularizing tendencies it unleashes is made clear by the distinction he introduces between the "liberal" nationalism of the nineteenth century, which was essentially a "liberal and liberating movement" seeking to establish national states and the nationalism of the twentieth century, "which is really a nationalistic

---

[112] Morgenthau, *Politics among Nations*, 268.
[113] Morgenthau, *Politics among Nations*, 268.
[114] Morgenthau, *Politics among Nations*, 195, 189, 191.
[115] Morgenthau, "The Evil of Politics and the Ethics of Evil," 15. In the same passage, Morgenthau actually uses Hobbes's expression when he designates the modern state as a "mortal God."

"Liberalism's Empty Skies": Morgenthau's Critique of Secularism

universalism."[116] This distinction, often coined by conservative thinkers eager to salvage nationalism after 1945, can be traced to Hans Kohn, whose *Idea of Nationalism* (1944) Morgenthau had read, and it fulfills a critical function for his line of argument, as it exonerates nationalism *per se* and shifts instead the responsibility on the secularizing tendency at work in the moral claims of the nation.[117]

Not surprisingly for a man who belonged in his youth to a dueling society and admired the aristocracy, Morgenthau had nothing against the former brand of nationalism. He conceived of the post-1848 nationalist awakening as a positive movement that was still compatible with and located within the ethical horizon of a common religious morality. In a review of Salo Wittmayer Baron's *Modern Nationalism and Religion* (1947), he clearly expressed this idea when, "paraphras[ing] Ranke's profound remark," he observed that in the nineteenth century, "each nationalism [was] equally close to God." By contrast, modern nationalism had simply displaced God and taken its place, thus exhibiting "the earmarks of an expansive religion which attempts to impose its own standards and institutions upon the rest of the world."[118] What is wrong, therefore, is not so much the establishment of states on a national basis, which Morgenthau considers "liberating," as the process of secularization that completely detaches politics from its religious background. Secularism is the real cause behind the transformation of nineteenth-century nationalism into "an expansive religion," a demiurgic force that has "many messianic facets"[119] and instills a "pseudo-religious fervor" in the aspirations for power of individual nations in the course of the twentieth century.[120] Only when it is uprooted from its embeddedness in the "concrete situation" of European Christendom, does politics assume the characteristics of moral abstractions and universal ideologies fit for global export. The state then loses sight of its concrete "national interest," and ceases to exist politically. The chapter of *Politics among Nations* on international morality ends with an eloquent denunciation of modern nationalism as a false religion only made possible in a secularized

---

[116] Hans J. Morgenthau, review of *Modern Nationalism and Religion* by Salo Wittmayer Baron, *Ethics* 59, no. 2 (1949): 148.
[117] Morgenthau cites Kohn in a 1945 review of *Nationalities and National Minorities* by Oscar I. Janowski. Kohn explicitly related the rise of nationalism to the secularization of politics in Europe, the combination of both being central to the rise of liberalism.
[118] Morgenthau, "Review of Modern Nationalism," 148.
[119] Morgenthau, "Review of Modern Nationalism," 148.
[120] Morgenthau, *Politics among Nations*, 268.

age: "carrying their idols before them, the nationalistic masses of our time meet in the international arena, each group convinced that it executes the mandate of history, that it does for humanity what it seems to do for itself, and that it fulfills a sacred mission ordained by providence, however defined. Little do they know that they meet under an empty sky from which the gods have departed."[121]

Morgenthau's analysis leaves no doubt as to the real nature of his argument: absolute secularization ends up transforming national emancipation into an "-ism," a universal ideology detached from any concrete political orientation and wedded to legal globalism and abstract humanitarianism. Liberal internationalism, as Morgenthau made clear in his review of Janowski, was one of these modern political religions brought into existence by the continued development of secularism: "Nationalism was the great liberating and pacifying force which would destroy autocratic government and unite those who belonged together by nature. For Woodrow Wilson, it had become the magic formula which, by removing the main cause of modern wars, would assure permanent peace."[122] Thus, it is not nationalism per se, but its secular variant that generated the moral abstractions that have replaced politics in liberal modernity. Secularism was for Morgenthau the root cause of idealism in foreign policy. The realist critique of idealism in international relations theory, and indeed realism itself, was essentially a critique of secularism.

Morgenthau's genius lies in having reformulated this critique in a way that made it acceptable to his new audience. The argument, however, was not new: secularism produces states that no longer relate to the concrete situation through a clear notion of national interest, since they live in moral abstractions and have no external principle of legitimacy. Morgenthau's defense of secular nationalism and his critique of any further secularization likely to transform the concrete orientation of the state into a political religion closely echoes with Schmitt's ambivalent attitude toward secularism. Secularization has weakened the state, deprived it of a notion of sovereignty, and made it unable to act in its own interest. This was exactly Schmitt's political theology – yet repackaged. And no packaging was better suited to postwar America than a critique of nationalism and ideologies. Political theology thus made its entry in the United States under the guise of a critique of

---

[121] Morgenthau, *Politics among Nations*, 196.
[122] Hans J. Morgenthau, review of *Nationalities and National Minorities*, by Oscar I. Janowsky, *Harvard Law Review* 59, no. 2 (1945): 301.

nationalism, a coating much better suited to its new audience than the quixotic disquisitions of a compromised German jurist.

THE AMERICANIZATION OF POLITICAL THEOLOGY

Realism's debt to an imported, un-American metaphysics of power could easily go unnoticed as it was seen as a pragmatic refusal of ideologies, and in that sense a very American thing indeed. Not only did the real origins of Morgenthau's critique of political religions drop out of sight, but he himself seems to have encouraged an understanding of realism as an indigenous tradition, by striving to recover within the history of the Republic a lost strand of political thought oriented by a clear vision of the national interest. While he chastised America for having lost the political wisdom characteristic of the early Republic, Morgenthau however pointed out that "beyond the political dilettantism (...) there has remained alive an almost instinctive awareness of the perennial interest of the United States" in the Western Hemisphere. He traced back this awareness to the Hamiltonian view that, in order to prevent any European encroachment in the hemisphere that would threaten their independence and freedom, the United States would have to pursue an active foreign policy of balance of power.[123] Realism was not only rooted in the nation's past, according to Morgenthau, but was indeed constitutive of it, and any emphasis on humanitarian values and moral ideals as drivers of US foreign policy was nothing short of a "revision" of American history.[124] As we shall see in the next chapter, one of the paradoxes of this narrative about American realism is that it would soon be vindicated by historians – yet by historians who were émigrés like Morgenthau and who sought to resituate realism within the broader *translatio* of a republican political culture from the Italian Renaissance to the American republic.[125]

But not everybody was convinced, it seems, and many among Morgenthau's fellow realists knew that much more was going on than

---

[123] Hans J. Morgenthau, "What Is the National Interest of the United States?" *Annals of the American Academy of Political and Social Science* 282 (1952): 1–7.
[124] Hans J. Morgenthau, "Another 'Great Debate': The National Interest of the United States," *The American Political Science Review* 46, no. 4 (1952): 965. For a similar attempt at recovering an "anti-rationalist" heritage in American political tradition, see also Jacobson, "Political Realism and the Age of Reason."
[125] See in particular Gilbert, *To the Farewell Address*, which is discussed in greater detail in the next chapter.

a mere exercise in the revision of US history. Kenneth Thompson later candidly acknowledged that Morgenthau had "translated certain European ideas to fit the American experience (...) to rethink and restate these ideas to accord with the realities of American democracy."[126] That his variety of realism was indeed so controversial clearly suggests that it was not well-established indigenous tradition. In many ways, like political theory, the emerging field of IR theory functioned as an *alien* critique of *national* intellectual traditions, fueled in particular by émigré scholars who continued in the United States a conversation the premises of which were clearly Weimarian.[127] The debates over realism – and in particular the so-called "First Debate" opposing idealism and realism – indicated in fact some degree of resistance to the grafting of an imported and illiberal tradition of political thought on American soil.

But the provenience of the smuggled wares did not go entirely unnoticed: many understood Morgenthau's strategy as an attempt at "Americanizing" a theology of power, and did not fail to detect the unmistakably Schmittian whiff exhaled by some of realism's core concepts. Some worried fellow realists tried to sever the links with these embarrassing antecedents. As early as 1949, Arnold Wolfers wrote a long article in which he tried to chisel out a distinction between Morgenthau's concept of "power politics" and what he called a dangerous "German view," in which he bundled together the tradition of *Staatsräson*, Ratzenhofer's *Geojurisprüdenz*, and a justification of enmity that he attributed to Schmitt.[128] The "nonperfectionist" ethics or "ethics of responsibility" implied in Morgenthau's notion of power politics, Wolfers claimed, meant instead that statesmanship always entailed moral choice, however imperfect, rather than the dictates of a reason of state detached from all morality. Yet, this distinction proved largely rhetorical, for what Wolfers called "moral choice" turned out to be nothing but a form of decisionism closely echoing the Schmittian concept of the political: in the end, "the concepts of amity and enmity

---

[126] Kenneth W. Thompson, *Masters of International Thought : Major Twentieth-Century Theorists and the World Crisis* (Baton Rouge: Louisiana State University Press, 1980), 88.

[127] Greenberg, *The Weimar Century*. See also, for a more specific focus on the social sciences, Gunnell, "American Political Science."; Hauptmann, "From Opposition to Accommodation."

[128] This was a surprising distinction, to the extent that Meinecke (whose work both Morgenthau and Wolfers did not ignore) conflated the reason of state with "power politics." Meinecke, *Machiavellism*, 409.

can be usefully employed to shed light on the context within which statesmen are forced to make their choices."[129] And indeed, scholars who later applied the techniques of rational choice to the study of international security did not fail to develop this intuition in a direction more congruent with the methodological expectations of social science departments. Leaving out of the picture any reference to Schmitt's theology, which would have made his argument more difficult to sustain, Wolfers concluded that the difference was between two ethical standards, a "nationalistic" view and a "nonperfectionist Christian or humanistic" one that he attributed to Morgenthau, Niebuhr, and others.[130] Once again, the critique of secularism conveniently masqueraded as a critique of nationalism.

Others, however, had fewer qualms with the intellectual pedigree of the nascent theory of international relations. A connoisseur of the non-liberal strands of European thought, in particular of Catholic conservatism, and a conservative himself, the political scientist Francis G. Wilson immediately perceived the theological element in Morgenthau's critique of liberal rationalism. He cautiously referred to Schmitt in relation to the theological background of Morgenthau's brand of realism, in which he recognized a congenial form of conservatism:

The realism of the conservative is not a defense of evil in the world, but it is a recognition of it as a constant factor. It is a belief that evil arises from the nature of man, not from a lack of more science or more education, however laudable these things may be. Carl Schmitt, of unhallowed memory, once argued that all the great political philosophers have insisted on the evil in the nature of man. Can we not cite most of the Christian thinkers, as well as Machiavelli and Hobbes for this contention, a contention based on empirical observation, as much as on the presuppositions of theistic philosophy?[131]

These examples are particularly suggestive of the cultural displacement going on at the time. They can be read as attempts at taking some distance from the most problematic aspects of realism, but also as indications of a real continuity with them. They are not so much symptoms of a direct influence of Schmitt (which remained uneven, limited, and often indirect) as they flag out a referential universe of IR that has been left out of official

---

[129] Wolfers, "Statesmanship and Moral Choice," 181.
[130] Wolfers, "Statesmanship and Moral Choice," 188.
[131] Francis G. Wilson, "The Scholar and the Inarticulate Premise," *The Western Political Quarterly* 2, no. 3 (1949): 320.

histories but that was still meaningful to the realists writing in the 1950s. In both cases, Schmitt is treated as a *persona non grata*, but only in order to salvage his vision of politics and sovereignty, which was essential to the development of a discipline built on the demise of international law and to the self-understanding of sovereign hegemony at a time when the United States was assuming a global role. Schmitt's influence thus operated by proxies (Augustine, Machiavelli, Hobbes, Christian realism, neo-orthodoxy, etc.) – something that comes across very clearly in Wilson's piece. It is remarkable that in both cases the condemnation of Schmitt is the prelude to a restatement of Schmitt through other means: Wolfers ends up endorsing decisionism as a theoretical framework for understanding international relations, and Wilson discards him only to replace him with the most prominent figures at the center of Schmitt's thought.[132] This explains why a number of Schmittian themes became so prominent in IR theory, once they had detached themselves from their author.

But Morgenthau's thinly veiled critique of secularism and the connection between early IR and political theology also resonated beyond this circle of *cognoscenti*, among individuals who had probably never read Schmitt or even heard about him. It was part of a conversation where the theologico-political was a readily available conceptual category that was not yet entirely removed from the discussion of international relations and provided a strong counterpoint to the rationalist perspectives on politics. The discussions that took place within the committee on theory convened by Kenneth Thompson and Dean Rusk at the Rockefeller Foundation in 1954 bear witness to the gradual autonomization of political theology from its Weimarian origins as it provided the intellectual foundations of international relations theory in the United States. Ultimately, the failure to articulate a scientific theory of international relations was certainly related to the anti-rationalist position of most participants. The junction between Schmittian political theology and neo-orthodoxy took place within this context of counter-Enlightenment critique, and it was exemplified by the deep convergence of views between Niebuhr and Morgenthau.[133] "The political theology of the 1920s ha[d] indeed an

---

[132] On Schmitt's evolving interpretation of Machiavelli, see Carlo Galli, *Lo sguardo di Giano: Saggi su Carl Schmitt* (Bologna: Il Mulino, 2008), ch. 3.

[133] There were, of course, major divergences between Protestant neo-orthodoxy and mid-century Catholicism, and theologians such as Tillich or Niebuhr have been at times critical of the latter: Tillich, for instance, reproached "romantic Catholicism" with its idealization of the medieval era, Paul Tillich and H. Richard Niebuhr, *The Religious Situation* (New York: Henry Holt & Co.,

affinity with the neo-orthodox fideism of the time," as Michael Zank writes, to the extent that they all proceeded from "a counter-critique of the Enlightenment critique of religion."[134] This counter-critique was the real, and to a large extent the only, content of IR theory, which developed essentially as a *critical* project, both epistemologically and politically. Not surprisingly, the tutelary figures of this project were Augustine and Burke, who were cited by more than one participant and in particular by Thompson during the 1954 meeting on theory.[135]

Retooled as a critique of "universalistic nationalism" and political religions by Morgenthau, Schmitt's critique of liberalism as an extreme form of secularism could circulate detached from its original context and recombined with other references. Niebuhr, for instance, made the same argument by drawing on Butterfield:

> recently the distinguished Cambridge historian, Herbert Butterfield, has analyzed the moral issue in international relations in such a way in his 'Christianity, Diplomacy and War' as to regard the element of moral pretension as a more persistent cause of conflict between nations than the competition between frankly avowed national interests. *It is Butterfield's thesis that in the absence of an authentic religion, which regards all men and nations as falling short before an ultimate divine judgement, political causes have generated moral pretensions of religious proportions. The self-righteous claims make for unlimited and irreconcilable wars.*[136]

By the late 1940s, Butterfield was indeed identifying proper historical thinking with Christian belief: The Christian notion that all men were sinners implied that it was wrong to look in history for instances of

---

1932), 144. But Schmitt can hardly be considered as a typical representative of Catholic conservatism, and was certainly not writing in the Thomistic perspective denounced by Tillich. On the other hand, the Catholic Jacques Maritain, who indeed saw in the crisis of the 1930s an opportunity for a new humanism based on organic and spiritual solidarities, considered Schmitt closer to the Protestant political theology of the *sacrum imperium* and to nationalist Protestant theologians like Wilhelm Stapel. Jacques Maritain, *True Humanism* (London: Geoffrey Bles: The Centenary Press, 1938), 92–93. And Schmitt's famous reference to Kierkegaard as a thinker of the exception in *Political Theology* hints at the affinities between his position and Protestant neo-orthodoxy. I am thankful to William Sheuerman for pointing out these aspects to me.

[134] Michael Zank, "Beyond the 'Theologico-Political Predicament:' Toward a Contextualization of the Early Strauss," unpublished paper, Boston University (2005), 2.

[135] "Conference on International Politics," May 7–8, 1954, Folder 70, Box 8, Series 910, RG 3, RF, RAC.

[136] Reinhold Niebuhr, "The Moral Issue in International Relations," Folder 69, Box 8, Series 910, RG 3, RF, RAC, p. 6. Emphasis mine.

individual or national righteousness. Christian historical consciousness was a natural antidote to Whig history.[137] It carried a vision of history as a glorious tapestry, a collective work made by many hands, all contributing to a design no one could claim to have known in advance:

> Instead of seeing the modern world emerge as the victory of the children of light over the children of darkness in any generation, it is at least better to see it emerge as the result of a clash of wills, a result which often neither party wanted or even dreamed of, a result which indeed in some cases both parties would equally have hated.[138]

For the same reason, this Christian sense of history had immediate political implications, and Butterfield thought, in Maurice Cowling's apt characterization, that "historical thinking could play a part in removing the intellectual blinkers that hampered international amicability."[139] By removing the sense of self-righteousness, the Christian approach to history and politics allowed for the equal respectability of national interests. In fact, Butterfield believed that European eighteenth-century diplomacy concentrated in a secularized form the wisdom of the Christian tradition and thus made possible the urbanity that allegedly characterized the international politics in pre-revolutionary Europe. When Koselleck reviewed his work in 1955, he could only see in it a version of what his mentor Schmitt had said about the deleterious effect of secularization when it led the state to conflate its finite interests with universal morality, and to engage in total wars.[140] The Christian understanding of history that gained momentum after 1945 was much more than a cultural mood: For the realists, it provided nothing less than the only possible foundation of a stable international order.

By thus relating their vision of politics to more or less articulated theological foundations, early realists were following *à la lettre* Schmitt's program of political theology. Their critique of international liberalism, in particular, by emphasizing its complete detachment from religion, was firmly rooted in the theologico-political tradition and in particular in the idea that the political ended when religion ceased to exist as an independent order of morality. The theological nature of these arguments was perfectly clear to the early realists, who were aware

---

[137] On the intersection between conservative historiography and realism, see Guilhot, "Portrait of the Realist as a Historian."
[138] Butterfield, *Christianity and History*, 28.
[139] Cowling, *Religion and Public Doctrine*, vol. 1, 245.
[140] Koselleck, "Rezension zur Herbert Butterfield."

of speaking as political theologians. The reception of their works and public pronouncements was not yet confined to specialized academic publics, and it was clear to many of them that their arguments resonated with theology more than with the social sciences. Shortly after publishing *Scientific Man vs. Power Politics*, Morgenthau wrote to Niebuhr that "the theological responses to the book have generally been very gratifying", contrarily to those coming from political scientists, who, he felt, did not understand him.[141] Even among his closest interlocutors, the reception of Morgenthau's works was filtered through layers of theological meanings, to the point that he was sometimes explicitly considered a "political theologian," a fact that was obscured by the place he later came to occupy in the political science canon. As late as 1959, his best student, Kenneth Thompson, could still describe him in the following terms: "Morgenthau's 'political theology' is in one sense at least unfinished business foreshadowed in *Scientific Man vs. Power Politics*, elaborated in *Dilemmas of Politics*, but not yet spelled out and given content in a form comparable to the writings of Augustine and Burke."[142]

As a result, a number of key concepts used to flesh out the realist vision of international politics were also understood as "secularized theological concepts." Such was, for instance, Morgenthau's notion of *animus dominandi*, directly borrowed from Augustine to describe the "lust for power," in which he located the source of evil and the impossibility of worldly perfection. Similarly, his concept of the "national interest" was an attempt at rethinking politics from the point of view of the concrete situation rather than on the basis of legal and moral abstractions. Reinstating the national interest meant embedding in the new discipline the point of view of sovereignty and thus recovering the capacity to make authoritative decisions. It meant ceasing to be a *stato neutrale ed agnostico* and reverting to a clear distinction between the sphere of interests and that of morality, to an awareness that there can be a real state only in relation to an external order of morality and historical meaning. In terms that were often indirect, but in no case uncertain, the founding fathers of IR theory located in the process of secularization the root cause of the moral abstractions that had led international politics into the disasters of the twentieth century. They found in a loosely articulated political

---

[141] Quoted in Daniel Rice, "Reinhold Niebuhr and Hans Morgenthau: A Friendship with Contrasting Shades of Realism," *Journal of American Studies* 42, no. 2 (2008): 260.

[142] Kenneth W. Thompson, *Christian Ethics and the Dilemmas of Foreign Policy* (Durham: Duke University Press, 1959), 134.

theology the bulwark against the dangers associated with the claims of moral self-sufficiency characteristic of a political modernity in which they discerned a worrying replacement of politics with technology, a fundamental indifference for values, and the incapacity to discriminate and make political decisions. Their insistence on concrete situations, on the material dimensions of power, and on the necessarily limited nature of political aims did not so much express a simplistic, empirical vision of politics as it emphasized the finite nature of the political against the backdrop of an eschatological fulfillment of human history that was beyond its reach. The fundamental concern defining realism was to ensure that the imperative of the political decision could be fulfilled even in the absence of absolute justifications, or rather especially in their absence, since such justifications are not available to human political practice. In that sense, realism was indeed premised on a political theology.

The concept of balance of power, which was not only the main pillar of IR theory but also experienced a political renaissance in postwar America, was probably the most salient instance of this political theology. With its introduction in American political science, the old Schmittian *katechon* thus completed its transformation into a secularized figure of academic IR. Yet, while in the late 1940s and 1950s the question of the balance was still formulated in terms of historical agency, the following decade would witness a dramatic transformation of the concept, triggered in particular by the possibility of nuclear war. Security studies would provide a new understanding of the balance of power devoid of theological content, and rational choice methodologies would offer a new and more "scientific" language for decisionism, better suited to the dominant representation of politics and sovereignty in an era of technological progress and to a liberal culture that had to outsource to logical models and computing machines the nasty business of undemocratic decision-making. Soon, abstract notions of "equilibrium," models of "deterrence" and other strategic "dilemmas" meant to withhold the chaos of nuclear holocaust would give the old *katechon* a new lease on life in IR departments – but this part of the story has to wait for Chapter 5.

3

The Making of the Realist Tradition: Felix Gilbert and the Reclaiming of Machiavelli

As part of the postwar counter-Enlightenment, realism faced a double challenge. First, it rejected the notion that politics could be "scientific" and as a result it sought to insulate political theory – or at least its application to international matters – from the social sciences. In an academic context where the scientific method reigned supreme, this obviously represented a major obstacle to the successful diffusion and adoption of political realism. How the realists eventually circumvented this obstacle and turned realism into a pseudo-science will be the subject of the next chapters of this book. But the second challenge that postwar realists faced was just as formidable. Deprived of scientific legitimacy, realism could not claim traditional legitimacy either. It represented a relatively recent ideological development that stemmed from the crisis of the 1930s and the collapse of liberalism. At best, it found its deepest roots in late nineteenth-century German historicism. It had no real historical antecedents, and when it initially looked for references in the past, it could only muster a few enemies of the French Revolution or the bishop of Hippo. And yet, realism was closely associated with the work of historians who took a critical view of modernity. It would not take long before these historians exhumed a "realist tradition" that gave political realism its *lettres de noblesse* and a pedigree it sorely lacked until then. Soon, Thucydides, Augustine, or Hobbes were conscripted to form a historical genealogy of modern realism stretching centuries if not millennia: a timeless wisdom was born. Sometimes on the rise, sometimes on the wane, realism became a trans-historical force associated with the comprehension of the true essence of politics independently of time and place. And among those who best managed to express this essence, one name resonated with particular force: Machiavelli. Like Machiavelli's Prince, who had to secure his power over a newly conquered realm by ruling as if his legitimacy was established on ancient traditions, the realists had to convince others that they were only keeping alive a much older political wisdom.

It is today a widely accepted idea that the Florentine secretary was the first modern realist.[1] Yet, this assumption was anything but obvious in the 1940s and 1950s, and certainly it was not taken for granted by the realists themselves, who entertained at best ambivalent views about Machiavelli when they did not continue the anti-Machiavellian tradition. Among Christian realists, in particular, his name still elicited intellectual bigotry and moralistic condemnations.

The gradual process by which Machiavelli became a realist is closely tied to the fortunes of political realism in America. The inclusion of Machiavelli within a realist canon in the making achieved two things that no other historical association could provide. First, it turned postwar realists into the legitimate heirs of a long and noble tradition of political thought, thus gliding over the more immediate and less appealing roots of realism in conservative or reactionary doctrines of the interwar period. More importantly, the inclusion of Machiavelli within a realist "tradition" corresponded to the renewal of the interpretation of his works that associated political expediency to a moral background constituted by the defense of republican freedom – a move that inaugurated a new and far-reaching historiographical program that spawned the paradigmatic notion of "republicanism." This republican Machiavelli provided a perfect ideological vessel for easing the acclimatization of realism within postwar America, and for reconciling it with the self-image of America as a republic embattled in a conflict that in many respects resembled the constant state of alert characteristic of Florentine politics in the *cinquencento*. The Machiavelli we know today is thus, in part, also a product of

---

[1] Besides being mentioned in any IR textbook, Machiavelli is commonly considered as a realist in scholarly works. See for instance Robert G. Gilpin, "The Richness of the Tradition of Political Realism," in *Neorealism and Its Critics*, ed. Robert Keohane (New York: Columbia University Press, 1986), 306; McQueen, *Political Realism in Apocalyptic Times*; Donnelly, *Realism and International Relations*; Janice Leung, "Machiavelli and International Relations Theory," *Glendon Journal of International Studies* 1, no. 1 (2000): 3–13; Jonathan Haslam, *No Virtue Like Necessity: Realist Thought in International Relations since Machiavelli* (New Haven: Yale University Press, 2002). A recent panel at the British International Studies Association was entirely dedicated to Machiavelli and his place in the realist tradition (BISA conference, Dublin, June 2014).

The Making of the Realist Tradition

the Cold War – and nothing illustrates this better than the intellectual and professional career of one of the greatest interpreters of his thought.

On the first of June 1919 in Berlin, as he was walking back from school along the Tirpitzufer Straße, a fourteen-year-old boy joined other passers-by gathering on the bank of the Landwehr Canal to observe a group of men retrieving a corpse from the water. The corpse, the men announced, was that of Rosa Luxemburg, who had been murdered by the *Freikorps* several months earlier and whose body had been dumped in the canal. The schoolboy was Felix Gilbert, who was to become one of the foremost Machiavelli scholars and Renaissance historians following his exile to the United States. Much later, as he recounted the episode in his memoirs, Gilbert confessed that while he disapproved of the brutal murder of the Spartakist leaders, he was "certainly pleased about the defeat of the revolt." In retrospect, he conjectured that his decision to join the Social Democratic Party was motivated by its role in restoring order.[2] But reminiscence is a slippery exercise, as Gilbert knew, and it is difficult to tell apart the benefit of hindsight from retrospective rationalization: The motives that the older Gilbert attributes to his younger self may also reflect a set of concerns – with stability, with power, with the illusions of revolutionary idealism, with change and history – that only took shape later and defined his subsequent career as a historian. In this short time-collapsing vignette, in which the historian looks back at himself as a child looking at the decomposing body of the Revolution, Gilbert offers a powerful image of the infancy of realism as an ideology associated with the vicissitudes of modernity and the deliquescence of the idea of progress, captured by the Nietzschean unforgiveness of childhood.

Published in 1965, *Machiavelli and Guicciardini* remains to this day a landmark in the literature on the political thought of the *cinquecento*. In the United States, where scholarship on the subject was scarce outside literary studies and art history until the arrival of German émigré historians, Gilbert's work contributed to renewing the interpretation of Machiavelli. Yet, the stature that Gilbert has achieved as a historian of the Renaissance has tended to obscure the fact that his work on Machiavelli has developed in close connection with an interest in foreign policy that has spanned his entire career. His calling as a historian came from an early engagement with diplomatic history, when, as a student, Gilbert took a job at the Foreign Office and worked on the publication of Germany's prewar diplomatic documents. This experience got him

---

[2] Felix Gilbert, *A European Past: Memoirs, 1905–1945* (New York: Norton, 1988), 4, 39.

"intrigued by the working of international relations," and he later approached Friedrich Meinecke with a dissertation subject on "The Origin of the Idea of Balance of Power in the Renaissance."[3]

Gilbert, in fact, was also an international thinker in his own right. After leaving Germany in 1933, he found a position at Princeton's Institute for Advanced Study as the assistant of Edward Mead Earle, one of the early American realists and a founder of security studies; by 1940, he had completed the first draft of a manuscript on the intellectual origins of US foreign policy, later published under the title *To The Farewell Address* (1961); he assisted Earle in composing the classic *Makers of Modern Strategy* (1943), to which he contributed a chapter on Machiavelli; in 1953, he coedited an imposing volume on interwar diplomacy, *The Diplomats 1919–1939*, which stood out as an orthodox exercise in political history in the midst of a general turn to cultural history, but also as a get-together of veterans from the Research and Analysis branch of the Office of Strategic Services where Gilbert served from 1943 to 1946 (Fritz Stern later described the volume as "largely an OSS operation in mufti"[4]); and while Gilbert published in historical journals, he wrote as an occasional contributor to *Military Affairs, World Politics, Political Science Quarterly, Social Research,* and *Foreign Affairs*. It is also by a stroke of luck that Gilbert became the historian we know and not an intelligence analyst: In 1946, after his wartime service in the OSS, Gilbert was unsuccessful at securing an academic position and he came close to joining the State Department's Office of Research and Intelligence at the invitation of his former OSS boss, Sherman Kent. At the last minute, Mead Earle's relentless campaign in favor of his protégé serendipitously opened the doors of Bryn Mawr college, allowing Gilbert to pursue his academic career.[5] More tellingly, in 1956, the Rockefeller Foundation sponsored Gilbert's archival research for *Machiavelli and Guicciardini* as part of its efforts to promote the academic development of international relations theory, not Renaissance studies.[6]

---

[3] Gilbert, *A European Past*, 50, 72–73.
[4] Fritz Stern, "German History in America, 1884-1984," *Central European History* 19, no. 2 (1986): 158.
[5] Felix Gilbert to Edward Mead Earle, February 1st, 1946, Folder "Correspondence, Gilbert, Felix, 1946", Box 16, Correspondence F-G, MC020, Edward Mead Earle Papers, 1894–1954, Public Policy Papers, Department of Rare Books and Special Collections, Princeton University Library.
[6] "Grant in aid to Bryn Mawr College," February 23, 1955, Folder 4137, Box 484, Series 200S, RG 1.2, RF, RAC.

It is difficult to disentangle Gilbert's Machiavelli from his own involvement with the emerging national security state. Gilbert offered a fresh interpretation of Machiavelli, one that was developed in parallel with his participation in the efforts to reform American foreign policy thinking through new approaches to international politics focused on power, national interests, and security. By casting Machiavelli as a republican and a realist, Gilbert contributed to the legitimation of power politics in terms that were fully congruent with American political culture and supportive of the United States' self-image as an embattled republic, at a time when the Cold War gave renewed urgency to older discussions about emergency powers and revived anxieties about the hindrance to effective decisions represented by public opinion and democratic deliberation. In the process, he also lifted the obstacles to the inclusion of Machiavelli into a realist "tradition" that allegedly culminated with postwar realism and its academic derivations.

The integration of Machiavelli into the fold of a realist tradition of power politics was made possible because Gilbert built upon the previous treatment of the subject by Meinecke in *Die Idee der Staatsräson in der neueren Geschichte* (1924). Yet, Gilbert put historical flesh on Meinecke's thesis at a moment when Meinecke and a number of German historians had taken their distances vis-à-vis Machiavelli after World War II. The "realist" Machiavelli had fallen out of grace in West Germany, where he was increasingly viewed as the precursor of a Schmittian vision of politics or the proponent of an amoral doctrine that had degenerated into what Meinecke himself now called the "mass Machiavellism" of the Nazi regime.[7]

One would look in vain for traces of this guarded attitude in Gilbert's work. In the United States, Meinecke's legacy survived and played out differently. In showing that Machiavelli was not the proponent of a scientific technology of government and of a manipulative political rationalism bereft of moral bearings, but a thinker who understood that history placed politics in a productive tension with values, Gilbert overcame the suspicions that had kept Machiavelli on the margins of the emerging realist mainstream. By foregrounding Machiavelli's anti-Medicean

---

[7] Friedrich Meinecke, *The German Catastrophe: Reflections and Recollections* [Die Deutsche Katastrophe], trans. Sidney B. Fay (Cambridge, MA: Harvard University Press, 1950), 51. See also Gisela Bock, "Meinecke, Machiavelli und der Nationalsozialismus" in *Friedrich Meinecke in Seiner Zeit*, eds., Gisela Bock and Daniel Schönpflug (Stuttgart: Franz Steiner Verlag, 2006).

credentials and his republican inclinations, he also made power politics safe for America by associating it with the defense of liberty. Long before John Pocock identified Florentine DNA in the genetic makeup of the American republic, Gilbert had inscribed Machiavellian realism within a tradition that flowed straight into American foreign policy.[8] Shaped in the experience of cultural displacement and in the context of the emerging national security state, Gilbert's Machiavelli provided a new historical narrative that reduced the chiasm between political realism and American democracy, as the latter was learning to cope with its new role in world politics.

MID-CENTURY MODERN? MACHIAVELLI AND THE POSTWAR REALISTS

The idea of a realist tradition supposes that a specific style of thought is transmitted through a direct lineage from the Renaissance to the present, and reclaimed by successive generations of thinkers. It refers to "a discriminated pattern of subsistence and change" that is not in the eye of the beholder but represents "a convention of the works themselves."[9] This is, for instance, what the *Oxford Handbook of International Relations* posits when it suggests that "political realists typically *claim to be part* of a tradition that stretches back, through Thomas Hobbes and Niccolò Machiavelli, to Thucydides."[10] In this view, modern realists avail themselves of their Florentine predecessor and locate themselves in a tradition he is supposed to have pioneered.

At first sight, this claim is plausible. In one of the earliest American textbooks of international relations, *International Politics*, originally published in 1933, Frederick Schuman suggested that "the rebirth of realism" in the West was associated with the writings of Machiavelli, who saw first and more clearly than anybody else "the realities of the State System."[11] A few years later, in a diagnosis of the interwar crisis that

---

[8] For a similar, albeit more extreme, interpretation of the historiography of "republicanism" in relationship to American global hegemony, see Pecchioli, *Dal "mito" di Venezia all' "ideologia americana."*

[9] John G. Gunnell, *Political Theory: Tradition and Interpretation* (Cambridge, MA: Winthrop, 1979), 96.

[10] William Wohlforth, "Realism," in *The Oxford Handbook of International Relations*, ed. Christian Reus-Smit and Duncan Snidal, (Oxford: Oxford University Press, 2009), 132, emphasis mine.

[11] Frederick L. Schuman, *International Politics*, 7th edn. (New York: McGraw-Hill, 1969), 63, 64.

today is widely considered to be an early realist manifesto, E. H. Carr described Machiavelli as "the first important political realist."[12] Yet, Schuman's and Carr's appear as tentative bids to define "realism" in a fashion congruent with their progressive views. Carr, in particular, located Machiavelli in a line of rationalistic thinkers who saw history as a sequence of cause and effect (Bodin, Hobbes, Spinoza) and thus conceived of "the possibility of a physical science of politics." He surmised that Machiavelli inaugurated a tradition that culminated in a "progressive" nineteenth-century realism that took for granted the rational nature of the historical process. Whether or not there existed such a tradition, locating Machiavelli in a line of thinkers that ended with Hegel and Marx made him incompatible with the basic assumptions of postwar realism, an intellectual movement that found its common denominator in the rejection of scientific conceptions of history and opposed the rationalistic illusions involved in the reduction of politics to a social science. By the time he was writing, Carr knew this sort of synthesis was no longer possible and he had to concede that Machiavelli's putative realism eventually "br[oke] down." Schuman and Carr represented isolated and, ultimately, unsuccessful attempts at building a tradition that refused to separate completely realism and idealism. They were also indicators of the common association of Machiavelli with a rationalistic and scientific vision of politics. By the same token, they give away the reasons why postwar realist thinkers never saw themselves as part of a "realist tradition" that would have included the Florentine.

Although few realists have written anything substantial about Machiavelli, those who did have consistently expressed a negative view of the Florentine. One of the most articulate statements about Machiavelli in this literature is *The Statecraft of Machiavelli*, published in 1940 by the British historian Herbert Butterfield, who later became the head of the British Committee on International Relations and presided over the development of the "English school" of International Relations.[13] A reflection on the possibility of scientific history by a professional historian, *The Statecraft of Machiavelli* addressed the notion that Machiavelli was the inventor of a new science of politics premised on the assumption that history was driven by laws that could be discovered and formulated as "a body of rules upon which

---

[12] Carr, *The Twenty Years' Crisis*, 63.
[13] On the English School, see Dunne, *Inventing International Society*.

governments should act."[14] Machiavelli, in other words, was a forerunner of the social sciences of government that the realists abhorred. As if this were not sufficient ground to dismiss the value of his writings, Butterfield contended that the "scientific flavor" of Machiavelli's writings was deceptive: The only historical science, for Machiavelli, was derived from the writers of Antiquity, not from the modern scientific method. He was "a channel for classical influence" rather than the precursor of modernity so often celebrated.[15] His mistake was to assume that he could offer generalizations about politics, while he also rightly recognized it as the world of "chance and change." "On shifting sands like these," Butterfield declared echoing the critique of Machiavelli by his contemporary Francesco Guicciardini, "no science of statecraft could find a hold."[16] Machiavelli had failed to see that the contingency of politics could not be captured in general terms and he was, in that sense, less modern than Guicciardini, "the modern observer standing already in the clear light of the day."[17]

This was a sobering assessment, which pointed at Machiavelli's lack of realism. His eyes riveted to the *exempla* handed down by Roman historians, steeped in the imitation of the Ancients, Machiavelli was looking past reality. Even his view of human nature was too doctrinaire to count as realist: "Machiavelli believed that human nature was thoroughly wicked, and such a judgment *makes us imagine* that he was a modern realist."[18] But nothing could be further from the truth for Butterfield: Machiavelli's indebtedness to the classics explained "the defective nature of [his] contact with the world" – a damning judgment coming from a realist.[19] What was left was a political philosopher whose alleged "science" of statecraft could not even redeem the loss of the moral horizon of politics in the Christian Middle Ages. Under the unforgiving gaze of the Christian historian, Machiavelli was still "Old Nick," the main culprit of a political modernity that had lost its cultural mooring in a universal Christian morality. Butterfield gave an academic voice to Christian anti-Machiavellism, and

---

[14] Herbert Butterfield, *The Statecraft of Machiavelli* (New York and London: Collie-Macmillan, 1960), 22.
[15] Butterfield, *Statecraft*, 63.
[16] Butterfield, *Statecraft*, 21, 18. See Francesco Guicciardini, *Ricordi*, 2012 edn. (Milano: Garzanti, 1999), 136.
[17] Butterfield, *Statecraft*, 46. A view still found, for instance, in Tuck, *The Rights of War and Peace*, 10.
[18] Butterfield, *Statecraft*, 62, emphasis mine.
[19] Butterfield, *Statecraft*, 94.

Mid-Century Modern? Machiavelli and the Postwar Realists

indeed sought to vindicate this tradition by suggesting that "the Anti-Machiavels and even the Elizabethan dramatists were not so willfully wide off the mark."[20] He was not alone in leading this charge. A similar diagnosis was formulated at about the same time by his German colleague Gerhard Ritter. Renewing the genre of Christian apologetics for the reason of state, Ritter, like Giovanni Botero four centuries earlier, suggested that while the logic of power was inescapable, it could be countenanced only if supplemented by the Christian values that Machiavelli had so brazenly trampled.[21]

A similar attempt at saving power politics *from* Machiavelli from a Christian realist perspective can be found in the writings of Reinhold Niebuhr. As he sought to establish a historical pedigree for postwar realism, Niebuhr suggested that "by general consent, the first great 'realist' in Western history" was not Machiavelli but Augustine.[22] It is significant that he chose to identify realism with a thinker who was in many ways the antithesis of Machiavelli and an intellectual authority used throughout medieval times to secure the articulation between politics and a universal notion of justice that Machiavelli was supposed to have undone.[23] For those who, like Niebuhr, led the revival of political Augustinianism in the 1940s and 1950s, Machiavelli represented indeed the archenemy and the root cause of the disasters of modernity, from moral relativism to political nihilism. His claim to fame was not to have been the first modern realist, as it is believed today, but to have been "the first in a long line of moral cynics in the field of international relations."[24]

Hans Morgenthau, who is widely considered to be the founding father of that field, has not given much attention to Machiavelli. *Politics among Nations* does not contain more than the occasional reference to Machiavelli's advocacy of expediency in politics. But an article published in 1945 in the journal *Ethics* provides clues about how he considered the man now believed to be his predecessor: "The Machiavellian Utopia" was indeed a scathing critique of the United Nations project. While Wilson's

---

[20] Butterfield, *Statecraft*, 10.
[21] Gerhard Ritter, *The Corrupting Influence of Power* [Die Dämonie der Macht], trans. F. W. Pick (Hadleigh: Tower Bridge Publications, 1952). The book was originally published in 1940 under the title *Machtsaat und Utopie* and revised after the war. On Ritter, see Samuel Moyn, "The First Historian of Human Rights," *The American Historical Review* 116, no. 1 (2011): 58–79.
[22] Niebuhr, "Augustine's Political Realism," 124.
[23] "If justice is left out, what are kingdoms except great robber bands?" Augustine, *City of God*, vol. 2, Loeb Classical Library (1963), 7.
[24] Niebuhr, "The Children of Light and the Children of Darkness," 165.

Fourteen Points were a "heroic and futile attempt to transform the political scene according to the postulates of liberal rationality," the Atlantic charter and the UN represented "a less heroic and ... no less futile attempt to mold political reality in the image of Machiavelli's thought." Why invoke Machiavelli in this condemnation of the successor institution to the League of Nations and associate his name with Wilsonian idealism? While the Wilsonians had thought that a rational international order could subsist on the basis of its own moral force, the men of Dumbarton Oaks, wary of the failure of their predecessors, placed their hopes on the mechanics of power for keeping the Wilsonian dream afloat. In doing so, Morgenthau contended, they only moved from the Wilsonian utopia to the Machiavellian one. Like Machiavelli, they deluded themselves in imagining that the dispassionate analysis of power was sufficient to sustain a project of political unification. The United Nations project was just as utopian as the call for the unification of Italy at the end of *The Prince*, to the extent that it was based solely on the cool-headed analysis of power politics: "it was utopian to believe," Morgenthau says of Machiavelli, "that a country divided into a great number of small sovereignties could be united by any one of those small sovereigns' clever handling of the mechanics of political action."[25] Both Machiavelli and the diplomats of Dumbarton Oaks had forgotten that the foundation of any legal order was not a technique of power, but a moral code. Machiavelli's amoralism made his calls for the unification of Italy utopian, since the science of politics that was supposed to serve this aim was premised on the valediction of morality. Walking in his footsteps, the latter day Wilsonians were "the epigones of Machiavelli." It is worth noting that the same equation of Machiavelli with power deprived of moral bearings provides the incisive closing of Morgenthau's review of E. H. Carr's main works: Like the diplomats of Dumbarton Oaks, Carr erred in thinking that a check to power could be found within the logic of power itself and not in a transcendent moral standard: "Mr. Carr," Morgenthau writes, "might have learned that lesson from the fate of the political romantics of whom the outstanding representatives are Adam Müller and Carl Schmitt. It is a dangerous thing to be a Machiavelli. It is a disastrous thing to be a Machiavelli without *virtù*."[26]

---

[25] Hans J. Morgenthau, "The Machiavellian Utopia," *Ethics* 55, no. 2 (1945): 145.
[26] Hans J. Morgenthau, "The Political Science of E. H. Carr," *World Politics* 1, no. 1 (1948): 134.

Mid-Century Modern? Machiavelli and the Postwar Realists

It is an even more forceful indictment of political rationalism that one finds in the writings of Raymond Aron, one of the founders of international relations theory in France and an intellectual correspondent and ally of the American realists.[27] While Butterfield was finishing *The Statecraft of Machiavelli*, Aron was writing three short pieces about Machiavelli that explored the legacies of Machiavellism in the twentieth century.[28] Following Mannheim, Aron saw in Machiavelli a precursor of totalitarianism.[29] Machiavelli's science of politics was essentially the "codification of a technique of tyranny" that served an elitist conception of power. The problem that Aron saw in Machiavelli was not that of deciding whether he was in favor of liberty or despotism, or which of the *Principe* or the *Discorsi* best expressed his own preferences, but precisely the fact that their author could discuss republics and tyrannies in the same way because his vision of politics was dissociated from any normative criteria: It took the form of an attitude that was "the attitude of the scientist, and of the technician that relies on the results of the scientist."[30] The conception of human nature that sustained the Machiavellian science of politics inevitably led to tyrannical rule. This science was nothing else, in the end, than a set of recipes for manipulating the *vulgum pecus*. The modern Princes were the Hitlers and the Mussolinis, who had inherited a realm in an illegitimate manner and needed to rely on Machiavellian advice to secure their rule.[31] Whatever his own political inclinations, Machiavelli was guilty of uprooting politics from its moral soil, which made him "probably the first among the intellectuals who effectively contributed to giving a good conscience to evil men."[32] Like Butterfield, Aron made him directly responsible for the tragedies of the twentieth century.

But closer to fascism, even an *über*-realist such as Carl Schmitt considered Machiavelli with suspicion, as the main culprit of the modern

---

[27] On Aron and the American realists, see Daniel Steinmetz Jenkins, "A Narcissism of Minor Differences or Something More?: A Reconsideration of the Difference between the Political Realism of Raymond Aron and Hans Morgenthau," (unpublished paper, Columbia University, 2013).

[28] Written between 1938 and 1940, these texts are published in Raymond Aron, *Machiavel et les tyrannies modernes* (Paris: Editions de Fallois, 1993). See Serge Audier, *Raymond Aron. La démocratie conflictuelle* (Paris: Michalon, 2004); Serge Audier, *Machiavel, Conflit Et Liberté* (Paris: Vrin, 2005).

[29] See Mannheim, *Ideology and Utopia*, 125.

[30] Aron, *Machiavel*, 61.

[31] Aron, *Machiavel*, 122.

[32] Aron, *Machiavel*, 368.

secularization of politics and its reduction to pure technique. The legitimacy deficit of modern politics could be traced back to his rationalistic vision of politics as a self-sufficient activity. Schmitt remained wary of a thinker whom he considered responsible for the loss of the connection with transcendence, and therefore the loss of authority and political capacity.[33] While he recognized that Machiavelli's view of human nature was similar to that of Hobbes, Bossuet, or de Maistre, he also felt that it did not lead to the construction of the absolutist state but to a form of politically indifferent technique of government that was abhorrent to him.[34] A Catholic, Schmitt was also more appreciative of the Baroque tradition of the reason of state, with its Jesuitical moral casuistry, than of the pagan naturalness of power characteristic of Machiavelli's thought.

This brief overview suggests that the realists were unanimously critical of Machiavelli. But it also shows that an important aspect of their anti-Machiavellism stemmed from the understanding of Machiavelli as a *technician* of politics: he offered a vision of politics as a sphere of strictly technical rationality, severed from the transcendent moral background of Christianity. Inheriting a long tradition of anti-Machiavellism, realism gave it a new edge under the form of a denunciation of Machiavelli's exacerbated political rationalism. Machiavelli was, in the end, a precursor of the social sciences and of their application to politics – which is precisely what realists opposed. This reading of Machiavelli also reflected a specific intellectual provenance, largely shaped by German idealism. Indeed, Morgenthau was not far off the mark when he had bundled Machiavelli together with the Wilsonian "idealists": Nineteenth-century German idealism had exonerated Machiavelli of the opprobrium laid upon him by the Elizabethan moralists and seen in him a precursor of political modernity. Fichte and Hegel had celebrated the Italian patriot exposing the necessity and morality of the national state. This reading found an influential outlet in the work of the Italian philosopher Benedetto Croce, for whom Machiavelli "discover[ed] the necessity and autonomy of politics, of politics as situated beyond, or rather beneath moral good and evil, of politics which has its own laws against which it is useless to rebel, and which cannot be exorcised and expelled from the world using holy water."[35] This interpretation of Machiavelli was still

---

[33] Galli, *Lo sguardo di Giano*, 84–87.
[34] Carl Schmitt, *Dictatorship* (Cambridge: Polity, 2014), 6–7.
[35] Benedetto Croce, *Etica e politica* (Milano: Adelphi, 1994), 292.

extremely influential in the Machiavelli scholarship for much of the 1940s and 1950s.[36] It was Croce's rationalist philosopher that the realists had in mind when they inveighed against Machiavelli, and they were certainly confirmed in their suspicion by the fact that he was admired by neo-Kantians, such as Ernst Cassirer, for whom Machiavelli was not so much a politician addressing historically circumscribed problems as "the founder of a new science of politics" who had done for the study of politics what Galileo had done for the study of nature.[37] If there was anything like a realist "tradition" in the aftermath of World War II, it not only did not include Machiavelli: It defined itself *against* him.

FELIX GILBERT AND RENAISSANCE "REALISM": FROM THE CINQUECENTO TO THE TWENTIETH CENTURY

A symptom of the changing perception of Machiavelli among international relations scholars can be gleaned from a review of the American edition of Butterfield's *The Statecraft of Machiavelli* that Felix Gilbert wrote in 1957. Except for an interesting analysis of Machiavelli's influence on Bolingbroke, Gilbert wrote, Butterfield essentially reproduced the traditional anti-Machiavellian argument for which the Florentine was "a teacher of artifice." How much consideration Gilbert thought this position deserved was reflected in the length of his review, which disposed of Butterfield's pamphlet in nine terse lines.[38] Such a dismissal was significant, because it did not come from a Renaissance historian working at several removes from international relations debates and with an unsteady grasp of what modern "realism" meant. Like Butterfield, Gilbert was involved in the emergence of international relations theory and security studies; he had also published extensively on foreign affairs and diplomacy. What this suggests is that anti-Machiavellism was no longer central to realism and that a reassessment of Machiavelli was underway that reflected the changing landscape of international thought in the 1950s.

A detailed biography of Felix Gilbert will probably not be available until his personal papers, held at the Hoover Institution archives, are open to researchers in December 2018. Yet, his publications, his own

---

[36] As noted in Eric W. Cochrane, "Machiavelli: 1940–1960," *The Journal of Modern History* 33, no. 2 (1961): 115.

[37] Ernst Cassirer, *The Myth of the State* (New Haven: Yale University Press, 1946), 128.

[38] Felix Gilbert, review of *The Statecraft of Machiavelli*, by Herbert Butterfield, *Renaissance News* 10, no. 3 (1957): 157.

recollections, and open archival documents provide enough elements to understand the context of his approach to Machiavelli and to assess his role in crafting an image of the Florentine palatable to his realist colleagues despite the notorious reputation Machiavelli had among them. It is indeed with Gilbert that Machiavelli becomes, for the first time and with the seal of authenticity that only a historian can provide, a forerunner of twentieth-century realism.

Felix Gilbert was born in 1905 in Berlin, the scion of an important Jewish family converted to Lutheranism in the nineteenth century, the Mendelssohns, a banking dynasty that had made outstanding contributions to German high culture (his great-grandfather was the composer Felix Mendelssohn-Bartholdy, and the eighteenth-century philosopher Moses Mendelssohn was one of his forebears).[39] His reminiscences about his childhood and about the reasons for his early embrace of history as a vocation follow a pattern not uncommon among members of his generation who, like his fellow *Berliner* Walter Benjamin, had witnessed the unraveling of the enchanted world of their childhood, only to find themselves suddenly propelled into the maelstrom that engulfed Europe in the 1930s. The regular succession of cozy summers in Charlottenburg or on the Traunsee in Austria gave way to a period of instability and uncertainty that overlapped with Gilbert's coming of age. "War, revolution, and social turmoil, in an interlocking chain, shaped the crucial years of my youth," he later wrote. For the young Gilbert, the choice of history was inseparable from the prevalence of politics in his immediate experience: politics was constant change and fluctuation, not the rational realization of transcendent or unquestioned values. "I felt ... that we belonged to a special generation, different from the ones that preceded and followed mine. Skeptical about the values of the past, we were also skeptical about the likelihood of stability in the future."[40] History, at least in the historicist tradition in which Gilbert was schooled, made it possible to cultivate this skepticism and functioned as a propaedeutic to political realism. Gilbert was indeed the product of an intellectual tradition in which historical consciousness was intrinsically tied to the development of the

---

[39] The main source for Gilbert's biography before 1945 remains Gilbert, *A European Past*. See the reviews by Carl Schorske and Dante della Terza: Carl E. Schorske, "Survivor of a Lost World," *New York Review of Books* 35, no. 17 (1988), online version http://www.nybooks.com/articles/1988/11/10/survivor-of-a-lost-world/ (last accessed January 11, 2017); Dante della Terza, "Il passato europeo di Felix Gilbert," *Belfagor* 44, no. 1 (1989): 689–95.

[40] Gilbert, *A European Past*, 26, 27.

modern national state and for which, therefore, the state was the primary subject of historical research: From the beginning, history was "mainly, almost exclusively, political history."[41] As a historian, Gilbert would remain an exponent of the Rankean tradition that saw history as the history of high politics – a disposition strengthened by Meinecke, who taught Gilbert that a historical topic was important for political reasons.[42] This connection between historiography, high politics, and international relations would remain a characteristic of Gilbert's scholarship throughout his life. Beyond what may appear as intellectual eclecticism, the constellation of themes that commanded his attention found its coherence in this early experience of crisis. The combination of writings on "diplomatic history, the history of historiography and political thought with special reference to the Italian Renaissance and nineteenth-century Germany" was typical of this intellectual generation, according to another émigré historian, Arnaldo Momigliano. In his judgment, this made Gilbert "the *premier* survival [sic] of a glorious phase of German culture."[43]

This concern with high politics took a concrete form early, when the economic crisis forced Gilbert, still a student, to take his first steps as a "professional" historian by taking a job at the Foreign Office to assist with the publication of Germany's prewar diplomatic documents. Gilbert went back to his studies in 1925, but with a confirmed interest in international politics and the intention to write a dissertation on "The Origin of the Idea of Balance of Power in the Renaissance."[44] Meinecke rejected it, arguing that the handwriting of that time made it extremely difficult to deal with archival documents, and suggested instead a thesis on Droysen, which Gilbert reluctantly embarked upon and completed in 1931, before being able to pursue his interest in the political thought of the Renaissance. This pursuit, however, would be resumed only during the exile into which Gilbert was forced in 1933.

The place of Machiavelli in Gilbert's *oeuvre* must therefore be resituated in the complex framework made up by Meinecke's impress on the understanding of Machiavelli, and the experience of exile. Gilbert resumed his work on the Renaissance, as he had left Germany for the

---

[41] Gilbert, *A European Past*, 27.
[42] Felix Gilbert, *History: Choice and Commitment* (Cambridge, MA: Belknap Press, 1977), 86.
[43] Arnaldo Momigliano, *Sesto contributo alla storia degli studi classici e del mondo antico*, vol. II (Roma: Edizioni di Storia e Letteratura, 1980), 770.
[44] Gilbert, *A European Past*, 72.

United Kingdom. He had initially hoped that the political thinkers of the Renaissance were "an 'international' subject," but he quickly realized that the history of the political ideas of the Renaissance was left to art or literary historians, with the result that in the history of *political* thought, the suspicion that Machiavelli was "an advocate of the devil" still lingered on.[45]

From his first writings on the Renaissance, Gilbert cast Machiavelli as a very different figure from the ideological foil that occasionally surfaced in the writings of the realists. Gilbert sought to understand Machiavelli by resituating him in the context of Florentine politics between the end of the fifteenth century and the first decades of the *cinquecento*. Machiavelli ceased to be a scandalous and isolated figure that smeared the pristine tapestry of Renaissance humanism to become a man of his time, fully immersed in the cultural atmosphere of his city. His political doctrine was no longer an idiosyncratic anomaly, but the expression of a diffuse political culture; the concepts and ideas that he adopted or revisited circulated widely in Florence and informed municipal politics as well as foreign policy.[46] His originality "did not consist ... in the ideas which he proffered," since they were not exclusively his own: "his contribution was to weave them together in such a way that a new vision of politics emerged."[47]

Much of this was pure Meinecke, in method but also in intent. Meinecke had turned to Machiavelli in the context of a "self-examination of historicism," as he sought to understand the impasse in which this tradition had thrown Germany. Nineteenth-century German idealism had seen in Machiavelli a thinker who expressed the "rational" aspect of the national interest and thus a particular moment in the dialectic that led to the rise of the ethical State. In this tradition, individuality and identity, reality and rationality, the interests of a particular state and the accomplishment of Reason in history were conflated. Seen from the perspective of the defeat of 1918, however, this sanctification of power

---

[45] Gilbert, *A European Past*, 172.

[46] "Machiavelli and Guicciardini ... proceeded from political and historical concepts which were the common property of a whole group of Florentine writers." Felix Gilbert, "Bernardo Rucellai and the Orti Oricellari: A Study on the Origin of Modern Political Thought," *Journal of the Warburg and Courtauld Institutes* 12 (1949): 102. See also Felix Gilbert, "Machiavelli and Guicciardini," *Journal of the Warburg Institute* 2, no. 3 (1939): 263–66.

[47] Felix Gilbert, *Machiavelli and Guicciardini: Politics and History in Sixteenth Century Florence* (New York: Norton, 1984), 159.

politics looked like a dangerous illusion. The notion of a *philosophy* of history, already challenged since Dilthey, was now in total disrepute for sanctioning power under the seal of rationality and morality. A critical reassessment was in order. This was Meinecke's main problem in *Die Idee der Staatsräson*: recovering a tradition of power politics that did not end up with the idealization of *Machtpolitik*, but that remained in tension with ethics and recognized the limitations of rationality.[48] In his search for a new articulation between politics and ethics that did not conflate them in the illusion that national power operated unwittingly for the realization of Reason in world history, Meinecke saw in Machiavelli the naturalistic, "realist" element of modern historical consciousness, aware of the contingency of politics and the limits of reason – an element that was utterly irreducible to idealistic syntheses. The permanence of war was no longer the sign of a Hegelian "cunning of reason," but suggested on the contrary an "incapacity" of reason, unable to "triumph by her own strength."[49] The last part of the book, moving from historical analysis to a critical diagnosis of the situation of Weimar Germany, was shaped by a concern that was no longer "the *legitimation* or the *justification* of history, but [the problem] of the responsibility of historical actors."[50] Meinecke sought to recover the problematic nature of the relationship between morality and politics, rather than considering history as the instance of its resolution. In doing so, he was challenging Croce's neo-Hegelianism, and this tension could only be exacerbated when it came to making sense of Machiavelli.[51] The Florentine secretary became the first exponent of a "reason of state," which, in Meinecke's view, acted as a countervailing principle to the idealistic force of mass politics, "a benefic ice-cooling on the heat that irradiates from nationalism."[52] Meinecke enrolled Machiavelli in a critique of nineteenth-century idealism and universalistic nationalism

---

[48] Meinecke, *Machiavellism*, 425. See also Carlo Antoni, *Dallo storicismo alla sociologia* (Firenze: Sansoni, 1973), 112–20.
[49] Meinecke, *Machiavellism*, 429.
[50] Fulvio Tessitore, *Interpretazione dello storicismo* (Pisa: Edizioni della Normale, 2006), 72.
[51] Meinecke observed that he and his German colleagues had experienced defeat and could see better "the terrible antinomy between the ideals of rational morality and the actual processes and causal connections of history," something that was lost on Croce because, as a victor, he stood "on the happier and sunnier side of life." Meinecke, *Machiavellism*, 432.
[52] Friedrich Meinecke, *Die deutsche Erhebung Von 1914* (Stuttgart: J. G. Cottasche Buchhandlung Nachfolger, 1915), 98, quoted in Antonio Negri, *Saggi sullo storicismo tedesco. Dilthey e Meinecke* (Milano: Feltrinelli, 1959), 211.

that would soon become a standard of realist thought. Machiavelli stood for a separation of politics from morality that acted as a safety valve preventing politics from descending into extremist forms of self-righteousness. He also became the indispensable starting point for responsible political reflection in the turmoil of the twentieth century.

Raised in the anti-Hegelian tradition of Ranke, Burckhardt, and Meinecke, Gilbert's Machiavelli was not an abstract rationalist, but the exponent of a culture that tied politics and ethics in ways that may have been contradictory, but that did not have to be resolved into a higher conceptual unity. No matter how scandalous Machiavelli's doctrine may have sounded, it was couched in a rhetoric inherited from the tradition of *specula principum*, a genre that he revisited but that tied his vision of politics to a cultural hinterland of debates about the moral qualities of the Prince that gave its specific meaning to his concept of *virtù*.[53] In light of this ethical background of Machiavelli's thought, Gilbert confidently asserted that "the view that he was a mere technician of statecraft can be considered obsolete, despite the attempts by Mosca, and more recently by Butterfield, to revive it."[54] Any notion of "amoralism" was thus historically inaccurate and could only be viewed as a contrived attempt to transform into a rigid philosophy a thought that was historical throughout. By refuting the idea that Machiavelli had formulated a pure "science" of politics, Gilbert also invalidated the interpretations that turned Machiavelli into the precursor of modern totalitarianism.

What was paradoxical, however, was that Gilbert consolidated Meinecke's intellectual legacy precisely when Meinecke himself had gone much further in his revision of historicism and taken his distances from Machiavellian realism. In his postwar diagnosis of the German tragedy, Meinecke indicted the degeneration of Machiavellism into a mass ideology. Far from having an "ice-cooling" effect, it now seemed that the *ragione di stato* itself had reached a point of incandescence at the contact of modern nationalism. The "daemonic," non-rational element in the reason of state was no longer the key to political greatness, but a force that had led first the German bourgeoisie and then the masses into an "intoxicated craze for power." By propelling ever-broader segments of the population into politics, the liberalization of government had

---

[53] Felix Gilbert, "The Humanist Concept of the Prince and *the Prince* of Machiavelli," *Journal of Modern History* 11, no. 4 (1939): 449–83.
[54] Felix Gilbert, "Political Thought of the Renaissance and Reformation: A Report on Recent Scholarship," *The Huntington Library Quarterly* 4, no. 4 (1941): 449.

"multiplie[d] the keys to the chest of poisons in which lie the essences of Machiavellism."[55] Not only had Meinecke's view of the tradition changed dramatically, but he now associated his distrust of power politics with Burckhardt's nostalgia for "the aristocratic character of the *ancien régime*."[56] The reference to the Basel historian, who had stood out as the counterpoint to the celebration of power politics by his Berlin colleagues, was anticipating a wider turn to Burckhardt in the postwar years. In a 1947 lecture on Ranke and Burckhardt given at the German Academy of Sciences, Meinecke had suggested that, between the two historians, it was Burckhardt, with his bleak view of power and the state, who was now more attuned to the present than his Berlin colleague, with his harmonious view of the "regulated progress of world history."[57] That Burckhardt actually viewed Machiavelli with admiration and even saw in him an anxiety about the ethical decline of political communities that echoed his own concerns was irrelevant: He was now the symbol of the rejection of Machiavellism and the power state, and as such he was swiftly conscripted into the Cold War fight against Soviet totalitarianism.[58]

Although he acknowledged his debt vis-à-vis Burckhardt, Gilbert refused to follow Meinecke all the way in this indictment of power politics and Machiavellism.[59] He rejected the idea that Ranke and Burckhardt were the opposite terms of an alternative and insisted on their complementarity, a view he defended at the end of his life in a small volume dedicated to the two historians.[60] More importantly, his studies on Machiavelli remained indefectibly wedded to the perspectives opened by *Die Idee der Staatsräson* despite Meinecke's later denunciation of "Machiavellism" as a pathology of the reason of state in the era of mass politics. Yet, it would be wrong to read into this divergence a discrepancy between Meinecke's concern for the present and a putatively more

---

[55] Meinecke, *The German Catastrophe*, 54, 52.
[56] Meinecke, *The German Catastrophe*, 52.
[57] Friedrich Meinecke, "Ranke Und Burckhardt," in *Aphorismen und Skizze zur Geschichte* (Stuttgart: K. F. Koehler Verlag, 1948), 147.
[58] On Burckhardt and Machiavelli, see Hugh Trevor-Roper, *History and the Enlightenment* (New Haven: Yale University Press, 2010), 256. On the Cold War context of the turn to Burckhardt, see Lionel Gossman, "Jacob Burckhardt: Cold War Liberal?" *The Journal of Modern History* 74, no. 3 (2002): 538–72.
[59] Gilbert, *Machiavelli and Guicciardini*, 4.
[60] Felix Gilbert, *History: Politics or Culture? Reflections on Ranke and Burckhardt* (Princeton: Princeton University Press, 1990), 62. For an overview of the Ranke-Burckhardt discussion, see J. L. Herkless, "Meinecke and the Rank-Burckhardt Problem," *History and Theory* 9, no. 3 (1970): 290–321.

historical perspective pursued by Gilbert. For most German historians since Burckhardt and Ranke, the Renaissance was not a specialized field of study, but the foundation of both the history of modernity and modern historiography. They "studied the Renaissance because of its essential contribution to the formation of modern Europe."[61] Gilbert was no exception and he had his own presentist concerns as he turned to Machiavelli, but they were markedly different from those of his West German colleagues.

One of Gilbert's concerns was provided by his first-hand experience of the failure to "maintain the state" (*mantenere lo stato*) that had led to the collapse of the Weimar republic. Machiavelli's relevance to contemporary politics had nothing to do with the intellectual lineage of totalitarianism, but on the contrary with a robust defense of liberty that avoided the pitfalls of idealism. In *Machiavelli and Guicciardini*, the crisis of idealistic representations of politics was illustrated at one extreme by the fall of Savonarola, and at the other by a waning faith in politics based on reason and by a positive view of power. The collapse of the Republic was seen as the failure of political rationalism, and the Medicean restoration was supported by a new generation of aristocrats who no longer believed in reason. They were, in Gilbert's pointed expression, "prophets of force."[62] Within a few decades, humanistic rationalism and the moralistic idealism of Savonarola had succumbed to the attack on reason and the unleashing of brute power. It is difficult not to hear in Gilbert's masterwork echoes of the intellectual and political climate in which it had matured over thirty years: a frail republican regime born out of international developments and military defeat; a period of unprecedented artistic expression and creativity and, at the same time, of political uncertainty and instability; a protracted constitutional crisis; a violent coup supported by "prophets of force" who abolished republican institutions ... One can only concur with Gabriele Pedullà when he observes that "the clash between rationalism and irrationalism that led to the triumph of the Medici is modeled after ... the direct experience of the conflict that had torn apart Germany during the 1920s and was brought to conclusion with the establishment of Nazism." Gilbert's Renaissance was indeed a "transfiguration" of Weimar.[63]

---

[61] Anthony Molho, "The Italian Renaissance, Made in USA," in *Imagined Histories: American Historians Interpret the Past*, eds., Anthony Molho and Gordon S. Wood (Princeton: Princeton University Press, 1998), 274.

[62] Gilbert, *Machiavelli and Guicciardini*, 129, 150.

[63] Gabriele Pedullà, "Machiavelli Dopo Auschwitz," introduction to *Machiavelli e Guicciardini*, by Felix Gilbert (Torino: Einaudi, 2012), xxix, xxvii.

Seen through the prism of Weimar, Machiavelli represented a political wisdom that could have saved the day and had much to teach to an embattled postwar liberalism. Equally distant from the "idealism" of Savonarola or the humanists and from the irrationalism of the "prophets of force" who had brought the Medici back into power, he stood for the capacity to rise up to the challenge of political emergencies, to act decisively in a timely manner, unconstrained by moral norms and accepted customs, yet within an ethical horizon defined by republican values. This was a Machiavelli critical of the powerlessness of rationalism and its incapacity to stop the rising tide of fascism – not the abstract rationalist of the pro-appeasement Carr. This did not make him an apologist of pure force, but the *ragione* that for him guided political action was a reason entirely exposed to contingency, and therefore limited in its purchase – yet it was precisely this limitation that ensured its connection to reality and its effectiveness. It was a reason that could not rise above its own historical situation, and which, as a result, could not serve as a transcendent justification of power. This was a historicist Machiavelli, yet redeemed from the sins of extreme historicism and the sanctification of power characteristic of the German idealist tradition. In outlining a paradoxical bond between the idealistic Savonarola and the Medicean advocates of force, who despite their fundamental differences found themselves united in a common attack on reason, Gilbert may have read into the Florentine *cinquecento* the combination of idealism and power politics that distinguished the historicist tradition he knew so well, while also seeking to exonerate Machiavelli from it.[64] For if the Machiavellian moment was coming to an end in West Germany, it was only dawning in America.

FROM GERMAN HISTORICISM TO AMERICAN REALISM: MEINECKE'S ATLANTIC LEGACY

It is difficult to understand the discrepancy between Machiavelli's dismal fate in postwar German historiography and his rising fortunes in American political science without keeping in mind the context in which Gilbert's scholarship developed from the late 1930s onward. Just like Machiavelli's *Prince*, Gilbert's mature work on Machiavelli began *post res perditas*, in exile, and in some ways as an offering of historical wisdom

---

[64] Gilbert, *Machiavelli and Guicciardini*, 150.

to the powers that be of his adoptive country.⁶⁵ As Meinecke reflected upon Machiavellianism from the dead end of the German *Sonderweg*, Gilbert was considering it from the perspective of a victorious power coming to terms with its world-political role, a perspective shaped by his participation in the nascent fields of security studies and international relations theory.

Shortly after arriving in the United States in 1936, Gilbert found a position at the Institute for Advanced Studies as the assistant of Edward Mead Earle (1894–1954).⁶⁶ A somewhat forgotten figure of international studies, Earle has been recently rediscovered as an early American realist and an influential academic entrepreneur who largely contributed to the emergence of security studies.⁶⁷ Trained in history, Earle shared the frustration of the "New Historians," who felt that rigorous source criticism and historiographical technique were not sufficient and that they needed to be able to address contemporary issues – a concern that Gilbert also shared.⁶⁸ The seminar that he started at Princeton in 1939, and in which Gilbert was a key participant for years, brought together an impressive roster of strategists, policymakers, political scientists, and historians in an effort to create "a new regime of inquiry" that would mobilize and integrate different disciplines in an effort to mainstream "national strategy" thinking in academia.⁶⁹ Much more than an interdisciplinary experiment, this was an ambitious ideological project that examined the conditions for a social, political, economic, and educational reform that would better prepare American society to confront its global duties in terms of its national interests. This propaedeutic consisted among other things in moving away from isolationism and reconciling oneself with the "role of force in international affairs."⁷⁰ Earle's project was, in effect, intellectual propaganda.

---

⁶⁵ Gilbert's first article on Machiavelli was published in 1937: Felix Gilbert, "Machiavelli in an Unknown Contemporary Dialogue," *Journal of the Warburg Institute* 1, no. 2 (1937): 163–66.

⁶⁶ Gordon A. Craig, "Felix Gilbert (21 May 1905 – 14 February 1991)," *Proceedings of the American Philosophical Society* 137, no. 1 (1993): 132.

⁶⁷ See David Eckbladh, "Present at the Creation: Edward Mead Earle and the Depression-Era Origins of Security Studies," *International Security* 36, no. 3 (2011): 107–41; Inderjeet Parmar, "Edward Mead Earle and the Rise of Realism in the United States Academy," *Manchester Papers in Politics* 3/01 (2000). See also the review of Eckbladh's article by Robert Vitalis, H-Dipl, International Security Studies Forum, June 15, 2012, available at: https://issforum.org/ISSF/PDF/ISSF-AR14.pdf (last accessed March 16, 2016).

⁶⁸ Gilbert, *A European Past*, 106.   ⁶⁹ Eckbladh, "Present at the Creation," 115.

⁷⁰ Parmar, "Edward Mead Earle," 2.

Machiavelli obviously had much to contribute to a project that advocated the "return to an earlier tradition that treated military problems as an inherent element in the science of government and politics."[71] Edited by Earle, Craig, and Gilbert in 1943, *Makers of Modern Strategy* opened with a chapter by Gilbert emphasizing that the connection between "military power" and "political order" was at the center of Machiavelli's thought. Something deeper, however, was at stake in this relation between the use of force and political institutions. The question of military might was indistinguishable from the question of the *ordinamenti*, of the concrete constitution of the polity, and Gilbert considered that the "grandiose theme" of the *Discorsi* was the interrelationship between Rome's rise to world power and its republican constitution.[72] The conditions of military success were not only a matter of strategy and tactics: They were rooted in politically organized civic virtue. The absolutistic tradition outlined by Meinecke did not preclude the possibility that power politics could be reconciled with democratic values and the defense of freedom. This possibility would rapidly take the shape of a new historiographical paradigm, "republicanism," which has since left its mark on political theory in the English-speaking world, and whose origins owe much to the ideological context of the 1950s in which Machiavelli was reinterpreted.

The relation between the pressing necessities of power politics and democracy was one of the central questions that Earle's Princeton seminar sought to address in its uphill battle to reformulate problems of national security away from isolationism and its putative role in ensuring America's political virtue. In this context, the problem formulated by Meinecke was entirely relevant and captured what was now an American dilemma. By building upon it, Gilbert was directly engaging the most pressing issues of American foreign policy-making. The difference, however, was that the dualism between politics and ethics that Meinecke associated with Machiavelli and which eventually led him to take sides in 1946 was less pronounced when considered from

---

[71] Edward Mead Earle, "The Princeton Program of Military Studies," March 1942, Box 24, Folder "Professional Activities – Princeton Military Studies Group – 1941," MC020, Edward Mead Earle Papers; 1894–1954, Public Policy Papers, Department of Rare Books and Special Collections, Princeton University Library, at 3.

[72] Felix Gilbert, "Machiavelli: The Renaissance of the Art of War," in *Makers of Modern Strategy*, eds., Edward Mead Earle, Gordon Craig, and Felix Gilbert (Princeton: Princeton University Press, 1943), 3.

Princeton. For in thinking historically about the Renaissance and its aftermath, Gilbert very much had America in mind.

In his memoir, Gilbert acknowledged that the seminar had a strong influence on his work and that "American foreign policy became a chief concern of [his]" in the late 1930s.[73] During the academic year 1939–1940, the topic of the seminar was "American isolationism," and Gilbert gave several talks on the subject, which he revised and eventually published under the title *To the Farewell Address* (1961). Although it does not invoke Machiavelli once, this slim volume provides an important backdrop against which Gilbert's Renaissance work developed from the late 1930s onward, and it played a crucial role in assembling the historical circuitry in which Machiavellism could circulate unimpaired by moralistic reservations. *To the Farewell Address* examined the two main tendencies of US foreign policy, isolationism and international Messianism, from the perspective of their antecedents in eighteenth-century European political thought. In effect, it was a painstaking attempt to uncover under the idealistic garb of Washington's Farewell Address what Gilbert presented as the basic realistic thrust of early American political thought about international affairs. He acknowledged that the Address ultimately reflected the basic tension in American ideas about foreign policy "between Idealism and Realism," yet he also suggested that they manifested themselves in different ways. The Address belonged to a type of document – "political testaments" – that were "closely tied to the eighteenth-century concept of power politics." What distinguished it was "the integration of idealistic assumptions" that came to conceal its realist bottom-line.[74] These conventional assumptions notwithstanding, nothing less than the entire "intellectual framework" of the recommendations on foreign policy "was that of the school of the interests of the state."[75] Far from being a cultural import, realism turned out to be as American as apple pie.

With realism thus safely lodged into the foundations of the American republic, it was possible to look at the reason of state with a more benevolent gaze. If Gilbert saw value in Machiavellism and the *ratio status* tradition even after Meinecke had repudiated it, it was because he was outlining an alternative historical path for this tradition, one that did not end up with the Nazi catastrophe but with the American republic. In many ways, *To Farewell Address* was a critical appendage to Meinecke's book

---

[73] Gilbert, *A European Past*, 176. [74] Gilbert, *To the Farewell Address*, 136.
[75] Gilbert, *To the Farewell Address*, 134.

and explored another trajectory of the *Idee der Staatsräson*, one that saw the tension between politics and ethics subside with the foundation of the American republic. By sketching a genetic connection between sixteenth-century Florence and the American republic, Gilbert paved the way toward the acculturation of Machiavelli in American political thought, and thus contributed to a more general movement that sought to establish the legitimacy of non-liberal and non-democratic forms of politics in the context of the Cold War. Machiavelli was no longer the forerunner of totalitarianism, but, on the contrary, a defender of republican liberty who directly spoke to the dilemmas of a democracy confronted with issues of national security, and in particular to the inescapable tension between its attachment to moral values and the necessity of survival – a tension exacerbated by the constant state of emergency of the Cold War. "The Cold War," John Lewis Gaddis noted, "transformed American leaders into Machiavellians"[76] – but while he may have simply meant that they showed a greater tolerance for expediency, there was a much deeper sense in which Machiavelli became central to the emergence of a new vision of politics that sought to overcome what was increasingly perceived as the limitations of liberal constitutionalism. As the foreign policy establishment developed new prerogative powers shrouded from public scrutiny and located outside traditional democratic institutions, its intellectuals provided fresh ideological justifications for political expediency. The late 1940s and 1950s saw the development of a new interest in "dictatorship," not as a counter-model but, on the contrary, as a specialized aspect of republics, as historians, political theorists, and constitutionalists sought to reduce the chiasm between democracy and the exercise of unaccountable decision-making power. Because it allowed navigation of this tension, the notion of "republicanism" was crucial to the acclimatization of dictatorial solutions in a democratic context, and Machiavelli became obviously central to this ideological operation.[77] All the ingredients of the "Machiavellian moment" were thus in place two decades before John Pocock published his *magnum opus*. The seeds of the republican paradigm were planted in the 1950s, when Hans Baron and

---

[76] John Lewis Gaddis, *The Cold War: A New History* (New York: Penguin, 2005), 165.
[77] On the dictatorial political imaginary of the 1950s, see Chapter 6. The implication of dictatorship in the republican paradigm is superbly highlighted by Andreas Kalyvas: Andreas Kalyvas, "The Sublime Dignity of the Dictator: Republicanism and the Return of Dictatorship in Political Modernity," in *African, American and European Trajectories of Modernity: Past Oppression, Future Justice?* ed. Peter Wagner (Edinburgh: Edinburgh University Press, 2015).

later Felix Gilbert assembled elements of historical continuity that facilitated the positive identification of Cold War America with the Florentine republic – an identification based on the assumption that these regimes acted essentially in self-defense, even though this implied, in the case of Baron, glossing over Florentine imperialism.[78] Gilbert, in particular, sought culturally efficient ways to reconcile political expediency with the defense of freedom. The historiography of republicanism – which later spawned an entire cottage industry in political theory – initially took shape among efforts to transform the self-image of the foreign policy establishment and its decision-making latitude in the context of the fight against Soviet "totalitarianism."[79]

FROM MODERN RATIONALISM TO RENAISSANCE DECISIONISM

The exposure to the "security dilemma" in the context of Earle's seminar and the wartime service in the OSS, in which the émigrés gained "an education in contemporary *Realpolitik* and an insight into the unvarnished process by which the political decision later studied by historians are made," undoubtedly helped crystallize the main themes of Gilbert's work, and in particular the vexed question of the relationship between power politics and moral norms, or, more generally, security and democracy.[80] They also help explain why he kept in sharp focus the aspects of Machiavelli's thought that made him a theorist of force and power, while they tended to be downplayed by other historians of the Renaissance involved in the rehabilitation of Machiavelli as a model republican.[81] For Hans Baron, Machiavelli was only a link in the transmission of "civic humanism" from the *trecento* all the way to Wilhelmine

---

[78] Mikael Hörnqvist, "The Two Myths of Civic Humanism," in *Renaissance Civic Humanism*, ed. James Hankins (Cambridge: Cambridge University Press, 2000).
[79] Pecchioli, *Dal "mito" di Venezia all' "ideologia americana,"* 164–65.
[80] Barry Katz, "German Historians in the Office of Strategic Services," in *An Interrupted Past: German-Speaking Historians in the United States after 1933*, eds., Hartmut Lehmann and James J. Sheehan (Washington, DC and Cambridge: German Historical Institute and Cambridge University Press, 1991), 139.
[81] On the downplaying of these aspects of Machiavelli, see the discussion in William J. Connell, "The Republican Tradition, in and out of Florence," in *Girolamo Savonarola: Piety, Prophecy and Politics in Renaissance Florence*, eds., Donald Weinstein and Valerie R. Hotchkiss (Dallas: Bridwell Library, Southern Methodist University, 1994).

Bürgertum.⁸² But as an early reader of Nietzsche, Gilbert was "more interested in his *Genealogy of Morals* because of its attack on bourgeois values than in his *Zarathustra*."⁸³ He saw in Machiavelli a healthy corrective to bourgeois values, which sometimes had to be infringed in order to be safeguarded. The reason of state tradition may have informed early American political thought, as *To the Farewell Address* suggested, but it was also distinct from America's liberal and democratic values and Gilbert made it clear that this separation was paramount and ought to be maintained.⁸⁴ The recovery of Machiavelli's thought was thus used to reintroduce in democratic practice a dimension of politics that was not bounded by it and had been traditionally associated with absolutism.⁸⁵

Yet, while he defended the idea that foreign policy should be exempt from the democratic strictures of domestic politics, Gilbert was also seeking to ease its acceptance. By emphasizing Machiavelli's anti-Medicean credentials and relating his considerations on the use of force to a normative background of humanist and republican traditions, he was suggesting the possibility of a less threatening and more functional relationship between prerogative power and established norms. Machiavelli's republicanism ultimately meant that political expediency was essential to the defense of freedom and thus normatively justified.

However, this reading of Machiavelli was up against a formidable obstacle, namely his association with a scientific, abstract, and rationalistic approach to politics, which had earned him the contempt of the postwar realists. Gilbert did much to change this, in particular by foregrounding the dimension of Machiavelli's politics that was restive to rationalization and formalization, and by dramatizing the "contrast between *ragione* and *Fortuna*," in which he saw the structuring force of sixteenth-century Florentine politics.⁸⁶ The vicissitudes that had led to the fall of the Medici in 1494 and the protracted crisis of the republic before its eventual collapse had strengthened the notion that politics was not about realizing a fixed template or an ideal order, or about following

---

⁸² Riccardo Fubini, "Renaissance Historian: The Career of Hans Baron," *The Journal of Modern History* 62, no. 3 (1992): 541–74. See also the discussion in Pecchioli, *Dal "mito" di Venezia all' "ideologia americana,"* 168–203.
⁸³ Gilbert, *A European Past*, 43.
⁸⁴ See his cautionary observations in Felix Gilbert, "Bicentennial Reflections," *Foreign Affairs* 54, no. 4 (1976): 635–44.
⁸⁵ Along these lines, see Athanasios Moulakis, *Republican Realism in Renaissance Florence: Francesco Guicciardini's Discorso di Logrogno* (Langham: Rowman & Littlefield, 1998), 2.
⁸⁶ Gilbert, *Machiavelli and Guicciardini*, 138.

universal rules, but about dealing with constant change and fluctuation.[87] Machiavelli's greatness was to have expressed this new historical consciousness better than any of his contemporaries.

But Gilbert went further and provided an astute reinterpretation of Machiavelli's rationalism. Here again, *To the Farewell Address* provides important clues. Gilbert drew a conventional opposition between power politics and the French Enlightenment: The target of the revolutionary thought of the eighteenth century was the "balance of power." The balance of power was the obstacle to all projects of perpetual peace and in the eyes of the political reformers of the eighteenth century, "foreign affairs showed most clearly the ills of a world not yet ruled by reason." But Gilbert was too much of a historian to assume that this clearcut opposition between power politics and the reformist philosophies of the eighteenth century was historically accurate or intellectually sound. If power politics "undisguised and untrammeled by moral values" was one aspect of the century, the other was the "scientific and systematizing spirit" that led politicians to believe that there existed "laws" of politics. This belief was not confined to revolutionary thinkers: It defined the mentality of the age and found supporters even among the realists. The result was that even advocates of power politics sought to express their philosophy in a rationalistic form: "even the power struggle among states was considered to have its laws. The attempt to discover these laws, *though condemned to futility because of an erroneous belief in the rationality of human society*," Gilbert went on, "resulted in a clearer insight into the nature of diplomacy and a sharper definition of its tasks."[88]

Gilbert did not hide his own skepticism vis-à-vis political rationalism and the idea that political knowledge could take the form of a "science," but he also considered that the Enlightenment had paved the way for the

---

[87] The notion that constitutional matters resolved themselves into political practice may have had a very specific resonance in the context of the early Cold War and its extension of the sovereign powers of government, but it came to Gilbert from the Tuscan school of historical realism, which influenced him. See Vittorio de Caprariis, *Francesco Guicciardini dalla politica alla storia*, ed. Istituto Italiano per gli Studi Storici (Napoli: Il Mulino, 1950); Antonio Anzilotti, *La crisi costituzionale della repubblica fiorentina* (Firenze: Lumachi, 1911); Rudolf von Albertini, *Das florentinische Staatsbewusstsein im Übergang von der Republik zum Prinzipat* (Bern: Francke, 1955). On Tuscan realism, see the introduction by Luigi Russo in Antonio Anzilotti, *Movimenti e constrasti per l'unità italiana* (Milano: Giuffrè, 1964), xxxi, as well as Nicola Ottokar, "Antonio Anzilotti," *Leonardo: Rassegna mensile della cultura italiana* 1, no. 1 (1925): 12–13. I am grateful to Anthony Molho for drawing my attention to their importance for Gilbert.

[88] Emphasis mine. Gilbert, *To the Farewell Address*, 92.

transformation of power politics into an intellectually coherent *doctrine*. Rationalism was not necessarily a rigid philosophy of politics: It was also a rhetorical convention that could be applied even to power politics and made it more persuasive. By the same token, it could be peeled off, leaving intact the fundamental insight of realism. Thus, "divested of its rationalistic exaggerations, the doctrine of the interests of the states contained a kernel of truth."[89]

Examined against the backdrop of *To the Farewell Address*, Machiavelli's rationalism in *Machiavelli and Guicciardini* becomes very different from the quality attributed to him as the founder of a new science of politics. Gilbert assigned a purely conventional meaning to Machiavelli's political rationalism. Certainly, his early articles were replete with the idea that Machiavelli was looking for "the laws behind political phenomena" and mentioned repeatedly his "passionate concern to discover the hidden laws of history's involutions."[90] Machiavelli's "basic approach [was] rationalistic" to the extent that his understanding of human nature made men's actions "calculable."[91] But none of this meant that he thought reason was a sufficient and reliable guide to politics. His rationalism was a rationalism humbled by defeat, weakened by the historical involution of 1512 and the increased awareness of the volatility and unpredictability of *Fortuna*. Machiavelli was fully "aware that conducing politics according to pure reason had limits." It was the non-rational part of the human psyche that allowed great politicians to impose their will on *Fortuna* and achieve glory.[92] The role of contingency and timeliness in politics ("*la qualità dei tempi*") was such that, in some circumstances, ratiocination had to give way to a decision taken in the absence of practical and normative certainty. Machiavelli was indeed "extremely critical of irresoluteness and delay. Determination and will power were the qualities which might prevail against all reason."[93] In the last instance, Gilbert placed the emphasis on the limited nature of Machiavelli's rationalism: immersed in the ever-changing "stream of history," politics was the realm of pure contingency and could not take the form of rule-following. Machiavelli's genius was to rely on rationalistic conventions to deliver a message that limited the purview of reason in

---

[89] Gilbert, *To the Farewell Address*, 103.
[90] Gilbert, "The Humanist Concept of the Prince," 450, 470.
[91] Gilbert, *Machiavelli and Guicciardini*, 156–57.
[92] Gilbert, *Machiavelli and Guicciardini*, 157, 198.
[93] Gilbert, *Machiavelli and Guicciardini*, 157.

political affairs, to formulate a rational approach to politics that took into account and gave pride of place to what was *not* rational: his greatness was in "reveal[ing] – more than anyone before or after him, that, at any time, politics is choice and decision."⁹⁴ And to add *gravitas* to this judgment, Gilbert sealed it with the epitaph engraved on Machiavelli's tomb in Santa Croce: "*tanto nomini nullum par elogium.*"⁹⁵

While this portrait of Machiavelli was the result of a careful philological and historical reconstruction, Gilbert's choice of words suggests that he was also reading Machiavelli in light of recent political debates. In an essay on Meinecke's study of the political ideas of German academics from the nineteenth to the twentieth century published shortly after *Machiavelli and Guicciardini*, Gilbert dealt once again with political thinkers who "emphasiz[ed] will and decision rather than intellect." These thinkers, however, were not Renaissance politicians, but none other than Carl Schmitt and Karl Mannheim.⁹⁶ The use of identical terms to describe both what Gilbert considered to be the defining feature of Machiavelli's thought and Schmitt's decisionism or Mannheim's rejection of the possibility of fully rationalizing politics cannot be discounted as an unfortunate coincidence. It was symptomatic of the tendency to use Machiavelli as a surrogate for discussing the issues raised by the decisionist thinkers of the interwar period, and in particular the legitimacy of extra-constitutional measures. The more or less explicit connection between Machiavelli and Schmitt's theorization of emergency powers was not casual: It was on the mind of a number of German thinkers eager to salvage from the Nazi episode what they considered to be the still valuable contribution of decisionism to modern politics. In Gerhard Ritter's *Machtstaat und Utopie*, for instance, Machiavelli appeared as a Schmittian for whom the essence of politics subordinates "all moral and human considerations to the friend-foe relationship."⁹⁷ While Ritter deemed his realism morally deficient, it nonetheless found redemption in the emergency situation, since "self-preservation is a moral duty."⁹⁸

---

⁹⁴ Gilbert, *Machiavelli and Guicciardini*, 200.
⁹⁵ "No homage could match such a name."
⁹⁶ Felix Gilbert, "Political Power and Academic Responsibility: Reflections on Friedrich Meinecke's *Drei Generationen deutscher Gerlehrtenpolitik*," in *The Responsibility of Power: Historical Essays in Honor of Hajo Holborn*, eds., Leonard Krieger and Fritz Stern (New York: Doubleday & Co., 1967), 406.
⁹⁷ Quoted in Bock, "Meinecke, Machiavelli und der Nationalsozialismus," 168.
⁹⁸ Ritter, *The Corrupting Influence of Power*, 183.

In the United States, this casuistic justification of power politics and emergency powers could be dispensed with because of the robustness and intrinsic virtue of the constitutional order. Despite fears to the contrary, the exceptional measures of the New Deal had shown that the basic democratic framework of American society could be safeguarded through, if not thanks to, forms of administered governance.[99] If Schmitt's theory of dictatorship elicited much interest from American political scientists in the postwar years, it was essentially because it seemed to establish a solid distinction between constitutional and unconstitutional dictatorship.[100] It is no coincidence, then, that a previous disciple of Schmitt such as Carl Friedrich also turned to Machiavelli with a polemical intent vis-à-vis liberal constitutionalism in order to illustrate the importance of preserving a space for the reason of state in the context of constitutional government.[101] His *Constitutional Reason of State* (1957) invoked Machiavelli precisely because only "pre-liberal" political thought considered with sufficient clarity the existential issue facing modern democracies.[102] A few years later, Friedrich would go back to Machiavelli in order to suggest that the republican reason of state generated its own morality and its own rationality.[103]

These debates were perfectly known to Gilbert. He praised Friedrich's 1957 book for "clos[ing] a gap which Meinecke had left" and exploring the problem of the reason of state beyond absolutism. Friedrich's merit was to point out that "the constitutional thinkers of the past were aware that an emergency situation might arise in which the maintenance of legality might involve great risks for the continued existence of

---

[99] Katznelson, *Fear Itself*. After the war, the "consensus historians" would contribute to showing that the New Deal did not represent a parenthesis in American history, but on the contrary that it was in line with the core liberal values of American society. See Jewett, *Science, Democracy, and the American University*, 283.

[100] See the discussion in Chapter 6.

[101] See Augustin Simard, "La raison d'Etat constitutionnelle," *Canadian Journal of Political Science/Revue canadienne de science politique* 45, no. 1 (2012): 163–84. For a subtle historical analysis of the differences between Machiavelli and the "reason of state" tradition, see Michel Senellart, *Machiavélisme et raison d'Etat* (Paris: Presses Universitaires de France, 1989).

[102] Friedrich, *Constitutional Reason of State*. On Schmitt's influence on Friedrich, see Hans J. Lietzmann, "Von der Konstitutionellen zur totalitären Diktatur. Carl Joachim Friedrichs Totalitarismustheorie," in *Totalitarismus. Eine Ideengeschichte des 20. Jahrhunderts*, eds., Alfons Söllner, Ralf Walkenhaus, and Karin Wieland (Berlin: Akademie Verlag, 1997).

[103] Friedrich, "On Rereading Machiavelli and Althusius."

a constitutional order."[104] Gilbert could only agree with a colleague who, like him, suggested that absolutism was not the only historical course for the reason of state: Friedrich too was cobbling together an Atlantic tradition of power politics that fed directly into the American present. In this alternative tradition, Meinecke's dualism between politics and ethics subsided. Friedrich indeed "argue[d] convincingly that the problem of the reason of state did not exist for Machiavelli." Unburdened by the tradition of liberal constitutionalism or by legal positivism, unaffected by a conflict between legality and legitimacy that did not yet exist, Machiavelli could advocate robust measures departing from political and moral customs because he envisaged politics in relation to the concrete, historical existence of a free community.

Here, then, was the starting point for recovering power politics beyond the moral dilemma framed by Meinecke. Reengaging historically with Machiavelli made it possible to retrieve from the wreckage of the twentieth century an important line of political thought traditionally associated with authoritarian politics, and to reconsider it without being blinded by liberalism, yet without following the absolutist tradition ending with the illiberal thinkers of the interwar years. Gilbert's Machiavelli was thus informed by, and fed into, a discussion about emergency powers going back to the 1930s now revived by anxieties about the capacity of democracies to meet the challenges of the Cold War.[105] Gilbert may indeed have been the first one to see in Machiavelli a form of "republican exceptionalism" that contributed to the acclimatization of power politics in American political thought.[106]

SAN CASCIANO-ON-HUDSON: THE FLORENTINE RECRUIT OF A NEW ACADEMIC DISCIPLINE

It is difficult to ascertain whether Gilbert himself conceived of his work as a direct contribution to the invention of a realist "tradition." He certainly framed Machiavelli in terms that were indigenous to the postwar discussion about "realism" and "idealism" in international politics.[107] And by

---

[104] Felix Gilbert, review of *Constitutional Reason of State: The Survival of the Constitutional Order*, by C. J. Friedrich, *The American Historical Review* 64, no. 1 (1958): 68.
[105] Katznelson, *Fear Itself*.
[106] This notion appears in Nomi Claire Lazar, *States of Emergency in Liberal Democracies* (Cambridge: Cambridge University Press, 2009), 24.
[107] Machiavelli established a "demarcation between himself and his 'idealist' predecessors." Gilbert, "The Humanist Concept of the Prince," 450. The last chapter of the *Prince* was

painting the portrait of a republican Machiavelli concerned with the political capacity for decisive action unimpaired by moralistic strictures or utopian rationalism, he definitely lifted the obstacles that had previously condemned the Florentine to the opprobrium of the postwar realists. Whatever Gilbert's intentions may have been, the fact remains that the academic entrepreneurs involved in the institutionalization of international relations theory after 1945 saw his work as sufficiently relevant to their project to sponsor it.

In 1956, the Rockefeller Foundation funded the archival groundwork for *Machiavelli and Guicciardini*. While a number of historians received such funding at the time, what is surprising is that Gilbert was funded under a grant program not devoted to history: The support he received came from the recently established Program in Legal and Political Philosophy, Kenneth Thompson's fiefdom and the most important institution behind the diffusion of a realist approach to international relations in the 1950s. It funded both Gilbert's research for *Machiavelli and Guicciardini* and his subsequent work on Meinecke, as part of an effort at clarifying "the origins of political realism." Born under Meinecke's auspices, raised in the cozy atmosphere of Mead Earle's Princeton seminar, Gilbert's Machiavelli ultimately matured under the benevolent nursing of Kenneth Thompson, the philanthropic patron of international relations theory and political realism in the 1950s.

One can only build conjectures about the first contacts between Felix Gilbert and the Rockefeller Foundation. The Foundation had supported the making of *The Diplomats*, but it seems that contacts were made through Craig rather than Gilbert. It seems safer to assume that his family's extensive social networks were involved. One of Gilbert's uncles, Albrecht Mendelssohn Bartholdy, was a professor of international law and, with Max Weber and the historian of warfare Hans Delbrück, an early proponent of the creation of a German institute for foreign policy at the Versailles conference. He eventually became the first director of the resulting *Institute für Auswärtige Politik*, which received Rockefeller Foundation funding during the interwar years, and in this capacity he was also a member of the Rockefeller Committee in Berlin.[108] Gilbert thus

---

probably appended at a later date because its "emotional idealism" did not fit with the preceding "realism." Felix Gilbert, "The Concept of Nationalism in Machiavelli's Prince," *Studies in the Renaissance* 1 (1954): 38, 39.

[108] Gilbert, *A European Past*, 84.

had a direct connection with the higher echelons of the Foundation, and a name that certainly elicited goodwill from its officers.

In any event, when he met with Kenneth Thompson, Gilbert found a receptive interlocutor. A first meeting in May 1954, meant to discuss the state of diplomatic history, revealed that Gilbert, whom Thompson thought was a "stimulating, thoughtful and imaginative scholar," was currently embarked upon a project focused on "16th century Italian international relations."[109] This meeting, of a fact-finding nature, paved the way for a second one, in which Gilbert probed the possibility of having the Foundation support the research sabbatical he needed to work on historical documents at the Warburg Institute in London and the *archivio di Stato* in Florence. Meeting again with Thompson in November 1954, Gilbert explained that he planned to spend the academic year 1955–56 working on Machiavelli's theory of politics. In the formal inquiry he sent a few weeks later, he presented his project as being focused on "the theory of international relations in the sixteenth century." He was very clear that his research in European archives would address a question of contemporary relevance. In studying the role of Machiavelli and Guicciardini, his purpose was to break with traditional scholarship, which treated them as isolated phenomena: "I am interested ... in investigating their thought from the point of view of clarifying the relationship between political science and historiography." Gilbert was touching upon a key issue that was at the center of the discussions surrounding the birth of IR theory. He was in fact emphasizing its relevance to the debates about the nature of political knowledge, caught between history and science, and its place in universities transformed by the behavioral social sciences. Much remained to be done, he continued, in order to understand the sixteenth-century "turning point toward realism." There was primarily a need to study the emergence of new political concepts, and he intended to work in particular on a new intellectual approach to foreign affairs, which had generated many of the notions still guiding twentieth-century diplomacy, from the "balance of power" to the notion of the state system. Here again, the point was to "elucidate the presuppositions which underlie the conceptual framework of our own political thought."[110]

---

[109] Interview with Felix Gilbert, Kenneth W. Thompson, May 17, 1954, Folder 4137, Box 484, Series 200S, RG 1.2, RF, RAC.
[110] Felix Gilbert to Kenneth W. Thompson, December 10, 1954, Folder 4137, Box 484, Series 200S, RG 1.2, RF, RAC.

Gilbert's request was strongly supported by the referees whom Thompson consulted upon Gilbert's suggestion, and who included both historians and political scientists (Gordon Craig, Sigmund Neumann, H. Stuart Hughes, Isaiah Berlin, Hans Morgenthau, Hajo Holborn), some of whom were former OSS colleagues. Morgenthau, who had tried a few years earlier to hire Gilbert at his Center for the Study of American Foreign Policy in Chicago to work on early US foreign policy (a task for which he finally recruited the Viennese historian Gerald Stourzh), had only praise for Gilbert and his project. While he had disparaged Machiavelli as a cynical utopian ten years before, he was now strongly supporting "a study of political realism in the 16th century" because of the considerable contemporary relevance it would have.[111]

But the most clear-sighted endorsement probably came from Gilbert's friend and former Meinecke student, the historian Hajo Holborn. Holborn was the first occupant – at 29 years – of the Carnegie-funded chair for the study of international relations at Berlin's *Hochschule für Politik*, and he had an immediate grasp of the stakes of Gilbert's work on Machiavelli for contemporary politics. He observed that in the Anglophone tradition, most of the work on the rise of modern political theory had focused on representative government and civil rights, overlooking the "absolutistic or power state." "A trail was blazed by Friedrich Meinecke's *Idea of the Raison d'Etat* [sic] but the book is not an answer to many of the problems implied ... " Gilbert's work was important because it would enrich "not only the knowledge of 16th century history but the orientation of our own political thinking."[112]

The other references were equally praiseful, and on the 23rd of February, the Rockefeller Foundation decided to award Gilbert a $5,400 grant for the study of "the origins of political realism." The additional information included in the grant docket stated that "the study of political science and international relations has been marked by an increasing interest in the principles and forces governing political conduct ... The early Florentine political realists including

---

[111] Hans J. Morgenthau to Kenneth W. Thompson, January 31, 1955, Folder 4137, Box 484, Series 200S, RG 1.2, RF, RAC.

[112] Hajo Holborn to Kenneth W. Thompson, January 31, 1955, Folder 4137, Box 484, Series 200S, RG 1.2, RF, RAC. See also Otto P. Pflanze, "The Americanization of Hajo Holborn," in *An Interrupted Past: German-Speaking Refugee Historians in the United States after 1933*, eds., Hartmut Lehmann and James J. Sheehan (Washington, DC and Cambridge: German Historical Institute, Cambridge University Press, 1991).

Machiavelli and Guicciardini were among the first to grapple with this problem."[113]

This was an important grant for several reasons. It was one of the early grants of the Legal and Political Philosophy program meant to strengthen international relations theory. Of course, Gilbert was in part facing the problem of all German refugee historians who had to "attract funding not specifically designed for their field," given the lack of prior international networks in history.[114] But historians such as himself or Holborn came to the United States already versed in the study of international relations and did not have to craft their projects in ways designed to meet the programing constraints of potential sponsors. It is clear that for Gilbert's referees, for the Rockefeller Foundation, and probably for Gilbert himself, the topic of *Machiavelli and Guicciardini* was directly connected to the question of political realism in the twentieth century and to the consolidation of a new approach to international politics. His proposal also came at the right time: Thompson had just convened the May 1954 meeting in an effort to oppose the reduction of the study of politics to a behavioral social science, blind to the contingency and uniqueness of historical situations. In this context, Gilbert provided a powerful antidote against the scientization of politics. His Machiavelli relied on rationalistic conventions to convey a historicist message that refused the resolution of politics into an abstract rationalism and kept it fully immersed "in the ever-moving stream of history."[115] But if politics could not be reduced to technical expertise, it could not be conflated either with democratic deliberation: "reason of state" or "security" considerations required the statesmanship of seasoned politicians, who understood that the logic of power and time occasionally demanded an expediency violating established norms. The rehabilitation of power politics via the Renaissance dovetailed with the ideological agenda of postwar realism, and in particular its repeated calls for insulating foreign policy from the liberal values it was meant to defend. It also provided realism with a long and prestigious historical tradition that enhanced its status and, more importantly, obfuscated its

---

[113] "Grant in aid to Bryn Mawr College," February 23, 1955, Folder 4137, Box 484, Series 200S, RG 1.2, RF, RAC.

[114] Karen J. Greenberg, "'Uphill Work': The German Refugee Historians and American Institutions of Higher Learning," in *An Interrupted Past: German-Speaking Refugee Historians in the United States after 1933*, eds., Hartmut Lehmann and James J. Sheehan (Washington, DC and Cambridge: German Historical Institute, Cambridge University Press, 1991), 100.

[115] Gilbert, *Machiavelli and Guicciardini*, 199.

direct antecedents in German historicism and in the interwar critiques of liberal democracy.

Felix Gilbert was the perfect embodiment of the new breed of academics auspicated by Edward Mead Earle, for whom "the grand strategy of American security" ought to be formulated, among other things, "in reference to our history, traditions and aspirations."[116] In Gilbert's view, Machiavelli stood for a tradition of power politics and an attachment to republican values both of which informed American political culture. If, as Judith Shklar once noted, "political realism [wa]s radical only in its rebellion against American traditions," then Gilbert did much to acclimatize it in America.[117] His scholarship is a reminder that all historical work is grounded in the present. His treatment of Machiavelli was not the independent corroboration by a historian of a realist tradition intuitively understood by international relations scholars, but an active force shaping this tradition and creating a new historical narrative for the reason of state, now redefined as "security." As a result, the notion of a long realist "tradition" must be turned on its head: Modern realism is not a distant legacy of a tradition inaugurated by Machiavelli; rather, it is the realist Machiavelli familiar to us who is the outcome of a moment in the historiography of the Renaissance partly shaped by the emergence of the national security state and its academic disciplines. Gilbert's scholarship must be resituated within the postwar realist movement, next to the work of Hans Morgenthau, John Herz, Reinhold Niebuhr, Herbert Butterfield, or Raymond Aron, and as part of the same effort to uphold the ideal of traditional diplomacy and to insulate foreign policy from both the democratization of politics and its transformation into scientific expertise. For sure, these ideas fared better now that they came in the garb of a majestic fresco of the Florentine *cinquecento*, rather than coated in the *chiaroscuro* of the realist counter-enlightenment or, worse, the darkest hours of the Weimar republic. If the power political state of the Renaissance was indeed a "work of art," as Burckhardt had suggested, then realism could claim a place of pride as one the highest achievements of European culture. Gilbert's feat was thus to generate a tradition where there had been none so far, and to fold into it a Machiavelli whom the realists still ostracized only a few years earlier, turning him indeed into the "first modern realist." *Tanto nomini nullum par elogium.*

---

[116] Edward Mead Earle, "The Princeton Program of Military Studies," 3.
[117] Judith N. Shklar, "Decisionism," in *Rational Decision*, ed. Carl J. Friedrich, Nomos (New Brunswick: Transaction, 1964), 12–13.

4

The Kuhning of Reason: Political Realism and Decision-Making after Thomas Kuhn

A SCIENCE OF FOREIGN POLICY DECISIONS?

With the benefit of hindsight, it seems that the suspicion of postwar realists vis-à-vis the scientific study of politics was the infantile disorder of international relations theory. In the words of Kenneth Waltz, who could arguably claim to be the legitimate heir to the postwar realists through a direct lineage, there was realist *thought*, but only neorealist *theory*. Only in the late 1970s – that is, once it assimilated Waltz's contribution – did the discipline premised on realist political wisdom upgrade to the status of science.[1] We will meet Waltz again in the last chapter of this book, but for now it is sufficient to note that something seems to have dramatically changed in the way political realists account for the knowledge they claim to hold. A theory born from the deliberate intent to insulate the study of politics from the scientific method and uphold traditional notions of politics as an "art" and not as a "science," as an exercise in "prudence" and *virtù*, has become one of the most formalized, mathematized, game-theoretical disciplines in political science departments, and probably one that is deeply attached to its status as a "science," drawing heavily on rational choice models.[2] How did realism come to embody the most "scientific" and "rational" approach to politics?

The rejection of political science was certainly a heavy handicap impairing the development of the discipline in the academic context of the 1950s and 1960s, won over by the appeal of behavioralism and a new

---

[1] Kenneth Waltz, "Realist Thought and Neorealist Theory," in *Realism and International Politics* (New York: Routledge, 2008).
[2] See for instance Bruce Bueno de Mesquita, *Principles of International Politics* (Thousand Oaks: CQ Press, 2014).

approach to social science promising to resolve everything into the notion of "system."³ In the mid-1960s, minor intellectual skirmishes erupted between historically minded, traditional realists and younger advocates of a sciency approach to politics eager to shore up their professional credentials in an age enraptured by rocket science. This squabble rapidly won the status of a defining moment for the discipline – known to the insiders as the "second debate" – which supposedly heralded the permanent return of international relations theory to the capacious house of high modernist social science.⁴ As we shall see in Chapter 5, however, this victory was a Pyrrhic one. The "science" that a new generation of realists was seeking to emulate was of a new kind, and fundamentally different from the kind of positivism abhorrent to orthodox realists. It was, in fact, hardly scientific – more of a hodge-podge of experimental protocols, modelization tools, and suggestive hypotheses for thinking about a problem. The result was not so much the disappearance of classical political realism as the emergence of a "new" realism that would ultimately find its most convincing interpreter in Kenneth Waltz.⁵

The notion of a gradual conversion of political realists to a scientific treatment of strategic and political issues conceals a more complex, and in part inverse, phenomenon: the transformation of dominant conceptions of science in a direction congruent with realism itself, away from previous beliefs in the existence of a superior domain of knowledge expected to generate a "truth" that could trump politics and thus orient it. As David Hollinger writes, invocations of science tell us "less about how science works than about the cultural conflicts in society at large."⁶

THE STRUCTURE OF A SCIENTIFIC INVOLUTION

A good indicator of this changing relationship between science and power is provided by the meteoric impact that the publication of Thomas Kuhn's

---

[3] Hunter Heyck, *Age of System: Understanding the Development of Modern Social Science* (Baltimore: Johns Hopkins University Press, 2015).
[4] The canonical interventions in this "debate" are: Hedley Bull, "International Theory: The Case for a Classical Approach," *World Politics* 18, no. 3 (1966): 361–77; Morton A. Kaplan, "The New Great Debate: Traditionalism Vs. Science in International Relations," *World Politics* 19, no. 1 (1966): 1–20; and the attack on scientific methods by Morgenthau: Hans J. Morgenthau, "Supplement: International Relations, 1960–1964," *Annals of the American Academy of Political and Social Science* 360 (1965): 163–71.
[5] See Chapter 6.
[6] David A. Hollinger, *Science, Jews, and Secular Culture: Studies in Mid-Twentieth-Century American Intellectual History* (Princeton: Princeton University Press, 1996), 157.

Structure of Scientific Revolutions in 1962 had on a discipline built upon the rejection of science and a deep suspicion vis-à-vis revolutions. There is indeed something utterly perplexing about the infatuation of international relations theorists with the work of Thomas Kuhn starting in the mid-1960s, not least because it was later followed by the rejection of the various shibboleths previously gleaned in the pages of *The Structure of Scientific Revolutions*, from "paradigms" to "incommensurability." It is almost as if the discipline went through a Kuhnian *Gestalt* switch, whereby the very things that international relations theorists initially found so exciting in Kuhn were suddenly jettisoned, leading an entire cohort of scholars to look for new idols among the ranks of the Popperian Kuhn-bashers gathered at the International Colloquium in the Philosophy of Science or in the "critical realism" movement associated with Rom Harré or Roy Bhaskar.[7] Rarely has an object of so much adulation become reviled so rapidly. In retrospect, these ambivalent feelings raise the question of what, exactly, Kuhn stood for in international relations theory. The question is compounded by the fact that the reasons for which the discipline embraced Kuhn in the first place were often self-contradictory.

Consider indeed the causes of Kuhn's initial popularity among IR theorists: for some, he provided a model for the history of science that could be applied with minor tweaks to political science and suggested that structural realism was indeed a scientific-grade theory of international politics.[8] For others, his sociological vision of science was a formidable weapon against "positivism," which could be putatively deployed against realism.[9] Philip Mirowski points out that for many in the social sciences,

---

[7] Terence Ball traced a similar trajectory of Kuhn within political science, before endorsing Lakatos like everybody else: Terence Ball, "From Paradigms to Research Programs: Toward a Post-Kuhnian Political Science," *American Journal of Political Science* 20, no. 1 (1976): 151–77. See also Imre Lakatos and Alan Musgrave, eds., *Criticism and the Growth of Knowledge*, Proceedings of the International Colloquium in the Philosophy of Science (Cambridge: Cambridge University Press, 1970); Heikki Patomaki and Colin Wight, "After Postpositivism? The Promises of Critical Realism," *International Studies Quarterly* 44, no. 2 (2000): 213–37; Fred Chernoff, "Scientific Realism as a Meta-Theory of International Politics," *International Studies Quarterly* 46, no. 2 (2002): 189–207.

[8] Arend Lijphart, "The Structure of the Theoretical Revolution in International Relations," *International Studies Quarterly* 18, no. 1 (1974): 41–74.

[9] Like all words in "-ism," positivism suffers from semantic fuzziness. Here, I will follow Ayer and consider "positivism" to be a diluted version of logical positivism according to which it is only "required that a statement be capable of being in some degree confirmed of disconfirmed by observation," A. J. Ayer, ed. *Logical Positivism* (New York: The Free

Kuhn offered a fresh departure from the algorithmic notion of rationality that was dominant at the time.[10] In IR, the notions of paradigms and incommensurability meant that there was no need to feel sorry about the state of a discipline marred by fragmentation, but that there was no need either to relinquish pretensions to scientific rigor.[11] And by enshrining the impossibility of validating or refuting a scientific paradigm on the basis of a set of neutral logical criteria, the incommensurability thesis played a protectionist role in carving out a space for the development of intellectual "infant industries" – such as transnational studies or international political economy – outside the realist mainstream and shielded them from criticism.[12] Some saw Kuhn as a revolutionary thinker, who encouraged "radical re-thinking, focused on 'deep' problems rather than ... the routine 'puzzle-solving'"[13]; yet this did not deter others to suggest that he had certainly set IR on a course leading toward "normal science" and its puzzle-solving powers.[14] All these contradictory assessments suggest each had their own Kuhn, who may have been a very different person from the author of *Structure*.

By the 1990s, however, the Kuhnfest had come to an end and the hangover was tangible. Yet, the reasons for ditching Kuhn were just as self-contradictory as those that had made him so popular in the first place. Many now claimed that Kuhn's model did not apply to the social sciences after all: the attempts at enlisting Kuhn to justify progress were simply a "misuse" of his work[15]; his sociology of science was inadequate to

---

Press, 1959), 14. This is in line with the use of the term in IR, for instance by Kenneth Waltz, when he attacks the "crassly positivist ideas" of those who think that theories must be evaluated with observations: Kenneth Waltz, "Foreword: Thoughts About Assaying Theories," in *Progress in International Relations Theory: Appraising the Field*, eds., Colin Elman and Miriam Fendius Elman (Cambridge, MA: MIT Press, 2003), ix, xii.

[10] Philip Mirowski, "What's Kuhn Got to Do with It?" *Social Epistemology* 17, nos. 2&3 (2003): 231.

[11] Steve Smith, "Paradigm Dominance in International Relations: The Development of International Relations as a Social Science," *Millennium: Journal of International Studies* 16, no. 2 (1987): 189–206.

[12] Ole Waever, "The Rise and Fall of the Inter-Paradigm Debate," in *International Theory: Positivism and Beyond*, eds., Steve Smith, Ken Booth, and Marysia Zalewski (Cambridge: Cambridge University Press, 1996).

[13] Michael Banks, "The Evolution of International Relations Theory," in *Conflict in World Society: A New Perspective on International Relations*, ed. Michael Banks (New York: St. Martin's Press, 1984), 15.

[14] Lijphart, "Structure."

[15] Brian C. Schmidt, "On the History and Historiography of International Relations," in *Handbook of International Relations*, eds., Walter Carlsnaes, Thomas Risse, and Beth A Simmons (London: Sage, 2013), 11.

understand the structure of IR as a discipline, although a few admirers felt nostalgia for the lost world of paradigms[16]; his reconstruction of the history of science was equally deficient.[17] Even worse, in the eyes of those who did not recognize themselves in realism, rather than facilitating the coexistence of various approaches in the discipline, Kuhn had played an essentially conservative role by consolidating realism into "normal science."[18] Unless what had happened was just the opposite: The "paradigm mentality" had fostered the "Balkanization" of international relations theory into small, fiercely independent territories.[19] As one can expect, the most unforgiving critics often happened to be former fans: After participating in the bacchanal and proposing an *über-Kuhnian* interpretation of the evolution of the discipline in 1987, Steve Smith later recanted by confessing that despite the original impression that paradigm-thinking was "liberating," it turned out to be "just another gate-keeping device for maintaining the status-quo."[20] Others followed suit and denounced the incommensurability thesis for being a "legitimating device [...] for theoretical fragmentation" that stifled criticism and thus, presumably, could only work to the benefit of a still hegemonic realism.[21] Besides, the discipline had moved on – unless, as

---

[16] Ole Waever, "The Sociology of a Not So International Discipline: American and European Developments in International Relations," *International Organization* 52, no. 4 (1998): 687–727. For a defense of Kuhn's usefulness for the history of IR theory, see John A. Vasquez, "Kuhn vs. Lakatos? The Case for Multiple Frames in Appraising IR Theory," in *Progress in International Relations Theory: Appraising the Field*, eds., Colin Elman and Miriam Fendius Elman, (Cambridge, MA: MIT Press, 2003) and Richard W. Mansbach and John A. Vasquez, *In Search of Theory: A New Paradigm for Global Politics* (New York: Columbia University Press, 1981), 12.

[17] Lucian Ashworth, "The Poverty of Paradigms: Subcultures, Trading Zones and the Case of Liberal Socialism in Interwar International Relations," *International Relations* 26, no. 1 (2012): 35–59.

[18] Kenneth E. Boulding, "Future Directions in Conflict and Peace Studies," in *Conflict: Readings in Management and Resolution*, eds., John Burton and Frank Dukes (London: Macmillan, 1990), 38, quoted in Thomas C. Walker, "The Perils of Paradigm Mentalities: Revisiting Kuhn, Lakatos, and Popper," *Perspectives on Politics* 8, no. 2 (2012): 433–51; Steve Smith, "The Forty Years' Detour: The Resurgence of Normative Theory in International Relations," *Millennium: Journal of International Studies* 21, no. 3 (1992): 489–506.

[19] Walker, "The Perils of Paradigm Mentalities," 443.

[20] Smith, "Development of International Relations"; Smith, "The Forty Years' Detour," 494.

[21] Colin Wight, "Incommensurability and Cross-Paradigm Communication in International Relations Theory: What's the Frequency Kenneth?" *Millennium: Journal of International Studies* 25, no. 2 (1996): 292.

some started to suspect, it had never really looked like the archipelago of insulated paradigms that IR scholars inebriated with Kuhn would have us believe it was: the so-called third debate between realism, pluralism, and structuralism may have never taken place.[22] These theoretical aggregates were far from incommensurable, as a result of which the notion of "paradigms" generated "deleterious effects" in a discipline better understood in conventional, ideal-typical Weberian terms.[23] In either case, only confusion had come out of the intemperate consumption of Kuhn.

One is tempted to put this dramatic reversal of fortune on the account of the more general waning of Kuhn's prestige in science studies, where the author of *Structure* has been for some time the object of much soul-searching into the reasons behind what many now view as an unwarranted intellectual success. Steve Fuller blames him for having produced a duplicitous version of science history meant to protect the patronage of science while generating accounts acceptable to all parties, and for having eased humanists and social scientists, among others, "into a post-modern mindset."[24] David Stove has excoriated Kuhn for being the founding father of postmodern irrationalism.[25] Philip Mirowski has pointed out his connection with operation research and the emergence of a science management regime shielded from public scrutiny and subservient to the needs of the Cold War establishment.[26] Even the more sympathetic accounts collected in a recent celebratory issue of the *Journal of Modern History* do not fail to emphasize Kuhn's fundamental ambiguities. By reproducing this pattern, it would not be the first time, after all, that the discipline of International Relations passively registers trends happening elsewhere. Yet, a number of things suggest that Kuhn has not been just a passing fad in IR.

It is common knowledge that international relations theorists have largely misused and misinterpreted Kuhn, but this diagnosis, along with the shift *en masse* to Lakatos, has prevented us to probe deeper into his actual impact. One of his legacies was surely to encourage the representation of IR as a congeries of contending "paradigms," despite the fact that

---

[22] Waever, "Rise and Fall."
[23] Patrick Thaddeus Jackson and Daniel H. Nexon, "Paradigmatic Faults in International-Relations Theory," *International Studies Quarterly* 53, no. 4 (2009): 919.
[24] Steve Fuller, *Thomas Kuhn: A Philosophical History for Our Times* (Chicago: The University of Chicago Press, 2000), 31.
[25] David Stove, *Scientific Irrationalism: Origins of a Postmodern Cult* (New Brunswick: Transaction Publishers, 2001).
[26] Mirowski, "What's Kuhn Got to Do with It?"

such a situation was not considered by Kuhn himself, who envisioned paradigms only in their succession and never really contemplated their simultaneity, and despite the fact that the "-isms" of IR theory can hardly qualify as genuinely Kuhnian paradigms. IR thus started to look very much like the fragmented world of sovereign states it sought to understand, rather than like a succession of epistemological empires. More surprisingly, Kuhn's capacity to serve agendas in every quarter of the discipline and in particular to support both the agenda of neorealists and that of their postpositivist critics suggests that the reception of *Structure* was a paradoxical factor of integration at a time of strong disciplinary divisions. As everybody could pick their own Kuhn, he became the point of intersection between allegedly incommensurable worldviews. It must be said that Kuhn himself was partly responsible for this state of affairs. The fact that there was a myriad of "possible Kuhns" to choose from in the absence of arbitration by Kuhn himself seems to vindicate those who, like Feyerabend, had suggested early on that Kuhn's ambiguity was "*intended* and that [he] want[ed] to fully exploit its propagandistic potentialities," or those who, like Terence Ball, claimed that while political scientists had taken *Structure*'s message to heart, "few can say with certainty what that message is."[27] Logical undecidability always means that the decision is, ultimately, political – something that, incidentally, was central to Kuhn's vision of science.

In tracing the "Kuhn effect" in IR, I want to clarify upfront that I am not seeking to adjudicate between erroneous and correct interpretations of Kuhn: instead, I am interested in is the reception of *Structure*, no matter how creative or abusive some interpretations have been. As long as Kuhn was invoked to make specific moves in the discipline, it did not matter whether the underlying interpretation of his theory was flawed or not, since it had real consequences. First, I want to suggest that the main reason for Kuhn's felicitous career in IR was that he offered a way out of the "second great debate" by providing an image of science that could accommodate realism's traditional suspicion vis-à-vis any form of robust rationalism. What *Structure* did was to explode the framework of classical realism, the exemplary – dare I say paradigmatic? – expression of which

---

[27] Kenneth L. Caneva, "Possible Kuhns in the History of Science: Anomalies of Incommensurable Paradigms," *Studies in History and Philosophy of Science* 31, no. 1 (2000): 87–124; Paul Feyerabend, "Consolations for the Specialist," in *Criticism and the Growth of Knowledge*, eds., Imre Lakatos and Alan Musgrave (Cambridge: Cambridge University Press, 1970), 199; Ball, "From Paradigms to Research Programs," 151.

was Morgenthau's *Scientific Man vs. Power Politics*, which was still premised upon a radical opposition between science and politics. *Structure* suggested that science too had its dark side, its irrational areas, and even its power politics. By suggesting that scientific revolutions were essentially a matter of power, Kuhn was applying something akin to realist principles in the field of epistemology. This did not only suggest that "science" was safe for realism after all: it also suggested that political realism was nothing short of a theory of scientific knowledge. To put it differently, if *Structure* proved so fascinating to a discipline that initially did not want to have anything to do with science, it is because it resonated, at some level, with realism itself. Kuhn's realism has so far remained the proverbial elephant in the room, and it took an outsider – a historian of science – to spell out the political implications of *Structure* that some realists had intuitively grasped.[28]

This leads us to the second argument developed in this chapter: If the Kuhn effect proved so important in IR, it may be because, as Steve Fuller aptly observed, "international relations is perhaps the one field in which Kuhn has been used to model not the field's research trajectory *but its very subject matter*," namely decision-making.[29] It is striking that while Kuhn was discussed by many international relations theorists, those who looked up to him in order to actually *explain* international politics were primarily concerned with establishing criteria of rationality for political decisions. Until then, as we have seen in previous chapters, the entire field of IR was premised on a "decisionist" vision of politics that emphasized the contingency and situatedness of politics in order to repel the notion that political conduct could take the form of rule following and that politics could be comprehended by scientific rationalism. Against the prior focus of the field of international law, postwar realism had drawn discretely on the critiques of legal positivism as a "scientific" codification of international relations: the rules of international law had no import for power relations, which were essentially a matter of decisions. No "science" of such decisions could ever obtain – only a prudence informed by historical knowledge. In this context, Kuhn was read in a very specific way: He was seen as offering an image of scientific rationality that could be used as a benchmark for politics because it also broke with legalism and the representation of science as a body of laws growing organically. Science too was now characterized by the uncertainty, relativity, and limitations found in political rationality. This is what made Kuhn so congenial to

---

[28] See Fuller, *Thomas Kuhn*, 170ff.   [29] Fuller, *Thomas Kuhn*, 175 fn. 72.

some IR theorists: he allowed them to be "scientific" without having to relinquish a single assumption of political realism. Two classics used to teach foreign policy decision-making in pol. sci. departments, Graham Allison's *Essence of Decision* (1971) or Robert Jervis' *Perception and Misperception in International Politics* (1976), thus used Kuhn to guard themselves *against* an over-rationalization of the process of decision-making while reaping the benefits of a "scientific" analogy. Kuhn himself was aware of the analogies between politics and his vision of science, and by remaining suggestively elusive as to their implications he left open the possibility of far-fetched interpretations. Much more than his role in shaping the self-image of the discipline, Kuhn's deep and lasting impact on IR was to reconcile scientific man with power politics by suggesting that the former was just another rank-and-file realist.

SCIENCE IS LIKE A BOX OF CHOCOLATES...

In order to understand the impact that *The Structure of Scientific Revolutions* had on international relations theory, it is useful to first set the stage on which Kuhn made his triumphal entrance in the discipline. Although the book was published in 1962, its digestion by IR started only after a brief physiological lag, during which it first reached the shores of political science and psychology, in particular as applied to strategic decision-making problems, where it was enlisted to build consensus around abstract behavioral models and secure the paradigmatic status of the notion of "system."[30] By the time Kuhn was metabolized by international relations theorists in the late 1960s, the discipline was in the throes of the internecine guerilla warfare known as the "second debate," which opposed "traditionalist" thinkers who defended the idea that politics was an existential and historical phenomenon escaping the strictures of scientific knowledge, and "behavioral" social scientists entranced by their recent discovery of cybernetics, general systems theory and games. The former insisted on the constitutive circularity of knowledge, which, even in its most rationalized manifestations, could not escape its situated historical condition, whereas the latter believed that scientific knowledge was defined precisely by its complete detachment from historical reality and its confinement to the netherworld of models and simulations. While

---

[30] For a first IR take on Kuhn, see Robert H. Davis, "The International Influence Process: How Relevant Is the Contribution of Psychologists?" *American Psychologist* 21, no. 3 (1966): 236–43.

the actual positions were probably much closer than it appeared at first sight and remained largely internal to the "realist" mainstream, the debate was dramatized as a radical opposition between "realism" (or "history") and "science," which explains why it remained largely inconclusive.[31]

While Steve Fuller has proposed to see Kuhn as an alter ego of "Chance," the main character in Jerzy Kozinski's novel *Being There*, whose simple pronouncements are taken as the expression of a profound wisdom, *Forrest Gump* may provide a better interpretive frame for Kuhn's influence in IR. Just as Gump finds himself caught in the midst of momentous historical events that he has nothing to do with, yet contributes to defining, Kuhn walked by chance into the discipline in the midst of the so-called second debate and unwittingly delineated a way out of it. While factions were fighting over the meaning of science and the role of history, he was conscripted by both sides to support their position – and he obliged ("I just be doin what I'm tole" says Gump to his football coach, and this may well be the key to Kuhn's success in all the different precincts of IR[32]). Kuhn offered indeed a version of science everybody could embrace: He vindicated the behavioralist claims to represent a truly scientific approach to international politics, not least by offering a perspective on the *history* of their discipline in which they featured as the vanguard of the scientific revolution. But he also seemed to give *epistemological* substance to their opponents' claim that any meaningful statement about international relations "must ... derive from a scientifically imperfect process of perception and intuition" rather than *ex tempore* laws or rules, and thus that even "science" was still expressing a partial perspective on the world.[33] Kuhn's formidable traction in the discipline was directly connected to the fact that he seemed to reconcile these arguments as the two faces of the same coin. Science was indeed premised on two different "truths" – one for the historians, one for the scientists – and this suddenly cast the second debate in a different light by suggesting that it was entirely moot. Just like Forrest Gump's biography is a conservative American pastoral leading up to the cultural reconciliation of a divided nation, Kuhn's two-decade-long marathon through IR secured the unity of the discipline during a time of deep divisions and ultimately reconciled the historically minded IR

---

[31] Cameron Thies, "Myth, Half-Truth, Reality or Strategy? Managing Disciplinary Identity and the Origins of the First Great Debate," in *International Relations and the First Great Debate*, ed. Brian C. Schmidt (New York: Routledge, 2012).
[32] Winston Groom, *Forrest Gump* (New York: Washington Square Press, 1986), 23.
[33] Bull, "International Theory," 361.

scholar with his rocket-scientist counterpart. Let us examine how the historical and the epistemological argument have been used.

It was in his capacity as historian of science that Kuhn was conscripted by those who advocated the mainstreaming of the behavioral science model. If the history of their discipline could be plausibly told as a paradigm-anomalies-scientific revolution sequence, then surely it was a science. In the mid-1960s, Kuhn thus starred prominently in the keynote speeches given by the presidents of the American Political Science Association: David Truman in 1965 and then Gabriel Almond in 1966 established a new historical interpretation of the development of the discipline. Beyond minute differences, the general canvass they offered was roughly the same: from the mid-nineteenth century to the 1930s, a first "paradigm" had prevailed, characterized by an unsophisticated empiricism premised on the parochial belief in the naturalness of "the separation of powers, checks and balances, and the mixed constitution." Its paradigmatic force was illustrated by the fact that even the challenges formulated at the end of the century – interest groups theory, administrative complexity, etc. – "were still prisoners of the theory" and were expressed in its language.[34] It took "experiences" falling "outside the implicit general agreement" as well as the accumulation of "anomalous findings" throughout the 1930s and after World War II to undermine it.[35] From their vantage point, Truman and Almond both concurred that "a new paradigm [was] developing in political science," and that it was defined by the concept of "system": "the introduction of the system concept represents a genuinely important step in the direction of science ... Taking place in the era of the scientific revolution it represents a surer thrust into the culture of modern science."[36]

Almond's view of the new political science contained two elements that predisposed it to be reproduced in the field of international relations. The first was that the traditional paradigm of the separation of powers in political science was, *mutatis mutandis*, easily translatable as a paradigm of the balance of power. The second was that the crisis and the subsequent scientific revolution leading to "systematic" science were premised on anomalies that, combined, amounted to "the disproof of the

---

[34] Gabriel A. Almond, "Political Theory and Political Science," *The American Political Science Review* 60, no. 4 (1966): 870, 873.

[35] David B. Truman, "Disillusion and Regeneration: The Quest for a Discipline," *The American Political Science Review* 59, no. 4 (1965): 865–73; Almond, "Political Theory and Political Science," 875.

[36] Almond, "Political Theory," 85.

Enlightenment historical predictions" – an assumption that could only resonate with the realist critiques of the Enlightenment.[37]

The first adaptation of this historical argument to IR was first made two years later by a student of Harold Sprout, Ronald Rogowski. Rogowski provided a historical reconstruction of IR in explicitly Kuhnian terms, which assumed that following the "profound anomaly" of World War I, the traditional reliance on international law as the master representation of international relations was displaced by an approach that stressed the relations between multiple actors and did not take for granted the spontaneous emergence of a balance of power. As investigations moved beyond the old legalistic vision, they gradually evolved all the attributes of an alternative paradigm, concerned with the "realities" of a balance that had to be maintained through the purposive decisions of statesmen. The debate between realists and idealists, Rogowski pointed out, was nothing but an "internal squabble" over the best ways to achieve this – it was just that "a victorious generation of 'realists' found it useful in mopping up to consign all 'idealists,' prescriptive international lawyers and altruistic students of international relations alike, to the same limbo." The result was the modern, realist paradigm of IR that "attained textbook status at Morgenthau's hands in 1948." This paradigm, however, came under attack a decade later as a variety of authors – Morton Kaplan, Richard Rosecrance, Charles McClelland, Thomas Shelling, Kenneth Waltz – analyzed international politics using approaches relying on the notion of "system."[38]

This reading seemed to be confirmed a few years later by Arend Lijphart. Walking in the steps of Almond but seemingly unaware of Rogowski's earlier piece, Lijphart suggested that the history of IR exhibited a "clear pattern" of development.[39] This pattern consisted in a "traditional paradigm" going back to Thucydides and based on the notion of sovereignty and anarchy. The last remnants of this paradigm were to be found in the writings of "traditionalist" realists such as Hans Morgenthau, Arnold Wolfers, Stanley Hoffman, or Raymond Aron.[40] Finessing the discrepancies between IR and Kuhnian "mature science," Lijphart suggested that something close to "normal science" obtained in the discipline until World War II, when the cumulative effect of

---

[37] Ibid.
[38] Ronald Rogowski, "International Politics: The Past as Science," *International Studies Quarterly* 12, no. 4 (1968): 406–08.
[39] Lijphart, "Structure," 41.   [40] Lijphart, "Structure," 53–54.

"discrepancies" between the traditional paradigm and reality displaced it and allowed for the emergence of new methods reflecting a fundamentally different perspective. What characterized these was that they no longer saw the world as anarchical, since they subsumed sovereign decisions and conflict under the all-encompassing concept of "system." A scientific revolution thus took place in the 1950s and saw the emergence of what he called the "behavioral paradigm." It is precisely because the second debate was a dialogue of the deaf – "the two schools are really looking at different worlds," Lijphart said[41] – that it was proof that a paradigmatic shift was taking place and a sure sign of the scientific normalization of IR. Years later, Waltz's *Theory of International Politics* would enshrine the new paradigm.

... YOU CAN PICK WHICHEVER ONES YOU LIKE

But if Kuhn provided fodder for those who defended the scientific normalization of IR, he also brought grist to their opponents' mill. While the former read Kuhn as an ally in their bid to establish a unique methodological standard built around the notion of "system," the latter saw in *The Structure of Scientific Revolutions* an attack on the last remnants of logical positivism and on the possibility of a neutral scientific language, and thus something to be deployed against the normalization of the discipline around a set of system-theoretical concepts. In political science, the Truman–Almond line was rapidly countered by Sheldon Wolin, in a judo move that turned Kuhn against its first promoters and impugned the behavioralists' pretense to dictate the terms of political research by pointing out that behavioralism was only one paradigm of political theory.[42] While some political scientists were afraid of the "nonrational and relativistic implications" of Kuhn's account of science and sought to counter them by reinstating validation criteria that they found in Lakatos, others simply embraced them.[43] The same thing happened in IR, where there was a real fear that any scientific normalization of the discipline would entrench an updated realism operating with the concept of "system" as the only legitimate "paradigm" at the expense of alternative

---

[41] Lijphart, "Structure," 63.
[42] Sheldon Wolin, "Paradigms and Political Theories," in *Paradigms and Revolutions: Appraisals and Applications of Thomas Kuhn's Philosophy of Science*, ed. Gary Gutting (Notre Dame: University of Notre Dame Press, 1980).
[43] Ball, "From Paradigms to Research Programs," 153.

approaches (a fear fueled by Kuhn himself, who had surmised that "it is precisely the abandonment of critical discourse that marks the transition to a science"[44]). No matter how implausible this conflation of realism with "normal science" was (not least because of realism's fundamental tension with the idea of a science of politics), it seemed to validate *a contrario* the notion that attacking positivist models of science was tantamount to pulling the rug under the realists' feet. The contribution of behavioralism, as Smith and many others believed, was indeed "to continue dominance by bringing the semblance of scientific rigor to Realism."[45] For these critics, realism and positivism were virtually conflated, since "realism in international relations inherited ... the presumption that the methods of natural science are the key with which to unlock the social world"[46] – an assumption that, as we shall see, turned out to be plain wrong. The odd result of all this was that "post-positivism" was somehow understood to be a bulwark against realism.

Those who did not recognize themselves in the emerging science of political "systems" thus found that Kuhn was a true *Janus bifrons*, who provided ammunition against those who used him to defend the agenda of a modernized, structural realism. In this new incarnation, Kuhn was also a constructivist thinker,[47] one for whom "the progressiveness of science lies not in the nature of the work scientists do" or its relationship to "reality" (however understood), "but in the control they exercise over how they recount their collective history."[48] The history of scientific progress told by Truman, Almond, Lijphart, and others suddenly appeared as an optical illusion, since for Kuhn each scientific revolution is followed by an "Orwellian" rewriting of history, which casts prior scientists as precursors of present ones, working on the same problems and contributing to the gradual emergence of the present paradigm (thus denying revolutions any function and making them "invisible").[49] Textbooks are rewritten, the work of previous scientists is "revised,"

---

[44] Thomas S. Kuhn, "Logic of Discovery or Psychology of Research?" in *Criticism and the Growth of Knowledge*, eds., Imre Lakatos and Alan Musgrave (Cambridge: Cambridge University Press, 1970), 6.
[45] Smith, "Paradigm Dominance," 202.
[46] Martin Hollis and Steve Smith, *Explaining and Understanding International Relations* (Oxford: Clarendon Press, 1990), 50.
[47] Tanja E. Aalberts and Rens van Munster, "From Wendt to Kuhn: Reviving the 'Third Debate' in International Relations," *International Politics* 45, no. 4 (2008): 720–46.
[48] Fuller, *Thomas Kuhn*, 28.
[49] Thomas S. Kuhn, *The Structure of Scientific Revolutions* (Chicago: The University of Chicago Press, 1996), 136–43. The comment on Orwell can be found on p. 167.

and history is "truncated" – but all for the good cause of normalizing current science: once this shift in perspective is adopted, history tells us that the current paradigm was, somehow, always in the making. Part of what made Kuhn exhilarating is that he was giving away this dirty little secret – histories of disciplinary progress are always deceptive – even though he was at the same time justifying Whig history as necessary to the proper operation of a scientific community.[50]

In any case, the disjunction between the official history of a discipline and its actual history contributed to relativize the behavioralists' scientific claims and to develop a more complex sociological argument about the capacity to establish paradigm dominance through non-scientific means. What mattered was that the validity of a scientific paradigm was not established through some universal or neutral logical criteria, but exclusively through institutional means, ranging from the control of educational programs to the inculcation of a Whiggish history to gullible aspiring scientists. If realism was still dominant, it was not because of some demonstrable theoretical superiority, but because, as Steve Smith put it, it was "the largest and most well-financed academic community."[51]

The notion that normal science depended on the capacity of specific groups to command consent had important epistemological consequences. Kuhn fascinated also because his model of science was premised on "an explicit rejection of the model of algorithmic decision theory."[52] Incommensurability between paradigms was not only a characteristic of the discontinuous historical development of science, as the advocates of behavioralism had assumed, but a fundamental epistemic structure in a discipline where different "schools" coexisted contemporaneously. This certainly thwarted the claim by neorealists that their approach was demonstrably superior on rational grounds, but it also eased the discipline into a relativistic mindset: since incommensurability implied that each paradigm defined its own criteria of validity and, between paradigms *tertium non datur*, the notion of truth and a strong concept of rationality were among the first casualties. Even though Kuhn's pronouncements remained ambiguous as he both "endorsed and qualified statements of

---

[50] Here again, the result was selective reading, and it is also from Kuhn that the critics of IR's potted history of "great debates" have taken some of their cues. See Schmidt, "History and Historiography," 9; John G. Gunnell, "Political Science on the Cusp: Recovering a Discipline's Past," *The American Political Science Review* 99, no. 4 (2005): 597–609.
[51] Smith, "Paradigm Dominance," 202.
[52] Mirowski, "What's Kuhn Got to Do with It?" 232.

anti-realism,"[53] his suggestion that the traditional notion of truth as *adaequatio rei et intellectus* was not a useful benchmark of scientific "progress" (since all this was in the end "in the eye of the beholder"[54]) was bought wholesale by the critics of realism and interpreted as a strong form of relativism. Michael Banks, for instance, saw in Kuhn somebody who argued that "there is no absolute truth."[55] Reality per se was not accessible, because it was only a kaleidoscopic effect of paradigmatic vision. There was no proof, no "evidence," that could be used to require submission to a realist paradigm now parading as "normal science," since evidence, as Steve Smith wrote following Kuhn's footsteps, "is evidence precisely, and only, because it fits within a theoretical framework."[56] It is not that these critics were against science: on the contrary; they were all too glad to accept Kuhn's description of science as a social practice built upon non-rational foundations, as this allowed them to suggest that realist principles only applied to the world realists saw.

By offering a multifaceted theory of science, Kuhn allowed advocates of scientific IR and their critics alike to hold on to their different notions of what defined the discipline, since these notions were equally valid. The "great debates" of the discipline had no solution in the sense of a demonstration that one side was right. When Ole Waever suggested in 1996 that the "third" or "inter-paradigm debate" had not taken place (because there were no agreed upon terms for debating), he was unwittingly picking up a well-established argument: Lijphart had written twenty years earlier that scientific revolutions "do end ... even though rational arguments are not the means to solve them."[57] As early as 1968, Rogowski had suggested that the "second debate" too was a non-debate, marred by the fact that both sides were captive of their own inarticulate and incommensurable assumptions about what counted as "facts."[58] The various "schools" of international relations simply inhabited parallel universes that hardly intersected. The seeds of the "post-positivist" moment that characterized IR in the 1980s and 1990s were thus planted three decades earlier, and Kuhn had much to do with it. In this perspective, any talk of progress was an Orwellian illusion, necessary to the proper

---

[53] Peter E. Gordon, "Agonies of the Real: Anti-Realism from Kuhn to Foucault," *Modern Intellectual History* 9, no. 1 (2012): 129.
[54] Kuhn, *Structure*, 163.   [55] Banks, "Evolution," 15.
[56] Smith, "Paradigm Dominance," 202.
[57] Waever, "Rise and Fall"; Lijphart, "Structure," 69.
[58] Rogowski, "International Politics," 415ff.

operation of scientific collectives and fit for ISA presidential speeches. But such "progress" could not be equated with the progress of Reason projecting its light over ever wider swathes of reality: Rationality became a circumscribed phenomenon, dependent upon the prior adoption of a certain perspective on the world, which, in turn, could not be justified in rational terms and could be preached only to the converted. The choice of a paradigm created its own justification in retrospect, on the basis of its efficiency and expediency in solving puzzles and "rationalizing" a set of phenomena – just as the exceptional political decision becomes legitimate in retrospect, when it succeeds in establishing a new stable order.

THE REALIST EPISTEMOLOGY OF THOMAS KUHN

Starting in the 1970s, however, assessments of Kuhn became somewhat mixed. Even though in 1989 Yosef Lapid could still suggest that the dawning postpositivist era in IR was premised upon "the possibility that, within limits, diversity of viewpoints might be fully compatible with scientific rationality and objectivity," this optimism was viewed with suspicion. "Paradigmatism" was considered a pathology that had blunted criticism and impaired scientific progress. [59] Less threatening figures like Lakatos were summoned to shore up the anti-positivist position while rescuing scientific rationalism, lest one would be accused of postmodernism and relativism. Last but not least, it was clear that the attack on positivism had failed to destabilize a realist mainstream made immune to criticism.[60]

These second thoughts, however, barely scratched the surface of what had really happened. It is true that the reaction against the project of turning IR into a behavioral science had failed to unsettle realism, but the reason was not because realism benefited from paradigmatic immunity. What the postpositivist critics of realism failed to understand is that the advocates of the "scientization" of realism in the 1960s and 1970s were not positivists. Flummoxed by the high-tech gimmickry of "system" theorists, with their

---

[59] Yosef Lapid, "The Third Debate: On the Prospects of International Theory in the Post-Positivist Era," *International Studies Quarterly* 33, no. 3 (1989): 236; Colin Wight, "Philosophy of Social Science and International Relations," in *Handbook of International Relations*, eds., Walter Carlsnaes, Thomas Risse, and Beth A Simmons (London: Sage, 2002), 31; Waever, "The Rise and Fall of the Inter-Paradigm Debate," 160ff.

[60] Wight, "Philosophy of Social Science and International Relations." On Waltz's refusal to provide a justification for realism, see also Guzzini, "Dilemmas of Realism," 548–51.

set theoretic games, their simulations, and their algorithmic schemata, their critics jumped to the conclusion that this had to be a resurgence of positivism – a conclusion that, unfortunately, has ever since been the accepted *doxa* in the discipline, with debilitating effects on any critical project. Yosef Lapid, for instance, mistakenly associated the scientific side of the "second debate" with "the ascendance of positivism in Western social science," while R. B. J. Walker saw Waltz as a die-hard advocate of the "positivist method," despite the latter's insistent claims to the contrary.[61] Hypnotized by the notion of "post-positivism," which had the unfortunate effect of implying – wrongly – that the past of the discipline was positivistic, many IR theorists showed little or no awareness that the kind of "science" peddled by Kaplan, Schelling, Riker, or Waltz had deep roots in cybernetics, with its celebration of artificiality and its ontological agnosticism, but not in positivism.[62] They also failed to notice the very explicit disclaimers of their opponents: Morton Kaplan, for instance, had candidly confessed that he was "not a positivist," and that system-models were self-referential constructs that bracketed out reality.[63] If anything, their neorealist successors were even more outspoken: Waltz's *Theory of International Politics* inherited from cybernetics a fuzzy relationship between theoretical models and reality: "theories do construct *a* reality, but no one can ever say that it is *the* reality."[64] Waltz pointed out that this kaleidoscopic nature of "reality," accessed only through incommensurable theories, implied that participants in debates over the empirical merits of different theories "are talking about different things while using the same terms for them."[65] This was a sufficient reason to distinguish his own theory from scientific positivism: it was fundamentally different from the "analytic method," which was "preeminently the method of classical physics and . . . often thought of as *the* method of science."[66] While Waltz did not elaborate upon this distinction, it is clear that the tension between realism and science had not

---

[61] Lapid, "The Third Debate," 237; R. B. J. Walker, "Realism, Change, and International Political Theory," *International Studies Quarterly* 31, no. 1 (1987): 66.
[62] See Chapter 6. On the ontological agnosticism of cybernetics, see Andrew Pickering, *The Cybernetic Brain: Sketches of Another Future* (Chicago: Chicago University Press, 2010).
[63] Morton A. Kaplan, "A Poor Boy's Journey," in *Journeys through World Politics: Autobiographical Reflections of Thirty-Four Academic Travelers*, eds., Joseph Kruzel and James N. Rosenau (Lexington: Lexington Books, 1989), 44.
[64] Kenneth Waltz, *Theory of International Politics* (Long Grove, IL: Waveland Press, 1979; repr., 2010), 9. The extent of Ross Ashby's influence on Waltz has yet to be studied in detail.
[65] Waltz, *Theory*, 11.
[66] Waltz, *Theory*, 39.

subsided with structural realism and was now taking the form of a rejection of positivism, which only became stronger in Waltz's later work. Rejecting Popper's falsification proposal, he attacked "positivism" by suggesting that falsifying a theory was made difficult by "the interdependence of theory and fact." As a result, "what is to be taken as evidence for or against a theory is always in question," and all one can do is go back and forth between theory and "an uncertain state of affairs that we take to be ... reality."[67]

The idea that realism would be destabilized by an attack on its putatively positivist foundations thus turned out to be a Quixotic fight against epistemological windmills. It not only failed miserably: It backfired. In deploying a Kuhnian arsenal, the postpositivist critics of the realist mainstream were unwittingly doing the groundwork for the enemy. By the time they started having second thoughts about Kuhn, it was too late: The enemy had crushed the gates, and science itself was now premised on realist principles. Kuhn, in fact, viewed science very much like realists viewed the world.

Arguments supporting Kuhn's affinities with political realism have been made on the basis of biographical considerations, in particular his association with James Conant at Harvard, closely studied by Steve Fuller. According to Fuller, it is through his mentor that Kuhn inherited a number of realist thought patterns, which he then sublimated into a theory of science.[68] It is indeed tempting to read back some of Kuhn's core tenets into Conant's vision of science – in particular, a political approach to science, shaped by the political and institutional imperatives of the Cold War, which acknowledged the importance of non-scientific decisions in scientific work, as well as the idea that there is "no such thing as *the* scientific method," in the sense of an algorithmic logic capable of endlessly generating theories from facts.[69] But Fuller does not specify the exact pathways of this influence, which he takes for granted as part of a general intellectual climate.[70] This being said, one does not need to delve deep into Kuhn's biography to make the case for the political

---

[67] Kenneth Waltz, "Evaluating Theories," *The American Political Science Review* 91, no. 4 (1997): 914, 916.
[68] On Kuhn's Harvard years, see also Joel Isaac, "Kuhn's Education: Wittgenstein, Pedagogy and the Road to *Structure*," *Modern Intellectual History* 9, no. 1 (2012): 89–107.
[69] Justin Biddle, "Putting Pragmatism to Work in the Cold War: Science, Technology, and Politics in the Writings of James B. Conant," *Studies in History and Philosophy of Science* 42, no. 4 (2011): 555.
[70] Fuller, *Thomas Kuhn*, 174. See the criticism by John G. Gunnell, "Ideology and the Philosophy of Science: An American Misunderstanding," *Journal of Political Ideologies* 14, no. 3 (2009): 317–37.

implications of *Structure*, since Kuhn himself made them explicit: "the genetic aspect of the parallel between political and scientific development," he wrote, "should no longer be open to doubt."[71]

While much has been written about Kuhn's role in shaping the self-image of the discipline as a congeries of "paradigms," little attention has been paid to these political analogies. One of the core propositions of *Structure* was that (scientific) authority was vested not in a system of rules, but in a (scientific) collective that *decided* to recognize certain rules as valid and had the means to *enforce* that decision. While this may have been an earth-shattering proposition for historians of science, it was hardly big news for political realists. Postwar realism too was premised on a break with representations of politics as a legalistic or rule-based activity: instead, realists suggested, understanding international politics meant shifting from the rationalism of legal structures to the messiness of power relationships. The shift from science to politics was not difficult: Kuhn was building upon a long historical tradition in Western thought, in which the concept of law, as "natural law," was for a long time common to jurisprudence and science with little by way of differentiation.[72] The move from a system of laws to power relations that was one of the subtexts of *Structure* certainly resonated with realists, since Kuhn was doing for scientific positivism what they had done earlier for legal positivism. The rejection of legalism was something that Kuhn shared with the realists.

This, in turn, raises the issue of the analogy between paradigm choice and political decision. On the one hand, Kuhn often describes the adoption of a new paradigm in terms of *Gestalt* switch, i.e. a process that is more of a passively registered change of perspective than an active decision. But Kuhn also cultivates ambiguity in this respect, and in many instances he explicitly presents paradigm change as a matter of "decision" or "choice," including between competing alternatives. The analogy between paradigm choice and political decision was not lost on IR theorists, notably on Waltz, who distinguishes between scientific decision and scientific law in *Theory of International Politics*.[73] Behind every paradigm thus lies a constitutive decision, prior to the system of rules it gives rise to,

---

[71] Kuhn, *Structure*, 93.
[72] Lorraine Daston and Michael Stolleis, "Introduction: Nature, Law and Natural Law in Early Modern Europe," in *Natural Law and Laws of Nature in Early Modern Europe: Jurisprudence, Theology, Moral and Natural Philosophy*, eds., Lorraine Daston and Michael Stolleis (Farnham: Ashgate, 2008).
[73] Waltz, *Theory*, 1–9.

in the same way a legal system is premised on an unconditioned, sovereign decision that by its very nature is exempt from its strictures. Kuhn himself warranted a judicial analogy by suggesting that a scientific paradigm, "*like an accepted judicial decision in the common law* ... is an object for further articulation and specification."[74] If anything, the oscillation between "*Gestalt* switch" and "decision" in *Structure* seems to suggest that the former qualifies the latter as non-rational, non-discursive, and non-deliberative. While for other philosophers of science, like Duhem, the choice between theories can be made on the basis of conventional or commonsensical deliberation even if there is "no logical or formal method" to arbitrate between them, Kuhn presented a more radical version of this argument by suggesting that there was no rational ground for comparing paradigms.[75]

But the analogy between paradigm choice and political decision cuts deeper, for in advancing an argument in which science rests on theory choices that cannot be accounted for rationally (Kuhn compares them to something akin to a religious conversion[76]), Kuhn ultimately conjures a vision of science that is disturbingly *equivalent* with the realist vision of politics. This convergence is better teased out when one examines the implications of "incommensurability," which built upon insights originally developed by Duhem and extended by Quine. By showing that any finite set of observations could be accommodated by an indefinite number of theories, Duhem had established that there were no scientific criteria for establishing the superiority of one theory over another. Quine later extended the "underdetermination of theory" proposition to linguistic sets, and suggested that it was impossible to stipulate unambiguous translation criteria between different languages, even when empirical correlations limit the set of meanings possibly intended: a central, authoritative, translation code could not obtain.[77] While in linguistic communication misunderstandings can abound and interpretations can be challenged without necessarily having dramatic consequences, this problem took

---

[74] Kuhn, *Structure*, 23.
[75] Fred Chernoff, "The Impact of Duhemian Principles on Social Science Testing and Progress," in *The Oxford Handbook of the Philosophy of the Social Sciences*, ed. Harold Kincaid (Oxford: Oxford University Press, 2012).
[76] Imre Lakatos, "Falsification and the Methodology of Scientific Research Programmes," in *Criticism and the Growth of Knowledge*, eds., Imre Lakatos and Alan Musgrave (Cambridge: Cambridge University Press, 1970). Lakatos famously depicted Kuhn as an ideologue for religious fanatics.
[77] Willard Van Orman Quine, *Word and Object* (Cambridge: MIT Press, 1960), 27.

The Realist Epistemology of Thomas Kuhn

a special urgency in science, where there was a need to secure a degree of stability required by "normal science" in the absence of a logically demonstrable foundation. The notion of incommensurability thus pointed at the problem of achieving a *stable* and *rational order* in the absence of an authoritative system of rules capable of adjudicating between paradigms.[78] But wasn't this precisely the core question that IR theory sought to address – stability in the absence of authoritative and centralized rules, order under conditions of anarchy?

In a very direct way, IR theory too was born as an answer to the problem of interpretive authority, when it emerged in the late 1940s and early 1950s as a critique of international law. Morgenthau had pointed precisely at the impossibility to stipulate a univocal and authoritative translation code lifting the indeterminacy of international law:

> We find that documents, such as the Covenant of the League of Nations and the Charter of the United Nations, present ... a problem which in this form is alien to domestic law. We are referring to the problem of ascertaining the meaning of the particular provisions of these documents. ... In the international field, it is the subjects of the law themselves which not only legislate for themselves, but are also the supreme authority for interpreting and giving concrete meaning to their own legislative enactments.[79]

For legal realists in general, the determination of the meaning and the applicability of legal rules were considered a matter of decision that could not be itself settled by the rules under consideration.[80] A conflict over which set of rules applies cannot be solved in a rule-based manner and may be settled by recourse to force. The very same logic underpins Kuhn's explanation of conflict between paradigms: There are no neutral procedures for resolving such conflicts, since any rational argument is conducted on the basis of a prior adherence to a paradigm: "the choice [between competing paradigms] is not and cannot be determined merely by evaluative procedures characteristic of normal science, for these depend in part upon a particular paradigm, and that paradigm is at issue. Each group uses its own paradigm to argue in that paradigm's defense."[81] Science and

---

[78] On the political implications of Quine's indeterminacy thesis, see David Golumbia, "Quine's Ambivalence," *Cultural Critique*, no. 38 (1998): 5–38; Fuller, *Thomas Kuhn*, 177 fn. 76.
[79] Morgenthau, *Politics among Nations*, 216–17.
[80] On the parallels between legal and political realism, see Olivier Zajec, "Legal Realism et International Realism aux Etats-Unis dans l'entre-deux-guerres," *Revue Française de Science Politique* 65, no. 5–6 (2015): 785–804.
[81] Kuhn, *Structure*, 94.

international relations thus faced the same problem: In the absence of a *tertium quid*, what counts as "facts" and the choice of the relevant procedures for addressing them cannot be established by rule-governed procedures, but through power relations. As Lakatos put it in his coruscating critique, in Kuhn's science, "truth is power."[82]

Kuhn's discussion of normal science and paradigm change is thus uncannily reminiscent of the world of politics. Scientific crises are indeed formally equivalent with international ones. Normal politics, like "normal science," takes place when the application of rules goes without saying; the rules are not in question and are tacitly agreed upon. In situations of "crisis," however, the determination of which rules apply and the correlate decision over their relationship to "facts" is precisely what is at stake and what cannot be established in a rule-governed fashion. Any adjudication of competing claims by rival countries (any choice between paradigms) cannot be done through rules. The rules of international law (the logic of scientific activity) do not provide a path to a solution because they must be interpreted, and the ultimate instance of interpretation is always party to the dispute (i.e. subscribes to a paradigm). Lest the reader believes these are wild extrapolations, I hasten to add that Kuhn leaves no doubt whatsoever about the equivalence of paradigm choice and political or constitutional decision: "like the choice between competing political institutions, that between competing paradigms proves to be a choice between incompatible modes of community life."[83] Hidden in plain sight in the pages of *Structure*, the political distinction between friend and foe had thus made its discrete entrance in science and was now becoming an *unconditioned premise* of scientific rationalism.

THE ELUSIVE ESSENCE OF (RATIONAL) DECISION

These analogies between paradigm choice and fundamental political decisions were not lost on international relations theorists. But as Kuhn became widely read in the discipline, the distinction between theory choice and political decision became blurry. For, in a realist world where the opponent's motives are uncertain and can be interpreted in a variety of ways, the "rational" course of action is entirely dependent on the prior adoption of an interpretive grid that helps make sense of that opponent's

---

[82] Lakatos, "Falsification," 93.
[83] Kuhn, *Structure*, 94.

moves. The problem for decision-makers thus becomes the problem of deciding between different sets of hypotheses or "models" that all make the enemy legible, yet in different ways and presumably with different practical consequences. To put it differently: in the uncertain world of realism, in a very fundamental way, the political decision *is* theory choice, and theory choice is a *political* problem. As a result, explaining decision-making too becomes a matter of choosing a paradigm.

The widespread interest in Kuhn among IR theorists working on decision-making certainly warrants Steve Fuller's observation that it is the only discipline in which Kuhn has been used not only to map the discipline itself, but also to conceptualize its very subject matter.[84] Again, these were often creative interpretations, but they would have been impossible if Kuhn's ambiguous formulations had not made them plausible. What IR theorists found in Kuhn was not so much a substantive orientation that influenced them – indeed, the whole discipline was already premised on decisionism – but an account of science that was compatible with it and gave it scientific status: By breaking with legalistic representations of science, Kuhn had effaced the distinction between science and politics that was at the basis of postwar realism.

The first and arguably most influential work amalgamating political decision and theory choice is Graham Allison's *Essence of Decision*, published in 1971. The book reflected the internal discussions of the "bureaucratic politics" group led by diplomatic historian Ernest May at Harvard's Institute of Politics, which operated as the research arm and intellectual beacon of the John F. Kennedy School of Government. It originated "at least in the spring of 1966" when the May group started to convene, and it represented the "still unfinished 'Evolving Paper' of [the May] Group."[85]

An in-depth analysis of the Cuban missile crisis based on first-hand information provided by key players in the decision process, *Essence of Decision* was an innovative book that did not have a central thesis but instead applied three different interpretive grids to the same material and outlined the payoffs as well as the blind spots of these "models." For each of these models, Allison provided a narrative "cut" of what the Cuban

---

[84] Fuller, *Thomas Kuhn*, 174–75 fn. 72. Fuller argues that if Kuhn appears to offer an "independent corroboration" of Jervis' argument, it is because Jervis is unaware of the "common ancestry" that relates Kuhn to him, i.e. Cold War realism.

[85] Graham Allison, *Essence of Decision: Explaining the Cuban Missile Crisis* (Boston: Little, Brown and Company, 1971), ix.

crisis looked like when it was interpreted through that particular lens. Yet, like the models, the narratives were not related in a logical fashion but simply juxtaposed as parallel versions of reality. The main purpose of the book was not to provide an ultimate pronouncement or to uncover the "truth" of what had actually happened, but rather to accommodate the flux and uncertainty of the actual decision-making process by shedding light on the taken-for-granted assumptions that inform our understanding of decisions. *Essence of Decision* thus sought to identify the "conceptual lenses" affecting foreign policy analysis, knowing that each of these lenses "magnifies, highlights, and reveals but also blurs or neglects," in an effort to "demonstrate how alternative conceptual lenses lead one to see, emphasize, and worry about quite different aspects of events like the missile crisis."[86]

Although Kuhn is not cited, his influence on Allison and on the May group in general, flagged out by Bruce Kuklick, surfaces in the minutes and documents of the group meetings.[87] In 1969–1970, Allison and his associates read Kuhn and saw in him a crucial ally as they developed a theory of decision that refused to arbitrate between incommensurable models. In particular, the reading of *Structure* led them to justify the dominance of the rational choice model, even though they sought to develop an alternative to it on the basis of its perceived flaws. Multiple examples of irrational decisions by leaders or nations were not cause for discarding the model: "it must be replaced with something better before we can realistically counsel the discontinuation of its use," Steinbruner wrote in a 1969 memo in reference to the resilience of normal science in the face of contradictory data. More importantly, the members of the group saw in Kuhn a justification for the equivalence of scientific and political rationality. In both cases, rationality obtained only within the framework of a prior decision: "The point to which Kuhn sensitizes us," Steinbruner went on, "is that in the most productive scientific disciplines, all work has been organized by a fundamental paradigm, i.e., a set of assumptions defining a family of models. *I believe that the argument can be made that the enterprise of making policy tends similarly to be organized by a fundamental paradigm.*"[88]

---

[86] Allison, *Essence*, v.
[87] Bruce Kuklick, *Blind Oracles: Intellectuals and War from Kennan to Kissinger* (Princeton: Princeton University Press, 2006), 166. See the documents in Harvard University, Institute of Politics-May Group, Core Group 1969–1970, UAV 708.8.
[88] Harvard University, Institute of Politics-May Group, Core Group 1969–1970, UAV 708.8, Memorandum by John Steinbruner, 10 April 1970, Harvard University Archives, pp. 10–11. Emphasis added.

The Elusive Essence of (Rational) Decision

For Harvard's policy wonks, the cognitive setup of policy-making made it akin to scientific practice: What Kuhn wrote about science could be transposed to politics without further qualifications. For the post-Kuhnian realists, the prerogative decision, taken under time constraints and within a context of normative and practical uncertainty, was suddenly expressing the same rationality as scientific activity. An implication of this popularized understanding of Kuhn was that in order to be "scientific," policy did not have to reach a higher degree of rationality, since an underdetermined decision remained its unfathomable basis.

This intellectual backstage explains the Kuhnian flavor of Allison's models of decision analysis. These decisional models are solipsistic entities that do not so much distort the perception of a reality "out there" as they constitute what counts as real and what counts as evidence: "what we see and judge to be important and accept as adequate depends not only on the evidence but also on the 'conceptual lenses' through which we look at evidence."[89] Even though Allison gestured toward the possibility of integrating the three models and repeatedly claimed he was subscribing to the standard formula of social scientific positivism *à la* Hempel, the structure of the book as well as the nature of the "conceptual lenses" under scrutiny undermined such claims.[90] Like Kuhn's paradigms, Allison's "models" led analysts to see different worlds and were, in the end, incommensurable: "while at one level three models produce different explanations of the same happening, at a second level the models produce different explanations of quite different occurrences."[91] The result was a string of contradictory statements and positions, which only got more confusing in the 1999 edition. In the end, the "grand model" that Allison auspicated and that was expected to integrate the different policy analysis paradigms into a general theory was "really a metaphor."[92] All that was left was the undecidable alternative between different tunnel visions, or rather a fundamental decision that was not dependent on a set of formal rules. By the same token, there were no criteria on the basis of which such a decision could be judged. According to Kuklick, much of *Essence* was intended to absolve the mistakes of the best and the brightest in

---

[89] Allison, *Essence*, 2.
[90] In the 1999 edition, Allison describes himself as a positivist, while Zelikow disavows positivism. Graham Allison and Philip Zelikow, *Essence of Decision: Explaining the Cuban Missile Crisis*, 2nd edn. (New York: Longman, 1999), 521; Kuklick, *Blind Oracles*, 165.
[91] Allison, *Essence*, 251.
[92] Allison, *Essence*, 275, quoted in Kuklick, *Blind Oracles*, 167.

government through a "stylish relativism," which suggested that any decision was dependent on prior assumptions, between which there was no way of arbitrating rationally. In the end, it was not possible to isolate the factors that had really generated the decision. The title of Allison's book and the John F. Kennedy quotation from which it is excerpted give away what may be the core message of *Essence*, namely that the political decision is ultimately an inscrutable *arcanum arcanorum*: "the essence of ultimate decision remains impenetrable to the observed – often, indeed, to the decider himself... There will be always the dark and tangled stretches in the decision-making process – mysterious even to those who may be most intimately involved."[93] *Essence* thus boiled down to a restatement of a traditional metaphysics of sovereignty, now refurbished with a scientific *imprimatur* authorized by Kuhn. Long confined to the darkest recesses of political theory before being reprocessed by IR in the postwar years, decisionism was now worming its way into the very definition of scientific rationality.

A similar example of an intellectual project that set out with positivist overtones but ended up endorsing Kuhnian perspectivism is Robert Jervis' *Perception and Misperception in International Politics*, published five years after Allison's book. The book is based on the assumption that "perceptions of the world and of other actors *diverge from reality in patterns that we can detect*"[94] – yet, the idea of measuring and understanding this "deviation" quickly unravels, as the distinction between "perceptions" and "misperceptions" gradually becomes meaningless, or at least makes sense only in retrospect, when the consequences of decisions tell them apart.

Along with *Essence of Decision*, *Perception* is the product of an intellectual context influenced by the impact of nuclear strategy on IR theory and the correlate shift of emphasis from material-military factors to the psychological factors involved in the "efforts to influence the decision to attack."[95] Psychology, and in particular *Gestalt* psychology, provided a perfect meeting ground with Kuhn's philosophy of science and its fascination with duck-rabbit problems. In this respect, *Perception* is superior to *Essence of Decision*, since it makes explicit what was largely implicit and inarticulate in Allison's book (but spelled out in the minutes and memos of the May group), namely the equivalence between theory choice in science and political decision in international politics. In his

---

[93] Quoted in Allison, *Essence*, vi.
[94] Robert Jervis, *Perception and Misperception in International Politics* (Princeton: Princeton University Press, 1976), 5.
[95] Davis, "The International Influence Process," 236.

attempt to specify "rational" criteria for decision-making, Jervis turned to what appeared to be the most constraining concept of rationality available, i.e. scientific rationalism: "I see no reason to believe," he suggested, "that political decision-makers are less rational, sophisticated, and motivated to understand their environment than are scientists."[96] But it's not just that political decisions should be evaluated according to the standards of rationality that had currency in science: Jervis' argument went further and was explicitly premised on the equivalence of scientific investigation with the cognitive process that informed political decisions (which, then, become the equivalent of a test of the theory or hypothesis behind it). The Kuhnian analogy between scientific communities and political ones was now given free rein and allowed to deploy all its effects, with due credits to Kuhn's *Structure*, which became the organizing reference of one of the key chapters of the book, dealing with "cognitive consistency and the interaction between theory and data."

The sustained analogy between scientists and decision-makers that runs through *Perception* allows Jervis to follow the Kuhnian script very closely and to posit the paradigmatic nature of perceptions in international politics: "in the interpretation of other states' behavior, and in the scientific laboratory, expectations create predispositions that lead actors to notice certain things and to neglect others."[97] This selective framing of reality, however, is perfectly *rational*, since the processes that consist in "fit[ing] incoming information into pre-existing beliefs ... characterize investigations in science."[98] This, in turn, means that in the face of unexpected or incoherent information, decision-makers will most of the time stick to their beliefs rather than revise them, just as paradigms are not challenged by discrete anomalies. Even seemingly irrational cognitive distortion (evidence is ignored or twisted to accommodate existing beliefs) is a rational feature of the decision, for at least two reasons. First, it does not produce inaccurate pictures of reality, since by virtue of the theory-dependency of facts, "evidence always permits multiple interpretations."[99] Second, just as "normal science" cannot operate and produce results if its fundamentals are permanently questioned, no sound decision can be taken if policy expectations are constantly changed and destabilized:

Like the scientist, the statesman who wants to create and maintain a view that has even minimal coherence will have to refuse to give full weight to evidence that others would see as discrepant with his beliefs ... in politics too, ignoring

---

[96] Jervis, *Perception*, 5. [97] Jervis, *Perception*, 145. [98] Jervis, *Perception*, 143.
[99] Jervis, *Perception*, 154.

discrepant information or assimilating it to pre-existing beliefs will perpetuate inaccurate images and maintain unsatisfactory policies, but these processes are necessary if decision-makers are to act at all.[100]

In good realist fashion, any decision results in a mixture of good and bad, and international politics knows only partial, tunnel visions that will never capture the "truth" of the situation. The only important question is to strike a balance between "stability" and "flexibility" of expectations or, in other words, to decide when normal science ought to proceed and when a paradigmatic revolution is in order. But Jervis' wholesale adoption of the Kuhnian model ends up blurring the distinction between a "correct" perception and a misperception, since the latter is perfectly rational and even necessary if decisions are to be made at all. The distinction, then, only makes sense in retrospect, after a paradigm shift that casts new light on prior "evidence": "because established theories give a coherence, interrelated view of reality, contradicting facts cannot be appreciated until the theory is displaced" and until, seen through new lenses, "the world looks different."[101] No judgment about the validity of specific inferences, therefore, can be dissociated from "the larger question of the merits of contending theories and images." But in the Kuhnified decision process analyzed by Jervis, these images are, like paradigms, incommensurable, and their merits cannot be adjudicated on the basis of a single set of rules: "the interaction between theories and facts renders difficult a debate on the merits of opposing paradigms, and, to a lesser extent, images."[102] In the end, like in Allison, no rational discussion of the "essence of ultimate decision" can be conclusive.

Remarkably, both books displayed feats of social scientific erudition and yet ended up reasserting the traditional vision of the sovereign decision as something that exceeds the bounds of rationality and thwarts any attempt at rule-based codification. Not that this limitation was specific to Allison or Jervis: Despite the vast resources poured into their development, the postwar decision sciences as a whole never delivered the goods they promised, and in particular a scientific formula for making

---

[100] Jervis, *Perception*, 161, 172. Jervis adds that "scientific investigation could not be carried out if men were too open-minded," p. 158.

[101] Jervis, *Perception*, 169, 167. Jervis later acknowledges that there is "no way to draw a neat, sharp line between that degree of holding to existing beliefs and disparaging information that is necessary for the intelligent comprehension of the environment and that degree that leads to the maintenance of beliefs that should be rejected by all fair-minded men," p. 177.

[102] Jervis, *Perception*, 171.

decisions.[103] This was certainly the case in the IR theory, where most of the work done on decision-making, including the more formal work of Schelling, Kahn, and others ended up emphasizing the importance of the non-formalizable elements of the decision. Yet, the real stakes of the engagement with Kuhn lay elsewhere.

What was really new in the adoption of Kuhn's *Structure* as the "paradigmatic" account of science by IR theorists was the complete transformation of the terms of debate within the discipline and the new articulation of science and politics that was thus made possible. In many ways, the postwar social science movement was also an attempt at bringing science and politics together by bringing science into politics and transforming politics into applied social science. This is what triggered the reaction of political realists, who believed like Morgenthau that "a science of politics deals with a subject that is existentially alien to it."[104] Until *Structure*, scientific man and the man of power politics were fundamentally at odds.

If IR theorists found so much to like in Kuhn, it is because rather than pressing scientific concepts onto politics, he did exactly the contrary and brought politics into science. After *Structure*, being a realist and subscribing to an ideal of scientific rationality was no longer impossible, since scientific rationalism now appeared to rest upon non-scientific premises and even a dose of power politics. As the tension between realism and scientific rationalism disappeared, the "second debate" lost its *raison d'être*. The tension between history and science also subsided: A Kuhnified vision of history as a repository of analogies – read: paradigm-reinforcing cognitive consistencies – informing perceptions represented nothing short of "a useful shortcut to rationality."[105] Science and politics apprehended the world in the same manner and with the same limitations. Adhesion to a partial and even flawed image of the world was *necessary* to make political decisions, just as the limitations of rationality were *necessary* to generate scientific knowledge. Kuhn was thus crucial in authorizing realism to claim the "scientific" credentials that the fledgling discipline had sought in vain since its inception, yet without relinquishing its vision of politics as a sphere of limited rationality. The price to pay, however, was the diffusion of a weakened concept of rationality that could never be opposed to political realism because it was already premised on it. Indeed, Kuhn's critique of the "textbook" version of the history of science was indeed nothing else than another critique of idealism.

---

[103] Erickson et al., *How Reason Almost Lost Its Mind*, 2013.
[104] Morgenthau, *Science*, 34.   [105] Jervis, *Perception*, 220.

Those who embraced Kuhn as a liberator did not see that by placing limits on rationalism (now confined within the limits of "normal science," which was itself premised on an underlying decision that dispensed with rational, rule-based justifications), he provided a perfect vehicle for the modernization of the old anti-rationalism of classical realism. More importantly, he was squaring the circle by reconciling a decisionist perspective with a rationalist one – a move indicative of the evolution of political science in the 1960s, which we briefly encountered when touching upon Carl Friedrich in the previous chapter. This had major consequences for the discipline: The impossible synthesis between politics and science, which had impaired the academic development of realism, was finally realized – yet the fiction of their difference was maintained (thanks to manipulative "official" histories, which Kuhn legitimated). Realists could fully embrace scientific rationalism now that it was premised on a form of realism.

In retrospect, it appears that those who welcomed "post-positivism" in the 1980s failed to understand the deep affinities that made Kuhn so compatible with realism. What is perplexing about this collective blindness is that this connection was there for anybody to see since the very beginning, and even a cursory look at Kenneth Waltz's, Graham Allison's, or Robert Jervis' classic works would have been sufficient to trigger some alarm bells. In any case, the idea that attacking positivism would amount to attacking realism proved to be delusional. Even at the height of the putative "inter-paradigm" debate of the 1980s, when realism seemed to be on the defensive and new approaches to international politics inspired by versions of liberalism and Marxism were emerging, the Kuhnian gloss used to describe that moment actually *consolidated* realism by turning it into a theory of knowledge. It no longer mattered what the actual extent of the realist school was compared to others: Realism reigned supreme as the fundamental cognitive structure of our relationship to the world. The critics of realism misunderstood its true nature: Realism has never been concerned with certain knowledge; on the contrary, it is a philosophy entirely premised on the limits of human knowledge and rationality. These cognitive limitations were, in fact, a defining element of IR theory for somebody like Morgenthau.[106] One may see better why classical realism

---

[106] Hans J. Morgenthau, "The Theoretical and Practical Importance of a Theory of International Relations," in *The Invention of International Relations: Realism, the Rockefeller Foundation and the 1954 Conference on Theory*, ed. Nicolas Guilhot (New York: Columbia University Press, 2011).

was not only able to survive, but actually thrived on the postwar notions of "bounded" rationality and other kinds of strictures that produced a much thinner concept of rationality than those associated in the past with enlightened Reason or scientific positivism. In this general context, Kuhn represented a very particular position, in which the weakening of rationality was not only meant to enable its algorithmic treatment (as in rational choice), but also made room for reintroducing the fundamental role of the non-rational in determining where and how rationality would be allowed to operate. Science was just a particular case of a more general dynamic in which value-conflict could not be adjudicated through rule-governed procedures. Of course, rationalism had a place in human affairs, but this place was now seen as necessarily circumscribed. It did not rid science or politics of the non-rational, power-driven element in it – if anything, the possibility of rationalism was premised on this element. This was a key tenet of classical realism, restated in the language of the philosophy of science. After decades of estrangement, scientific man could finally embrace power politics without compromise, for Kuhn had shown that, unbeknownst to him, he had been a realist all along.

5

Cyborg Pantocrator: At the Origins of Neorealism

"Computing machines become the modern substitutes for the *Volksgeist* or the *Vernunft*."
  Bruno Leoni, "The Meaning of 'Political' in Political Decisions,"
  Political Studies 5, no. 3, 1957: 233.

"Even if time and prudence, the patience of knowledge, and the mastery of external conditions were by hypothesis without limits, the decision would be structurally finite, however late it is taken – a decision of urgency and precipitation, acting in the night of non-knowledge and non-rule."
  Jacques Derrida, *Force de Loi* (Paris: Galilée, 1994): 58.

Reporting on the latest developments of systems theory in a 1967 issue of the magazine *Science News*, Jonathan Eberhart wryly observed that this thriving field of research, which had "all the trappings of a full-fledged science," was in the process of redefining diplomacy. The State Department had recently established a Center for International Systems Research, where, to the dismay of their more traditionalist colleagues, some over-enthusiastic analysts entertained the ultimate machine dream: a "fully automated foreign policy."[1] While even at the time this prospect certainly seemed spurious – Eberhart considered that system analysis amounted to "computerized hair-tearing" – more disturbing applications were given serious consideration elsewhere, such as the infamous "doomsday machine" devised at the RAND Corporation by nuclear strategist

---

[1] Jonathan Eberhart, "About the Systems System," *Science News* 91, no. 1 (1967): 19.

Herman Kahn and given its game-theoretical credentials by Thomas Schelling.[2] In any event, the anecdote is revealing of the degree to which political and strategic questions had been recast as technical problems by the 1960s and of the hopes placed in what Sonja Amadae has called the "objectivization of political decision procedures."[3]

These hopes were a defining trait of the period and they expressed a momentous transition in the dominant conceptions of political decision-making, away from Morgenthau's educated "hunches" and toward exact, formally specified protocols supposed to facilitate decision-making and limit its arbitrariness. The books examined in the previous chapter are a good indicator of this transition. There are a number of reasons for which the 1960s saw a flourishing of attempts at placing political decisions on more rational foundations, and thus, increasingly, into the hands of scientists. Recently, Hunter Heyck has enumerated some of these reasons: the behavior-focused vision of "high modern" social science and its intent to make decisions observable by detaching them from the deciding subject; the idea that industrial society was infinitely more complex and thus required new methods for decision-making, better adapted than the limited computation capacities of individual subjects; and the role of new patrons for scientific research.[4] These are important reasons, which bear witness to the transformation of the social sciences, yet others may be added in relation to a broader context. Why was the era replete with fantasies of automated decisions? Why did decision-making, and in particular *political* decision-making, become a core focus of the social sciences? While the notion was practically absent from political science until 1945 (if we except "decisions" as legal decisions made in courts), the number of articles focusing on "decision-making" in political science (and economics) journals started increasing exponentially after World War II.[5] Political decision-making was a new concern for the academic profession. This quantitative trend was reflected in the changing conceptions of

---

[2] Schelling suggested that automated enforcement provided an edge in bargaining situations where the credibility of threats was crucial. Thomas Schelling, "The Strategy of Conflict," *The Journal of Conflict Resolution* 2, no. 3 (1958): 203–64.

[3] Amadae, *Rationalizing Capitalist Democracy*, 185. On the question of automated, algorithmic decision-making, see Erickson et al., *How Reason Almost Lost Its Mind*.

[4] Heyck, *Age of System*, 138–39. On the role of patrons, see Solovey, *Shaky Foundations*.

[5] See the figures in Nicolas Guilhot and Alain Marciano, "Rational Choice as Neo-Decisionism: Decision-Making in Economics and Political Science After 1945," in *Scientific Imperialism: Exploring the Boundaries of Interdisciplinarity*, eds., Uskali Mäki, Adrian Walsh, and Manuela Fernández Pinto (London: Routledge, forthcoming).

the discipline's identity. From the historical and legal study of governmental institutions or procedures, political science became a discipline dedicated to the systematic and formal study of decisional processes. William Riker, for instance, claimed that "the subject studied by political scientists is decision-making."[6] He was echoed by Herbert Simon, for whom decision-making was "not ... some highly special aspect of the political process, but ... its central core."[7] Obviously, much more than disciplinary issues was at stake given the magnitude of such efforts at understanding and rationalizing political decisions. The rise of "rational choice" – which, it should be said, is not a method but a loose label designating a variety of different, albeit overlapping, intellectual projects – was tightly connected to a diffuse anxiety about politics and political decisions that had several sources.

First, as already mentioned, the postwar era was a time of widespread doubts about the capacities of democracies to operate efficiently in situations of crisis and about the "rationality" of their citizens.[8] The social sciences, generally speaking, suggested that individuals were *not* rational: acting out of emulation or conformity, governed by irrational drives, manipulated by opinion-makers, reacting mechanically to signals, the social individual could not be trusted to act rationally. "Many postwar political scientists," Andrew Jewett writes, "expressed profound doubts about the average citizen's capacity to take an active political role, even through the limited avenue of informed voting."[9] And even if one assumed that individuals could act rationally, one of the major results that economics generated in the 1950s was to demonstrate that there was no satisfying way of translating this individual rationality at the collective level.[10] A collective decision could not be rational, unless it entailed a degree of coercion or an ultimate authority that overrode the collective itself – something that, incidentally, fitted well with traditional critiques of democratic decision-making often found among realists. This

---

[6] William H. Riker, *The Theory of Political Coalitions* (New Haven: Yale University Press, 1962), 11.

[7] Herbert A. Simon, "Political Research: The Decision-Making Framework," in *Varieties of Political Theory*, ed. David Easton (Englewood Cliffs, NJ: Prentice-Hall, 1966), 15.

[8] Katznelson, *Fear Itself*.

[9] As result, Jewett adds, "by the 1960s, the social sciences had, to varying degrees, pivoted from the public to the federal government as their ultimate audience." Jewett, *Science, Democracy, and the American University*, 358, 342.

[10] Kenneth Arrow, *Social Choice and Individual Values* (New Haven: Yale University Press, 1951); Kenneth Arrow, "A Difficulty in the Concept of Social Welfare," *Journal of Political Economy* 58, no. 4 (1950): 328–46.

image of irrational publics seemed to find confirmation in recent history, as Germany and Italy had democratically produced regimes that either pretended to embody "true" democracy or to supersede it.[11] Second, the development of nuclear arsenals – and in particular of thermonuclear bombs – seemed to give, for the first time, a concrete content to the suggestive yet vague Schmittian metaphors of sovereignty ultimately taking the form of the "decision upon the exception": the possibility of ordering a nuclear strike, and even more so a thermonuclear one, was the possibility of an absolute and absolutely sovereign decision, unprecedented historically and utterly deprived of a normative or juridical framework. Finally, the Cold War itself required a new understanding of authority and a new tolerance for decision-making practices that fell short of any form of democratic accountability in the name of "security."[12]

In this context, it was crucial to define non-arbitrary criteria for making such momentous decisions lest they ushered in new forms of authoritarianism. Nuclear decisions, for instance, were not only undemocratic by virtue of being dictated by scientific and military considerations rather than public deliberation: As we shall see in chapter 6, they were also *constitutional* decisions that entailed important consequences for the nature of the regime, and in particular a turn toward authoritarianism. It was thus important, in a country that represented itself as the cradle of liberal constitutionalism, to find a language that could justify restricted forms of decision-making without drifting into the murky waters of antiliberalism. "Rational" choice was precisely a way of legitimating decisions that, while maybe not democratic, were not entirely arbitrary in the sense that they could allegedly command unanimous consent from the part of rational beings. The notion of rational choice was germane to entrenched representations of America as a liberal polity. Game theory, as William Riker aptly saw, entailed the promise of reconciling the predictability of decisions with the idea of individual freedom: While traditionally the social sciences' emphasis on generalization and determinacy seemed incompatible with human freedom, "game theory offer[ed] a way out of this dilemma by combining the possibilities of generalization

---

[11] On the theoretical issues raised by self-abdication, see Ivan Ermakoff, *Ruling Oneself Out: A Theory of Collective Abdications* (Durham: Duke University Press, 2008).
[12] The tensions between political realism and liberal constitutionalism were already present in NSC-68 (1950), a document mostly reflecting Paul Nitze's views, which advocated the suspension of some liberal values and guarantees in the struggle against Communism. Lewis Gaddis, *The Cold War*, 164–65.

and free choice."[13] At the same time, rational choice legitimated decisions taken away from, and without the participation of, an informed and active public.

The paradox of "rational choice" and irrational subjects was thus only too apparent. In rational choice, the "rationality" is an attribute of the decision itself, not of the deciding subject, who cannot be trusted to act rationally if left to her own devices: The "chooser" no longer matters, only the design of the decision protocol does.[14] By implication, this meant that good decisions not only did not have to reflect the preferences of the citizens at large, but could attain rationality only by being insulated from them. As an intellectual project that directly flowed from the crisis of democracy and of the belief in rational publics, rational choice was perfectly adapted to a brand of political theory that had always considered democracy as detrimental to high politics, since it assumed a degree of coercion as a condition for attaining rationality. Decisions could be made rational only if they were constrained – by institutions, by authority, by protocols.[15] The notion of "bounded rationality" coined by Herbert Simon perfectly captured this intuition by suggesting that rationality could only exist in a concrete, and therefore limited, fashion.[16] It was also reinforcing, at a deeper level, the idea that "freedom does not exist without limits."[17] This conclusion was also valid at the international level: In the conditions of the Cold War, the defense of freedom implied, by necessity, its limitation. The rise of rational choice was also the rise of "authoritarian liberalism."

International relations theory was central to these developments. Its distinctive feature, starting in the late 1950s, was the development of various rational choice methodologies, ranging from system analysis to game theory or conceptual borrowings from the cybernetic toolbox, which, collectively, appeared to be "decision sciences." This chapter explores the gradual colonization of political thought by these methodologies and outlines some of its consequences. It sheds light on a key episode

---

[13] William H. Riker, "The Entry of Game Theory into Political Science," in *Toward a History of Game Theory*, ed. E. Roy Weintraub (Durham: Duke University Press, 1992), 210.

[14] Heyck, *Age of System*, in particular ch. 4.

[15] Bruno Leoni, "The Meaning of 'Political' in Political Decisions," *Political Studies* 5, no. 3 (1957): 225–39.

[16] On bounded rationality see M. Klaes and E. M. Sent, "A Conceptual History of the Emergence of Bounded Rationality," *History of political economy* 37, no. 1 (2005): 27–59.

[17] Heyck, *Age of System*, 134.

in the formative stage of the discipline, which, however, is curiously absent from histories of political theory and international thought, despite its decisive role in the subsequent rise of "neorealism," analyzed in greater detail in the next chapter.[18] This may be because its historians are content with considering this episode as a minor aspect of the "second debate," which we already encountered in the previous chapter, i.e. the turf battle in the 1960s between classical realists steeped in history and philosophy, and younger scholars eager to develop the credentials of the field in an era of unbridled optimism about the prospects of a methodologically unified social science. The notion that, sometime in the mid-1960s, political realists lost their bid to keep the theory of international politics immune from behavioral social science is a distorted view of what happened, insensitive to the changing meaning of "science" for those who wanted to establish the analysis of international politics on scientific foundations. True, realism was defined in large part by the assumption that politics was an art and could never be a science modeled after physics. On the face of it, the triumph of systemic theories and rational choice methods thus seemed to signal the end of classical realism, or at least a temporary setback in the unending tension between what some commentators have recently considered the two constitutive pillars of American foreign policy thinking: politics-as-art vs. politics-as-science.[19] But two important qualifications must be made.

First, what really ended was the "classical" stage of realism, not realism itself. The debates of the 1960s, the stakes of which were by no means exclusively methodological, were actually the birth pangs of a new realism, conventionally called "neorealism," which we will explore in greater detail in the next chapter. Neorealism was realism redux, but alleviated from the metaphysical burden attached to it – whether a definition of human nature or a theological vision of sovereignty – and augmented with cybernetic prosthetics. The robust methodological discussions of those years were fueled by conflicts between different generations of scholars over the legitimate credentials of authority and the nature of scholarship, but emphatically *not* by deep divisions over political realism or even the fraught relationship between rationality and politics. Again, for the

---

[18] There is a surprising dearth of analysis of the cybernetic influences on IR theory, despite the role of cybernetics in the emergence of neorealism in the 1970s.
[19] David Milne, *Worldmaking: The Art and Science of American Diplomacy* (New York: Farrar, Straus & Giroux, 2015).

advocates of rational choice or cybernetic systems, there was nothing contradictory in assuming just like their realist mentors that man was *not* a rational being.

Second, the fact that "science" was brandished indiscriminately by a younger generation of international relations theorists did not mean, as old realists feared, that it signaled a return to the Enlightenment tradition of political rationalism that they had successfully defeated. "Science" is a very elastic notion, and what international relations theorists meant by it is not immediately obvious, while the reference to equally flexible notions of "behavioralism" or "positivism" does not yield much insight.[20] A closer look at the new scientism of international relations theory reveals that it had not much to do with the tendency to model the social sciences after physics or to assume that history was driven by discoverable "laws." More importantly, it also suggests that this novelty was totally lost on the old realist guard, whose members believed that they were fighting a resurgence of nineteenth-century-style liberalism and economic thinking now parading under the banner of science. It is more accurate to see the second debate as a *misunderstanding*, fueled in part by generational differences and by a misreading of what "science" stood for, perpetuated to this day by standard accounts of the discipline. What international relations theorists eager to do "science" had in mind was, essentially, an intellectual project fundamentally informed by cybernetic representations of reality.

The cybernetic turn in political science had major consequences. It triggered unlimited hopes: the scalability of cybernetic concepts across different classes of problems pointed toward a possible unification of theory and the enhancement of administrative rationality.[21]

---

[20] The point is made by both Brian Schmidt and Colin Wight. See Schmidt, "History and Historiography"; Wight, "Philosophy," 29. On behavioralism, see the nuanced historical analysis by Adcock in Mark Bevir and Robert Adcock, "The History of Political Science," *Political Studies Review* 3, no. 1 (2005).

[21] It is not possible to survey the literature within the scope of this book. For a general overview of the cybernetic movement, see James R. Beniger, *The Control Revolution: Technological and Economic Origins of the Information Society* (Cambridge: Harvard University Press, 1986); Steve Joshua Heims, *The Cybernetics Group* (Cambridge: The MIT Press, 1991); Ronald R. Kline, *The Cybernetics Moment: Or Why We Call Our Age the Information Age* (Baltimore: Johns Hopkins University Press, 2015). See also in particular Mirowski, *Machine Dreams* and Peter Galison, "The Ontology of the Enemy: Norbert Wiener and the Cybernetic Vision," *Critical Inquiry* 21, no. 1 (1994): 228–66; Peter Galison, "The Americanization of Unity," *Daedalus* 127, no. 1 (1998): 45–71. On the role of machines, see N. Katherine Hayles,

But the cybernetic turn also raised some issues. The first can be stated as a question: What happens to political realism when politics is moved to the confined atmosphere of the research lab – that is, when it no longer refers directly to a "concrete situation," which according to political realists from Carl Schmitt to Hans Morgenthau is the touchstone of true politics, but to an artificial environment? The decision sciences of the nuclear age were closely related to the rise of simulation as a research protocol, which destabilized a number of previous assumptions about what constituted political "reality." Despite the vogue of political gaming, Monte Carlo experiments and other exercises in "social science fiction," the greatest challenge to this new way of thinking politically was "the problem of realism."[22] If the objectivization of political decisions primarily took the form of their simulation, what sense could be made of "realism" once the boundaries between the real and the artificial became porous? Would it still make sense to talk about "politics"?

A related issue was that the scientific approach to foreign policy decisions led to a re-description of statecraft and sovereign decisions in terms of rational decision-making or "rational choice." This was nothing short of revolutionary in a realist discipline still premised on a decisionist understanding of politics – one that did not ground politics in a higher natural order accessible to reason but in a pre-rational *animus dominandi* and in primordial decisions discriminating between friend and foe that could never be fully comprehended by political rationalism, let alone political *science*. Developing a science of decision-making applied to sovereign decisions was an exercise seemingly fraught with contradictions, as some commentators realized early on: If the goal of the theory was to determine "the freely arrived-at and non-caused perceptions of the individual decision-maker," the task was "impossible" since it implied that the non-caused phenomenon of sovereignty was somehow conditioned since it took the form of rules or laws.[23] One can better judge why realists saw the very idea of "decision sciences" as a contradiction in

How We Became Posthuman: Virtual Bodies in Cybernetics, Literature, and Informatics (Chicago: The University of Chicago Press, 1999) and Paul N. Edwards, *The Closed World: Computers and the Politics of Discourse in Cold War America* (Cambridge, MA: The MIT Press, 1996).

[22] Sharon Ghamari-Tabrizi, *The Worlds of Herman Kahn: The Intuitive Science of Thermonuclear War* (Cambridge: Harvard University Press, 2005), 165.

[23] As pointed out early on by Robert A Gorman, "On the Inadequacies of Non-Philosophical Political Science: A Critical Analysis of Decision-Making Theory," *International Studies Quarterly* 14, no. 4 (1970): 399. I am grateful to Robert Jervis for bringing this reference to my attention.

terms, which blended two incompatible intellectual traditions: one that associated science with normality, regularity, and laws, and another that located the political in the exception or the unique.

But the realists' eagerness to preserve a historicist understanding of political decisions, indexed to historical individuality and situational uniqueness, may have prevented them from observing that their opponents did not so much seek to make politics rational (and obliterate sovereignty) as to tailor rationality so that it fit power politics. That is, in substance, what cybernetics made possible: One did not have to pronounce upon the true nature of politics to study it scientifically. It was enough to produce satisfying analogs of political situations that could be subjected to formal and mathematized treatments. Tellingly, this form of scientism entailed no assumption of rationality on the part of political actors and did not signal a return to political rationalism.[24] On the contrary, like classical realism, neorealism was pushing back against any strong notion of rationality applied to politics – except that, unlike classical realism, it did so on seemingly scientific grounds. The attempt to overcome the limits imposed by strong notions of rationality would also become explicit in the subsequent development of decision theory, as in Steinbruner's classic *Cybernetic Theory of Decision-Making*, which presented cybernetics as an alternative to rational choice, and conflated cybernetics with realism by defining cybernetic "purpose" as "survival" in a context of high "uncertainty."[25]

UNRAVELING THE SECOND DEBATE

The realists' contempt for the idea of social *science* and the attempt at insulating the study of politics from the development of a general science of social behavior eventually clashed with the ambient techno-scientific culture of Cold War academia. Given the epistemic foundations of the discipline, however, the first calls for analyzing international politics as a "system" or building "models" based on "hypotheses about relations between variables" lending themselves to "empirical verification" were met with skepticism if not outright contempt by realists who considered that theory could never understand the true essence of politics as an existential engagement with a *concrete* situation. What seemed to be lacking from the new wave of formal theorizing was reality itself. As system theorists constantly emphasized, in order to be scientific

---

[24] On the rationality assumption, see Chapter 6, pp. 241–242.
[25] John D. Steinbruner, *The Cybernetic Theory of Decision: New Dimensions of Political Analysis* (Princeton, NJ: Princeton University Press, 1974), 18, 62–65.

a theory had to be "closed" onto itself, and this closure came with a hefty price tag: "once you close a theory, you are no longer making direct statement about the world but are working out of the internal logic of a system."[26] To many older scholars who had weathered the crisis of the 1930s and had a taste of the real thing, this certainly seemed like a hydroponic version of politics. The problem was stated in a particularly cogent form by Hedley Bull, one of the central figures of the "English school" of international relations: for him, the advocates of science were "committing themselves to a course of intellectual puritanism that keeps them (...) as remote from the substance of international politics as the inmates of a Victorian nunnery were from the study of sex."[27]

Although these issues eventually gave rise to polemical exchanges, framing this moment as a debate between a "realist" approach to politics and a "scientific" or "positivistic" one that ultimately redefined the field may be more problematic than it seems. First off, many advocates of the "scientific method" had the most orthodox realist pedigree and never called into question the specificity and the separateness of international politics as a field. While the old realist guard was certainly wary that the application of the scientific method entailed the risk of subsuming politics under an all-encompassing concept of social action applying to everything from economic transactions to face-to-face interactions, the zealots of scientific IR proved remarkably open to the idea that politics was indeed different from other social activities to the extent that it dealt with division and not integration. By the late 1950s, the Parsonian project of a general theory of social action had failed in its bid to unify the social sciences, and this failure was even more pronounced in a field entirely organized around the absence of a central authority ensuring the integration of different social subsystems.[28] Neither political scientists such as William Riker nor economists such as Charles Kindleberger, nor even systems theorists

---

[26] Kaplan, "A Poor Boy's Journey," 44.
[27] Bull, "International Theory," 366. See also the criticisms by Morgenthau, "Reflections," 443; Morgenthau, "Supplement: International Relations, 1960–1964," 171; Barrington Moore, "The New Scholasticism and the Study of Politics," *World Politics* 6, no. 1 (1953): 122–38; and the response by Morton Kaplan, "The New Great Debate."
[28] Joel Isaac, *Working Knowledge. Making the Human Sciences from Parsons to Kuhn* (Cambridge: Harvard University Press, 2012); Klausner and Lidz, *The Nationalization of the Social Sciences.*

such as Morton Kaplan, intended to fold IR into some generic science of social behavior.[29]

One of the surprising things about this debate over method, therefore, was the consensus over the specificity of international politics as a sphere that was not characterized by social integration. But to make things worse, it seems that the advocates of "science" entertained ambiguous notions of what "science" stood for. The fact that one of the most vocal advocates of the new approach to the study of international politics, Morton Kaplan, insisted that he was an "antipositivist" should give pause to those who see the second debate as the clash between the speculative inclination of early realism and a form of scientific positivism.[30] Traditionalist IR scholars were critical of the idea of social science understood as *social physics*. But so were their opponents, and the kind of science of politics they advocated was anything but based on a naturalistic philosophy. What most "scientific" versions of IR had in common at the time was some degree of reliance on game theory, and game theory was essentially understood as an *alternative* to social physics, if not its *opposite*. While the statistical study of phenomena treated human actions as nature and looked for law-like regularities, thus emptying social phenomena from their meaningful and purposive content by apprehending them from the outside, as it were, game theory reintroduced the perspective of interiority by focusing on choice, uncertainty, preferred outcomes, and the maximization of expected utility. "Concepts of choice, calculation of outcomes, and preference are extraneous to social physics (...) In a way, then, the theory of games is an approach diametrically opposed to that of social physics," Anatol Rapoport wrote in his influential 1955 treatise *Fights, Games, and Debates*, where game theory was introduced following a chapter entitled "Critique of Social Physics."[31] As a matter of fact, few international relations theorists subscribed to a social physics approach, and those who occasionally did, like George Modelski for instance, were arguably *not* protagonists of the

---

[29] Charles P Kindleberger, "International Political Theory from Outside," in *Theoretical Aspects of International Relations*, ed. William T. R. Fox (Notre Dame: University of Notre Dame Press, 1959), 75; Riker, *The Theory of Political Coalitions*, viii–ix.

[30] Kaplan, "A Poor Boy's Journey," 48. To my knowledge, only Stefano Guzzini has picked up the fact that "systems theory" and the kind of "empiricism" based on statistical correlations did not sit well together. Guzzini, *Realism*, 32–33.

[31] Anatol Rapoport, *Fights, Games, and Debates* (Ann Arbor: The University of Michigan Press, 1960), 109.

debate against realists. The same thing goes for the participants in the Correlates of War Project at the University of Michigan (J. David Singer, Kenneth Boulding, Anatol Rapoport, etc.), who were associated with the new *Journal of Conflict Resolution*: They may have shared a similar scientific outlook with Schelling, Kaplan, and others, but they were still steeped in a tradition of peace research that located them on the outer margins of IR. Morton Kaplan, on the other hand, grounded his analysis of the international system on game theory and cybernetics. The extensive tribute he paid to physics against the antiquarian study of statecraft was the prelude to some important qualifications, and in particular to an emphasis of the differences between "mechanical" systems, for which the toolbox of physics was perfectly adapted, and "ultrastable" systems that counteracted or even anticipated external circumstances, for the study of which "the deterministic models of physics obviously are inappropriate."[32] Other strategists such as Bernard Brodie or Thomas Schelling were just as cautious regarding the relevance of physics to the study of politics. Schelling's contribution to strategic thinking is best known for its emphasis on the non-formal elements of games that distinguish game theory from other scientific programs. If "the mathematical structure of the payoff function should not be permitted to dominate the analysis," it is because the properly *strategic* principles cannot be entirely captured by the formal properties of the game and involve such things as traditions, value-systems, tacit knowledge, focal points, shared norms, or subjective uncertainties about the extent to which norms are shared and all other kinds of subtleties that fell outside the realm of physics.[33] In short, the late-1950s calls for a "scientific" approach to IR should be seen in the continuity of the earlier rejection of "social physics" by the founding fathers of the discipline.[34] But if there were few causes for theoretical disagreement, what triggered so much debate? In true realist

---

[32] Kaplan, "The New Great Debate," 7.
[33] Schelling, "The Strategy of Conflict," 256–57.
[34] It is in fact surprising how much Schelling's insistence that "there is (...) no way that an analyst can reproduce the whole decision process either introspectively or by an axiomatic method. There is no way to build a model for the interaction of two or more decision units" echoes Morgenthau's emphasis on the limits of theory: "A theory of international relations, to be theoretically valid, must build into its theoretical structure, as it were, those very qualifications which limit its theoretical validity and practical usefulness." Schelling, "The Strategy of Conflict," 257; Morgenthau, "The Theoretical and Practical Importance of a Theory of International Relations," 265.

fashion, the causes of the second debate must be sought not in the pristine skies of theory, but in the nitty-gritty of social authority.

THE "COOL YOUNG MEN" OF INTERNATIONAL POLITICS

In order to understand what was at stake in the debate about system approaches to international politics in the 1960s, one should probably take seriously the observation by R. Duncan Luce and Howard Raiffa, the authors of the standard game theory manual of the time, that during wartime "considerable activity developed in scientific, or at least systematic, approaches to problems that had been previously considered the exclusive province of men of 'experience.'"[35] Game theory was indeed one of the primary beneficiaries of this redistribution of authority. The buildup of nuclear arsenals detached strategic thinking from experience acquired in the battlefield or in actual political decisions and relocated it within laboratories and research centers where war scenarios of a new kind were staged within entirely hypothetical models and simulated through gaming.[36] The research lab lavishly endowed by military or philanthropic sponsors displaced the academic department or the policy forum as a site of policy-making. In the wake of the wartime collaboration between researchers and the military, a new cadre of civilian researchers claimed authority in strategic matters on the basis of their scientific expertise. It was, in the words of Thomas Schelling, nothing short of "a new academic profession," which eventually "moved in 1961 into the Establishment, the Departments of State and Defense."[37] It is this move, in large part, which triggered the so-called second debate, as "cool young men" theorizing about the nuclear doomsday invaded a field previously defined by an older generation of scholars whom they considered irredeemably tethered to a pre-scientific age.

Early realists were indeed slow to catch up with the implications of nuclear weapon systems for their conceptions of war and peace.[38]

---

[35] R. Duncan Luce and Howard Raiffa, *Games and Decisions: Introduction and Critical Survey* (New York: John Wiley & Sons, 1957), 3.
[36] Ghamari-Tabrizi, *The Worlds of Herman Kahn*; Daniel Bessner, "Weimar Social Science in Cold War America: The Case of the Political Game," *Bulletin of the German Historical Institute* 54, *Bulletin Supplement* 10 (2014).
[37] Thomas Schelling, "A Tribute to Bernard Brodie and (Incidentally) to Rand," in *RAND Paper Series* (Santa Monica: RAND Corporation, 1979), 1.
[38] Craig, *Glimmer of a New Leviathan*; Kaplan, *Wizards of Armageddon*; Kuklick, *Blind Oracles*.

The crisis of classical realism was the crisis of an approach that had been primarily defined by the "explicit reliance on the exercise of judgment" rather than certified technical skills.[39] Whether one had read Meinecke or had a stint at the Policy Planning Staff mattered little to the technicalities of nuclear strategy, and the atomic bomb's first casualties were certainly the political theologians whose bid for influence was based upon their claims to know the ineffable mysteries of statecraft. The methodological disputes of the "second debate" may thus be seen as the sublimated form of a more prosaic challenge to their authority claims, in a context where the place of historical knowledge within an increasingly technical academic culture was becoming uncertain.[40] It is not fortuitous that Morgenthau wrote some of his most acerbic critiques of the decline of American democracy at the time of this methodological debate: According to him, the development of modern science and its increasing entanglement with government had dramatically transformed the nature of political decision-making. The ascendancy of a scientific and technological elite in the process of government and the increasingly esoteric nature of the knowledge it possessed had displaced the sites of decision-making and circumvented entirely democratic control: Power had "shifted from democratically responsible officials to certain technological elites, military and scientific, which are not democratically responsible. In consequence, popular participation in and control over the affairs of government have drastically decreased."[41] Worse, the science that preempted the political process did not express a morally superior ground capable of constraining power: Scientific advisors "transform themselves of necessity into political actors of first importance." Morgenthau perfectly captured the post-Kuhnian understanding of science when he suggested that in the process of being caught in political decision-making discussions, the arguments of scientific elites "subtly change their character. They become political and depend for their success as much upon the political skills and outside political support of their proponents as upon their scientific soundness."[42] The shift toward political decisions shielded from public scrutiny was compounded by the institutional setup of the Cold War alliance between science and power: "this naturally secretive character

---

[39] Bull, "International Theory," 361.
[40] For a contemporary take on the changing landscape for historical disciplines, see E. K. Francis, "History and the Social Sciences: Some Reflections on the Re-Integration of Social Science," *The Review of Politics* 13, no. 3 (1951): 354–74.
[41] Morgenthau, *Truth and Power*, 215. [42] Morgenthau, *Truth and Power*, 231.

of scientific knowledge, removing it from both executive understanding and democratic control, is accentuated by the artificial barriers of secrecy with which politically and militarily relevant knowledge has been surrounded."[43] It did not seem to matter that Morgenthau himself was unelected and unaccountable when he was advising the State Department in the late 1940s. The defense of democracy now offered him a convenient – if quite novel – position from which he could extend the fight against science that was the trademark of political realism.

That the authority and nature of expertise was at stake is further suggested by the overlap between intellectual positions and social trajectories characterizing this debate and clearly distinguishing the "tough-minded and expert new men, taking over an effete and wooly discipline" from old school realists.[44] The early realists were usually born around the turn of the century: Morgenthau was born in 1904, Niebuhr in 1892, Fox in 1912, Nitze in 1907, Kennan in 1904. Theirs was a generation who had come of age in the 1930s and experienced the intense divisions and traumas of the time. Some had nurtured a pessimistic and conservative vision of politics all along. Others had gone through a process of conversion: Reinhold Niebuhr had moved away from the progressive orientation of the Social Gospel and joined the conservative fray of Protestant neo-orthodoxy. William Fox had started as an internationalist and an isolationist, trained at Chicago in the Charles Merriam tradition of value-free social science and believing that "the power politics system could be reformed by strengthening international organizations," until the Munich crisis dispelled his prior illusions and led him to cross over to the dark side of the force.[45] Most of these scholars were trained as historians, lawyers, or political scientists. Even their younger disciples, such as Stanley Hoffman (b. 1928) or Kenneth Thompson (b. 1921), were steeped in different varieties of historicism: Hoffman called for a "historical sociology" of international relations inspired by Weber, while Thompson found his intellectual bearings in Toynbee.[46] These early realists tended to have

---

[43] Morgenthau, *Truth and Power*, 233.
[44] Bull, "International Theory," 362.
[45] "Not until I went to Princeton on the eve of the entry of the United States into World War II did I move beyond a 'war-as-pathological-behavior' approach." William T. R. Fox, "A Middle Western Isolationist-Internationalist's Journey toward Relevance," in *Journeys through World Politics: Autobiographical Reflections of Thirty-Four Academic Travelers*, eds., Joseph Kruzel and James N Rosenau (Lexington: Lexington Books, 1989), 235–36, 238.
[46] Stanley Hoffman, "International Systems and International Law," *World Politics* 14, no. 1 (1961): 205–37.

their strongholds at Columbia, Chicago, or Acheson's State Department. They also included a number of émigré scholars who brought European intellectual traditions at odds with American social science to bear upon the study of politics. Either they had never supported the project of a social science of politics, or, like the apostate Fox, they had reneged on it.

By contrast, the advocates of a "science" of international politics were often born in the 1920s, which means that the defining period for their intellectual training was the 1940s.[47] Few had a direct experience of military operations, but the war socialized them into new forms of research organization, characterized by interdisciplinary teams structured around specific issues defined by external funders. The fluid circulation of scholars across porous disciplinary boundaries set the pattern for the postwar cyborg sciences, based on *ad hoc* collaboration between social scientists, engineers, psychologists, mathematicians, physicists, or biologists. Those who hoped that the analysis of international relations and foreign policy decision-making could ever be a science were the direct result of this collaborative regimen. Beyond the important differences in their normative orientation toward conflict, one particular experience cemented this group: They all had bathed in the intellectual placenta of cybernetics.

In this respect, the intellectual trajectory of Morton Kaplan is typical. Trained in political science and psychology, Kaplan discovered cybernetics while working on postwar US foreign policy at the Brookings Institution in 1954. He spent the following year at the Center for Advanced Study in the Behavioral Sciences at Palo Alto, in the company of luminaries of cybernetics, game theory, and economics such as Ross Ashby, Howard Raiffa, or Jacob Marschak, whose influence explains his subsequent fascination with homeostatic systems.[48] But Kaplan was not the only one brokering between IR and cybernetics, and Palo Alto appears to have been one of the main incubating sites for the cyborg turn in IR theory. Kenneth Boulding, who had crossed over from chemistry to economics and was the driving force behind the creation of the *Journal of Conflict Resolution* at the University of Michigan in 1955,

---

[47] Morton Kaplan (b. 1921), J. David Singer (b. 1925), William Riker (b. 1920), and Thomas Schelling (b. 1921). There were notable exceptions: Bernard Brodie (b. 1910), Anatol Rapoport (b. 1911), and Karl Deutsch (b. 1912) – but Rapoport and Deutsch were émigrés and not quite representative of mainstream game theory. Brodie may have been influential within the field of security studies but his impact on IR was modest. On him, see Betts, "Should Strategic Studies Survive?"

[48] See his reminiscences in Kaplan, "A Poor Boy's Journey."

enjoyed a stint at the Center the same year as Kaplan, along with another rising star of game theory, Anatol Rapoport, and the main proponent of a behavioral science of politics, Harold Lasswell.[49] The following year, 1956–1957, was an even greater vintage for the hybridization of IR with gaming techniques on the fertile hills of Palo Alto. The Center hosted Harold Guetzkow, the director of the Social Science Laboratory at Carnegie Mellon University, then the fiefdom of his old friend Herbert Simon.[50] Trained in biology at Chicago and in psychology at the University of Michigan, Guetzkow had already developed a strong interest in simulations by the time he joined the Center. His year in Palo Alto was crucial in the development of a project that would later be known as the Inter-Nation Simulation (INS), probably one of the most advanced human-computer political interfaces of the time, developed at Northwestern with the support of the Air Force Office of Scientific Research (AFOSR) and the Advanced Research Projects Agency (ARPA) of the Department of Defense. While at the Center, Guetzkow became the leader of a study group on simulated international processes that included Richard C. Snyder, Charles McClelland, Wilbur Schramm, and Karl Deutsch, all of whom made significant contributions to the cybernetic turn in international relations theory.[51] Snyder became chair of the political science department at Northwestern, where he co-directed the INS experiment with Guetzkow in 1957. McClelland contributed to connecting the original project of developing a "theory" of international relations with the quest for formalization. A transfuge from traditional IR, Deutsch had developed an intellectual connection to Norbert Wiener back in 1942 at MIT.[52] Another member of the group was Hans Speier, an

---

[49] Kenneth E. Boulding, "An Apologia," in *Journeys through World Politics: Autobiographical Reflections of Thirty-Four Academic Travelers*, eds., Joseph Kruzel and James N. Rosenau (Lexington: Lexington Books, 1989); Philippe Fontaine, "Stabilizing American Society: Kenneth Boulding and the Integration of the Social Sciences 1943–1980," *Science in Context* 23, no. 2 (2010): 221–65.

[50] Herbert A. Simon, "Maintaining the Peace," in *Theories, Models, and Simulations in International Relations*, ed. Michael D. Ward (Boulder: Westview Press, 1985).

[51] Harold Guetzkow, "Simulated International Processes: An Incomplete History," in *Simulated International Processes: Theories and Research in Global Modeling*, eds., Harold Guetzkow and Joseph J. Valadez (Beverly Hills: Sage, 1981), 13; Michael D. Ward and Daniel Guetzkow, "Obituary: Harold Guetzkow, 1915–2008," *Footnotes* 37, no. 1 (2009), www.asanet.org/sites/default/files/savvy/footnotes/jan09/obit.html#ob it_2 (last accessed January 12, 2017).

[52] Karl W. Deutsch, "A Path among the Social Sciences," in *Journeys through World Politics: Autobiographical Reflections of Thirty-Four Academic Travelers*, eds., Joseph Kruzel and

émigré sociologist who headed the Social Science Division of the RAND Corporation and was promoting the development of political gaming.[53]

Just as Kaplan's career was defined by his encounter with cybernetics, the political scientist William Riker woke up from the dogmatic slumber of traditional pol-sci when he read Lloyd Shapley and Martin Shubik's 1954 paper on the measurement of power using statistical mathematics. Riker's game-theoretical work on political coalitions, which extended this application to international politics but also built critically upon Kaplan's *System and Process*, was entirely written in Palo Alto in 1960–1961.[54] And although its role in the incubation of game theory and systems theory cannot be properly addressed within the confines of this chapter, the RAND Corporation in Santa Monica provided another important site of exchange between strategic thinking and IR theory. "System analysis" was a hallmark of RAND in these years, and Kaplan's program was heavily influenced by it. While it represented a milieu relatively insulated from academia (and, for that matter, of pretty much every social institution including its sponsor, the Air Force), and despite internecine rifts between its Social Science Division and its "hard" branches dealing with mathematics or engineering, RAND was nonetheless instrumental in popularizing gaming and systems theory within a proximate circle of IR scholars interested in problems of military strategy. It had ties to Yale, where it had recruited Bernard Brodie from the Institute for International Studies in 1951, and Thomas Schelling from the economics faculty. And RAND researchers John Kennedy, Robert Chapman, Olaf Helmer, Lloyd Shapley, Joseph Goldsen, and Milton Weiner, as well as Hans Speier, collaborated closely with Guetzkow and his team from Northwestern on the development of political gaming.[55]

The advocates of science also had a powerful outlet with the *Journal for Conflict Resolution* founded in 1955 at the University of Michigan (first issue 1957). The new publication initially managed to muzzle the divisions

---

James N. Rosenau (Lexington: Lexington Books, 1989). On Deutsch's contribution to cybernetics, see Kline, *The Cybernetics Moment*, 143–46.

[53] Herbert Goldhamer and Hans Speier, "Some Observations on Political Gaming," *World Politics* 12, no. 1 (1959): 71–83. On Speier, see Daniel Bessner, *Democracy in Exile: Hans Speier and the Rise of the Defense Intellectual* (Ithaca: Cornell University Press, 2018).

[54] Amadae, *Rationalizing Capitalist Democracy*, 161–63; Riker, *The Theory of Political Coalitions*.

[55] Harold Guetzkow, "A Use of Simulation in the Study of Inter-Nation Relations," in *Simulation in International Relations: Developments for Research and Teaching*, eds., Harold Guetzkow, et al. (Englewood Cliffs, NJ: Prentice-Hall, 1963), 26fn22.

between peace researchers and strategists, federating them under the banner of methodological progress. In 1958, it published as a single issue Schelling's influential manifesto, *The Strategy of Conflict*, which reintegrated empirical analysis within game theory and emphasized the communication component of conflict, thus paving the way toward closer integration between international relations theory, the study of social communication, and formal methods.[56] The Mental Health Research Institute at Michigan (staffed by Rapoport, Boulding, and Mead, among others) also played a role in the diffusion of systems theory among political scientists, in particular through the work of David Easton, who attended the MHRI Staff Theory Seminar. Through RAND, the Center for the Advanced Study of the Behavioral Sciences, and the *Journal of Conflict Resolution*, a methodological toolbox packing a new language of politics was thus released within IR theory where it empowered a new generation of scholars.

On closer scrutiny, however, the generational opposition providing the sociological foundations of the "second debate" conceals as much as it reveals. First, it significantly downplays the bitter divisions running among the "scientists" themselves, split between the strategists, like Schelling or the early Brodie, and the peace researchers, like Boulding, Singer, or Rapoport, who blended ethical considerations into the study of conflict. As Hedley Bull observed at the time, "far from facing the outside world with a united front, [the advocates of the scientific approach] commonly regard one another with the hostility of leaders of Marxist sects."[57] These divisions were not only just as significant as the opposition between the "scientific" and the "traditional" approach to international politics: They also blurred its front lines. By disconnecting their models of strategic rationality from any moral considerations and never moving beyond the narrow horizon of their axiomatic sets, the pure strategists and the systems theorists could claim to be more rigorously scientific than the peace researchers. But by the same token, they were also more "realist", since the Michigan peaceniks appeared as a modernist reincarnation of an earlier "idealism" striving to find an engineering fix to international conflict. Michigan thus hosted "the aggressive come-back of the pacifist psychosociologists," a new species of Wilsonians, as it were, yet "armed with equations and experimental games," in the words of a French realist.[58]

---

[56] Schelling, "The Strategy of Conflict." [57] Bull, "International Theory," 362–63.
[58] Pierre Hassner, *La violence et la paix. De la bombe atomique au nettoyage ethnique* (Paris: Seuil, 2000), 83.

Conversely, Rapoport did not fail to see that some strategists such as Kaplan or Kissinger were reproducing the tenets of classical realism under a new scientific language; tellingly, he called them "neotraditionalists."[59] That the distinction between "realism" and "behavioralism" was far from watertight is further suggested by the frequent collusion between "scientists" and "traditionalists." The two scholars who did the most to usher international relations theory into its scientific age, Morton Kaplan and Kenneth Waltz, were students of William T. R. Fox (the first at Temple University in 1939, the second at Columbia after the war). They were also participants in such realist cenacles as the 1956–57 interuniversity seminar on theory held at Columbia, along with others who would later contribute to the formalistic study of political decisions, such as Burton Sapin, Glenn Snyder, and Robert W. Tufts.[60]

At this stage, what is left of the idea of a "second debate"? The 1960s certainly saw a bitter fight over the legitimate *style* of political scholarship, but this fight was emphatically not a disagreement over the core *principles* of political realism. Tellingly, those who did not subscribe to these principles (such as the group behind the *Journal of Conflict Resolution*) were not protagonists in the debate. The discussion triggered by the increasing reliance on game-theoretic or systemic approaches did not reflect either a process of colonization of political science by economics or economic thinking.[61] It was largely an internal development, whose main players – Kaplan, Schelling, Snyder, etc. – had a legitimate realist pedigree or were fellow travelers. This explains why the continuity with the main tenets of classical IR theory – the pursuit of the national interest defined in terms of power, the state as the primary unit of international politics, the themes of sovereignty and prudential rationality – was uninterrupted. As Sonja Amadae writes, "the first 'rational actor' as conceptualized in game theory and the decision sciences was a nation-state locked in the icy and treacherous grip of the Cold War."[62] Even in the high-tech precinct of the IR program at Northwestern, where Harold Guetzkow and Richard Snyder started developing the INS simulation in 1957, classical realism provided many of the assumptions drawn from the "verbal literature" and translated into program code.[63]

[59] Anatol Rapoport, *Strategy and Conscience* (New York: Harper & Row, 1964), 180–86.
[60] Fox, *Theoretical Aspects*, x.
[61] Guilhot and Marciano, "Rational Choice."
[62] Amadae, *Rationalizing Capitalist Democracy*, 77.
[63] Guetzkow, "Simulated International Processes," 19.

In his retrospective genealogy of the evolution leading from the original INS to the upgraded International Processes Simulation (IPS), Paul Smoker observed that the core of the original simulation involved a restatement in formal language of what was still a set of competing nation-states following the precepts of Morgenthau and Schwarzenberger about power politics.[64] A generation of newcomers thus carried over formal methodologies into the nascent field of IR, which was established around a realist understanding of the political and still in search of a "theory." Far from opposing "realists" and "behavioralist," therefore, the second debate was largely a contest over the legitimate language for articulating a realist theory of politics. In that sense, it signaled an *expansion of realism* beyond its original networks.

Meanwhile, this fact was lost on the old IR guard. The thrust of its critique of the scientific approach targeted the fallacious analogy between the natural and the social sciences, under the assumption that political phenomena are essentially defined by their value-content and their meaning in historical context. What traditional realists saw in the "new scholasticism" of the 1950s was the return of a naturalistic rationalism. Niebuhr thus warned that "the clear refutation of the policies, which rest upon the presupposition that human history can and must be mastered, had not deterred bold scientists in the liberal world from projecting various scientific programs for manipulating historical events as if they were in the dimension of nature."[65] Similarly, Morgenthau approached system analysis and game theory through the lens of his previous attack against the emulation of physics in political science; he dismissed these new developments by referring to his *Scientific Man vs. Power Politics*, which according to him settled the discussion.[66] Classical realists did not register the changing nature of what "science" meant for their younger disciples: essentially, they misread the turn to cybernetic concepts as a new instantiation of traditional economic thinking. In this respect, Morgenthau's reaction has exemplary value:

What characterizes contemporary theories of international relations is the attempt to use the tools of modern economic analysis in a modified form in order to understand international relations. Their mainstay is quantification. The use of

---

[64] Paul L. Smoker, "The International Processes Simulation," in *Simulated International Processes: Theories and Research in Global Modeling*, eds., Harold Guetzkow and Joseph J. Valadez (Beverly Hills: Sage, 1981), 102.
[65] Niebuhr, *Christian Realism*, 11.
[66] Morgenthau, "Reflections," 441.

terms such as 'systems analysis,' 'feedback,' 'input,' and 'output' (to mention only a few common and easily accessible ones) is revealing, for these concepts were first developed by economic theory.[67]

This was a fundamental misunderstanding of the situation. Being neither versed in the subtleties of game theory or system analysis, nor cognizant of their cyborg genealogy, the realist old guard was totally unaware that these tools provided advocates of a "science" of international relations with a way *out* of the *Methodenstreit* fought in the 1930s and 1940s over the fundamental differences between the physical and the human. Morgenthau had tellingly declared that the scientific approach was particularly inapt to deliver insights when it was applied to "phenomena which are determined by historic individuality, *rational* or moral *choice*," unaware that the notions of choice and rationality were precisely the core of the scientific approach.[68] It is hard to overstate the extent to which the emerging paradigm was defined by its capacity to incorporate notions that were deemed ontologically incommensurable with the formal specifications going under the label of "science." As early as 1948, the Weberian sociologist Theodore Abel had published an article ominously entitled "The Operation called *Verstehen*," which was a weathervane indicating the coming intellectual storm. Not only was the epistemological exceptionalism of the human sciences indefensible, Abel suggested, but the long-held distinctions supposed to shield them from the scientistic dreams of operation research and cybernetics could no longer be relied upon.[69] The world as the realists knew it, neatly divided between the solid reality of human nature and the corrosive artifact of technology, was unraveling. Waging a rearguard battle against a specter of the past, the old realists did not see the revolution brewing: Inspired by methods that formalized the process of decision as a set of operations involving calculative capacities and enabling its simulation through technical artifacts, the scientific approach had collapsed the boundary between the physical and the human, making the entire discussion about scientific reductionism moot.[70] This was probably the most important achievement of the decision sciences: once detached from the deciding subject, the political decision itself was amenable to a "scientific" treatment and

---

[67] Morgenthau, *Truth and Power*, 244.
[68] Morgenthau, "Reflections on the State of Political Science," 442, emphasis mine.
[69] Theodore Abel, "The Operation Called Verstehen," *The American Journal of Sociology* 54, no. 3 (1948): 211–18.
[70] For a discussion of the obsolescence of reductionism in the cyborg sciences, see Mirowski, *Machine Dreams*, 13–14.

could be reproduced in a laboratory setting.[71] But neither did the postwar realists realize how much this new science of international relations owed to their own metaphysical view of the sovereign decision, and to a non-perfectionist conception of politics now parading as the minimax. The second debate was in fact a huge misunderstanding, for "scientific" IR was a blessing in disguise for realism.

KAPLAN'S CYBORG, OR WHAT SYSTEMS THEORY DID FOR IR

In order to understand the cyborg turn of international relations theory in the late 1960s, it is necessary to start from the *Ur*-debate over the fundamental differences between the methods of the human sciences and those of the natural sciences. To the extent that the IR "scientists" were trained in the 1940s, this debate was part of their academic regimen. E. H. Carr, Morgenthau, and many others had inveighed against the temptation to hand the field over to the social sciences, and their arguments were constitutive of IR theory. It should come as no surprise that references to this debate provide the exordium to most methodological reflections. Practically every statement written at the time by the advocates of scientific IR starts by acknowledging the insurmountable hurdles preventing the application of the method of the natural sciences to the study of politics, and their tribute to physics often sounds like a longing for the unattainable object of desire. William Riker has probably gone further than anybody else in listing such difficulties: "Numerous obstacles stand in the way, however, of direct emulation (...) human action is itself enormously more complex than the motion of things (...) As a consequence of these obstacles, the behavioral sciences are *sciences* only by the kindly tolerance of university faculties who are willing to put up with our pretensions and ambitions in appropriating the name."[72] Morton Kaplan did not lag far behind, and opened his defense of the scientific approach by conceding that "systems embodying purpose cannot be studied by the methods ordinarily used by physicists."[73] "We must give up the hope," he wrote, "that a theory of international politics can have either the explanatory or the predictive power of a 'hard' science."[74] Similar voices were heard even

---

[71] Heyck, *Age of System*, in particular chapter 4.
[72] Riker, *Theory of Political Coalitions*, 3–6.
[73] Kaplan, "The New Great Debate," 2.
[74] Morton A. Kaplan, "Problems of Theory Building and Theory Confirmation in International Politics," in *The International System: Theoretical Essays*, eds., Klaus Knorr and Sidney Verba (Princeton: Princeton University Press, 1961), 20.

at the RAND Corporation, where Bernard Brodie was the first to admit that "the nature of political science is determined by a subject matter which is fundamentally different from the subject matter of the physical sciences."[75]

But these lyrical *ouvertures* lamenting the irreducible distance between the natural and the political were usually followed by a *molto allegro* movement bridging the gap with the help of various cybernetic props. For it was hard to take "no" as an answer in those years, especially since the scientific bride came with a lofty dowry from its Establishment family, usually under the form of lavish funding from the Air Force or the Ford Foundation. Newly minted researchers in international relations theory were therefore confronted with a conundrum: Everything invited them to do "science," but their masters had also taught them that politics had nothing to do with it. But what if they could find an object-like *proxy* for politics? What if they could *simulate* politics with devices that were entirely amenable to scientific treatment, without having to take a position on the *nature* of the political itself? What if they could have it both ways?

The solution to this problem was a moment of intellectual epiphany for Morton Kaplan, who first introduced a systems theory perspective in mainstream IR. It took the form of a transformative encounter with cybernetics in 1954, when Kaplan read Ross Ashby's book *Design for a Brain* while working on US foreign policy at the Brookings Institution. The encounter with Ashby led him "to see things differently" and played a "major role" in his subsequent formulation of the problem of the balance of power.[76] Ashby belonged to a small group of early British cyberneticians often grounded in psychiatry and primarily interested in understanding the brain as an adaptive system.[77] *Design for a Brain* was based on the assumption that some mechanical systems (which Ashby called respectively "homeostatic" and "ultrastable") could behave adaptively, and hence that the brain could be understood as a machine that coped with changing circumstances.[78] Although Ashby was strictly concerned with the logic of corrective behavior at the individual level and did not make the leap into macroscropic applications, he placed no limits

---

[75] Bernard Brodie, *Scientific Progress and Political Science* (Santa Monica: The RAND Corporation, 1956), 9.
[76] Kaplan, "A Poor Boy's Journey," 43.
[77] On Ashby, see Pickering, *The Cybernetic Brain*.
[78] William Ross Ashby, *Design for a Brain*, 2nd (revised) edn. (New York: John Wiley & Sons, 1960).

on them. This encounter with cybernetics was a defining moment for Kaplan, as it provided a solution to his previous search for an "operational code" of statecraft without, however, having to either endorse or discard realist metaphysics.[79] It was also path-breaking for the future development of the discipline. For if the presence of value-oriented purpose was what made politics impervious to the method of physics, as Morgenthau, Carr, Niebuhr, and others never tired of repeating, this essential distinction no longer held. For "suitably defined (...) purpose need not distinguish the physical from the human," Kaplan suggested, before providing a typical example from the cybernetic literature, namely an automatic pilot with a reverse wiring system ensuring level flight through negative feedback: "Although the operation of the automatic pilot in this case differs from human purpose in two important respects – lack of consciousness and simplicity of the system – it has much in common with it."[80]

It is worth dwelling for a moment on Kaplan's example of the autopilot, for it packs a number of interlocking themes. First, it is a paradigmatic statement that enshrines the importance of servomechanical theory for political science, by recycling what by then had become clichés of the cybernetic literature. The aeronautical reference was also a common birthmark of systems theory, characteristic of its early years spent under the motherly care of the Air Force. Second, it bears one of the main hallmarks of the cyborg sciences, namely "the breaching of the ramparts between the Natural and the Social, the Human and the Inhuman."[81] By collapsing these domains into each other, the servomechanical imitation of goal-attainment behavior allowed for the fluid circulation of anthropocentric categories between the organic and the inorganic, at any level of complexity. As Ashby wrote, "once it is appreciated that feedback can be used to correct any deviation we like, it is easy to understand that there is no limit to the complexity of goal-seeking behavior which may occur in machines quite devoid of any 'vital' factor."[82] It is essential to understand that this possibility was itself a feedback effect of

---

[79] See Morton A. Kaplan, "An Introduction to the Strategy of Statecraft," *World Politics* 4, no. 4 (1952): 548–76. Draft chapters of *System and Process in International Politics* (1957) were read and vetted by an impressive roster of scholars coming from cybernetics (Ashby), economics (Beckmann, Hoselitz, Shubik), physics (Platt), mathematics (Raiffa), besides political scientists and sociologists. Morton A. Kaplan, *System and Process in International Politics* (New York: John Wiley & Sons, 1957), 19.

[80] Kaplan, "The New Great Debate," 2.   [81] Mirowski, *Machine Dreams*, 12.

[82] Ross Ashby, *Design for a Brain*, 55.

a prior critique of purposiveness as a form of explanation. The notion of feedback was initially used to rid scientific descriptions of any teleological causation. Only then did "goal-seeking" come back as a mere *metaphor* that cut both ways. For once it became possible to describe goal-seeking without reference to willful purpose, by the same token, "having 'explained away' foresight, goal-directedness, and so on, [it was possible to] apply these anthropomorphic notions without misgivings in explaining behaviour of systems to which we would be reluctant to ascribe these faculties 'seriously.'"[83] Before the rise of system theory, "notions of teleology and directiveness appeared to be outside the scope of science and to be the playground of mysterious, supernatural or anthropomorphic agencies."[84] Once purpose or value-orientation no longer had to refer to the unfathomable depths of a conscience, nothing prevented the study of politics from becoming a cyborg science. The old debate over the specificity of politics was entirely circumvented, since what took place was an ontological flattening whereby radically different entities were made commensurable if not equivalent through a notion of "systems." If power was "the ability to attain goals," as Kaplan suggested, then it could be replicated by systems displaying all the external characteristics of goal-seeking. As a result, one could think of a "political system" without taking a position over the nature of power or the value-content of politics, since power understood as "the ability to attain goals" could be entirely specified in operational terms.[85] In *System and Process*, "systems" became the measure of all things: A declaration of war thus became equivalent to a viral breach of the immune system, a military chain of command was similar to neural communication, and the balance of power was not fundamentally different from a thermostat or indeed life itself.[86] Politics, immunology, neurology, or avionics certainly dealt with very different objects, but it did not matter since, ultimately, the true nature of these objects could be black-boxed. The distinctive trait of the cybernetic approach was that it did not pronounce upon the essence of what it understood as a system, and postulated instead "an ontology of unknowability."[87] Essentially, this meant that once IR theory started thinking of international politics as a system, it was no longer

---

[83] Anatol Rapoport, *General System Theory: Essential Concepts & Applications* (Tunbridge Wells: Abacus, 1986), 186.
[84] Ludwig von Bertalanffy, *General System Theory: Foundations, Development, Applications* (New York: George Braziller, 1968), 45.
[85] Kaplan, *System and Process*, 12.   [86] Kaplan, *System and Process*, 4–5.
[87] Pickering, *The Cybernetic Brain*, 23.

fundamentally concerned with the real, not least because the real had become disturbingly conflated with its own simulation.

REALITY SHOW AT NORTHWESTERN

By providing an analog for international power politics, the notion of "system" paved the way for the ubiquitous reliance on simulation, certainly one of the defining features of international relations theory in the 1960s. But simulation is a fuzzy thing: At a first level it provided the very epistemic basis for "scientific" IR and nothing short of a theory of knowledge. In order to be observed, the relevant features of political reality had to be sampled and abstracted from their thick shell of historical complexity, and sampling was already understood as something akin to simulation, if not identical with it.[88] A truly scientific knowledge of politics, in a sense, was always a simulation. In a closely related sense, simulation was also understood as a "model of a system" distinguished by its operational dimension and allowing for the *in vitro* manipulation of its key variables.[89] It was an "operable representation."[90] At yet another level, simulation took the form of games where players, who could be humans or machines or an assemblage of both, played out the different possibilities offered by a system of rules: "physical and/or biological representations of systems which attempt to replicate sociopolitical processes."[91] Finally, simulations were also used as pedagogical tools for teaching diplomacy and international affairs, and are still widely used for this purpose in international curricula and foreign service schools.

It is also important to emphasize that the notions of system, simulation, and games were characterized by their fluidity and, at least in IR theory, formed a set of tightly enmeshed ideas echoing each other. Game theory was fundamentally tied to system analysis when it came to military or political issues, since it made visible the interdependence of two decision centers, which then could be represented as forming a unit of higher

---

[88] Richard C. Snyder, "Some Perspectives on the Use of Experimental Techniques in the Study of International Relations," in *Simulation in International Relations: Developments for Research and Teaching*, eds., Harold Guetzkow, et al. (Englewood Cliffs, NJ: Prentice-Hall, 1963).

[89] Sidney Verba, "Simulation, Reality, and Theory in International Relations," *World Politics* 16, no. 3 (1964): 491.

[90] Guetzkow, "A Use of Simulation," 33.

[91] Richard A Brody, "Varieties of Simulations in International Relations Research," in *Simulation in International Relations: Developments for Research and Teaching*, eds., Harold Guetzkow, et al. (Englewood Cliffs, NJ: Prentice-Hall, 1963), 191.

complexity: it "ma[de] explicit the assumptions employed with respect to the nature of the international system."[92] Any game-theoretical schematic, therefore, can be seen as representing a system and its variables, just as much as it is also a simulation. The fortune of simulations and gaming in IR were also tied to the expansion of the game-theoretical program beyond formalism and toward empirical testing suggested by Thomas Schelling.[93] To the extent that most situations of political conflict could be understood as n-person non-zero sum games that by definition do not have a mathematical solution, the staging of the game was required to compensate for this built-in element of indeterminacy by generating the missing information or developing an intuitive sense of how the "system" was operating.[94]

Although games and simulations promised to bridge the gap between the systemic "metamodel" and political "reality," the latter notion had become increasingly fuzzy in the meantime.[95] Games, it turned out, were not so much allowing reality to inform the experiment as they generated cyborg actors. In this respect, the INS undertaken at Northwestern by Guetzkow was revealing. As human players representing fictitious nations took decisions on the basis of domestic situations generated by the program, it quickly appeared to the organizers that they were "acting as surrogates rather than as experimental subjects in their own right." "Our simulation," Guetzkow realized, "was not (...) a laboratory counter-part of field behaviors."[96]

To the extent that humans players acted as system-generated proxies rather than selves, these surrogates were also conforming to the need to "close" theoretical constructs as formulated by Kaplan. In both epistemic and material ways, the INS simulation room was thus tightly sealed off to prevent any intrusion of reality, just like today's reality shows (Figure 5.1). The only scientific way to understand politics was as

---

[92] Kaplan, *System and Process*, 167.
[93] On Schelling, see in particular Mirowski, *Machine Dreams*, 367–69 and Esther-Mirjma Sent, "Some Like It Cold: Thomas Schelling as a Cold Warrior," *Journal of Economic Methodology* 14, no. 4 (2007): 455–71.
[94] Schelling, "The Strategy of Conflict," 257; Thomas Schelling, "Experimental Games and Bargaining Theory," in *The International System: Theoretical Essays*, eds., Klaus Knorr and Sidney Verba (Princeton: Princeton University Press, 1961); Ghamari-Tabrizi, *The Worlds of Herman Kahn*, 161–65.
[95] Richard E. Quandt, "On the Use of Game Models in Theories of International Relations," *World Politics* 14, no. 1 (1961): 69–76.
[96] Guetzkow, "Simulated International Processes," 16.

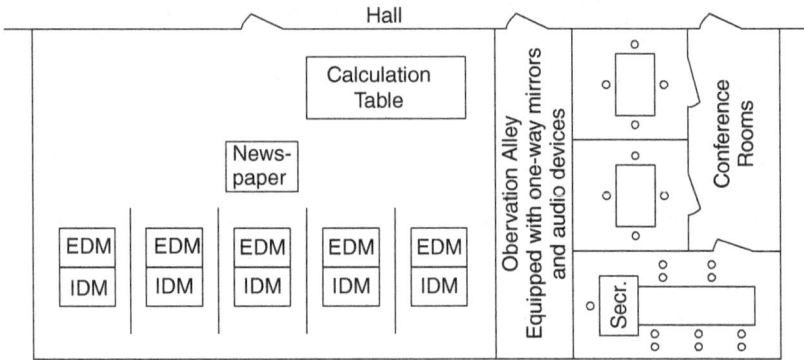

FIGURE 5.1 Simulation room, integrated circuit, computer, or reality show TV studio?
The INS gaming room at Northwestern (reprinted from Harold Guetzkow, "A Use of Simulation in the Study of Inter-Nation Relations," in *Simulation in International Relations: Developments for Research and Teaching*, ed. Harold Guetzkow et al. (Englewood Cliffs, N. J.: Prentice-Hall, 1963), 30.)

a simulacrum, and this understanding was then projected upon all politics: History itself became a reality show illustrating the operation of different systemic models; it was nothing but "the great laboratory within which international action occurs," except it was a bigger, better equipped lab featuring the most vivid and realistic simulations.[97]

Needless to say, these ontological displacements of "reality" precipitated a crisis of classical political "realism."[98] It is not so much that they reflected some kind of idealism or a principled critique of realism: rather, they determined its gradual obsolescence. Realism still provided the intellectual matrix for many advocates of the new science of international politics. Kaplan, for instance, "still found the concept theoretically useful" when he wrote his first professional article in 1952, but he later confessed he "had jettisoned it" by the time he wrote *System and Process*.[99] The scientific approach could dispense with a strong notion of reality and yet still produce a quasi-identical version of politics (albeit a synthetic one). For realism was not only a vision of politics, but also a bleak view of human *nature*, rooted in the drive for power, which was ultimately unfalsifiable and metaphysical. A concretion of nineteenth-century psychology, historicism, and interwar

---

[97] Kaplan, *System and Process*, 3. On spillover effects between reality and experiment, see in particular Rebecca M Lemov, *World as Laboratory: Experiments with Mice, Mazes, and Men* (New York: Hill and Wang, 2005).
[98] Ghamari-Tabrizi, *The Worlds of Herman Kahn*, 165–74.
[99] Kaplan, "An Introduction"; Kaplan, "A Poor Boy's Journey," 46.

political theology, realism dragged along a heavy dose of speculative thinking that kept it on the margins of the postwar reinvention of academia on the model of the wartime R&D lab connected to governmental centers. This was arguably a problem from the very first attempts at establishing the new discipline on a realist footing. In early international relations theory, much of the theoretical activity sought to cope with this situation and to dispense with such cumbersome foundations. Formulating a realist vision of politics without reference to human nature was already a problem that some classical realists had tried to address.

Yet, the solution offered by Kaplan, Guetzkow et al. promised even greater pay-offs. It solved the problems of the speculative and metaphysical foundations of realism by getting rid of foundations altogether. One could represent politics *as if* it were organized around the drive for power, without subscribing to all the metaphysical paraphernalia of classical realism. Out of fashion in the forward-looking 1960s, the Augustinian *animus dominandi* that drove the destitute creature of the realists were now replaced with the feedback servomechanisms animating a goal-seeking cyborg freshly released from its incubating pod.[100] As a result, world politics looked exactly the same, but there was nothing to feel sorry about.

Of course, the reliance on simulations offered a stark contrast with the previous ontological claims to speak for human nature or the essence of power. But one should be wary of accepting realism's pretense to access the true nature of things, and consider the second debate as a contest between different accounts of what counted as "real," and by extension of different authoritative fictions. As James Der Derian points out, "realism has built a life out of the transformation of fictions, like the immutability of human nature and the apodictic threat of anarchy, into facticity."[101] Once this is acknowledged, it is clear that nothing stood in the way of realism accomplishing the opposite movement and turning facticity into a second level meta-fiction, made of simulations, models, and games. This

---

[100] Cybernetics was quite compatible with such psychoanalytical themes: see Orit Halpern, "Dreams for Our Perceptual Present: Temporality, Storage, and Interactivity in Cybernetics," *Configurations* 13, no. 2 (2005): 283–319. On Nietzsche's influence upon Morgenthau, see Frei, *Morgenthau*; Michael C. Williams, "Morgenthau Now: Neoconservatism, National Greatness, and Realism," in *Realism Reconsidered: The Legacy of Hans J. Morgenthau in International Relations*, ed. Michael C. Williams (Oxford: Oxford University Press, 2007).

[101] James Der Derian, *Virtuous War: Mapping the Military-Industrial-Media-Entertainment Network* (New York: Routledge, 2009), 36.

newly acknowledged fictitiousness proved to be liberating, for it meant that the power maximization principle could now be detached from the heavy ballast of human nature and transported across a wide range of situations. This may have been Realism-lite – a heavily processed intellectual nutrient for sure – but it allowed everybody, including the weaker stomachs, to enjoy the exhilarating taste of realism without having to digest its heaviest metaphysical ingredients, some of which were past their consumption date after 1945.

THE UNBEARABLE LIGHTNESS OF THE DECISION

In retrospect, the transformation of realism from a political anthropology into the operational code of politics appears to have been the major precondition for the scientific objectivization of political decision procedures. Decisions were indeed central to game-theoretic or systemic approaches to IR: In *System and Process*, Kaplan defined the political system as an articulated but unified decision-making procedure[102]; Riker suggested that the entire field of political science was contained within the Morgenstern-Von Neumann theory of *n*-person games because "the subject studied by political scientists is decision-making" and political decisions are made by and within groups, and are therefore a matter of coalition-formation.[103] Decisions were also important in early realism, which associated them with a metaphysics of sovereignty. The difference was that conditions of rationality could now be specified for political decisions, at least to a degree allowing for measuring deviations from rationality standards. "Rationality" thus took the center stage in a discipline that so far had thrived on the uneasy relationship between rationalism and politics. The transformation of realism, in a sense, was also the transformation of decisionism into "rational choice."

But was this a genuine revolution? One would look in vain for a stable definition of rationality in the IR literature: The notion seems to have been more of a Schellingian tacit focal point than an explicit standard.[104] A useful synthesis is the 1961 article by Sidney Verba on "Assumptions

---

[102] Kaplan, *System and Process*, 13–14.
[103] Riker, *Theory of Political Coalitions*, 11.
[104] The game-theoretical literature has systematically tended to operate with a very thin notion of rationality often conflated with transitivity or has produced only ambiguous and unsatisfactory definitions of it. See Amadae, *Rationalizing Capitalist Democracy*, 127; Rapoport, *Strategy and Conscience*, 166; and more generally Erickson et al., *How Reason Almost Lost Its Mind*.

of Rationality and Non-Rationality in Models of the International System." Coming from a scholar attuned to the cybernetic themes of social communication and published in the 1961 special issue of *World Politics* dedicated to systemic approaches to IR, Verba's essay is an important landmark in the redeployment of realism in the 1960s. After distinguishing between "irrational" decisions caused by idiosyncratic psychological drives and "rational" ones based on cool-headed "means-ends calculation," Verba went on to specify what conditions were conducive to rationality in the handling of international affairs. In line with the assumptions behind simulations and games, Verba saw rationality essentially residing in the *insulation* of the decision-making process: "the greater the involvement of an individual in a situation, the greater will be the effect of non-logical and predispositional influences."[105] This understanding of rationality was compounded by its conflation with "transitivity." In the game-theoretical literature, transitivity referred to consistency in the ranking of preferences: If I prefer A to B and B to C, then I also prefer A to C. In many organizational settings, and in particular in policy matters where decisions were collective, such consistency could hardly obtain: Ordering utilities for individuals was already problematic, but doing so for collectives was simply impossible, which obviously compromised the rationality of collective decisions.[106] Lurking in the background of Verba's argument, the Arrow theorem about the impossibility of rational social choice already functioned in political science and IR as an incentive to associate even more closely rationality with the non-conditioned nature of the political decision – or, to put it differently, with its sovereign and authoritative nature. The problem, then, was to identify social settings where a situation of unconditioned decision-making insulated from external inputs could be approximated so as to make decisions more rational. The deviation from rationality standards observed whenever decisions were entangled in a dense web of institutional determinations

suggests the importance of decision-making or, at least, decision-recommending outside of a bureaucratic context. Means-ends rationality as a process of decision-making is more closely approximated in research and in decisions that are 'unattached' rather than bureaucratic. The search for policy alternatives by unattached intellectuals is less inhibited by organizational coalitions (...)

---

[105] Sidney Verba, "Assumptions of Rationality and Non-Rationality in Models of the International System," *World Politics* 14, no. 1 (1961): 99–100.
[106] Verba, "Assumptions of Rationality," 111.

Unattached intellectual research, therefore, can introduce a higher level of means-ends rationality into foreign-policy decision-making.[107]

The cadre of defense intellectuals to which Verba himself belonged thus reimagined themselves as members of a Mannheimian "free-floating" intelligentsia securing the possibility of disinterested knowledge and therefore of rational decision-making. Yet, they were "unattached" in a concrete but different way, as the Cold War science regime, with its military-corporate-philanthropic nexus and its patterns of funding, shielded them from social influences under multiple layers of institutional protection.[108] Insulated from the pressures of public opinion, scrutiny, and accountability, they were in a better position to express the "rational" element of the decision than true decision-makers exposed to volatile publics. Verba was in fact articulating a widespread assumption of the nascent decision sciences: Far from underscoring the limitations of game-theoretical models, the introduction of bureaucratic complexity in research designs only served to validate these models, as it was meant to account for the *deviation* from rationality observed in real life. Reality was coming short of its own simulation. Originating at RAND out of the need to explain irrational resources allocation of the Soviet defense system, the "bureaucratic politics" paradigm spread through IR via the "May Group" at Harvard, which, from 1966 onward, spawned various research projects on the impact of organizational factors on political decisions, and in particular *The Essence of Decision*, which we encountered in the previous chapter.[109] Only when the decision was uprooted from its immediate organizational environment and from the uninterrupted jetstream of events and its multiple chains of causation to be relocated in the netherworld of simulation rooms, wargaming, and prisoner's dilemmas, did it upgrade to the status of "rational choice." By the same token, however, rationality was coming dangerously close to being conflated with an attribute of sovereignty, namely its unconditioned nature.

This surreptitious entanglement of rationality and sovereignty characteristic of game theory did not go entirely unnoticed. In his "Notes on the observation and measurement of political power," Herbert Simon could

---

[107] Verba, "Assumptions of Rationality," 115–16.
[108] Mirowski, *Machine Dreams*, 156–61; Heyck, *Age of System*, 51–80; Solovey, *Shaky Foundations*. On defense intellectuals, see Bessner, *Democracy in Exile*.
[109] Marc Trachtenberg, "Strategic Thought in America, 1952–1966," *Political Science Quarterly* 104, no. 2 (1989): 321–22.

only point out that power evoked disturbing "pre-Humeian and pre-Newtonian notions of causality" in a scientific world converted to symmetrical functional interrelations.[110] Closer to IR, Karl Deutsch developed further the political implications, which, according to him, haunted the notion of transitivity. Suggesting that there were games where transitivity did not apply and where "A take B, B takes C, but C takes A," he suggested that such "loop patterns of dominance" could be found, for instance, "in the relationship of the British Parliament to the prime minister." He went on: "the simple notion of sixteenth- and seventeenth-century lawyers, that there must always be one single supreme law-giver or 'sovereign' in a country, contains the hidden assumption that the political decision system of each country must be transitive."[111] Transitivity thus functioned as a powerful conceptual interchange seamlessly weaving together the semantics of rationality and sovereignty around shared meanings such as "unattachment," non-caused determination, or indeed transitivity itself. Similarly, the axiomatic closure of game-theoretical analysis was both a condition of rationality of the decision at hand and a formalism akin to traditional figurations of sovereignty as an instance *qui nulli subest*. The ambivalence of these notions and the fact that they were also *political metaphors* suggest that, as it was staged in scientific IR theory, rationality increasingly took on the attributes of sovereignty. This meant that rational choice could only be a sovereign decision, but also that it was rational *because* it was absolutely sovereign, and that any limitation, bureaucratic or otherwise, on this sovereignty implied a lesser degree of rationality. Abandoning any strong or naturalistic notions of a transformative rationality constraining sovereign power from outside, the postwar science of international relations derived rationality from the realist bedrock of the sovereign decision in a context of high uncertainty and potential conflict. In the end, by construing the political decision as an absolute origin eschewing any prior determinations, a *terminus ab quo* conjuring a low-level rationality out of pure conflict, the language of rational choice resonated with uncanny echoes of a Schmittian decisionism for which the sovereign decision sprung "from the normative nothing and a concrete disorder."[112]

---

[110] Simon, "Notes on the Observation and Measurement of Political Power," 503.
[111] Karl W. Deutsch, "Game Theory and Politics: Some Problems of Application," *The Canadian Journal of Economics and Political Science* 20, no. 1 (1954): 77–78.
[112] Carl Schmitt, *On the Three Types of Juristic Thought* (Westport, CT: Praeger, 2004), 62. It should be noted that cybernetic research was often justified by decisionist arguments. The origins of cybernetic machines, for instance, lay in Norbert Wiener's desire to be "of

Fifth Deterrence Game

The fifth deterrence game is exactly the same as the fourth deterrence game with the addition of a research and development program. We assure now that both players are trying to develop better bombs and better concrete for their cellars. It is clear that if one player gets a substantial lead on the other player, so that for example his bomb is certain to wreck his energy's cellar making it impossible for the other to retaliate, then the quality of the game will change drastically. Under these circumstances it behooves both players to have extremely large research and development programs and to follow up all

FIGURE 5.2: R&D as ultimate deterrence: Kahn's Fifth Deterrence Game From Herman Kahn and Irwin Mann's *Game Theory*, RAND, p. 63. Courtesy of RAND Corporation. Full report accessible at http://www.rand.org/pubs/papers/P1166.html (last accessed January 17, 2017)

By the 1960s, political realism was in the midst of a profound mutation of its forms and of its languages. It no longer expressed itself primarily in the religiously inflected idiom of political theology and sovereignty – it had "quietly secularized itself"[113] – nor did it present itself as a historical knowledge or wisdom. Its secularization meant that it had dropped its traditional opposition to science: political realism now came clad in the sophisticated and often abstruse schematics of game theory, general systems, and cybernetics. Yet, what has gone largely unnoticed is that this new "scientific" apparatus had nothing to do with previous epistemologies that saw in every science a derivation of physics.

By the same token, however, science itself was sucked into the iterative loops of the strategic decision and lost control over its creature, as R&D became entirely subsumed under the mind game called deterrence, where it was reduced to the component of a strategy mix (Figure 5.2). Science

---

use during the emergency" (quoted in Galison, "The Ontology of the Enemy," 228.). Kaplan also used decisionist language when he suggested that "we cannot wait for the law of averages to work in our favor" to make decisions informed by an imperfect theory of systems. The idea that a bad decision is better than no decision is always the telltale sign of decisionism. Kaplan, *System and Process*, 550.

[113] Jones, "Christian Realism," 371.

was no longer "speaking truth to power," as even an old realist such as Morgenthau still liked to believe: Now, power was the truth of science, and science provided it with its new symbols, insignia, and dramaturgy. Neorealism was in fact decisionism with a vengeance: a doctrine of sovereignty that equated power and rationality, a totalizing vision of politics that no longer recognized an outside of politics in an all-encompassing system, and a set of decision-making technologies modeled after the sovereign decision and adapted to the constant state of emergency called the Cold War.

6

The Americanization of Realism: Kenneth Waltz, the Security Dilemma, and the Problem of Decision-Making*

"All masters of decision are dangerous."
Kenneth Waltz, *Foreign Policy and Democratic Politics: The American and British Experience* (Boston: Little, Brown & Co., 1967), 267.

"The decisionist is out to de-ideologize politics entirely."
Judith Shklar, "Decisionism," in *Rational Decision*, ed. Carl Friedrich (New York: Prentice-Hall, 1964): 15.

We saw in the previous chapter how a "new" political realism emerged in the 1960s – a realism supported by an entirely new intellectual style, no longer associated with conservative political theory or with traditionalist critiques of modernity but, on the contrary, with modernist social science. Neorealism, however, did not depart from classical realism in terms of its fundamental ideological worldview, its distrust of democracy in foreign policy matters, or its assumption that rationality was the prerogative of a small class of seasoned statesmen, now retooled as defense intellectuals armed with academic credentials and abstruse forms of expertise.[1] Yet, it justified it in seemingly non-ideological terms, as a scientific and logical requirement devoid of political significance and based upon the objective

---

* This chapter is a largely rewritten version of an essay co-authored with Daniel Bessner. It however retains a lot of the original insights developed in collaboration with him. I am extremely grateful to Daniel for allowing me to reproduce it here in a modified form. The idea of neorealism being the solution to the anti-liberal orientation of classical realism through the elimination of the decision-maker first emerged in discussion with Daniel.
[1] Bessner, *Democracy in Exile*.

and dispassionate consideration of the strategic element in international relations. It would take a few more years, however, until the publication of Kenneth Waltz's *Theory of International Politics* in 1979, for neorealism to achieve full ascendency within the discipline and forever eclipse previous forms of political realism. Neorealism offered a version of realism where the actors were no longer directly relevant and disappear behind the overall "system" of international politics, thus displacing foreign policy decisions outside the purview of IR theory. Since, neorealism has become the basic intellectual regimen taught to cohorts of students enrolled in international relations courses, at least in the United States.

That realism achieved dominance precisely when it seemed to have severed its ties to political decision-making is not the least of the paradoxes of neorealism. The reasons for its intellectual success are also puzzling. While *Theory of International Politics* is hailed as a major theoretical breakthrough in the efforts to establish realism on scientific foundations, the book has never been the object of much historical curiosity or efforts at contextualization.[2] It stands as a sort of towering *terminus ab quo* in the literature, a self-standing work of theoretical brilliance, whose intellectual origins are left vague, not least by Waltz himself, who shrouded the origins of his theory in the ineffable mysteries of creative inspiration.[3] Yet, even a cursory glance at the influences at work in *Theory of International Politics* suggests that it is not the watershed it is considered to be, but a rather conventional exercise within the context of political science at the time. The intellectual sources of neorealism appear both in *Theory of International Politics* and in an embryonic version of the book published in the 1975 *Handbook of Political Science*.[4] The references that Waltz found most useful to develop his own approach to international relations include major cybernetic treatises such as Ross Ashby's *Design for a Brain* (1952) – which was enormously influential for international relations theorists and which we already encountered in the previous chapter – or Norbert Wiener's bestselling *Cybernetics*

---

[2] For a broader analysis of the origins of *Theory of International Politics*, see Daniel Bessner and Nicolas Guilhot, "How Realism Waltzed Off: Liberalism and Decisionmaking In Kenneth Waltz's Neorealism," *International Security* 40, no. 2 (2015): 87–118.

[3] For Waltz, "a brilliant intuition flashes, a creative idea emerges. One cannot say how the intuition comes and how the idea is born." Waltz, *Theory*, 9.

[4] Kenneth Waltz, "Theory of International Relations," in *Handbook of Political Science: International Politics*, eds., Fred I. Greenstein and Nelson W. Polsby, Handbook of Political Science (Reading, MA: Addison-Wesley, 1975).

(1948) and a number of other important contributions to cybernetic theory.[5] In other words, *Theory of International Politics* belonged to a wider body of political science scholarship that applied cybernetic insights (when not simply cybernetic terminology) to political problems. Earlier examples include works we already encountered in previous chapters, notably Morton Kaplan's *System and Process in International Relations* (1957), Graham Allison's *Essence of Decision* (1971), and John Steinbruner's *The Cybernetic Theory of Decision* (1974). *Theory of International Politics* was in fact a late addition to this broader intellectual movement, and therefore not a particularly original work. What is even more puzzling is that it appeared precisely when the cybernetic movement had entered its terminal crisis.[6] Why, then, did Waltz's *oeuvre* achieve the status it did?

Without discounting the role of Waltz's incisive style and intellectual brilliance in securing the iconic status of *Theory*, the reasons for the success of neorealism lie in the long history of realism in the United States, and in particular in obstacles toward its integration in the political-cultural mainstream, which *Theory* managed to lift. Waltz provided a reformulation of some basic principles of traditional realism, as some commentators have noted.[7] But it would be wrong to understand this reformulation exclusively as a methodological step forward. It sanctified the reconciliation of power politics and science and ironed out in the process major ideological issues associated with power politics, in particular the undemocratic implications of realism.

THE DILEMMA BEHIND THE SECURITY DILEMMA

The systemic vision of international politics that is the hallmark of *Theory of International Politics* extends and reformulates prior structural representations of international relations made possible by the adoption of the "security dilemma" as a core concept of realist thought. A standard notion of international relations theory, the security dilemma designates the inescapable situation in which states are locked as their search for security is inevitably perceived as a threat for others: "many of the means

---

[5] Waltz, *Theory of International Politics*, 40, fn; Waltz, *Theory of International Politics*.
[6] Kline, *The Cybernetics Moment*.
[7] Thus Robert Keohane: "The significance of Waltz's theory ... lies less in his initiation of a new line of theoretical inquiry or speculation than in his attempt to systematize political realism into a rigorous, deductive systemic theory of international politics." Robert O. Keohane, "Realism, Neorealism and the Study of World Politics," in *Neorealism and Its Critics*, ed. Robert O. Keohane (New York: Columbia University Press, 1986), 15.

by which a state tries to increase its security decrease the security of others."[8] The security dilemma was given pride of place in Waltz's 1959 *Man, the State, and War*, and a more systemic turn in *Theory of International Politics*. The notion, however, had been elaborated much earlier by American and British classical realists, particularly John Herz and Herbert Butterfield. Trying to move away from theologically inflected references to a vague "human nature," Herz had attempted to reformulate realism in situational rather than in psychological terms around the so-called security dilemma. The reason threats would never cease to emerge and conflicts would always be fought no matter the degree of rationality applied to the treatment of political problems, Herz suggested, had nothing to do with old metaphysical ideas about a flawed human nature. Rather, it was the uncertainty about the intentions of others, an uncertainty inherent to the human condition itself, which fueled an unending search for security that, ironically and tragically, only compounded uncertainty. The measures we take to ensure our security may be seen by others as the expression of offensive intentions, thus leading them in turn to increase their power in view of guaranteeing their security, in a vicious cycle that could spiral out of control at any moment and erupt into open conflict. A few years later, considering the implications of the thermonuclear revolution in similar terms, Thomas Schelling provided an example of this process of escalation and of the inherent risk of nuclear doom that was all the more frightening for coming clad in the cold logic of Schelling's nuclear reveries: "he thinks we think he'll attack; so he thinks we shall; so he will; so we must."[9] Once it is acknowledged that political units are seeking their own security in a context in which the motives of others were uncertain, whether or not they are animated by a drive for power, is, according to Schelling, "immaterial," since the objective situation leads them, "whether they want to or not (...) to play the power game."[10]

At about the same time, Herbert Butterfield had provided a similar sociological justification for his Christian vision of the human predicament. He started with a hypothetical situation in which equally virtuous Western and Eastern blocs want to avoid war but are also unsure about the intentions of the other party, "each beset by the devils of fear and

---

[8] Robert Jervis, "Cooperation under the Security Dilemma," *World Politics* 30, no. 2 (1978): 169.
[9] Schelling, "The Strategy of Conflict," 207.
[10] Herz, "Idealist Internationalism," 161.

suspicion." Here, Butterfield suggested, was "the absolute predicament and the irreducible dilemma." As a result, "the greatest war in history could be produced without the intervention of any great criminals who might be out to do deliberate harm in the world. It could be produced between two Powers both of which were desperately anxious to avoid conflict of any sort." This situation pointed at "an intractability that can exist in the human situation itself." "Here, in other words, is the mathematical formula – or perhaps one of the formulas – for a state of things which produces what I should call the tragic element in human conflict ... this condition of absolute predicament or irreducible dilemma lies in the very geometry of human conflict. It is at the basis of the structure of any given episode in that conflict."[11]

The security dilemma moved away from the theological-moral background of realism, and did much to transform international political theory into social science. It allowed the theorist to dispense with any notion of "evil" rooted in human nature and deploy a realist worldview ridden of its pessimistic, conservative theology. In the eyes of Herz at least, this move made possible the development of a gentler realism, one in which the recognition of a common condition allowed for an identification with and an understanding of the objectives of the other – an empathy of sorts that constituted the very basis of traditional diplomacy. For him, the reformulation of the human condition as a "security dilemma" seemed to delineate a way out of Schmittian ontologies of absolute enmity.[12] And yet, according to later reminiscences by Herz himself, it was also a way of incorporating precisely such notions, or at least a sense of the immanent presence of power and conflict that always lay beneath the surface of normality, into a more acceptable framework tied to the defense of liberal institutions.[13]

Neither the older notion of international "anarchy," which can be traced back to interwar writers, nor a metaphysical reference to a morally stained human nature, the security dilemma provided a way of thinking about power politics, i.e. politics dictated by necessity and survival, within a rationalist framework and in the context of a commitment to

---

[11] Herbert Butterfield, *History and Human Relations* (London: Collins, 1951), 19–20.
[12] Herz, *Vom Überleben*, 161.
[13] "I myself, starting from a political realism of Hobbesian, Machiavellian or Schmittian variety, in the late 1930s began to develop a theory of what I called 'realist liberalism' [which] is the only way to incorporate what is valuable and important in Carl Schmitt into minimally decent and civilized politics." Herz, "Looking at Carl Schmitt," 311.

liberalism.¹⁴ But Herz's intellectual trajectory also suggests that the security dilemma was one aspect of the transformation of liberalism in a more robust or authoritative direction. It gave a rationalistic spin to prior decisionistic notions, by establishing on sociological or structural foundations the intractable nature of critical political decisions, rather than on anti-rationalistic, anti-liberal ones. This rationalistic take on decisionism was eventually extended into even more formal renditions of the security dilemma, under the form of the Prisoner's Dilemma, which would provide the ultimate avatar of international anarchy in the discipline.¹⁵

Yet, considering the security dilemma only from the narrow point of view of its iconic status in the discipline of international relations prevents us from grasping all its implications for liberal politics. The security dilemma wove together in a seamless fashion both international concerns and possible infringements on or limitations of liberal constitutionalism domestically. In a 1950 article, political scientist Clinton Rossiter addressed the issue of the kind of regime the US state would need to become after a nuclear attack on its territory. He pointed out that nuclear theorists and strategic thinkers had not given any serious consideration to the constitutional implications of nuclear war. Yet, a nuclear attack against the country would leave in its wake a surviving population and, presumably, an emergency government. This government, Rossiter suggested, would be necessarily "some form of executive-military dictatorship." Dictatorship was the ever-present constitutional possibility characteristic of the nuclear age, an age in which "the absolute weapon will have brought absolute government."¹⁶ As a result, Rossiter continued, it was necessary to prepare ourselves for emergency dictatorship, in particular by locating it firmly in the normative framework of constitutional democracy. Making sure that a future dictatorship was as efficient as possible and remained bound by a commitment to the survival of democracy was nothing short of "one of the great objects of American statesmanship."

---

[14] For an early formulation of international anarchy, see Goldsworthy Lowes Dickinson, *The European Anarchy* (New York: Macmillan, 1917).

[15] Some IR theorists consider that the Prisoner's Dilemma is a "sufficient description for international issues." See e.g. Duncan Snidal, "Relative Gains and the Pattern of International Cooperation," *The American Political Science Review* 85, no. 3 (1991): 723. For a detailed analysis of the Prisoner's Dilemma in relation to international politics, see Amadae, *Prisoners of Reason*.

[16] Clinton Rossiter, "Constitutional Dictatorship in the Atomic Age," *The Review of Politics* 11, no. 4 (1949): 396, 398.

Rossiter provided a series of criteria and suggestions for his constitutional dictatorship – institutional templates, legal provisions, temporal and task-oriented limitations – all meant to insure against the evolution of the dictatorship into permanent, unconstitutional rule. These criteria did not – and probably could not – totally alleviate the concerns about the concrete possibility that a dictatorship become "sovereign," to use Carl Schmitt's nomenclature, and usurp its initial mandate, but that need not detain us here.[17] What matters is the general orientation of Rossiter's study. For his constitutional dictatorship was not just a constitutional scenario: It introduced an authoritarian imaginary in the democratic present. The very existence of nuclear arsenals, Rossiter pointed out, necessitated preemptive constitutional adjustments, special legislation, the creation of restricted shadow committees and emergency organizations – a constitutional preparedness or contingency plan of sorts. Rossiter had previously dedicated a book to the history of constitutional dictatorship that has since become a classic and saw its sales sky rocket again after 9/11. Both his future scenario of post-nuclear political dystopia and his historical study of the Roman origins of constitutional dictatorship and the subsequent practice of emergency government in France, Germany, Great Britain, and the United States were part of a wider intellectual movement that sought to rehabilitate a strand of authoritarian political theory in the wake of wartime government and in the context of the governmental challenges posed by the Cold War. Besides Rossiter, this movement included such figures as Carl Friedrich, his student Fredrick Watkins, or the political scientist Edward Corwin, who wrote substantial works on the subject, but interest in dictatorship also picked up among historians.[18]

Friedrich, in particular, brought to this discussion knowledge of the German debates of the 1930s and did much to acclimatize the notion of dictatorship to the postwar American context.[19] In the 1920s and 1930s,

---

[17] In the end, Rossiter had to fall back onto a faith in the democratic values of the citizens as the ultimate protection against the descent into tyranny.

[18] Carl J. Friedrich, *Constitutional Government and Democracy: Theory and Practice in Europe and America* (Boston: Ginn and Company, 1950); Friedrich, *Constitutional Reason of State*; Watkins, *The Failure of Constitutional Emergency Powers under the German Republic*; Edward Corwin, *Total War and the Constitution* (New York: Alfred A. Knopf, 1947).

[19] On Friedrich, see Simard, "La raison d'Etat constitutionnelle"; Michel Senellart, "Le problème de la raison d'Etat constitutionelle selon C.J. Friedrich," in *Raison(s) d'Etat(s) en Europe. Traditions, usages, recompositions*, ed. Brigitte Krulic (Bern: Peter Lang, 2010); Greenberg, *The Weimar Century*.

he had developed an interest in prerogative powers and produced a theory of "constitutional dictatorship" that shared a number of fundamental assumptions with Carl Schmitt's analysis of "commissarial dictatorship."[20] Not only did Friedrich know and admire Schmitt, but both men shared a similar understanding of constitutionalism and an elitist conception of democracy (associated, in the case of Friedrich, with the teaching of his mentor Alfred Weber in Heidelberg, and an unwavering faith in the virtues of rational bureaucracies).[21] Like Schmitt, Friedrich justified the extension of presidential powers on the basis of Article 48 of the Weimar constitution and the dissolution of the Reichstag.[22] They saw the possibility of saving *in concreto* the constitution through extra-legal means as a necessity embedded in the very concept of constitution. The constitutionalization of politics, for them, indexed politics to a fundamental decision that could be defended against corrosive social processes and existential threats. Constitutionalism could not be conceived without the built-in possibility of a "constitutional dictatorship" that limited democracy and allowed for "the strengthening of executive decisionism" against the division of powers.[23] After the war, in a review of Bertrand de Jouvenel's book *Sovereignty*, Friedrich acknowledged in passing that he "himself was more inclined towards ... 'decisionism' some twenty years ago than he is now."[24]

Even though Friedrich had distanced himself from Schmitt during the 1930s, he still adhered to this decisionist understanding of the constitution, while Schmitt eventually drifted into Nazi apologetics and dispensed with constitutionalism altogether. Friedrich's 1937 book *Constitutional Government and Politics* thus proposed a decisionist conception of the constitution and included a chapter on constitutional dictatorship. Its revision and update in 1950 gave Friedrich the opportunity to adapt his theory of constitutional dictatorship to the new international context. He

---

[20] Friedrich's distinction between "constitutional" and "totalitarian" dictatorship mirrored exactly Schmitt's distinction between "commissarial" and "sovereign" dictatorship.
[21] See Bessner, *Democracy in Exile*.
[22] In an early analysis of this episode, Friedrich called Schmitt's discussion of this issue in *Die Diktatur* "epoch-making" and acknowledged that he was "indebted for important suggestions for the general analysis" given in the article. Carl J. Friedrich, "Dictatorship in Germany?" *Foreign Affairs* 9, no. 1 (1930): 129. But starting with the 1941 reedition of his 1937 treatise, eager to dissociate himself from the disgraced jurist, he declared *Die Diktatur* "a partisan tract." Friedrich, *Constitutional Government and Democracy*, 664.
[23] Lietzmann, "Von Der Konstitutionellen Zur Totalitären Diktatur," 183.
[24] Carl J. Friedrich, "Sovereignty: An Inquiry into the Political Good by Bertrand De Jouvenel," *The American Political Science Review* 53, no. 1 (1959): 183.

considerably expanded the chapter on constitutional dictatorship by adding a discussion of "military government," largely informed by his own experience in the American Office of Military Government in Germany (OMGUS) after the war.[25] Military government offered a powerful illustration of the positive relationship between constitutional dictatorship (of which military government was an instance) and democracy: it was dictatorship employed to re-establish constitutionalism. Constitutional dictatorship was again a topical issue, and the emergency powers employed by the Allies in Germany to restore constitutionalism differed "only in degree" from the policies necessitated by the Cold War, since "[the] antidemocratic forces, whether Communist or Fascist, have created in the past and continue to create a state of universal emergency throughout the world community by their appeal to force."[26] In order to confront "the world revolutionary situation" of the time, Friedrich suggested, like Rossiter before him, to face coolly the possibility of relying on such governmental arrangements in the eventuality of a conflict between the United States and the Soviet Union: The hope that war would not break out between the two hegemonic contenders "should not prevent students of constitutionalism, as it did in the past, from formulating basic policy for military government as an important phase of any possible future war between a world 'half free and half slave.'"[27]

The dictatorship literature of the late 1940s and 1950s did not only extend a discussion initiated by Schmitt and others in Weimar: It also built upon the experience of crisis in the United States and on the New Deal, which inaugurated new ways of thinking about emergency governance and its constitutional implications, and triggered some interest in – and sometimes a positive appraisal of – the performance of dictatorial regimes in Europe.[28] Even before Roosevelt was elected, calls for addressing the situation through expanded executive powers were heard across the nation. Walter Lippmann called for "strong medicine" and the granting of "extraordinary powers" to the new president, which he described to Roosevelt as "dictatorial powers."[29] While these dictatorial powers were requested in order to deal with an economic emergency, they were explicitly conceived on the basis of an analogy with war and international

---

[25] Friedrich, *Constitutional Government and Democracy*, 588–96.
[26] Friedrich, *Constitutional Government and Democracy*, 594.
[27] Friedrich, *Constitutional Government and Democracy*, 595.
[28] Schivelbusch, *Three New Deals*, New York.
[29] Quoted in Katznelson, *Fear Itself*, 118–19.

The Dilemma behind the Security Dilemma

politics.³⁰ The kind of powers deemed to be necessary were those employed when facing an external enemy. The postwar literature on dictatorship only exacerbated these tensions between the necessities of foreign policy and liberal constitutionalism as it brought these American and foreign experiences to bear upon the intellectual climate of the Cold War. It reformulated the problems of emergency powers and constitutional dictatorship in reaction to the nuclear confrontation between two superpowers, and in the process blurred entirely the distinction between domestic and international "security." Political theorists such as Rossiter and Friedrich were perfectly aware that "internal and external security get hopelessly mixed up with each other."³¹ This indicates that the "security dilemma" was the specific form that the discussion about emergency powers and the limitations of liberal constitutionalism took in the field of international relations. Friedrich suggested as much when he wrote that the "totalitarian challenge" forced constitutional thinkers to address what he called the "security problem," by which he meant the issues of constitutional dictatorship or constitutional "reason of state."³² The security dilemma pointed to a sphere of existential danger requiring decisions to be taken with a view to expediency, i.e. as purely technical-instrumental decisions dependent on the behavior and the strategies of potentially hostile political entities, and emphatically *not* on the nature of constitutional arrangements or the provisions of international law.³³ This "dictatorial" aspect of foreign policy was already present in classical realism, as we saw earlier, notably in the writings of Morgenthau and his indictment of the American inclination to see law or democracy as the ultimate foundations of politics (but also, more prosaically, in the authoritarian orientation of some of his fellow realists, such as Arnold Wolfers).³⁴ It is because the statesman has to deal with existential threats that he may have to act regardless of established procedures. Morgenthau's conception of statesmanship was indeed one that often implied a charismatic leader, sensitive to the *kairos* of political time, capable of resolute action in the

---

³⁰ Katznelson, *Fear Itself*, 121–22. ³¹ Friedrich, *Constitutional Reason of State*, 2.
³² Friedrich, *Constitutional Reason of State*, viii. On the evolution from "constitutional dictatorship" to "constitutional reason of state" in Friedrich's thought, see the discussion in Senellart, "Le problème de la raison d'Etat."
³³ In his definition of the commissarial dictatorship, Schmitt points out that the institution dictatorship is indifferent to legality (it does not replace it) because it is confined within the domain of technical means of expediency. It only aims at reinstating the conditions of the normal operation of law. In it, "only the goal governs." Schmitt, *Dictatorship*, 8.
³⁴ See Chapter 1, pp. 60, 64–65.

face of absolute uncertainty, and dictating the way forward in times of crisis – a conception echoing the Schmittian mystique of sovereignty:

> The decision of the statesman has three distinctive qualities. It is a commitment to action. It is a commitment to a particular action that precludes all other courses of action. It is a decision taken in the face of the unknown and the unknowable ... The statesman ... must be capable of staking the fate of the nation upon a hunch. He must face the impenetrable darkness of the future and still not flinch from walking into it, drawing the nation behind him ... He is the leading part in a tragedy, and he must act his part.[35]

The security dilemma considerably updated this vision: It still placed the emphasis on the intractability of decisions, on the role of concrete judgment, but it also set the stage for considering political decisions in purely strategic terms dictated by security imperatives. It is fair to say that, like Schmitt's dictatorship, the security dilemma was oriented exclusively toward "rationalism, technicality and the executive."[36] It carried into international relations theory a set of arguments about the limitations or suspension of constitutional provisions for certain kinds of political decisions, while repackaging these arguments in the emerging vocabulary of "security studies" and justifying such decisions on the basis of their "rationality." Whether in historical reconstructions, such as Carl Friedrich's *Constitutional Reason of State*, or in the development of rational choice, "rationality" became in the 1950s and 1960s the new foundation for political decision-making not subject to democratic constraints or constitutional restrictions.[37] As we saw in the previous chapter, the staging of the security dilemma in terms of rational choice did not diminish but, on the contrary, justified the full autonomy of decisions taking that form and the suspension of any kind of control over them.[38] As one of the political scientists invited to contribute to the *Rational Decision* volume edited by Carl Friedrich in 1964 put it, "how can a government be both rational and representative? It is notorious that what is rational is not necessarily representative of the people and is unlikely to be so."[39]

---

[35] Morgenthau, *The Restoration of American Politics*, 102–03.
[36] Schmitt, *Dictatorship*, 9.
[37] Friedrich rightly conflated "reason of state" and "security." Much of his work in the 1950s and 1960s can be seen as an effort to re-describe traditional reason of state and decisionism in terms of their rationality. See Friedrich, "On Rereading Machiavelli and Althusius," 180.
[38] See pp. 214–216.
[39] Harvey Mansfield, "Rational and Representation in Burke's 'Bristol Speech'," in *Rational Decision*, ed. Carl J. Friedrich (Piscataway, NJ: Transaction 1964), 197.

It is indeed in the name of strategic considerations that theorists promoted a new governmental project aimed at strengthening executive powers. Pondering the international situation, Rossiter proposed nothing short of a reorganization of the constitutional edifice: "it is obvious that any overhauling of this government's weapons of constitutional dictatorship is only one small part of a larger and more essential whole – the renovation of the entire constitutional structure and the creation of a national government capable of dealing resolutely and effectively with the bewildering problems of this twentieth-century world."[40] Morgenthau did not say anything different when he advocated the reorganization and the strengthening of the executive.[41] In fact, he lavished praise on Rossiter's dictatorial meditation, dubbing it a "relief": here was a political scientist who understood that the dilemmas that paralyzed democracies when they had to face existential threats could not be solved with the tools of the "social engineer" but had to be addressed with the wisdom bequeathed by the historical record. If, as Morgenthau surmised, there was an "irreversible trend toward [dictatorship] in all democracies," then Rossiter was making an important contribution to the adjustments democracies needed to do in order to accommodate that trend.[42]

WHO DECIDES? CLASSICAL REALISM, DIPLOMACY, AND THE QUESTION OF FOREIGN POLICY

While constitutional theorists were aware of the connection between the security dilemma and dictatorial decisions, international relations theorists seem to have ignored it. This is all the more surprising, since while the exceptional situation is the exception for domestic politics, it is considered the normal state of affairs in international relations. But things may not be what they seem at first sight, and there are indications that the authoritarian orientation of classical realism constituted, at least for some theorists, a cultural and political problem plaguing the discipline. First among them was Kenneth Waltz, whose *Theory of International Politics* can be read as an attempt to sever the connection between the security dilemma and illiberal conceptions of politics.

---

[40] Rossiter, *Constitutional Dictatorship*, 307.
[41] Morgenthau, *The Restoration of American Politics*, 300–07.
[42] Hans J. Morgenthau, "Constitutional Dictatorship. By Clinton L. Rossiter," *American Journal of Sociology* 54, no. 6 (1949): 566.

In the late 1940s and 1950s, Morgenthau's classical realism swept through the emergent discipline of international relations. One of the major scholars to respond to Morgenthau was Kenneth Waltz, then a professor at Swarthmore College who had received his PhD in political theory from Columbia University in 1954. He was the rapporteur and youngest member of the working group that, under the leadership of William T. R. Fox, developed the first formulations of a realist "theory" of international relations at Columbia in 1956–1957. The proceedings of the working group were eventually published in 1959 in the collective volume *Theoretical Aspects of International Relations*, edited by Fox. In his dissertation, later published as *Man, the State, and War*, Waltz famously identified three "images" of war's causes discussed by political philosophers: the first explained war with reference to human nature, the second through state regimes, and the third referred instead to the international system, and specifically to international anarchy. Even though he diplomatically criticized Morgenthau for relying on the first "image," his objections were epistemological, not substantive. He also praised Morgenthau for emphasizing the "necessary imperfections of all social and political forms," the "limits of possible political accomplishment," and "the inescapable necessity of balance-of-power politics."[43] Waltz thus appeared as a perfectly orthodox realist – and in many ways, he was.

Yet, one thing that was absent from Waltz's early work was precisely the kind of calls for strong leadership and unaccountable decision-making capacities that regularly surfaced in the realist literature. In *Politics among Nations* and a number of later essays, Morgenthau repeatedly called for the establishment of a new diplomatic elite capable of learning the rules of international relations he provided. For him, the "international disorder" of the twentieth century was the direct outcome of the decline of diplomacy: "the traditional methods of diplomacy have been under continuous attack since the First World War and have to a considerable extent been discarded in practice since the end of the Second World War."[44] While liberals had considered traditional diplomacy a leftover of the *ancien régime*, for Morgenthau, the "restoration" of US politics needed nothing short of the restoration of the diplomatic arts that had

---

[43] Kenneth Waltz, *Man, the State, and War* (New York: Columbia University Press, 1954), 30, 34.

[44] Morgenthau, *The Restoration of American Politics*, 199, 198.

come under attack as politics had become more democratic. Morgenthau's calls for a return to eighteenth-century diplomacy were not the lonely grousing of an embittered conservative: He was echoed by other realists, including historians such as Gordon Craig and Felix Gilbert, who also lamented the disappearance of a diplomatic tradition eroded by democracy.[45]

This longing for classical diplomacy had an important anti-democratic dimension. Classical realists asserted that decision-makers must be unconstrained by ignorant publics incapable of understanding international relations. Morgenthau frequently criticized the public's interference in foreign policy issues: For him, the main issue faced by American presidents was "the incompatibility between the rational requirements of sound foreign policy and the emotional preferences of a democratically controlled public opinion."[46] The calls for the restoration of diplomacy also ran the risk of making classical realism politically irrelevant. Indeed, such calls turned out to be pure nostalgia in an era of massive expansion of governmental bureaucracies and interstitial foreign policy research organizations like the RAND Corporation. The realist program also suffered from a lack of specificity. While classical realists called for a diplomatic corps comprising wise men aware of the tragic contingency of politics, they never described who these men were supposed to be. For all his lyricism, Morgenthau could not identify his idealized statesmen in the 1950s and 1960s. All he could do was lament the complexity of anonymous political bureaucracies that undermined the capacity to decide, advocate a simplification of the processes of the executive branch, and chastise all US presidents from Roosevelt to Kennedy for what he regarded as their irresoluteness.[47]

Although Waltz was socialized into classical realism's intellectual framework, he departed from it in at least one fundamental respect. Throughout Waltz's extensive publishing record, there is no nostalgic call for traditional diplomacy and even less for unaccountability in foreign

---

[45] Craig and Gilbert wrote as "the age in which diplomats held the fate of nations in their hands" had passed, and looked wistfully at a practice that was spawned by the absolute state and finished "assailed from the democratic, as well as from the totalitarian side" during the interwar period. Gordon A. Craig and Felix Gilbert, eds., *The Diplomats 1919–1939* (Princeton: Princeton University Press, 1953), 3, 7.
[46] Morgenthau, *The Restoration of American Politics*, 106.
[47] See for instance Hans J. Morgenthau, *The Decline of Democratic Politics*, vol. 1 of *Politics in the 20th Century* (The University of Chicago Press, 1958), 380–89; Morgenthau, *The Restoration of American Politics*, 300–07.

policy decisions, no advocacy of authoritative leadership, no gesturing toward constitutional dictatorship. Instead, it seems that he dropped out of his work the very notions that would support "dictatorial" conclusions. In *Man, the State, and War*, Waltz adumbrated the possibility of framing balance-of-power in terms of game theory, "using the concepts of von Neumann and Morgenstern."[48] As we saw previously, the kind of "rationality" implied in game theory and more generally rational choice was characterized essentially by its restricted nature and was in tension with any notion of collective decision. Rational choice is such only by virtue of being immune from the normal and open political and bureaucratic processes characteristic of decision-making in a democratic context, and abstracting itself from them. In that sense, rational choice approaches to international relations also provided a vehicle for the rehabilitation of a decisionist vision of politics. This continuity was identified early on, in particular by Judith Shklar, who, as a student of Frederick Watkins and Carl Friedrich, was well versed in the discussion of prerogative powers and dictatorship. Writing about the main intellectual trends of the mid-1960s, she observed that "the most prevalent form of decisionism is … centered on the all-important realm of foreign policy," with postwar realism as its primary vehicle.[49] But what makes Shklar's essay illuminating is that she postulates a direct, if conflicted, lineage going from the decisionist orientation of classical realism to the systemic approach that came to define Waltz's neorealism. Shklar suggested that it was precisely the diplomatic nostalgia of realism, the "decisionist" imaginary of a few actors holding the balance in their hands and choosing between distinct alternatives, that became appealing to system theorists because it reduced the decision-making process to a few actors insulated from wider politics. The small scale inherent to classical realism's nostalgia for diplomacy actually paved the way for the modelization of policy-makers' interactions using formal methods:

> A theory of statesmen pursuing something as vague as the national interest has not proven acceptable to theorists of a more systematic turn of mind. Decisionism, however, has a vast appeal, precisely because the vision of a limited number of political actors engaged in making calculated choices among clearly conceived alternatives is an essential basis for any theory that wishes to reduce international complexities to systematic, diagrammatic form.[50]

---

[48] Waltz, *Man, the State, and War*, 201.   [49] Shklar, "Decisionism," 11.
[50] Shklar, "Decisionism," 13.

Far from breaking with the authoritarian and decisionist aspects of classical realism, rational choice made them unrecognizable as it reformulated them in terms of their intrinsic "rationality," coating them in a scientistic outlook. This is the path on which Waltz could have embarked in his early work when, in *Man, the State, and War*, he saw promise in the deployment of rational choice approaches. Yet, twenty years later this possibility was entirely absent from *Theory of International Politics*, which had opted for a theoretical framework that not only dismissed rational choice, but was explicitly developed *against* it.

DEMOCRACIES AND FOREIGN POLICY

It is a common misconception that because he "blackboxes" states in *Theory of International Politics*, Waltz was uninterested in the nature of regimes and never looked into the foreign policy-making process. He himself concluded *Man, the State, and War* by saying that the "first" and "second" images were important indicators of the forces that shaped international politics. There is also evidence that Waltz had a normative commitment to democracy and liberalism that set him apart from classical realists – beginning with his 1967 publication of *Foreign Policy and Democratic Politics*, a comparative case study of foreign policy performance in the United Kingdom and the United States entirely dedicated to the relationship between democracy and foreign policy. *Foreign Policy and Democratic Politics* argues that democracies are as capable of making effective foreign policies as totalitarian regimes. This was an important argument, since it rejected the notion of "totalitarian advantage" directly associated with the realist arguments in favor of constitutional dictatorship.[51]

It is important to take notice of the slightly dissonant note that *Foreign Policy and Democratic Politics* struck in the realist literature. Indeed, the notion that foreign policy performance could be determined by domestic institutions largely seems to contradict Waltz's later writings. More importantly, the assumption that "the kind of foreign policy a nation pursues is determined by the kind of domestic institutions it possesses" was ridiculed by classical realism and Morgenthau associated it with the rejection of diplomacy as a separated and independent sphere of action.[52]

---

[51] See Bessner, *Democracy in Exile*.
[52] Morgenthau, *The Restoration of American Politics*, 199.

Why would Waltz engage in an exercise that clearly flew in the face of the realist tradition to which he belonged?

As Michael Williams has suggested, *Foreign Policy and Democratic Politics* makes sense only when one realizes that it is a sustained defense of liberal democratic values and liberal policy-making.[53] Williams demonstrates that neorealism sought to address domestic issues but also to engage directly with the vexed question of the relationship between democracy and security. Indeed, on a closer reading, *Foreign Policy and Democratic Politics* is a proximate response to the anti-democratic arguments offered by Walter Lippmann in his 1955 *The Public Philosophy*, which themselves emerged from Lippmann's earlier works from the 1920s, in particular *Public Opinion* and *The Phantom Public*. Waltz attacked Lippmann's "aristocratic distrust of mass electorates," a distrust that classical realists shared and, for those who came to the United States in the 1930s, developed in dialogue with Lippmann's earlier books.[54] From the 1920s onward, Lippmann questioned the ability of public opinion to guide decisions-makers, and in the 1950s asserted that uninformed public opinion was directly responsible for the poor governance of liberal democracies. In democratic regimes, he suggested, the masses had acquired a "power which they are incapable of exercising," while governments had lost the power they needed, resulting in "an enfeeblement, verging on paralysis, of the capacity to govern."[55]

Lippmann's critique of liberalism as the main cause behind the loss of authority of the state and the incapacity to act in a timely and effective way was extending the prewar critiques of parliamentarianism and party politics that were characteristic of anti-liberal, conservative thought. The "devitalization of the governing power" was for him a direct consequence of the rise of party politics and interest groups.[56] *The Public Philosophy* shared and reinforced a number of classical realist concerns. Both anti-public ideologues like Lippmann and classical realists like Morgenthau lambasted the illusions of nineteenth-century liberalism, the deleterious effects of democratization on governmental authority,

---

[53] See for instance Michael C. Williams, "Waltz, Realism and Democracy," *International Relations* 23, no. 3 (2009). Daniel Bessner and I are very much indebted to Michael Williams for his reading of Waltz.

[54] Kenneth Waltz, *Foreign Policy and Democratic Politics: The American and British Experience* (Boston: Little, Brown and company, 1967), 13. For a further discussion of this dialogue, see Bessner, *Democracy in Exile*.

[55] Lippmann, *Public Philosophy*, 14–15.

[56] Lippmann, *Public Philosophy*, 14–15.

the blinding effect of universalistic ideologies, the debilitating role of public opinion, the irrationality of the public, and so on. Morgenthau, unsurprisingly, had only praise for Lippmann's book.[57] Lippmann was connected to the realist movement and participated in the first meeting convened to discuss the development of a realist theory of international relations.[58] Moreover, Lippmann's references in *The Public Philosophy* were primarily in the realm of foreign policy.[59] In *Foreign Policy and Democratic Politics*, Lippmann served as an intellectual proxy for classical realism.[60] It is in dialogue with Lippmann that Waltz's discomfort with the anti-democratic implications of classical realism clearly emerges, and that neorealism takes shape as a compromise solution.

Yet, if *Foreign Policy and Democratic Politics* was a direct response to Lippmann's argument that the dire condition of his time was "connected with grave errors in war and peace that have been committed by democratic governments," it was also a circumstantial and provisional answer.[61] Waltz limited himself to two case studies, and was unable to articulate a vision of international relations that complemented his focus on the policy-making process. The next step consisted in developing a theoretical response of general value, which is the task he embarked upon with *Theory of International Politics*.

Waltz did not simply reject the critique of democratic publics, restate democratic principles, or offer a defense of public rationality. On the contrary, he had no issues with the classical realist critique of the public's irrationality – in fact, *Theory of International Politics* was entirely based on the rejection of the "rationality assumption," i.e. the notion that political actors act "rationally" in the sense of having at their disposal extended calculative capacities. What Waltz seemed unwilling to do,

---

[57] "Representative government," he wrote in his review of *The Public Philosophy*, "tends to become paralyzed government." Morgenthau, *The Restoration of American Politics*, 64.
[58] Lippmann's diagnosis of the incapacity of the democratic public to make foreign policy decisions made him an obvious ally of the early proponents of a realist "theory" of international relations: "Strategic and diplomatic decisions call for a kind of knowledge – not to speak of an experience and a seasoned judgment – which cannot be had by glancing at newspapers, listening to snatches of radio comment. Watching politicians perform on television, hearing occasional lectures, and reading a few books." Lippmann, *Public Philosophy*, 14–15.
[59] Paul Roazen, "Introduction to the Transaction Edition," in *The Public Philosophy*, by Walter Lippmann (New Brunswick: Transaction Publishers, 1989), xvii.
[60] Morgenthau too thought that while the formulation may be exaggerated, there was something true to the statement that "a democratically conducted foreign policy is of necessity bad foreign policy" Morgenthau, *Dilemmas of Politics*, 326.
[61] Lippmann, *Public Philosophy*, 14–15.

however, was to draw the anti-democratic implications of this critique for decision-making. He was thus facing a dilemma: How was he to reconcile the classical realist *Weltanschauung* with liberal principles and policy-making in a democratic context? How could one develop a theory of international politics based upon the security dilemma without endorsing a non-democratic conception of foreign policy? How was it possible to escape the dictatorial implications of rational choice theory? The solution Waltz arrived at consisted in circumventing entirely the problem of decision-making and developing a theory that treated the aggregate outcome of foreign policy decisions – that is, international politics as a whole – as a self-contained system whose logic of operation could be described without prescribing any form of decision-making and without relying on a notion of rationality that was tethered to decision theory and its anti-democratic implications.

NEOREALISM: A CYBERNETIC THEORY OF DECISION-MAKING WITHOUT DECISION-MAKERS

The intellectual sources of neorealism that Waltz cites in *Theory of International Politics* and in the more succinct version of his approach published in the 1975 *Handbook of Political Science* include von Bertalanffy's *General System Theory* (1968), Ross Ashby's *Design for a Brain* (1952) as well as *Introduction to Cybernetics* (1956), Norbert Wiener's *Cybernetics* (1948) and some of David Easton's publications on systemic functionalism in political science, along with a number of methodological papers.[62] These texts were each foundational to the development of cybernetics and system theory in general, and they situate *Theory of International Politics* squarely within the cybernetic tradition.

Situating *Theory of International Politics* in the context of the cybernetic movement makes it possible to understand Waltz's work in relation to both rationalist theories of decision-making and to the decisionist undertones of classical realism. *Theory of International Politics* was part of a broader cybernetic trend in political science, along with other international relations books. Earlier examples in the field include Morton Kaplan's *System and Process in International Relations* (1957),

---

[62] Waltz, *Theory of International Politics*, 40, fn.

Graham Allison's *Essence of Decision* (1971), or John Steinbruner's *The Cybernetic Theory of Decision* (1974). All these books sought to make the study of international relations more "scientific" while addressing immediate political issues, and in particular the issues of policy formulation and decision. In the 1960s and 1970s, cybernetics and system theory appealed to political scientists because they offered an alternative to rationalistic theories of decision and seemed to be better adapted to the unprecedented growth of governmental bureaucracies and to the challenge organizational complexity represented for policy research. The most important problem international relations theorists confronted was that, in the new institutional era, political decisions were the largely impersonal outcomes of exceedingly complex procedures that traditional models of decision-making, which implied a centralized decision-maker, a set of transitive preferences, and a linearity of the decision process, were unable to explain.

Perhaps the most appealing characteristic of cybernetics and system theory for Waltz was that they moved away from notions of decision and choice. Indeed, they were explicitly conceived as an alternative to "rational choice" models and operated from "a theoretical base fundamentally different from rational theory."[63] They rejected formal decision theories, and game theory in particular, as better-suited to an ideal world where alternatives were known and the capacity to compute them (i.e. rationality) widely available. In the real world, system theorists claimed, choices were made in a murkier fashion, and actual alternatives were infinitely superior to the limited computing capacities of human actors, who were obviously not "rational." Vicarious learning, trial-and-error were really how individuals navigated complex environments – not the transparent and neatly organized decisional trees of rational decision theory. Organizational and bureaucratic processes were also part of the decisional machinery. In fact, they contributed to reducing massively, through institutionalized routines, the number of choices one was confronted with.[64]

---

[63] Steinbruner, *The Cybernetic Theory of Decision*, 13. This is also very clear in Allison's book. That system theory was explicitly recognized as an alternative to rational choice is yet another reason why it is a misconception to think that Waltz subscribed or needed to subscribe to a "rationality assumption." On this question, see von Bertalanffy, *General System Theory*, 8.

[64] Simon, "Political Research." See also Herbert A. Simon, *Administrative Behavior: A Study of Decision-Making Processes in Administrative Organization*, 3rd edn. (New York: Free Press, 1976).

In their own way, system theorists echoed the critique of rational choice theories made by classical realists from the late-1940s forward, but in a new, formal and non-ideological language.⁶⁵

System theory, for its part, made it possible to explain the outcome of thoughtful, strategic decisions without assuming any underlying deliberative thought process, any "rationality" or indeed any notion of intention or purpose. As Steinbruner declared, "much of the work [in cybernetics] ... has been directed precisely at the problem of explaining highly successful behavior (usually called adaptive) without assuming elaborate decision-making mechanisms."⁶⁶ To do so, system theory and cybernetics shifted the emphasis from teleological, outcome-driven models to models that emphasized process and recipe-following, while being deprived of any form of entelechy. Servomechanics, feedback loops, and other physical analogies were deployed to explain efficient adaptive behavior without ascribing any rationality to political actors, or indeed, taking much account of the actors.⁶⁷ Before the rise of system theory, to quote one of Waltz's sources, "notions of teleology and directiveness appeared to be outside the scope of science and to be the playground of mysterious, supernatural or anthropomorphic agencies."⁶⁸ Cybernetics made it possible to replace decisions with mechanistic processes. Goal-seeking behavior, as Ross Ashby had explained, was now understood on the basis of organizational patterns totally deprived of willful purpose or self-determination.⁶⁹ Self-steering could be represented as a process entirely devoid of teleology and will. To put it differently, decisional outcomes could be replicated, modelized, or simulated without assuming a central and omnipotent decision-maker. This is a crucial aspect of *Theory of International Politics*: System theory enabled Waltz to describe international politics without any recourse to a concept of decision. How decisions were made no longer mattered, since cybernetic models made it possible to describe their outcomes without implying purpose, intention, or rationality. As Shklar clearly saw, "system" and "decision" were really two mutually exclusive

---

⁶⁵ See Daniel Bessner, "Organizing Complexity: The Hopeful Dreams and Harsh Realities of Interdisciplinary Collaboration at the Rand Corporation in the Early Cold War," *Journal of the History of the Behavioral Sciences* 51, no. 1 (2015): 31–53.
⁶⁶ Steinbruner, *The Cybernetic Theory of Decision*, 48.
⁶⁷ Cybernetics focuses on "recipes" or "performances" rather than "ontologies": it produces an outcome through a sequential process, but without a model of the world or of the environment. It is adaptive. The outcome is not conceptualized in advance – only produced through a series of operations, and only these operations are specified ex ante.
⁶⁸ Von Bertalanffy, *General System Theory*, 45. ⁶⁹ Ross Ashby, *Design for a Brain*, 55.

ways of talking about the same thing. In the system approach, whether the concept of decision was considered an old anthropomorphic notion tied to obscure forces, or an unrealistic assumption of rationality, it could be jettisoned altogether in favor of anonymous adaptive processes. The new approach to international politics associated today with neorealism was, in fact, already present in a number of cybernetic essays.[70]

Theory of International Politics thus rested on methodological choices that excluded any "rationality assumption," i.e. the idea that humans were rational actors, pursuing consistent preferences in an instrumentally economic way. Neorealist theory, Waltz wrote in *TIP*, "requires no assumption of rationality or of constancy of will on the part of all the actors."[71] Foreign policy making is "such a complicated business," he later asserted, that "one cannot expect of political leaders the nicely calculated decisions that the word 'rationality' suggests."[72] This was a standard line from the intellectual repertoire of cybernetics. And in one of his last interviews, Waltz even confessed that he had no idea what the expression "rational actor" meant.[73] John Mearsheimer is thus

---

[70] The idea that "first image" theories of politics – i.e. theories explaining war by reference to decision-makers – had become obsolete was already present in von Bertalanffy: "Earlier periods of history may have consoled themselves by blaming atrocities and stupidities on bad kings, wicked dictators, ignorance, superstition, material want and related factors. Consequently, history was of the 'who-did-what' kind – 'idiographic,' as it is technically known. Thus, the Thirty-Years War was a consequence of religious superstition and the rivalries of German princes; Napoleon overturned Europe because of his unbridled ambition; the Second World War could be blamed on the wickedness of Hitler and the warlike proclivity of the Germans." Von Bertalanffy, *General System Theory*, 45.
[71] Waltz, *Theory*, 118.
[72] Waltz, "Reflections," 43.
[73] It is worth quoting the passage at length, because it suggests the abyssal gap that distinguishes a system approach from rational choice theory: "I do not even know what 'rational actor' means empirically. A rational actor assumption may enter into a theory but has no direct, empirical representation. One can define rationality only within narrow settings, as for example in game theory, where one can define what a rational actor is and work out some outcomes under assumed conditions. Of course economists presuppose that economic actors are rational. People of course in a very loose sense prefer to do less work and get higher rewards. That is a good way of putting it now, but there is no reason in economics to think that a bunch of actors are going to be rational. Some of them are going to do better than others; some are going to be a lot smarter; some are going to be a little bit luckier than others; some are going to be better at cheating than others. All those things affect outcomes, but rationality – in its empirical form – has really little to do with it. The notion of rationality is a big help in constructing a theory, but one has to go back and forth between the theory and what goes out in the real world. But in the real world, does anybody think 'I'm rational, or you're rational'? Let alone, that *states* could be rational? It has no empirical meaning." www.theory-talks.org/2011/06/theory-talk-40.html (last accessed June 9, 2016).

absolutely right when he suggests that Waltz's putative rationality assumption is a perplexing case of collective self-delusion among IR theorists, who have usually overlooked both the context in which Waltz was writing and the intellectual sources that informed *Theory of International Politics*.[74] One reason for the persistence of this disciplinary canard is that IR scholars have tended to assume that Waltz adopted classical microeconomic foundations for his theory, and in particular the notion of a rational actor. This is partly misleading. He actually made it clear that his theory of international politics was not modeled after the neoclassical model assuming rational actors acting in perfectly competitive markets (to the extent that such a model would end up with harmonious equilibria requiring no policing, as some critics have noticed[75]): To the extent that he drew inspiration from economic theories, his reference was the theory of oligopolistic markets.[76] But there was a much more formidable obstacle that kept Waltz from adopting the rational actor assumption, and indeed one that came straight from microeconomics, namely Arrow's impossibility theorem. Even for the new economists of rational choice, the fact that a decision was political made it de facto either irrational or authoritarian.[77] As collectives, states were either irresolute or irrational if they were democracies, or their foreign policy decisions had to be insulated from the democratic process in order to attain rationality. In other words, the rationality assumption would have brought Waltz back exactly where he did not want to be, namely in the chorus of classical realists calling for the reinstatement of pre-liberal, pre-democratic foreign policy practices. His explicit reluctance to accept the notion that states could be rational points directly to the state of the discussion after Arrow and to the ideological implications of the rationality assumption.

The move away from rational choice and toward "systems" had therefore deeper motivations than a mere desire to reduce politics to something akin to a natural phenomenon and to turn international relations theory into a natural science. The adoption of system approaches by IR theorists was directly tied to their ideological discomfort with classical realism. Like Waltz, system theorists retained a deep anxiety

---

[74] John J. Mearsheimer, "Reckless States and Realism," *International Relations* 23, no. 2 (2009): 241–56.
[75] Randall Schweller, "Neorealism's Status Quo Bias: What Security Dilemma?" *Security Studies* 5, no. 3 (1996): 90–121.
[76] Kenneth Waltz, "International Politics Is Not Foreign Policy," *Security Studies* 6, no. 1 (2007): 54–57.
[77] Leoni, "The Meaning of 'Political'."

about the nature of decision-making in democracies. Steinbruner captured these fears when he wrote that:

> a society traditionally concerned with constraining government in the interests of avoiding tyranny must now concern itself with effectiveness. Even if it could be fully accomplished, it would no longer be acceptable merely to follow the established principles of democracy to trust that the outcomes of such a process will be the best attainable, or even acceptable ... Achieving effective performance without stumbling into some new form of tyranny is a major issue of coming decades.[78]

The same concerns were popularized the following year by the report of the Trilateral Commission on the governability of democracies. It sought to delineate a way out of a presumed crisis of authority determined by the democratic surge and the corresponding weakening of government due to its responsiveness to a widening range of social interests, without advocating forms of authoritarian command.[79] In the political context of the mid-1970s, a context in which long-standing anxieties regarding democratic performance were reinforced by emerging doubts about the governance of complex societies, system theory and cybernetics promised policy efficiency without authoritarianism. Systemic theories of politics directly, if implicitly, built upon the conservative critiques of democracy formulated by Lippmann and Morgenthau, now reformulated as crises of government "overload," while avoiding classical realism's anti-democratic implications.[80] Cybernetics provided a theory of decision-making adapted to complex societies for which the traditional mechanisms of liberal democracy were deemed obsolete or inefficient. Yet it also offered a reassuring prospect to liberals: There may have been no way for a rational public to generate good decisions, but neither was there a need for an authoritarian decision-maker who would approximate the prescriptions of "rational choice." Both were chimeras. Political pluralism and social complexity could be maintained, executive power could be decentralized, and the calls for dictatorial crisis-management that had grown louder among political theorists since the end of the war could be

---

[78] Steinbruner, *The Cybernetic Theory of Decision*, 6–7.
[79] Michel Crozier et al., *The Crisis of Democracy: Report on the Governability of Democracies to the Trilateral Commission*, The Triangle Papers (New York: New York University Press, 1975).
[80] Easton, for instance, introduced his notion of "system" against what he saw as a movement back to traditionalism in politics – a movement of which he considered the primary exponent to be Michael Oakeshott. See David Easton, *The Political System: An Inquiry into the State of Political Science* (New York: Alfred A. Knopf, 1953).

ignored. System theory replaced anthropocentric decision-making with abstract, large-scale organizational processes that did not rely on individual capacities or rationality. The benchmark of "rationality," to the extent that this notion retained any importance, was no longer a subjective attribute of the individual decision-maker, but a property of the system denoting its capacity for adaptation and survival. For these reasons, system theorists could accept the critical realist position on public opinion while paying lip service to liberal democratic norms.

System theory provided Waltz with an obvious solution to the political dilemma he had inherited from classical realism. On the one hand, it took for granted the inadequacy of traditional notions of liberal-democratic decision-making for the governance of complex societies. It thus accommodated the realist critiques of democracy. But on the other hand, instead of calling for an authoritative decision-maker, it equated policy effectiveness with systemic adaptive properties. The nature of the decision-making process no longer mattered. This provided Waltz with theoretical vindication, as it supported his claim in *Foreign Policy and Democratic Politics* that democracies were just as capable of effective foreign policy decision-making as authoritarian regimes. As units of the same system, these two regime types were caught in an adaptive process of learning and deviation-correction: discrete "decisions," per se, mattered little in a structure where the system itself was the ultimate shape of reality and enforcer of the "correct" course of action.

In sum, system theory made it possible to leave behind the focus of sovereign decision-making evident in Morgenthau's and other classical realists' works. They presented Waltz with several advantages. First, they elided the thorny question of political personnel. Who made decisions was no longer a question one had to worry about – the system would take care of itself. Waltz successfully excised out of political realism the need to think about decision-making in ways that ran counter to liberal constitutionalism. Decisions were simply made invisible in *Theory of International Politics*. Second, unlike rational choice models, system theory coped with what Steinbruner called "structural uncertainties," the very uncertainties about the rules of the game that Morgenthau desired to teach decision-makers. Third, system theory abandoned the need for rationality, whether that of a rational public or of a rational decision-maker, and thus remained in line with realism's basic assumptions. Finally, system theory placed a premium on state-conservation and stability in general: As such, it was also very much in the air du temps as an ideology of bipolar stability, which helped explain the rise of détente.

BIPOLARITY AND DEMOCRATIC BALANCING

Waltz's views about bipolarity expressed in *TIP* relate directly to the broader discussion about the capacity of democracies to wage an effective foreign policy. They also represent another major difference between neorealism and classical realism. Morgenthau, for instance, had a very critical view of the Cold War and he had pointed at bipolarity to prove the instability of the postwar international system. Waltz, in contrast, highlighted bipolarity as a stabilizing factor in international politics. This difference must be understood in light of diverging views about the relationship between democracy and foreign policy. The theoretical arguments Waltz uses to defend bipolarity are well known: In a multipolar system, the balance of power dear to both him and the classical realists is too uncertain. The making and undoing of alliances, the identification of threats, the expectations of leadership, and the flexibility of the balance introduce too many unknowns in policy calculations, which increases the risk of misperceptions and hence the outbreak of war.[81] Bipolar systems, Waltz asserts, are more stable for three reasons. First, they simplify balancing. Second, they make it easy to identify threats. Third, they create constant pressure in favor of balancing, whereas in multipolar systems such pressures are reduced.

Waltz's preference for bipolarity was not simply a case of political quietism or conservative acquiescence to the state of geopolitics circa 1975. It was part of the ongoing conversation about decision-making triggered by classical realism's calls for the restoration of diplomacy and the limitation of democracy. By rejecting the large-N balance of power associated with multipolarity, Waltz implicitly rejected traditional diplomacy: "with more than two states, the politics of power turn on diplomacy by which alliances are made."[82] In contrast, for Waltz, diplomacy had no role to play in bipolar systems. This particular understanding of the concept of balance in Waltz has not been noted by the commentators of his work. In a bipolar system diplomacy is atavistic, since "where two powers contend, imbalances can be righted only by their internal efforts."[83] In other words, the balancing act takes place essentially in the domestic arena: economic policies, research and development,

---

[81] "In the great-power politics of multipolar worlds, who is a danger to whom, and who can be expected to deal with threats and problems, are matters of uncertainty." Waltz, *Theory*, 170.
[82] Waltz, *Theory*, 165.
[83] Waltz, *Theory*, 163.

education, culture, everything becomes engulfed in the systemic logic of bipolar stability.[84] Waltz's analysis of bipolarity was thus a major reason for him not to heed the calls for the restoration of traditional diplomacy coming from classical realists.

Neorealism dispensed with a theory of foreign policy because Waltz assumed that any policy decision in the domestic or international sphere was relevant to the overall systemic process. Focusing on a subset of decisions and transforming them into the reserved turf of a specialized cadre of unaccountable decision-makers was ultimately meaningless. Morgenthau, in the end, was right to claim that relating foreign policy to domestic institutions was the symptom of "an intellectual attitude hostile to diplomacy."[85] And this was Waltz's attitude: For him, the illiberal recipes of classical realism were obsolete in the age of hegemonic bipolarity and high industrial modernity. In the systemic imaginary of neorealism, the ordinary operation of domestic institutions replaced diplomacy. And this, Waltz had earlier suggested in *Foreign Policy and Democratic Politics*, was not a problem, since democracies were as good at making decisions as authoritarian regimes. The open airing and public discussion of policies even made democracies better at sifting out foolish options.[86] As more complex and articulated subsystems, to put it in the cybernetic terms of *Theory of International Politics*, democracies were perfectly capable of rapid adaptation to changing environments and thus at maintaining system stability. They coped with the security dilemma just as well as any other regimes, and they did not need to develop authoritarian formulas or constitutional dictatorships to achieve security.

The historical context in which Waltz wrote *Theory of International Politics*, both in terms of the international situation and in terms of the ideological divergences internal to realism, is crucial for understanding neorealism's origins and success. The era of détente and the ensuing period of stability gave credibility to systemic theories that were entirely organized around the maintenance of equilibrium and the conservation of given states (in the physical sense): The arch-model of the system in cybernetic theory was indeed Ross Ashby's "homeostat," a contraption

---

[84] A civil rights judiciary decision becomes just as important as an official delegation traveling abroad: "Vice President Nixon hailed the Supreme Court's desegregation decision as our greatest victory in the Cold War," Waltz wrote approvingly in 1964. Waltz, "The Stability of a Bipolar World," 100.
[85] Morgenthau, *The Restoration of American Politics*, 199.
[86] Waltz, *Foreign Policy and Democratic Politics*, 311.

that recovered a situation of equilibrium every time the prior equilibrium was disturbed. The widely accepted notion that industrial democracies were experiencing a crisis of governance because the traditional processes of will-formation were ill-adapted to the complexity of policy-making in the modern world also helped lead to the rise of systemic theories that broke with simplistic representation of politics in terms of discrete "decisions." By the same token, his embrace of systems allowed Waltz to move realism beyond its previous concern with decision-makers and to de-ideologize the discussion of foreign policy by turning it into a matter of process, not substance. Neorealism broke entirely with the dictatorial imaginary attached to the security dilemma and with linear, transitive, and, ultimately, authoritarian visions of sovereign decision-making. It thus brought realism into the fold of American liberalism.

Ironically, given the theoretical gymnastics that went into Waltz's development of neorealism, the defense of democracy it offered was decidedly a weak one. If Waltz could assert that democracies were just as good as authoritarian regimes, it was not because democracy was just as, or more, just or effective, but because it was irrelevant. While classical realists insisted on curtailing liberal democracy by insulating foreign policy decisions from the public, neorealism saved democracy by making it inconsequential. Neorealism provided a theory of international politics that did not require a theory of foreign policy-making nor pronouncements upon the organization of powers in society since it rested on the assumption that ultimately the system would take care of itself. It made decision-making invisible by replacing it with an entirely different representation of politics.

Neorealism thus belonged to a longer conversation about the decision-making capacity of liberal democracies that stretched back to the interwar years and across the Atlantic. Waltz was reacting to the illiberal assumptions of classical realism and its elitist and conservative ideology of decision-making. Classical realism, however, provided Waltz with a theoretical opening to create a purely formal theory. For all their hemming and hawing about the sovereign decision-maker, Morgenthau and other classical realists never specified who, exactly, should make decisions. This lacuna enabled Waltz to take the next logical step and transform this absence of content into a pure formalism and a theory of international politics that circumvented the problem of decision-making altogether.

Yet Waltz was unable to remove the "decisionist" problem completely. Even if decisions were made invisible, neorealism did not suppress the need for them. In fact, whenever he pronounced upon decision-making,

Waltz returned to traditional realist themes, such as the need for good judgment or a sense of history. Paradoxically, his formal theory of international politics remained an instrument of policy to be supplemented in real historical time by a sense of the situation: "A theory is an instrument used in attempting to explain 'the real world' and perhaps to make some predictions about it. In using the instrument, all sorts of information, along with a lot of good judgment, is needed."[87] Judgment, of course, was what classical realists desired to improve in decision-makers.

The system-theoretical replacement of decisions by system processes was ultimately a deliberate obfuscation of the real decision-making process that attempted to protect liberal democracy while carving out a political space immune to it. This proved an impossible task. Who decides, perhaps the central question of international politics – which Waltz himself admitted – remained shrouded in mystery. Neorealism was Waltz's effort to rid realism from its ideological ballast by providing a scientific spin on the question of executive decision-making that made realism's conservative assumptions non-threatening to liberals. The replacement of decisional outcomes with formal system effects was meant to shape preemptively the range and content of political decisions while remaining silent about the identity of the decision-making group. Nonetheless, as Shklar pointed out, the new systemic theories of international politics were also elitist theories, though they preferred sanitized references to "decision makers" instead of any mention of an "elite." To the extent that decision-making in international matters had become a cybernetic process of adaptation to a changing environment, it was better performed by those who understood the workings of the system and were perceptive to the constraints it created. The character of the system was all the decision-maker needed to know before formulating policy preferences. In the end, one of the core realist tenets, the need to shield foreign policy decision-making from the public and entrust it to a small cadre of realist politicians and advisers, was preserved, but without the vocal critiques of democracy that were its correlate in classical realism.

---

[87] Waltz, "International Politics Is Not Foreign Policy," 56. On the sense of history, see Waltz www.theory-talks.org/2011/06/theory-talk-40.html.

Index

Abel, Theodore 205
After Utopia (Shklar) 6, 46
Agamben, Giorgio 96–97
Allison, Graham 160, 175–78
Almond, Gabriel 162–63
Amadae, Sonja 203
American Political Science Review 36–37
Arendt, Hannah 82
Aron, Raymond 10, 125
Arrow, Kenneth 242
Ashby, Ross 207–8, 240
'Assumptions of Rationality and Non-Rationality in Models of the International System' (Article, Verba) 214–16
Augustinism, of political realists 70–71, 80–83, 123
authoritarian liberalism 188
authority 22
automatic pilot example 208–9
Ayer, A.J. 154

balance of power 94–97
  European 95–96
  in international relations theory 98, 114
  Morgenthau on 93–94, 95, 98–99
  in political realism 95–96
  providence notion in 96–99
  Schmitt on 93, 95
  theological influences on concept of 99
Ball, Terrence 154, 158
Banks, Michael 167

Baron, Hans 139–41
Bartholdy, Albrecht Mendelssohn 147
behavioralism
  in international relations theory 51, 60–61, 162
  in political science theory 164
  realist criticism of 55–56, 57–58
Bellow, Saul 11
Bennett, John C. 79–80
Berlin, Isaiah 16
  as political realist 17, 63–64
Bertalanffy, Ludwig von 241
Bessner, Daniel 236
bipolarity notion, in international relations theory 245–47
Bouglé, Célestin 44
Boulding, Kenneth 199–200
Brecht, Arnold 32
Brodie, Bernhard 199, 206–7
Bull, Hedley 193, 202
Burckhardt, Jacob 132–33
bureaucratic politics paradigm 216
Butterfield, Herbert 15, 65–66, 71
  Christian realism of 74
  on European history 96
  on Machiavelli 121–23
  secularization critique of 111–12
  on security dilemma 223–24

Carr, Edward Hallett 79, 120–21
  Morgenthau on 124
Cassirer, Ernst 127
Catholicism, conservatism in 110–11

Center for Advanced Study in the Behavioral Sciences (Palo Alto) 199–200
Center of International Studies (Princeton) 51, 52
Center for the Study of American Foreign Policy (University of Chicago) 49
Chicago, University of
  international relations at 49, 51–52
  liberalism criticism at 83
choice
  and paradigm change 171–73
  rational 22, 186
    in international relations theory 188–89, 191–92, 234, 235
    in political decision-making 23–24, 187, 188, 230
Christian realism 73–75
  anti-Machiavellism of 116, 121–23
  Enlightenment criticism of 83
Christianity
  history approaches of 111–12
  revival of intellectual interest in 76–77, 78–79
clarity, Schmitt on 85
Cold War
  and balance of power concept 95–96
  and bipolarity notion 245–47
  and democratic decision-making 187, 228
  Machiavelli as product of 116–17, 139–40
  Schmitt on 92
  scientific/rational politics in 22–24
Columbia University, international relations at 52, 62, 232
computers, use of 184
Conant, James 170–71
Conference on International Politics (1954) 53–62, 63, 110–11
conflicts, international
  between European states 92
  rationality in solving of 42–44
conservative realism 4
constitutional dictatorship 225–30
counter-Enlightenment critiques 67
  Christian realist 83
  in international relations theory 110–11
  in political realism 12–17, 64, 66–67
Cowling, Maurice 112
Craig, Gordon A. 233

crises
  decisions needed in times of 20
  see also emergency powers
Croce, Benedetto 126
Crowling, Maurice 71
Cybernetic Theory of Decision-Making (Steinbruner) 192
cybernetics 169, 209, 240
  application of 192
  in international relations 190–91, 199–200, 217–18, 222
  see also systems theory

decision-making 184, 220
  political 20–21, 61
    in international relations 159, 214, 239
    paradigm change as 171–73, 174–83
    rationality in 176, 178–81, 185–88, 214–16, 225
    and democracy 186–88, 197–98
    rational choice 23–24, 187, 188, 230
    Schmitt on 86, 144–45
    scientific analysis of 205–6
    and systems theory 239–41
decisionism 144–45, 220
  in international relations theory 159, 175–78, 214, 217–18, 234, 247
defensive liberalism 46, 68
democracy
  and dictatorship 139, 225–30
  and foreign policy 53–54, 141, 229–30, 235–38
  neorealism on 235–36, 244, 247
  political realism on 233, 235–36
  and power politics 137–38
  promotion of 5
  rational decision-making in 186–88, 197–98, 230
  realist critique of 15, 53–54, 242–44
  scientific 14
  and security 140
Derian, James Der 213
Derrida, Jacques 20, 184
Design for a Brain (Ashby) 207–8
deterrence, and game theory 218–19
Deutsch, Karl 199, 200, 217
Dewey, John 14
dictatorship
  and democracy 139, 225–30
  rehabilitation of 25–26

Index

diplomacy, traditional 53
  calls for return to 232–33
  rejection of 245–46
discrimination, capacity for 86
Duhem, Pierre 172–73
Dunn, Frederick 38

Earle, Edward Mead 118, 136, 151
Easton, David 243
Eberhart, Jonathan 184
economics
  international relations theory inspired by 204–5, 242
  providence in 97, 98
  and realism 6
  as science 11
elitist theories 248
emergency powers
  and constitutional government 145–46, 228–29
  Schmitt on 144–45
émigré scholars from Germany
  and American international relations theory 45–46, 108
  legalistic approaches of 45–46
  Schmitt's influences on 81–83
Enlightenment
  politics freed from religion in 69
  and power politics 142
  realist criticism of 12–17, 64, 66–67
  Christian 83
  and international relations theory 110–11
Epp, Roger 76
Essence of Decision (Allison) 160, 175–78
ethics
  and politics 131–32
  and Machiavelli 132, 138–40
Europe
  balance of power in 95–96
  history of 67–68, 91–94, 101–2
  legal order of 91–94, 102–4

fascism 15, 32
  see also Nazism
feedback notion, in systems theory 208–9
Feyerabend, Paul 158
Ford Foundation, Behavioral Sciences Program of 58

foreign policy
  automated 184–85
  and democracy 53–54, 141, 229–30, 235–38
  neorealism on 235–36, 244, 247
  political realism on 233, 235–36
  rationality in 42–44
Foreign Policy and Democratic Politics (Waltz) 235–36
Forrest Gump analogy, and Kuhn 161
Fosdick, Dorothy 71
Foucault, Michel 10
Fox, William T.R. 52, 62–63, 198, 203, 232
French Revolution, decline of the West caused by 67–68
Friedrich, Carl
  on authority and rationality 22
  on constitutional dictatorship 226–28, 229
  on neoliberalism 6
  on political science in United States 28, 29
  on reason of state 145–46, 230
Fuller, Steve 157, 159, 170–71, 175

Gaddis, John Lewis 139
game theory 23
  application of
    in international relations 194–95, 196, 210–11, 218–19, 234
    in social sciences 187–88
Germany
  émigré scholars from
    and American international relations theory 45–46, 108
    legalistic approaches of 45–46
    Schmitt's influences on 81–83
  idealism in 126–27, 130
    criticism of 131–32
  Machiavelli disliked in 119
  political science in 60
  Weimar Republic in 87
    collapse of 134
    democratic decision-making in 227
Gilbert, Felix 117–18, 128–29, 151
  on diplomacy 233
  on Machiavelli 117–18, 119–20, 127–28, 129–30, 132–40, 141–44, 146–47, 151
  Rockefeller Foundation sponsorship for 147–48, 149–51
  Thompson's endorsement of 148–49

Guetzkow, Harold 200
Guicciardini, Francesco 122
Gunnell, John 120
Gurian, Waldemar 39–40, 82
  on international relations discipline 40, 69

Hallowell, John 78–79
Hayes, Carlton 79
Herring, Pendleton 49
Herz, John 1, 82, 223, 224
  political realism of 3–4, 224
Heyck, Hunter 185
historical tradition of political realism 115–17
historicism 128–29
  in international relations 198–99
  Machiavelli interpretations of 135
history
  academic discipline of 10, 13–14
  Christian understanding of 111–12
  European 67–68, 91–94, 101–2
  God/providence in 96–97
  political 128–29
  possible order in 96
  of republicanism 25–26
  of science 63, 153–60
Hoffmann, Stanley 30, 198–99
Holborn, Hajo 149
Hollinger, David 153
Horton, Walter Marshall 69, 79, 80
humanity, Schmitt on 90
Hutchins, Robert Maynard 83

idealism
  criticism of 131–32
  Machiavelli's place in 126–27, 130
ideologies, of political realism 4
incommensurability 166, 172–73
Institute of International Studies (Yale) 47, 52
Institute of War and Peace Studies (Columbia University) 52
Inter-Nation Simulation (INS) 200, 211–12
international law
  and international relations 56–57, 173
  sociological approaches to 45–46
international order, peaceful, promotion of 42–44
international relations
  academic discipline of 28–29, 37–38, 40
  development of 14, 76
  Rockefeller Foundation support for 45, 46–47, 48–50, 118, 147
  emergence of 8–9, 43–44, 55, 173
  and political science 28–38
  theory 30, 38–39, 40–42, 48
    balance of power concept in 98, 114
    bipolarity notion in 245–47
    conference on (1954) 53–62, 63, 110–11
    decisionism in 159, 175–78, 214, 217–18, 234, 247
    emergence of 62–68, 237
    Kuhn's impact on 153–60, 161–62, 163–68, 173–83
    criticism of 168
    Machiavelli's role in 148–51
    neorealism in 220–22, 233–35, 238–44, 247
    political realism in 4–7, 20, 21, 45–46, 53–68, 182–83
      German émigré scholars' influence on 45–46, 108
    science in 152–53, 158–59, 164–65, 166–67
    postpositivist 168–70, 182–83
    rationality/rational choice in 230, 234, 235, 241–42
    Schmitt's influences on 84–87, 109–10
    science in 55–56, 152–60, 190, 194–96, 206–7
    'second debate' in (traditionalist-behavioralist) 160–61, 164, 189, 190, 197, 203–4, 206
    security dilemma in 222–31
    systems theory in 184–85, 188–89, 190–92, 196, 199–200, 201–2, 206–10, 234
      internal divisions 202–3
      and rationality 214–17, 241
      realist/neorealist responses to 192–99, 203–6, 212–14, 218, 238–44
      simulations and games 200, 210–12, 218–19, 234
    theological elements in 72–76, 98
internationalism, scientific 44
isolationism, in American foreign policy 137–38

Jervis, Robert 98, 160, 175, 222–23
  on international relations theory 178–80

Index

Jewett, Andrew 14, 186
Journal of Conflict Resolution 201–2

Kahn, Herman 218–19
Kaplan, Morton 199–201
  antipositivism of 194
  on realism 212
  and systems theory 169, 195, 203, 206, 207–8, 209, 214, 217–18
katechon metaphor (Schmitt) 90–91, 98–99
Katznelson, Ira 12
Kelsen, Hans 3–4, 33–34, 69
  on religion and politics 70
  Shklar's critique of 46
Kennan, George 53, 74
Keohane, Robert 222
Kirk Report 40–41, 47–48
Knorr, Klaus 29
Kohn, Hans 105
Kort, Fred 30–31, 34
Koselleck, Reinhart 74, 86, 112
Koskenniemi, Martti 75
Kuhn, Thomas, influence of
  on international relations theory 153–60, 161–62, 163–68, 173–83
    criticism of 168
  on political realism 170–73, 182
Kuklick, Bruce 176, 177–78

Lapid, Yosef 168, 169
Lasswell, Harold 29–30, 32–33, 58
Law and Society Association (US) 45–46
Lazarsfeld, Paul 10, 11
leaders/leadership, decision-making by 20–21
legal order, European
  collapse of 102–4
  history of 91–94
legal positivism 33–34, 46
  Schmitt's criticism of 87, 90
legalism
  criticism of 48
  in international relations 45–46
Leoni, Bruno 184
Lerner, Daniel 58
liberal Protestantism 77
liberal realism 3–4
liberalism
  authoritarian 188
  criticism of
    Christian 76–77, 83
  by Lippmann 236–37
  realist 112–13
  by Schmitt 87, 89
  defensive 46, 68
  democratic values of, and rationality 243–44
  of political realists 15–16
  as secularism's extreme form 111–12
  and social sciences 14–15
  of Waltz 236
  see also neoliberalism
Lijphart, Arend 163–64, 167
Lippmann, Walter 15, 54
  liberalism critique of 236–37
Luce, Duncan R. 196

McClelland, Charles 200
Machiavelli, Niccolò
  Christian realist critique of 116, 121–23
  and Cold war/security policies 116–17, 139–40
  Gilbert on 117–18, 119–20, 127–28, 129–30, 132–40, 141–44, 146–47, 151
  and international relations theory 148–51
  Meineke on 130–32
  Morgenthau on 123–24, 149
  as political realist 4, 25, 115–17, 120–21, 149–51
  political realist critique of 121–27
  on politics 19, 132
Machiavelli and Guicciardini (Gilbert) 117–18, 134, 143–44, 147
Makers of Modern Strategy (Earle ed.) 137
Man, the State and, War (Waltz) 232, 234
Mannheim, Karl 19–20
Mansfield, Harvey 230
Maritain, Jacques 111
May, Ernest 175
Mearsheimer, John 241–42
Meineke, Friedrich 119, 145–46
  influence on Gilbert 133–34
  on Machiavelli 130–32
  on power politics 132–33
methodologies
  in international relations 48, 55–56, 57–58
  in political science 29–30
  quantitative 29–30, 35
  scientific, in social sciences 78

Meyer, Donald B. 78
military
  government 227–28
  and politics 137
Mirowski, Philip 154–55, 157
modernism, reactionary 85
Momigliano, Arnaldo 129
morality, and politics 131–32
Morgenthau, Hans J. 33–34
  on balance of power 93–94, 95, 98–99
  on Cold War 245
  on democracy 53–54
  and foreign policy 237
  on dictatorship 231
  on diplomacy 232–33
  on Enlightenment 67
  on fascism 15
  influences on 82
    of Schmitt 84–85, 100–1
  on international relations academic discipline
    and political science 30, 31, 35, 38, 40
    and science/social sciences 55–56, 57
    theory of 8–9, 49–50, 54–55, 58–59, 61–62, 109, 204–5
  on law/international law 173
  on Machiavelli 123–24, 149
  on national interest 113
  on politics 113
    decision-making in 18, 21–22, 197–98
    and science 18, 22–23, 59–60
  on secularization 99–107, 110
  on statesmanship 229–30
Mosely, Philip 49
multipolarity, dangers of 245

national interest 113
nationalism, Morgenthau's critique of 103–6
Nazism, political realist sympathies for 64–65, 66
neo-orthodoxy 77–78, 111
neoliberalism, and political realism 5–7
neorealism 24, 192
  emergence of 189–90, 218–19, 246–47
  on foreign policy and democracy 235–36, 244, 247
  in international relations theory 220–22, 233–35, 241, 246
  and decisionism 247

security dilemma as central notion in 222–31
  and systems theory 192, 238–44
Neumann, Franz 36
New Deal 145, 228–29
Niebuhr, Reinhold 52, 62, 198
  Augustinism of 123
  criticism of
    on secularization 111
    on social sciences 56, 63, 78
    on systems theory 204
    on international relations theory 58
  political realism of 67, 71, 80
Nitze, Paul 56, 187
Nomos of the Earth (Schmitt) 91–94
nuclear capabilities
  and rational/democratic decision-making 187
  and security dilemma 223
nuclear war, and constitutional dictatorship 225–26

Oakeshott, Michael 243

Palo Alto, Center for Advanced Study in the Behavioral Sciences in 199–200
paradigm change
  and international relations theory 173–83
  as political decision-making 171–73, 174–83
paradigm-thinking, in international relations theory 155–58, 162, 163–64, 165–66
Parsons, Talcott 57–58
peace researchers, and systems theory 202
peaceful international order, promotion of 42–44
Perception and Misperception in International Politics (Jervis) 160, 178–80
philanthropic foundations, peaceful international order promoted by 42–44
political decision-making 20–21, 61
  in international relations 159, 214, 239
  paradigm change as 171–73, 174–83
  rationality in 176, 178–81, 185–88, 214–16
    and democracy 184, 186–87, 197–98
  rational choice 23–24, 187, 188, 230

Index

scientific analysis of 205–6
and systems theory 239–41
political history 128–29
political philosophy, study of, in United States 49
political realism 4
  balance of power concept in 95–96
  behavioralism critique of 55–56, 57–58
  Christian and theological influences on 69–71, 73–75, 79–80, 112–13
    Augustinism 70–71, 80–83, 123
  contemporary/modern 1–3, 4–7, 26
  as counter-Enlightenment movement 12–17, 64, 66–67
  on democracy 15, 53–54, 242–44
  and foreign policy 233, 235–36
  historical tradition of 24–25, 115–16, 120
    Machiavellism in 4, 25, 115–17, 120–21, 149–51
      criticism of 121–27
  in international relations theory 4–7, 20, 21, 45–46, 53–68, 182–83
    science in 152–53, 158–59, 164–65, 166–67
    and systems theory 192–99, 203–6, 212–14, 218, 234
  Kuhn's influence on 170–73, 182
  on politics, rationality in 18–22
  postpositivist critique of 168–70, 182–83
  in United States 17, 22, 25, 26, 107
    and Rockefeller Foundation 44–49
  see also neorealism
political religions 78, 89
political science
  decision-making studies in 185–87
  in Germany 60
  and international relations 28–38
  theories and methodologies of 29–30, 35
    behavioralism 164
political theology
  Americanization of 107–14
  of Schmitt 87, 88–90
Politics among Nations (Morgenthau) 103–6
politics/the political
  Augustinian views of 80–81
  and ethics/morality 131–32
  and Machiavelli 132, 138–40
  and military 137
  power 132–33, 137–38, 142, 150

  rational/scientific 10, 12, 14–15, 23, 34–37, 63
    Christian realist criticism of 74
    in Cold War period 22–24
    Machiavelli as founder of 121–23, 125, 127
    invalidation of 132, 141–44
    and political realism 18–22, 24, 192
  and religion
    Enlightenment ideas on 69
    political realism on 69–71
    Schmitt on 85–86
  and science 207
    Kuhn on 170–71, 181, 182
  security issue in 1–3
  and sociology 10–11
positivism 154
  legal 33–34, 46
    Schmitt's criticism of 87, 90
  political realist critique of 168–70, 182–83
  scientific 31–34, 44–45
postpositivism 168–70, 182–83
power
  analysis of 216–17
    in political science 34–37
  balance of 94–97
    European 95–96
    in international relations theory 98, 114
    Morgenthau on 93–94, 95, 98–99
    in political realism 95–96
    providence notion in 96–99
    Schmitt on 93, 95
    theological influences on 99
  and science 158–59
power politics 132–33
  and democracy 137–38
  and Enlightenment 142
  rehabilitation of 150
Princeton University, international relations at 51, 52, 60–61
Prisoner's Dilemma 225
progress, scientific 166–68
Protestantism
  liberal 77
  neo-orthodoxy in 111
providence notion 96, 98
  in balance of power 96–99
psychology, in international relations theory 178

quantitative methods
  in international relations 48
  in political science 29–30, 35
Quine, William Van Orman 172–73

Raiffa, Howard 196
RAND Corporation, system analysis
  by 201
Ranke, Leopold von 133
Rapoport, Anatol 194, 199, 202–3
Rasch, William 91
rational choice 22, 186
  in international relations theory 188–89,
    191–92, 234, 235
  in political decision-making 23–24, 187,
    188, 230
rationality/rationalism
  in decision-making 176, 178–81, 185–88,
    214–16, 225
  and democracy 184, 186–87, 197–98,
    243–44
  in foreign policy 42–44
  in international relations theory 214–17,
    241–42
  limits of 183
  of Machiavelli 141–44
  in politics 10, 12, 23, 34–37, 63
    Christian realism on 74
    political realism on 18–22, 24, 192
realism
  Tuscan 142
  see also Christian realism; political
    realism
realist liberalism 3–4
reality, and theoretical models 169–70
reason of state 145–46, 230
  and liberal constitutionalism 145–46
relativism, criticism of 31–34, 40
religion
  political 78, 89
  and politics
    Enlightenment ideas on 69
    political realism on 69–71
  secular 77
republicanism 139
  historiography of 25–26, 140
Riker, William 186, 187–88, 201,
  206, 214
Ritter, Gerhard 123, 144
Rockefeller Foundation
  Gilbert sponsored by 147–48, 149–51

international relations program of 41–42,
  45, 48–49, 118, 147
  and Morgenthau 49–50
  political realism supported by 44–49
  scientific internationalism supported
    by 44
Rogowski, Ronald 163, 167
Rossiter, Clinton 225–26, 231

Sandelius, Walter 36
Schelling, Thomas 23, 185, 195, 196,
  202, 223
Scheuerman, William 84, 100
Schmidt, Brian 98
Schmitt, Carl 35
  on balance of power 93, 95
  on dictatorship 229
  on emergency powers/political decision-
    making 86, 144–45
  on European legal order, history of 91–94
  influences of
    on Friedrich 226–27
    on Herz 3–4
    on international relations theory
      84–87, 109–10
    on Morgenthau 21, 84–85, 100–1
  on political realism 75–76, 81–83,
    112–13
  katechon metaphor of 90–91, 98–99
  on Machiavelli 125–26
  and Protestant political theology 111
  on secularization/political theology
    87–90, 106, 112
Schuman, Frederick L. 120
science 32
  age of (1950s) 9–10, 11
  historical/history of 63, 153–60
  in international relations theory 55–56,
    152–60, 190, 194–96, 206–7
  Kuhn on 153–60, 166–68, 170–71
  and politics 10, 12, 14–15, 59–60, 63, 207
    Kuhn on 170–71, 181, 182
    see also scientific politics
  and power 158–59
scientific internationalism 44
Scientific Man vs. Power Politics
  (Morgenthau) 22–23
scientific politics 30–31, 205–6
  Machiavelli as founder of 121–23, 125, 127
  invalidation of 132, 141–44
  neo-orthodox criticism of 78

Index

scientific positivism/rationalism, criticism of 31–34, 44–45
secular religion 77
secularization 72
  liberalism as extreme form of 111–12
  Morgenthau's critique on 99–107, 110
  neo-orthodox criticism of 77–78
  Schmitt's critique on 87–90, 106, 112
security
  centrality in politics 1–3
  and democracy 140
security dilemma, in international relations theory 222–31
Shklar, Judith
  on counter-Enlightenment 6, 16
  on political realism 46, 151, 234
  on power politics 35
  on system theory 240–41, 248
Simon, Herbert 186, 216–17
simulations, in international relations 200, 210–12
Smith, Steve 156, 167
Smith, Thomas Vernor 36–37
Smoker, Paul 203–4
Snyder, Richard C. 200
social sciences
  application of methods of, in international relations 48, 55–56, 57–58
  decision-making/rational choice in 185–88
  and liberalism 14–15
  realist criticism of 13, 57–58
  scientific nature of 9, 23
  criticism of 78, 154–55
  game theory 187–88
  Kuhn on 153–60
  in United States 49, 70–71
socialism, and politics 10
sociology
  and international law approaches 45–46
  and politics 10–11
  of science 153–60
sovereignty
  doctrine in international relations 76
  and liberalism/secularization 88, 89
  Morgenthau on 101–2
  and rationality 217
Speier, Hans 200–1
Statecraft of Machiavelli (Butterfield) 121–23
states
  European, conflicts between 92
  liberal, Schmitt's criticism of 87
statesmanship, Morgenthau on 229–30
Steinbruner, John 176, 192, 240, 243
Sternhell, Zeev 17
Stove, David 157
The Strategy of Conflict (Schelling) 202
structural realism 169–70
Structure of Scientific Revolutions (Kuhn), impact on international relations theory 153–60, 176, 181
System and Process in International Politics (Kaplan) 208, 214
systems theory
  application of
    in international relations 184–85, 188–89, 190–92, 196, 199–200, 201–2, 206–10, 234
  internal divisions 202–3
  and rationality 214–17, 241
  realist/neorealist responses to 192–99, 203–6, 212–14, 218, 238–44
  simulations and games 200, 210–12, 218–19, 234
  and democracy critique 242–44
  see also cybernetics

Taubes, Jacob 89, 99
theology
  in international relations theory 72–76, 98
  balance of power concept 99
  political
    Americanization of 107–14
    of Schmitt 87, 88–90
  political realism influenced by 71, 112–13
  progressive, in American social sciences 70–71
Theory of International Politics (Waltz) 24, 171, 221–22, 231, 237–38, 241–42
Thompson, Kenneth W. 49–52, 56, 147, 198–99
  on Enlightenment 66
  Gilbert endorsed by 148–49
  on international relations theory 48–49, 56, 58, 62
  on Morgenthau 108, 113
Tillich, Paul 110–11

time, political 19
To the Farewell Address (Gilbert) 138–39, 142
totalitarianism
  as Enlightenment's ultimate result 15, 16
  political realism on 66–67
  see also dictatorship; fascism
Toynbee, Arnold 93–94
transitivity 215, 217
Truman, David 162
Tuscan realism 142

Union Theological Seminary (Columbia University) 52
United Nations project, political realist rejection of 123–24
United States
  balance of power role of 93–94
  constitutional government in, and emergency powers 145
  foreign policy of
    isolationism and international Messianism in 137–38
    Machiavelli fitting in 120, 138–40
  liberal foundations of political system of 14
  political realism in 17, 22, 25, 26
    in American political tradition 107
    Machiavelli in 116–17
  political theology in 107–14
  social sciences in 49, 70–71
utopianism
  rejection of 67
  of United Nations project 123–24

value-relativism, criticism of 31–34, 40
Verba, Sidney 214–16
Vitalis, Robert 14
Voegelin, Eric 69
Von Bertalanffy, Ludwig 241

Walker, R.B.J. 169

Waltz, Kenneth 62–63, 169, 203, 231–32
  on bipolarity 245–47
  on decision-making 220
  on foreign policy and democracy 235–36, 244, 247
  on international relations theory 72, 171
  liberalism of 236
  neorealism of 24, 152, 221–22, 233–35, 238, 241, 246, 247
  on rationality/rational choice 235, 241–42
  and systems theory 169–70, 238, 240
war, causes of 232, 241
Weaver, Ole 167
Weimar Republic 87
  collapse of 134
  democratic decision-making in 227
West, decline of, French Revolution as cause of 67–68
White World Order, Black Power Politics: The Birth of American International Relations (Vitalis) 14
Wiener, Norbert 217–18
Williams, Michael 101, 236
Wilson, Francis G. 109
Wilsonian idealism, realist criticism on 123–24
Wolfers, Arnold 60–61
  on international relations as academic discipline 38, 55
  Nazi sympathies of 64–65
  on power politics 35, 108–9
  Schmitt's influences on 82
Wolin, Sheldon 164
Wood, Bryce 47–48
Wright, Quincy 30, 34, 51–52

Yale University, international relations at 47, 52, 60–61

Zank, Michael 110–11